W9-BKB-702

Helping Young Children Learn Language and Literacy:
Birth through Kindergarten

Helping Young Children Learn Language and Literacy: Birth through Kindergarten

Third Edition

Carol Vukelich
University of Delaware

James Christie
Arizona State University

Billie Enz
Arizona State University

PEARSON

Boston   Columbus   Indianapolis   New York   San Francisco   Upper Saddle River
Amsterdam   Cape Town   Dubai   London   Madrid   Milan   Munich   Paris   Montreal   Toronto
Delhi   Mexico City   Sao Paulo   Sydney   Hong Kong   Seoul   Singapore   Taipei   Tokyo

Vice President, Editor-in-Chief: *Aurora Martínez Ramos*
Editor: *Erin K. L. Grelak*
Editorial Assistant: *Michelle Hochberg*
Vice President, Director of Marketing: *Margaret Waples*
Executive Marketing Manager: *Krista Clark*
Production Editor: *Annette Joseph*
Editorial Production Service: *Nesbitt Graphics, Inc.*
Manufacturing Buyer: *Megan Cochran*
Electronic Composition: *Nesbitt Graphics, Inc.*
Art Director: *Jayne Conte*
Cover Designer: *Suzanne Duda*

Credits and acknowledgments borrowed from other sources and reproduced, with permission, in this textbook appear on appropriate page within text. Photos on pages 26, 50, 75, 85, 108, 124, 156, 170, 176, 177, and 195 were provided by the authors.

Cover image: © Yellow Dog Productions/Lifesize/Getty Images

Copyright © 2012, 2008 Pearson Education, Inc., 501 Boylston Street, Boston, MA, 02116. All rights reserved. Manufactured in the United States of America. This publication is protected by Copyright, and permission should be obtained from the publisher prior to any prohibited reproduction, storage in a retrieval system, or transmission in any form or by any means, electronic, mechanical, photocopying, recording, or likewise. To obtain permission(s) to use material from this work, please submit a written request to Pearson Education, Inc., Permissions Department, 501 Boylston Street, Boston, MA, 02116, or email permissionsus@pearson.com.

10 9 8 7 6 5 4 3 2 1 BRG 15 14 13 12 11

www.pearsonhighered.com

ISBN-10: 0-13-231636-6
ISBN-13: 978-0-13-231636-1

ABOUT THE AUTHORS

Carol Vukelich is the Director of the Delaware Center for Teacher Education and the Hammonds Professor in Teacher Education at the University of Delaware, where she teaches courses in early literacy and teaching writing. Her research interests include early literacy development and children's writing development. Dr. Vukelich is coauthor of *Teaching Language and Literacy: Preschool through the Elementary Grades*, 4th ed. (Pearson, 2011). She has been director of three Early Reading First projects: the Delaware Early Reading First project, the Opening Doors to Literacy project, and the Unlocking Doors to Enhanced Language and Literacy project.

James Christie is a Professor of Social and Family Dynamics at Arizona State University, where he teaches courses in play and early language and literacy development. Dr. Christie has coauthored *Play, Development, and Early Education* (Allyn & Bacon, 2005) and *Teaching Language and Literacy: Preschool through the Elementary Grades* (Pearson, 2011). He has been codirector of three Early Reading First projects: the *Arizona Centers of Excellence in Early Education* in San Luis, AZ; the *Mohave Desert Coalition* in Bullhead City, AZ; and *Pump Up the Volume in Preschool* in Gallup, NM.

Billie Enz is Professor Emeritus for the Mary Lou Fulton Teacher's College at Arizona State University, where she continues to teach emergent language and literacy courses. She is a Co Principle Investigator of Arizona's First Things First External Evaluation team. She is currently the Executive Director of Educare Arizona. Her research interests include early language and literacy development and parent involvement. Dr. Enz is the coauthor of *Teaching Language and Literacy: Preschool through the Elementary Grades*, 4th ed. (Pearson, 2011). She is also the president of New Direction Institute, a nonprofit organization for infant development and parent education.

CONTENTS

chapter 7   Teaching Early Reading Skills   146

chapter 8 **Teaching Early Writing**   **169**

chapter 9 **Assessing Young Children's Language and Early Literacy: Finding Out What They Know and Can Do**   **190**

PREFACE

This book is about teaching the language arts—about facilitating reading, writing, speaking, and listening development for children, ages birth through kindergarten. The language arts are essential to everyday life and central to all learning. Through reading, listening, writing, and talking, children come to understand the world and gain the ability to communicate effectively with others. This book explains how young children's language and literacy develop and how early childhood teachers can help children become fluent, flexible, effective users of oral and written language.

New to This Edition

This edition:

- Updates information in each chapter (135 new references were added and 125 of the 483 references in the second edition were deleted).
- Adds a new chapter on organizing the classroom and creating time schedules that maximize children's learning opportunities (see Chapter 4). In previous editions, aspects of these chapters were embedded with content on that aspect of the language and early literacy curriculum. For example, the information on the creation of the writing center was embedded with the teaching of writing chapter. In our own use of the book in our work with preservice and in-service teachers, we discovered that this arrangement was not as effective as having information about how to organize the classroom environment and the time schedule to support the children's language and literacy learning in one chapter. A print-rich classroom and time for learning is a necessary condition for the information in Chapters 5 through 9 to be meaningful. This chapter also includes two new diagrams, one of a classroom and one of a library center.
- Recognizes the importance of early childhood teachers knowing how to meet the needs of children whose home language is not English because an increasing number of English language learners (ELLs) are entering early childhood classrooms. Strategies for teaching English language learners are added in several chapters (see Chapters 2, 4, 5, 6, 7, and 9). Each of these sections helps readers understand how to take the information learned in the earlier portion of each chapter and apply it to teaching English language learners. Colleagues who are experts in teaching English language learners prepared these sections for this edition. Three of these special features (Chapters 2, 5, and 9) are new to this edition.
- Recognizes the importance of early childhood teachers connecting with their young learners' families. A new chapter, Chapter 3, focuses on how children's knowledge of print develops and the key role families play in this ongoing process. While much of the information presented in this chapter appears in various locations in earlier editions, in this edition we organize this content more effectively in a single chapter. In addition, we add a case study of a young English-speaking child's early literacy acquisition. This allows readers to compare and contrast this child's early literacy acquisition with that of a Spanish-speaking child. Readers see how home environment influences children's language and literacy development. In addition to this new chapter, we add a Family Focus feature in several chapters (see Chapters 4, 5, 6, 7, 8, and 9). With the exception of the information presented in Chapter 9 regarding

reporting children's progress to their parents, each of these special features presents information new to this edition.

■ Stresses the importance of national and state standards in prekindergarten and kindergarten education by including exemplars of language and early literacy content standards in Chapters 5, 6, 7, and 8. In previous editions we have included examples of specific states' prekindergarten standards; in this edition, we pull examples from various states' prekindergarten standards and include examples from the recently approved Core Content State Standards for kindergarten.

■ Places more emphasis on children with special needs. Chapters 4, 5, 6, and 7 contain special features that describe how instructional strategies can be modified to meet the needs of children with different disabilities. Some of the special feature content was present in earlier editions; other special feature content (e.g., see Chapter 6) is new to this edition.

■ In this edition, we have eliminated the focus on using literacy to learn, a portion of Chapter 10 in the second edition. Early childhood programs include full courses on integrating all aspects of the curriculum into a meaningful, comprehensive program for young learners. What we could do in a few pages could not do justice to the rich body of knowledge on this topic. We also eliminated the emphasis on national early literacy policies and initiatives in Chapter 1 in the second edition. A reviewer questioned the appropriateness of this section, wondering how it set the tone for the remainder of the book.

Detailed changes to each of the chapters:

In Chapter 1 the focus is shifted away from national early literacy policies and initiatives to providing an overview of the language and early literacy field and the setting forth the principles that guided the authors in their writing of the book. While the role of parents in their young children's development and learning was present in previous editions, in this edition this role is highlighted. We've added a new principle to our set of basic principles of effective literacy instruction, one that acknowledges the importance of early childhood teachers forming relationships with parents.

Chapter 2 describes how language develops between birth and age 5. It provides new views of how language theories interact as the child develops and updates the language milestones for children birth to age 5. Several new techniques caregivers and parents might use to support children's language development are shared. New brain research is helping us learn much about children's language development; our colleague Sandra Twardosz describes how experience influences the developing brain. Recognizing the increasing number of children in early childhood classrooms who arrive at preschool and kindergarten speaking a language other than English, we asked an expert on English language learners, Luisa Araújo, to share her expertise with our readers on how young children learn two languages (called simultaneous bilingualism).

Chapter 3, new to this edition, focuses on family literacy and language development, specifically on how language and literacy develop in the home. A highlight of this chapter is case studies of two children's language development, one describing an English-speaking child's and the other a Spanish-speaking child's language and literacy development. In addition, the chapter includes new special features on ways parents can enhance their children's language development.

Chapter 4 also is new to this edition. Its focus is on organizing classroom space and time to support young children's early language and literacy learning. Information spread across several chapters in the earlier editions has been consolidated into this chapter, and new information has been added reflecting the latest research on classrooms' physical environment. A new diagram of a well-designed classroom layout is included to illustrate this new research.

Chapter 5 focuses on research-based instructional strategies for facilitating young children's early language learning. Because we know that language is central to children's later success as readers, this chapter provides many descriptions of ways teachers might facilitate children's early language learning. Because growth in vocabulary is so important, new research-based strategies are described to explicitly teach vocabulary. Teachers' talk with children is important, so this chapter provides descriptions of how a teacher might create opportunities for reciprocal discussions and conversations.

Chapter 6 consolidates information from previous editions of this book and adds new information on how to share books with young children. This edition includes a much stronger emphasis on sharing expository books with young children because the literature is clear on the importance of children learning the text structures of expository, as well as narrative, texts. Comprehension is a key element in national and state standards; exemplars of these standards are provided in this chapter. Because of comprehension's research-based importance to children's success as readers, this chapter provides a strong emphasis on extended reading activities that support children's story retelling and hence their comprehension skill development. In addition, it describes new research-based strategies in how to read to young children in ways that support their comprehension and print knowledge development. Two new special feature sections highlight the adjustments teachers should make to storybook reading experiences to make them most meaningful for English language learners and children with special needs. A new Family Focus feature on sharing instructional materials offers families guidance in sharing literature with their children.

Chapter 7 focuses on the latest scientifically based reading research (SBRR) related to the teaching of early reading skills. A new sequence of phonological awareness skills is shared, based on the recent research of Chris Lonigan and his colleagues. Instructional strategies have been reorganized to align with this sequence. As in previous editions, this chapter addresses, with updated information, instructional strategies in each of the core reading areas: phonological awareness, print awareness, and alphabet knowledge. Each core reading skill area includes exemplars of new national and state standards that young children should know and be able to use effectively. The chapter also includes three new special features: one on selecting print-salient books to teach print awareness, one on new strategies for teaching the core early reading skills to English language learners, and one on creating a book nook and author's corner at home.

Chapter 8 provides updated references, reflecting the new information on teaching writing, and consolidates the content from earlier chapters on young children's development as writers. Consistent with Chapters 5, 6, and 7, this chapter provides a new boxed feature of typical national and state pre-K and kindergarten writing standards. It includes a new Trade Secrets feature on scaffolded interactive writing, new instructional ideas for teaching handwriting to young children, and a new Family Focus feature on helping parents discover how to use everyday home events as opportunities for their young children to learn about the purposes and audiences for writing.

Chapter 9 focuses on assessing young children's language and early literacy skills. We struggled with the placement of this chapter. Should it be first or last? In the end, we decided that readers needed to know something about the research-based strategies they should use to teach language and early literacy and what children needed to know and be able to do before they could think about assessment. We acknowledge that, in teaching, assessment comes first. We advocate an assess-plan-teach-assess model. This chapter consolidates the content from many different chapters in the earlier editions on assessing young children, updating the information as appropriate. We recognize that teachers must know about on-demand and ongoing assessment tools; we provided updated information regarding both kinds of data collection tools. Assessing children whose home language is not English sometime requires that adjustments be made. Therefore, we include a new special feature on strategies for assessing English language learners. Finally, we end with a special feature on sharing assessment results with parents.

Themes

Children are at the center of all good language and literacy teaching. This principle underlies the four themes that run throughout this book: blending emergent literacy and scientifically based reading research into a high-quality program, respect for diversity, instructionally linked assessment, and family involvement.

Our first theme acknowledges the two very different views on how to teach language and literacy to young children, emergent literacy and scientifically based reading research. We believe that both approaches to early literacy instruction have their advantages. Emergent literacy programs provide opportunities for children to learn about literacy on their own and with help from the teacher and peers. Learning can occur at the appropriate pace for each child and build on what he or she already knows. This approach provides children with rich opportunities to acquire oral language and to move through the developmental progressions in emergent reading and writing. The downside to this approach is that not all children are ready or able to take full advantage of these learning opportunities. These children have a tendency to "fall through the cracks" in emergent literacy programs and make very little progress. Such children need to be explicitly taught vocabulary, phonological awareness, alphabet, and concepts of print before they can fully profit from the learning experiences in an emergent literacy program. The book describes how children acquire language and literacy knowledge in many different contexts, how teachers can design authentic classroom opportunities for using oral and written language, and how teachers can design developmentally appropriate ways to explicitly teach the core skills that have been found to be predictive of later reading achievement.

Our second theme is respect for diversity. Children's personal experiences, both at home and at school, are important factors in learning. In our diverse society, children come to school with vastly different backgrounds, both in terms of life experiences and language. This diversity needs to be taken into account when designing instructional activities for children and in evaluating children's responses to these activities. Illustrations of how teachers can work effectively with diverse learners can be found throughout this book. This new edition includes special features at the end of most chapters that explain how to adapt instruction for English language learners and children with special needs. Every child comes to school with a wealth of information about how written and spoken language works in the real world. Teachers must discover what each student already knows to build on that student's knowledge through appropriate classroom activities.

Because we recognize that assessment cannot be separated from good teaching, instructionally linked assessment is our third major theme. We introduce the principles of assessment-guided instruction in Chapter 1. Chapter 9 focuses on assessment and describes strategies that teachers can use to understand children's language and literacy knowledge in the context of specific learning and teaching events. Chapter 9 also describes how standardized tests can be used to document how well schools, and now individual teachers, are doing their jobs. This "accountability" function of assessment is becoming increasingly important in the current political climate, so it is crucial that teachers understand how to interpret the results of these standardized assessment instruments. So, assessment-guided instruction is our third theme. Find out what children know and can do—and plan instruction based on each child's needs.

The fourth theme running through this edition is the importance of the family in young children's language and literacy development. The family and the home environment shape children's early language and literacy experiences—the sounds and words they hear, the storybooks read to them, the experiences they have with written language. Connecting home and school is critically important. In several chapters, we include descriptions of how early childhood teachers can connect with families and engage caregivers in their children's school or center. The aims are twofold—to provide effective communication strategies to share information with and receive information from caregivers about the children and to provide suggestions for what families might do to support and celebrate language and literacy learning in the home.

New! CourseSmart eTextbook Available

CourseSmart is an exciting new choice for students looking to save money. As an alternative to purchasing the printed textbook, students can purchase an electronic version of the same content. With a CourseSmart eTextbook, students can search the text, make notes online, print out reading assignments that incorporate lecture notes, and bookmark important passages for later review. For more information, or to purchase access to the CourseSmart eTextbook, visit www.coursesmart.com.

In *Preparing Teachers for a Changing World*, Linda Darling-Hammond and her colleagues point out that grounding teacher education in real classrooms—among real teachers and students with actual examples of students' and teachers' work—is an important, and perhaps even an essential, part of training teachers for the complexities of teaching in today's classrooms. MyEducationLab is an online learning solution that provides contextualized interactive exercises, simulations, and other resources designed to help develop the knowledge and skills teachers need. All of the activities and exercises in MyEducationLab are built around essential learning outcomes for teachers and are mapped to professional teaching standards. Utilizing classroom video, authentic student and teacher artifacts, case studies, and other resources and assessments, the scaffolded learning experiences in MyEducationLab offer preservice teachers and those who teach them a unique and valuable education tool.

For each topic covered in the course, you will find most or all of the following features and resources.

Connection to National Standards

Now it is easier than ever to see how coursework is connected to national standards. Each topic on MyEducationLab lists intended learning outcomes connected to the appropriate national standards. Additionally, all of the activities and exercises in MyEducationLab are mapped to the appropriate national standards and learning outcomes.

Assignments and Activities

Designed to enhance student understanding of concepts covered in class and save instructors preparation and grading time, these assignable exercises show concepts in action (through video, cases, and/or student and teacher artifacts). They help students deepen content knowledge and synthesize and apply concepts and strategies they read about in the book. (Correct answers for these assignments are available to the instructor only under the Instructor Resource tab.)

A+RISE As part of your access to MyEducationLab.

A+RISE®, developed by three-time Teacher of the Year and administrator, Evelyn Arroyo, gives new teachers in grades K-12 quick, research-based strategies that get to the "how" of targeting their instruction and making content accessible for all students, including English language learners.

A+RISE® Standards2Strategy™ is an innovative and interactive online resource that offers new teachers in grades K-12 just in time, research-based instructional strategies that:

■ Meet the linguistic needs of ELLs as they learn content
■ Differentiate instruction for all grades and abilities

- Offer reading and writing techniques, cooperative learning, use of linguistic and non-linguistic representations, scaffolding, teacher modeling, higher order thinking, and alternative classroom ELL assessment
- Provide support to help teachers be effective through the integration of listening, speaking, reading, and writing along with the content curriculum
- Improve student achievement
- Are aligned to Common Core Elementary Language Arts standards (for the literacy strategies) and to English language proficiency standards in WIDA, Texas, California, and Florida.

IRIS Center Resources

The IRIS Center at Vanderbilt University (http://iris.peabody.vanderbilt.edu), which is funded by the U.S. Department of Education's Office of Special Education Programs (OSEP), develops training enhancement materials for preservice and in-service teachers. The Center works with experts from across the country to create challenge-based interactive modules, case study units, and podcasts that provide research-validated information about working with students in inclusive settings. In your MyEducationLab course, we have integrated this content where appropriate.

Course Resources

The Course Resources section on MyEducationLab is designed to help students put together an effective lesson plan, prepare for and begin their career, navigate their first year of teaching, and understand key educational standards, policies, and laws. The Course Resources tab includes the following:

- The **Lesson Plan Builder** is an effective and easy-to-use tool that students can use to create, update, and share quality lesson plans. The software also makes it easy to integrate state content standards into any lesson plan.
- The **Preparing a Portfolio** module provides guidelines for creating a high-quality teaching portfolio.
- **Beginning Your Career** offers tips, advice, and other valuable information on
  - *Resume Writing and Interviewing*: Includes expert advice on how to write impressive resumes and prepare for job interviews.
  - *Your First Year of Teaching*: Provides practical tips to set up a first classroom, manage student behavior, and more easily organize for instruction and assessment.
  - *Law and Public Policies*: Details specific directives and requirements teachers need to understand under the No Child Left Behind Act and the Individuals with Disabilities Education Improvement Act of 2004.
- **Longman Dictionary of Contemporary English Online**. Make use of this online version of the CD-ROM of the Longman Dictionary of Contemporary English—the quickest and easiest way to look up any word while you are working on MyEducationLab.

Certification and Licensure

The Certification and Licensure section is designed to help students pass their licensure exam by giving them access to state test requirements, overviews of what tests cover, and sample test items. The Certification and Licensure tab includes the following:

- **State Certification Test Requirements**. Here, students can click on a state and will then be taken to a list of state certification tests.
- Students can click on the **Licensure Exams** they need to take to find
  - Basic information about each test
  - Descriptions of what is covered on each test
  - Sample test questions with explanations of correct answers
- **National Evaluation Series™** by Pearson. Here, students can see the tests in the NES, learn what is covered on each exam, and access sample test items with descriptions

and rationales of correct answers. They can also purchase interactive online tutorials developed by Pearson Evaluation Systems and the Pearson Teacher Education and Development group.

■ **ETS Online Praxis Tutorials**. Here, students can purchase interactive online tutorials developed by ETS and by the Pearson Teacher Education and Development group. Tutorials are available for the Praxis I exams and for select Praxis II exams.

Visit www.myeducationlab.com for a demonstration of this exciting new online teaching resource.

Acknowledgments

Many outstanding educators helped us write this book. In a series of new special features, Luisa Araújo, Myae Han, Sohyun Han, Sarah Hudelson and Irene Serna describe how teachers can help English language learners become bilingual and biliterate. Karen Burstein. Tanis Bryan, Cevriye Erfgul, and Laura Justice, experts in special education, wrote special features on meeting the needs of children with special needs. Like us, they sat before their computers for many days. Thanks, colleagues!

Many classroom teachers shared their secrets, showing how theory and research link with quality classroom practice. We are grateful to Doreen Bardsley, Chris Boyd, Virginia Emerson, Kathy Eustace, Colleen R. Fierro, Debby Helman, Dawn Foley, Debhra Handley, Cory Hanson, Phoebe Bell Ingraham, Maureen Jobe, Lisa Lemos, Donna Manz, Noreen Miller, Silvia Palenzuela, Cyndy Schmidt, Karen Valentine, and Bernadette Watson. We are also grateful to the many prekindergarten teachers in our Early Reading First projects. From these teachers and others like them, we have seen how exciting language and literacy learning can be when teachers and children are engaged in purposeful language arts activities. From them and their students, we have learned much.

Several of our colleagues played a role in the construction of this book through their willingness to engage us in many conversations about children's language and literacy learning. Never unwilling to hear our ideas and to share their own, colleagues like Kathy Roskos, John Carroll University; Susan B. Neuman, University of Michigan; Jay Blanchard, Cory Hansen, and Nancy Perry at Arizona State University; and Bonnie Albertson, Martha Buell, Christine Evans, Myae Han, and Sohyun Han, University of Delaware, have greatly helped us frame our arguments. We would also like to thank the reviewers of this edition who provided valuable feedback: Jane M. Gangi, Manhattanville College; Barbara Krol-Sinclair, Granite State College; and Elaine Van Lue, Nova Southeastern University. The students we have nurtured and taught, both young children and college students, also have influenced the development of our ideas. Their questions, their talk, their play, their responses, their enthusiasm—each one of them has taught us about the importance of the language arts in our lives. Their positive response to our ideas fueled our eagerness to share those ideas more broadly.

Finally, our families have helped us write this book. Our grandchildren and grandnieces and grandnephews are providing wonderful examples of their use and enjoyment of oral and written language. The stories of their journeys to being competent language users brings life to the research and theory discussed in our book. Mary Christie, Don (Skip) Enz, and Ron Vukelich gave us time to write but also pulled us from our computers to experience antique shows, museums, trips, home repairs, life. And then, of course, there is our extended family— our parents, David and Dorothy Palm, Art and Emma Larson, Bill and Jeannine Fullerton, John and Florence Christie—who provided our early reading, writing, speaking, and listening experiences and helped us know firsthand the joys of learning and teaching the language arts.

Foundations of Language and Literacy

In recent years, the field of literacy has been thrust into the spotlight. New studies, consensus reports, and national literacy policies have all had a significant impact on literacy instruction in America. Additional financial resources have been funneled into the literacy field. The resulting research has increased our knowledge about literacy and the teaching of reading. This research, detailed in chapters throughout this book, has identified the (a) key language and early literacy skills preschool children need to know and be able to use if they are to become successful readers and (b) effective instructional strategies that teachers of young children need to use to support their young learners' language and literacy development. Funded initiatives have provided incentives for educators to begin using these new research-based strategies to teach young children the key skills.

This book draws on current research and best practices, blending the previously held theory and research-based instructional practices that have proved successful in supporting children's reading, writing, and speaking development with the new scientifically based reading research. Our goal is to provide teachers with the foundations—the core content and the best-practice teaching strategies—needed to provide high-quality reading, writing, and speaking programs for young children. We begin this book with a brief description of the beliefs and the research base of our view on the teaching of reading to young children.

BEFORE READING THIS CHAPTER, THINK ABOUT . . .

- Your beliefs about how young children first learn to read and write. At what age do children begin to learn about literacy? Is knowledge about reading and writing transmitted from adults to young children, or do children construct this knowledge on their own?
- Your beliefs about effective language and literacy instruction. How can teachers best help young children become skilled speakers, listeners, readers, and writers?
- Your memories about how you learned to talk, read, and write. Do you recall, for example, reading cereal labels at an early age? Do you recall writing messages to loved ones?

FOCUS QUESTIONS

- How is the emergent literacy perspective different from the scientifically based reading research perspective on young children's early literacy learning?
- What principles should guide teachers' teaching of language and literacy?

Language and Literacy: Definitions and Interrelationships

The terms *language* and *literacy* can be defined in many ways. Language can be defined very broadly as any system of symbols that is used to transmit meaning (Bromley, 1988). These symbols can consist of sounds, finger movements, print, and so on. Literacy also has several different meanings. It can refer to the ability to create meaning through different media (e.g., *visual literacy*), knowledge of key concepts and ideas (e.g., *cultural literacy*), and the ability to deal effectively with different subject areas and technologies (e.g., *mathematical literacy, computer literacy*).

Because the topic of this book is early childhood language arts—the part of the preschool curriculum that deals with helping children learn to speak, listen, read, and write—we use school-based definitions of these terms. Language refers to oral language (communicating via speaking and listening), and literacy refers to reading and writing (communicating through print). However, as we describe how children grow in both these areas, it will become obvious that language and literacy acquisition are closely tied to the total development of the child—learning to think, to make sense of the world, to get along with others, and so on.

While we have organized this book into separate chapters on oral language and literacy, we know that the two types of language are integrally connected and related to each other. Oral language provides the base and foundation for literacy. Oral language involves first-order symbolism, with spoken words representing meaning. Written language, on the other hand, involves second-order symbolism that builds on the first-order symbolism of oral language. Printed symbols represent spoken words that, in turn, represent meaning. Do you see the connections between language and literacy?

One obvious connection between oral and written language is vocabulary. For a reader to recognize and get meaning from text, most of the words represented by the text must already be in the reader's oral vocabulary. If the reader can recognize most of the words in the text, context cues might be used to figure out the meaning of a few totally unfamiliar words. Similarly, a writer's choice of words is restricted by his or her oral vocabulary.

Catherine Snow and her colleagues (1991) point out a less obvious, but equally important, link between oral language and literacy. They point out that oral language is actually an array of skills related to different functions. One set of skills is relevant to the negotiation of interpersonal relationships and involves the child's ability to engage in face-to-face conversations (contextualized language). Another involves the ability to use language to convey information to audiences who are not physically present (decontextualized language). Decontextualized language plays a vital role in literacy because it is the type of language that is typically used in written texts.

Children gain experience in these different aspects of language through different activities. They become skilled at contextualized language by engaging in conversations with others, whereas they gain skill at decontextualized language by listening to stories and by engaging in explanations and personal narratives and by creating fantasy worlds (Snow et al., 1991). It is not surprising, therefore, that research has shown that children with rich oral language experiences at home tend to become early readers (Dickinson & Tabors, 2000) and have high levels of reading achievement during the elementary grades (Wells, 1986).

The relationship between literacy and oral language becomes reciprocal once children become proficient readers. Extensive reading begins to build children's oral language capabilities, particularly their vocabulary knowledge. Cunningham and Stanovich (1998) present evidence that people are much more likely to encounter "rare" unfamiliar words in printed texts than in adult speech, and Swanborn and de Glopper's (1999) meta-analysis of studies on incidental word learning revealed that during normal reading, students learn about 15 percent of the unknown words they encounter. The more children read, the larger their vocabularies become.

Because this book deals with the early stages of literacy development, the relationship between oral language and literacy is primarily one way. Anything teachers can do to build children's oral language skills, particularly their vocabulary knowledge and ability to deal with decontextualized language, will also benefit children's literacy development. So even if a school's primary mission is to boost young children's literacy skills, attention also needs to be given to building children's oral language abilities.

BOX 1.1

Definition of Terms

Common core standards: Define the knowledge and skills that students must attain in each content area (e.g., English language arts, mathematics, science)

Decontextualized language: Removed from the everyday and tangible experiences; listener must build ideas from the words alone

Emergent literacy perspective: The view that children begin learning about reading and writing at a very early age by observing and interacting with adults and other children as they use literacy in everyday life activities

Phonemic awareness: Phonemes are the smallest units of sound in a language. English consists of about 41 phonemes. Phonemic awareness refers to the ability to focus on and manipulate these phonemes in spoken words (official definition from *www.nationalreadingpanel. org/FAQ/faq.htm#1*).

A Continuum of Instructional Approaches

Emergent Literacy Approach

The field of prekindergarten language and early literacy instruction has witnessed a debate between the proponents of two very different views of how to teach reading. On one side are the supporters of the *emergent literacy approach*. During the 1990s, pre-K reading had largely escaped the bitter debate that was raging at the elementary level. Emergent literacy was the predominant view of early reading and writing, and most conceptions of best practice stemmed from this meaning-centered perspective. According to this view, children begin learning about reading and writing at a very early age by observing and interacting with adults and other children as they use literacy in everyday life activities. For example, young children observe the print on cereal boxes to select their favorite brands, watch as their parents write notes and read the newspaper, and participate in special literacy-focused routines such as storybook reading with a parent or older sibling. On the basis of these observations and activities, children construct their own concepts about the functions and structure of print and then try these out by engaging in emergent forms of reading and writing, which often are far removed from the conventional forms adults use. Based on how others respond to their early attempts, children make modifications and construct more sophisticated systems of reading and writing. For example, early attempts at writing often shift from scribbles to random streams of letters (SKPVSSPK) and to increasingly elaborate systems of invented spelling such as *JLE* for *jelly* (Sulzby, 1990). Eventually, with lots of opportunities to engage in meaningful literacy activities, large amounts of interaction with adults and peers, and some incidental instruction, children become conventional readers and writers.

Proponents of emergent literacy believe that, if provided the right kind of environments, experiences, and social interactions, most children require very little formal instruction to learn to read and write. Early childhood language arts programs based on the emergent literacy perspective feature the following components:

- Print-rich classroom settings that contain large numbers of good children's books; displays of conventional print (e.g., alphabet friezes, charts written by teachers); functional print (e.g., helper charts, daily schedules, labels); student writing; play-related print (e.g., empty cereal boxes in the housekeeping dramatic play center); and the like.
- Frequent storybook reading by the teacher with lots of student interaction
- Shared reading of big books coupled with embedded instruction on concepts about print (e.g., book concepts such as *author* and *title* and the left-to-right sequence of written language)
- Shared writing experiences in which the teacher writes down oral stories dictated by children
- Projects and/or thematic units that link language, reading, and writing activities together
- Opportunities for children to engage in meaningful reading and writing during "center time" activities and a family literacy component

Emergent literacy proponents contend that these types of emergent literacy experiences build on what children have already learned about written language, provide a smooth transition between home and school, and help to ensure initial success with learning to read and write. The teacher's role is to provide the materials, experiences, and interactions that enable children to learn to read and write. Direct instruction on skills such as alphabet recognition and letter–sound relationships is used only with children who fail to learn these skills through meaningful interactions with print.

Scientifically Based Reading Research Approach

By 2002, initiatives such as Good Start, Grow Smart (2002), and Early Reading First (see *http://www2.ed.gov/programs/earlyreading/index.html*) pushed a skills-based approach to early literacy instruction, often referred to as scientifically based reading research (SBRR), into prominence. Perhaps the most valuable contribution of the SBRR movement has been identifying the "core" knowledge and skills that young children must have to become successful readers (Snow, Burns, & Griffin, 1998). Longitudinal studies have shown that preschool-age children's oral language (expressive and receptive language, including vocabulary development), phonological awareness, and alphabet knowledge are predictive of reading achievement in the elementary grades. Print awareness, which includes concepts of print (e.g., left-to-right, top-to-bottom sequence), book concepts (author, title), and sight word recognition, has also been found to be positively correlated with reading ability in the primary grades (National Early Literacy Panel, 2008).

SBRR investigators have also focused on identifying effective strategies for teaching this core literacy content to young children. One of the most consistent research findings is that core early literacy skills can be increased via explicit, systematic instruction. This instruction can often take the form of games and other engaging activities, but it also contains the elements of direct instruction: explanations, teacher modeling, guided practice, and independent practice.

SBRR instruction occurs in large and small group settings. Large-group instruction occurs during "circle time," when the entire class sits on the floor near the teacher, and may include:

- Songs, such as "Down by the Bay ("Polka Dot Tail")," coupled with instruction on rhyme production ("Did you ever see a whale with a polka-dot . . . (tail), down by the bay.") [SBRR skill—phonological awareness]*
- Storybook reading, coupled with instruction on vocabulary (after reading "Did you ever see llamas eating their pajamas, down by the bay," the teacher asks, "Does anyone know what a llama is?") [SBRR skill—oral language]
- Alphabet charts with a poem for each letter that contains many examples of the "target letter." For example, after reading a chart poem for the letter *a* ("Andy Apple went out to play, Andy Apple had a bad day. He got bit by an ant and he forgot his address. Now Andy is full of dismay!"), the teacher asks children to come up and point to the words that contain the letter *a* [SBRR skill—alphabet knowledge]
- Every-pupil response activities in which all children have a chance to respond at the same time. For example, the teacher might say a series of words, some of which begin with the /p/ sound and some of which do not. Children hold their thumbs up if a word starts with sound of /p/ [SBRR skill—phonological awareness]

Instruction can also be conducted in small groups. The advantage is that if an activity requires that one child respond at a time, all children get multiple opportunities to participate. For example, using a pocket chart, a teacher can give a small group of children each a high-frequency-word flash card (*my, the, is, big, fast*) or a rebus picture card (*truck, cat, girl, house*). After reviewing the words on the cards, the teacher can help the children build sentences by saying words and placing cards in the chart ("My cat is big," "The truck is fast," "My house is big"). The SBRR skill being worked on here is print awareness.

* "Polka Dot Tail," words and music by Michael Melchiondo and Aaron Freeman © 1997 Warner-Tamerlane Publishing Corp. (BMI), Browndog Music (BMI) and Ver Music (BMI). All rights on behalf of Browndog Music (BMI) and Ver Music (BMI) and administered by Warner-Tamerlane Publishing Corp. (BMI). All rights reserved. Used by permission.

Children also need opportunities to practice and consolidate what has been taught in large and small group settings. This practice usually occurs during an "activity" time when children work individually or in small groups in learning centers. This requires that the teacher link the center activities to the skills taught in the curriculum.

Blended Instruction: A "Value-Added" Approach

Both the emergent literacy and SBRR approaches to early literacy instruction have their advantages. Emergent literacy programs provide opportunities for children to learn about literacy on their own and with help from the teacher and peers. Learning can occur at the appropriate pace for each child and build on what he or she already knows. This approach provides children with rich opportunities to acquire oral language and to move through the developmental progressions in emergent reading and writing. The downside to this approach is that not all children are ready or able to take full advantage of these learning opportunities. These children have a tendency to "fall through the cracks" in emergent literacy programs and make very little progress. Such children need to be directly taught vocabulary, phonological awareness, alphabet, and concepts of print before they can fully profit from the learning experiences in an emergent literacy program.

We advocate instruction that blends together the key components of both approaches (see Figure 1.1). This approach features the print-rich classroom, storybook reading, shared writing, projects/units, and meaningful center-based literacy activities advocated by proponents of emergent literacy, coupled with direct instruction and practice on core language and literacy skills featured in the SBRR approach. So blended instruction is a "value-added" approach to early literacy instruction, combining the best aspects of the emergent literacy and SBRR perspectives.

Fortunately, we are not alone in this view. Our review of the comprehensive pre-K early literacy curriculum developed since 2002 revealed that most of these curricula developed are blended programs. All have been strongly influenced by the SBRR perspective and use the term *scientifically based* in their promotional literature. These new instructional programs place heavy emphasis on the "big four" science-based skills: oral language, phonological awareness, alphabet knowledge, and print awareness. Explicit instruction on these skills in large and small group settings is also now a standard feature, though the nature and intensity of this instruction varies from program to program. These programs also include the main components recommended by emergent literacy: frequent storybook reading, print-rich classroom environments, and center activities that involve reading and writing. Special Feature 1.1 describes the blended program that is being used in a pre-K program in Arizona.

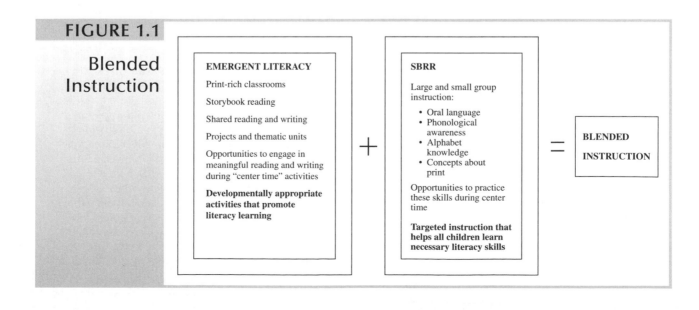

FIGURE 1.1

Blended Instruction

EMERGENT LITERACY

Print-rich classrooms

Storybook reading

Shared reading and writing

Projects and thematic units

Opportunities to engage in meaningful reading and writing during "center time" activities

Developmentally appropriate activities that promote literacy learning

+

SBRR

Large and small group instruction:

- Oral language
- Phonological awareness
- Alphabet knowledge
- Concepts about print

Opportunities to practice these skills during center time

Targeted instruction that helps all children learn necessary literacy skills

=

BLENDED INSTRUCTION

The Arizona Centers for Excellence in Early Education Project

The Arizona Centers for Excellence in Early Education (ACE[3]) was an Early Reading First project that served children in twenty Head Start and state-funded preschools in San Luis and Somerton, Arizona. The vast majority of these children were learning English as a second language. Like all Early Reading First projects, the primary goal of ACE[3] was to promote preschoolers' readiness for kindergarten by teaching them "science-based" early reading skills: oral language, phonological awareness, alphabet knowledge, and concepts of print.

The program used a commercially published curriculum, *Doors to Discovery* (Wright Group/McGraw-Hill, 2002), which is a good example of a blended early literacy program. The *Doors* program is organized into one-month "explorations" or units that focus on topics that appeal to young children, such as transportation, nature, food, and school. The ≈*Doors* curriculum consists of three interrelated components:

- **Large Group Time.** Song and rhyme posters are used as a "warm-up" and to teach phonological awareness (e.g., rhyme recognition). This is followed by shared reading of big books in which the teacher encourages children to read along and engage in book-related talk. Three shared-reading books are used in each unit: a narrative storybook, an informational book, and a concept book. When stories are initially introduced, the teacher does a "picture walk" to introduce key concepts and vocabulary. Instruction on concepts of print, phonological awareness, and alphabet knowledge are incorporated into the shared-reading sessions.
- **Discovery Center Time.** During a 60-minute period, children engage in self-selected activities in a variety of learning centers, including dramatic play, art, blocks, writing, mathematics, and science. Many of these activities are linked to the theme and to the stories that are read during shared reading. The teacher manual contains lists of theme-related Wonderful Words to be used with the children while they are engaging in center activities. These centers are stocked with theme-related literacy props and materials, providing children with a print-rich environment. For example, during the unit on transportation, the dramatic play center is turned into a gas station. Props include a gas station sign (e.g., *Chevron*) and a cardboard gas pump with a label (*gas*) and numerals to represent the gallons and cost of gas that is pumped.

- **Small Group Time.** During the second 10-minute segment of Discovery Center Time, the teacher meets with small groups of students and conducts a vocabulary lesson using an Interactive Book: a wordless big book that contains a number of illustrations related to the unit theme. For example, *Our Big Book of Driving,* which is used in the unit on transportation, contains pictures of different types of vehicles (bus, ambulance, motorcycle), parts of a car (door, tire, speedometer), and a scene of a busy intersection. Children are encouraged to discuss the pictures (initially in Spanish and then in English).

Once a week, during the third 10-minute segment of Discovery Center Time, the teacher also taught a small group lesson using Our Big Scrapbook, a blank big book. In a variation of the language experience approach or shared writing, the teacher wrote down children's oral language while they watched. The subject of the children's dictation was usually photographs of children's play activities or the children's artwork. For example, children maybe drew pictures of the type of vehicle that their parents drove. Each child then dictated a sentence ("My mom drives a blue van"), which the teacher wrote below the picture. The children's contributions were then pasted or taped to the blank pages of the scrapbook. Completed scrapbooks were placed in the classroom library center for children to read during the center time.

A positive feature of this program is the way the different components and activities were linked to the current theme. The following vignette occurred during a unit on building and construction:

During large group circle time, the teacher and children sang a song that had to do with building a tree house. The teacher paused to point out the words that rhymed in the song and then encouraged the children to come up with other words that ended with the same rhyming sound. She also focused on several tool-related vocabulary terms: *hammer* and *nail*. Next, the teacher did a shared reading lesson with a big book about building a doghouse. Before reading the book with the children, she did a "picture walk," engaging the children in a discussion about objects in the photos in this informational book. The teacher focused children's attention on several tool vocabulary terms: *hammer, nail, saw, measuring tape,* and *safety goggles.* Then the teacher read the book and encouraged the children to read along. Some were able to do so because of the simple text and picture clues. During center time, several children chose to play in a dramatic play center that was set up as a house construction site. There was a "house" made out of large cardboard boxes. In addition, there were toy tools (hammers, saw, measuring tape, level), safety goggles, hard hats, some golf tees that were used as make-believe nails, and several signs ("Hard Hat Area," "Danger," "Construction Site"). Two girls and a boy spent thirty minutes in the center, using the toy tools to measure, plan, and build the house. During this play, they used the target vocabulary repeatedly and

also explored the uses of the tools. For example, when the boy attempted to use the toy saw without first putting on his safety goggles, one of the girls reminded him to put on the goggles. The dramatic play center was used as a means to provide children with an opportunity to practice and consolidate the vocabulary and concepts that were being taught in the instructional part of the curriculum.

Of course, how teachers implement a curriculum has a big influence on how appropriate and effective the curriculum will be for specific groups of children. Susan Neuman and Kathy Roskos (2005) give an observation that they made in a preschool using a commercially published early literacy curriculum that fits our definition of a "blended" program. The classroom did have a print-rich environment. However, the instruction that Neuman and Roskos observed was not developmentally appropriate for the 3 1/2- and 4-year-old children who were participating in the lesson. Here is a vignette that describes the lesson (Neuman & Roskos, 2005, p. 22):

The local school administrator recommends an exemplary school for us to visit. We watch a day unfold in a room filled with print. The walls are adorned with words; pocket charts, alphabet letters, numbers, signs, and environmental print claim every available space. A Big Book stands ready in the circle area, accompanied by a pointer for tracking print. The children sit "station style," with "quiet hands and feet," in their designated space in the circle and sing "Stop, Look, and Listen" along with their teacher. The day is about to begin.

Taking flash cards in hand, the teacher begins, "Good morning, Charley. Do you know the first two letters of your name?" Charley moves tentatively to the board and slowly writes *C* and *H*. Moving to the next child, then the next, the teacher follows a similar routine. Some 14 children later, she reviews many of the letters, asking children to spell the names of the helpers of the week. The days of the week are next, and children repeat them in chorus. They compare the letters in Monday to the letters in Tuesday, then Tuesday to Wednesday, and Tuesday to Thursday. What follows is the Counting Calendar and "My, oh my, it's the 30th of the month," and so the children count each day up to 30. And finally with an "I like how you're listening" some 45 minutes later, circle time is about to end. Even so, the transition allows for one last teachable moment focusing on the *t-t-t* in teacher, the *m-m-m* in *Ms.*, and the */j/* in *j-j-jingle*.

This vignette shows that it is possible to take a blended curriculum and skew it one way or the other—resulting in too little or too much instruction. There is nothing inherently wrong with the activities themselves: writing the letters in children's names, spelling the names of classroom helpers, reciting the days of the week, comparing the letters in the days of the week, counting, and sounding out the initial sounds in words. In fact, with a few modifications, each of these activities could have been a very effective lesson. The problem is that the lesson contained all of these activities, making the lesson much too long for 3- and 4-year-olds. These instructional activities could have been shortened (e.g., writing the beginning letters in several children's names, but not all 14!) and spread across several days.

The challenge, then, for early childhood educators is to carefully plan and teach the key elements through meaningful experiences. Our goal is to provide teachers with research-based information on how to combine the emergent literacy and the scientifically based reading research perspectives to create a balanced, effective early literacy program—one with meaningful experiences and with direct, developmentally appropriate instruction in the key early literacy areas.

A Blended Literacy Instructional Program

We believe that the two perspectives need to be interwoven to provide preschool children with a high-quality, effective reading, writing, and speaking program. We believe that both views make significant contributions to such a program. Children need meaningful interactions with print in print-rich environments and in books. They need social interactions with their peers and their teachers in literacy events. They need many opportunities to engage in meaningful reading, writing, and speaking events. In addition, they need explicit instruction in reading, writing, and speaking skills.

By combining the two perspectives, we have created a set of basic principles of effective literacy instruction. We believe these principles should guide how children are taught spoken and written language in preschool.

Effective Early Childhood Teachers Provide Children with a Print-Rich Classroom Environment

High-quality literacy programs require a literacy-rich environment with many materials to support children's learning. Such environments include materials for children's exploration and manipulation, meaningful print to guide children's learning, physical space organized to support children's movement about the classroom and engagement with the materials, and reading and writing materials embedded appropriately in nearly all activity. A print-rich environment is central to children's learning about language and literacy.

Rich physical environments do not just happen; the creation of a classroom environment that supports children's learning, teachers' teaching, and the curriculum requires forethought. Some characteristics of this type of classroom environment include a well-stocked library corner and writing center, lots of functional print, theme-related literacy props in play areas, and displays of children's writing. This type of environment offers children opportunities to talk, listen, read, and write to one another for real-life purposes.

Effective Teachers Demonstrate and Model Literacy Events

Children will try to do what others do. Therefore, demonstrating and modeling literacy events will lead to children imitating these events. When a teacher reads books to young children, children independently pick up the books and say words in ways that would lead a listener to think they are reading. The children sound as though they are reading words, yet their eyes are focused on the illustrations. When children see parents and teachers using print for various purposes—writing shopping lists, looking up information in a book, and writing notes—they begin to learn about the practical uses of language and to understand why reading and writing are activities worth doing.

Effective Teachers Explicitly Teach Children Skills That Research Supports as Key Elements of Reading, Writing, and Speaking

Scientifically based reading research has identified key skills of early and later reading. This literature (e.g., NELP, 2008) tells us that early language and literacy instruction should focus on the core content—the knowledge, skills, and dispositions that are predictive of later reading success (i.e., oral language, phonological awareness, alphabet knowledge, concepts of print, and comprehension). There is a rich body of language development research to help teachers understand the key features of language (e.g., phonology, syntax, semantics, pragmatics). In each area, a rich literature identifies research-based instructional strategies for teaching children these skills, elements, and features. Many of these instructional strategies call for teachers to explicitly teach children—large groups of children, small groups of children, and individuals. In all instances, the strategies used should be appropriate for the age of the children.

Effective Early Childhood Teachers Provide Opportunities for Children to Work and Play Together in Literacy-Enriched Environments

Of course, teachers are not the only people in the classroom environment who offer demonstrations of literacy. Creating a "community of literacy learners" is often suggested in the professional literature. A child selects a book to "read" because his or her peers have selected the same book. Children talk to each other about books they are reading or have had read to them. Children turn to each other for information and help in decoding or spelling words. "How do you spell *morning?*" "What's this word say?"

Several researchers have documented what happens when teachers create a play environment where children can demonstrate for, or coach, each other. The following peer-to-peer interaction illustrates how one child coaches another child about how to spell her name:

> Abby is pretending to be the receptionist for the veterinarian office. She is seated at the entrance to the office. Behind her is the waiting area with chairs, toys, and children's books for reading to the sick pets while patients wait to be called for their turn to see the doctor. Antwon enters with his sick pet (a stuffed animal).

> *Abby:* WAIT! I have to sign you in to see the doctor. What's your baby's name?
>
> *Antwon:* Ginger.
>
> *Abby:* How do you write that?
>
> *Antwon:* 'G' (*Abby writes a lower case 'g'.*) No, it's the big kind. (*Antwon forms an upper case G with his finger on the table. Abby writes a G.*) Good.
>
> *Abby:* What next? [*Antwon coaches her through 'N', 'G', 'R', stretching the letter's sound and forming the letter on the table.* What's wrong with him?
>
> *Antwon:* HER! She doesn't feel good. She has a fever.
>
> *Abby:* Go sit there and wait to be called.

When teachers value children's contributions and celebrate what they know, children see the strengths in each other. Within such a supportive climate, children practice what they know and take the risks necessary for learning to occur. This kind of environment encourages young children to learn from themselves, from each other, and from the teacher.

Effective Early Childhood Teachers Link Literacy and Play

The previous example of children's teaching each other how to spell occurred in literacy-enriched play settings in a kindergarten classroom. Here is another example. The play setting was a park. The teachers and the children generated ideas for the dramatic play setting. There needed to be a place to fish, so the water table became the fishing pond labeled "Lum's Pond" after the nearby pond. Fish and fishing poles were made in the art center. Paper clips were attached to the fish and magnets to the end of the string attached to the fishing pole. Soon children were reeling in fish. But to fish one needs a fishing license. A form was created and placed in the writing center. Park rangers ensured that no one fished who did not have a license. Soon the children needed clipboards with paper; tickets had to be issued to children caught fishing without a license.

And so the setting developed. Because the tools of literacy were available to the children, they began to incorporate print into the dramatic play theme in very natural and real-world ways. They wrote for many purposes (e.g., to control others' behavior, to share stories of vacation experiences, to reserve a tent). They read books and each other's writing. They talked "park" talk, negotiating their various "camping/park" schema to create a new shared schema. Within this play setting, they had the opportunity to practice the literacy events they had witnessed in the world outside the classroom and to add to their knowledge about literacy. Enriching play settings with appropriate literacy materials provides young children with important opportunities for literacy learning and for practicing language and literacy. Play is central to children's learning.

Effective Early Childhood Teachers Encourage Children to Experiment with Emergent Forms of Reading and Writing

As we blend the two perspectives, it is important for teachers to allow children a "risk-free" environment where they practice and integrate new skills they are learning with what they already know. Years ago, young children were not considered to be writing until they were writing conventionally; that is, correctly forming the letters and spelling the words. They were not considered to be reading until they could correctly recognize numerous printed words. In the 1970s, Marie Clay (1975) and Charles Read (1971) helped us understand emergent forms of writing and reading. We learned that children construct, test, and perfect hypotheses about written language. Their research led to Elizabeth Sulzby and her colleagues' (Sulzby, 1985a, 1985b; Sulzby, Barnhart, & Hieshima, 1989) creation of developmental sequences that children pass through on their way to becoming conventional readers and writers.

Today, outstanding early childhood teachers do not expect young children's notions of writing and reading to conform to adult models of correctness. They expect children to experiment with print: to scribble, to make marks that look something like letters, to write strings of letters, and so forth. They expect children to look at pictures and "read" a story with an oral telling voice, to look at pictures and "read" a story with a written story voice, to attend to print and "read" in a written story voice, and so forth. Through such explorations, children create meaning and communicate. Their teachers support their explorations with materials and with comments. Their teachers confirm when their hypotheses about print are correct.

Effective Early Childhood Teachers Provide Opportunities for Children to Use Language and Literacy for Real Purposes and Audiences

Most research on learning supports the proposition that knowing the reason for a learning situation and seeing a purpose in a task helps children learn. By the time children come to school or the child care center, many have experienced a wide variety of purposes for writing to various audiences. If children are allowed to experiment with paper and pencils, these purposes will begin to show up in their early attempts at writing. They will write letters and messages to others, jot down lists of things they need to do, and make signs for their doors warning intruders to stay out.

Similarly, by the time children come to school or to the child care center, many have experienced many opportunities to read for real purposes. They have shopped in grocery stores—and sometimes screamed when their mothers refused to purchase the cereal box they "read" and wanted. They have told the car driver who slowed but didn't come to a full stop at the stop sign that "dat means stop!" They have enjoyed their personal "reading" of a book read and reread many times to them by an adult. They have pointed to the sign written in linear scribble and hung, just like their teenage sibling's sign, on their door and shouted, "Can't you read? It "says, 'Keep out!'" They have "read" the address on an envelope collected at the mailbox and said, "You won't like this one. It's a bill!"

Notice how many of these reading and writing opportunities are literacy events woven into the events of daily life. The event defines the purpose of the literacy activity.

Effective Early Childhood Teachers Make Use of Everyday Activities to Demonstrate the Many Purposes of Reading and Writing

Are they cooking tomorrow? The teacher reads the recipe today with the children, and together they make a list to help them remember the food items that need to be purchased at the grocery store. Did a parent or community person volunteer in the classroom? Together they write a thank-you note. The teacher might add special paper to the writing center so that individual children might write individual thank-you notes or letters. Effective teachers can provide young children with numerous opportunities to engage in purposeful reading and writing activities.

Effective Early Childhood Teachers Read to Children Daily and Encourage Them to Read Familiar Books on Their Own

Living in a print-rich world provides children with many opportunities to read *contextualized* print. That is, children form hypotheses about what words say because of the context in which the words are embedded. As described in other sections of the chapter, children learn to read cereal boxes, stop signs, and the McDonald's sign early in life. While making such connections with print is important, young children also need multiple experiences with decontextualized print. Susan Neuman and Kathy Roskos (1993, p. 36) explain the meaning of decontextualized print:

> written language [that] has meaning apart from the particular situation or context of its use. The meaning of decontextualized print is derived from the language itself and from the conventions of the literary genre. . . . Over time, [children] develop a frame, or sense of story, . . . a mental model of basic elements of a story.

Reading stories to children is one of the best ways to familiarize them with decontextualized print. Effective early childhood teachers plan numerous opportunities for storybook reading experiences. These teachers read aloud daily to individual children, small groups of children, and the whole class. Hearing stories read aloud, however, is not enough for children. Studies have shown the importance of talking about the books read (Heath, 1983; Whitehurst & Lonigan, 1998). Many teachers begin their read-alouds by engaging children in a discussion related to the story they are about to read. While reading, the teacher might invite the children to make comments, to share reactions, or to ask questions. After reading, the teacher will likely engage the children in a discussion aimed at extending their understanding of the story. This framework for read-alouds has been called a "grand conversation" (Clay, 1991) and more recently has been referred to as holding "extratextual conversations" (Cabell, Justice, Vukelich, Buell, & Han, 2008). Such conversations help children understand how to process the decontextualized text found in books.

Effective Early Childhood Teachers Know the Nation's and Their State's Birth-to-Kindergarten Standards and Provide Instruction Linked to These Standards

Standards? What are they? Standards define the knowledge and skills that children, all children, must attain. They clarify and raise expectations. Because they identify what all children must know and be able to do, they define what is to be taught and what kind of child performance is expected.

By the mid- to late 1990s, most states had developed standards defining what K–12 students should know and be able to do. By 2004, states had begun to develop standards for their preschool children. These standards were aligned with the state's K–12 standards. The goal was to help all early childhood educators prepare young children to be ready to learn when they arrived to kindergarten. In 2009, 48 states joined together, under the leadership of the Council of Chief State School Officers and the National Governors Association, to create K–12 standards in English language arts and mathematics that help ensure that all students are college and career ready by the end of high school. Statements like the following are typical of English language arts standards for young children:

- Recognize and name the letters in their name (a preschool standard)
- Define what authors and illustrators do (a preschool and kindergarten standard)
- Retell a familiar story (a kindergarten standard)

Throughout this book we provide examples of standards for preschool and kindergarten children.

As this book goes to press, groups representing various early childhood organizations have come together to discuss developing national birth to kindergarten standards. The aim is to ensure that all children have the skills necessary for kindergarten. While teachers of young children want their young learners to be successful in kindergarten and in life, some are concerned about the impact of standards on the preschool curriculum and teachers' instructional practices. Will instruction become drill based? Will play-based learning be lost? What happens to the preschoolers who are unable to meet the standards? Other teachers of young children believe that standards will be used wisely by good preschool teachers, that skills will be taught in developmentally appropriate ways, and that standards help teachers know what is expected of them.

All teachers must know their state's language and early reading standards. In select chapters throughout the book, we include example standards appropriate to that chapter's content in a special feature.

Effective Early Childhood Teachers Use Multiple Forms of Assessment to Find Out What Children Know and Can Do

Is the child's development following the expected trajectory? Is the child acquiring the core-content early literacy skills? Today teachers use standardized measures and ongoing progress monitoring tools to assess children's progress in acquiring the crucial elements or core content skills.

Not so very long ago, the literacy field recommended against the use of standardized tests, particularly with young children and particularly paper-and-pencil group-administered tests. For example, the 1998 International Reading Association and National Association for the Education of Young Children joint statement stressed the importance of teachers obtaining reliable and valid indications of children's knowledge, skills, and dispositions. The two organizations caution teachers against the use of standardized tests only and encourage teachers to gather evidence of what their children know and can do through classroom-based real-life reading and writing tasks. With knowledge from such tasks, teachers can better tailor their instruction to their children's needs.

This joint statement also advised teachers of young children to use multiple indicators to assess and monitor children's development and learning. We concur.

However, the field now also acknowledges that standardized assessments, assessments like the Peabody Picture Vocabulary Test (Dunn & Dunn, 1997), the Individual Growth and Developmental Indicator (IGDI) (Early Childhood Research Institute on Measuring Growth and Development, 2000), or the Phonological Awareness Literacy Screening (PALS) (Invernizzi, Meier, Swank, & Juel, 1999), can provide teachers with valuable information. Repeated use of the same instruments allows teachers to chronicle children's development over time. However, neither standardized nor informal, ongoing assessment should be used alone. When multiple sources of data are used, then the likelihood of an accurate understanding of children's literacy knowledge and learning is increased (IRA/NCTE, 1994).

Teachers use both kinds of assessment to improve their instruction. Teachers must gather information, analyze the information, and use what they learn to inform their instruction. In fact, that is a key purpose of assessment. The Assess-Plan-Teach-Assess model must be central to teachers' classroom assessment procedures.

Effective Early Childhood Teachers Respect and Make Accommodations for Children's Developmental, Cultural, and Linguistic Diversity

Children arrive in the classroom with different individual language and literacy needs. Our challenge is to offer good fits between each child's strengths and needs and what we try to give the child. The instruction we provide needs to dovetail with where children are developmentally and with their language and culture.

Some children will come to school having learned how to talk in ways that are consistent with their teachers' expectations; other children will not. In other words, the ways in which we make meaning and use words are dependent on the practices shared by the members of our community—the words chosen; the sentence structures used; the decision to talk after, or over, another's comment; and so on. Given our increasingly diverse communities, composed of many different cultures, teachers are more challenged than ever before to understand what this diversity means for their teaching and for their children's learning. Teachers must teach in ways that allow their children to work to their strengths—and these strengths are going to be related to children's cultural backgrounds.

It is only since the 1980s that researchers have investigated early literacy learning in nonmainstream homes and communities. In a pioneering study, Shirley Brice Heath (1983) described how children growing up in one working-class community learn that reading is sitting still and sounding out words—following the rules—whereas children in another working-class community learn that being able to tell a story well orally is more important than being able to read written texts. These conceptions of literacy were quite different from those found in children from middle-class families. The important question is, should these types of cultural differences be viewed as deficits that must be "fixed" for children to succeed in school, or should these differences be viewed as positive characteristics that teachers can take advantage of when helping children learn language and literacy? Throughout this book, we give pointers on providing culturally sensitive language and literacy instruction.

A significant and growing group of diverse learners are second-language learners. The population of U.S. children who speak English as a second language was estimated at 3.5 million in the year 2000 and is projected to grow to 6 million by 2020 (Faltis, 2001). Nearly 30 percent of the children participating in Head Start programs in 2005 spoke a language other than English (Office of Head Start, 2005).

Of this group, those children who speak little or no English are referred to as limited English proficient (LEP) or English language learners (ELL). Other children are bilingual and can speak both English and their native language with varying degrees of proficiency. These children's native language might be Spanish, Portuguese, Japanese, or some other world language. We have included several sections in subsequent chapters of this book that focus on English language learners. From these features, readers will learn which strategies presented in this book are appropriate for use with children whose primary language is a language other than mainstream English and which strategies need to be adapted to meet the needs of these children.

Effective Early Childhood Teachers Recognize the Importance of Reflecting on Their Instructional Decisions

The importance of "learning by doing," standing back from each teaching/learning event to learn from one's teaching, is not new. John Dewey (1938) is usually credited with proposing the importance of this activity and Donald Schon (1983) with reintroducing the idea into the educational literature. When teachers reflect, they take an active role in studying the impact of their instructional decisions on their children's development and learning. They identify questions to be answered or problems to be solved. They gather information from the professional literature. They secure examples of their children's work and their teaching. They carefully analyze these documents to understand the changes that need to be made to support every child's learning. Not all of such reflections will be on past actions (retrospective); some might be on the potential outcomes of future actions (anticipatory), while others will be "in action" while teaching (contemporaneous) (van Manen, 1995). To reflect is to make teaching problematic: to consider and reconsider the procedures for technical accuracy (e.g., the procedural steps to follow while conducting a guided reading lesson), the reasons for instructional actions and outcomes, and the underlying assumptions of actions that ensure that all children learn (e.g., curriculum mandates that affect teacher decision making or inequities that inhibit student learning).

Effective Early Childhood Teachers Build Partnerships with Families

Almost all parents want to support their children's learning of literacy, but many are unsure of the best way to begin. Similarly, most parents and other primary caregivers vastly underestimate the importance of their role in helping children become competent language users.

Research over the past few decades has consistently demonstrated that families provide the rich social context necessary for children's language development (Black, Puckett, & Bell, 1992; Field, Woodson, Greenberg, & Cohen, 1982; White, 1985). The thousands of hours of parent–child interactions from the moment of birth through the preschool years provide the foundation for language. Researchers (e.g., Hart & Risley, 1995) have documented that such factors as the family's socioeconomic status have a significant effect on the number of parent/child interactions children experience, with children from welfare homes hearing many fewer words during their preschool years than children from professional homes. If words were dollars, children from different socioeconomic homes would have significantly disparate bank accounts.

Likewise, parents play a critical role in helping children learn about print. Being read to at home has a significant effect on children's later reading achievement (Enz, 1992). Unfortunately, many parents do not have the resources or literacy legacy to offer their children (Enz & Foley, 2009). As with oral language, research suggests that this is especially true for low-income homes (Christian, Morrison, & Bryant, 1998; Griffin & Morrison, 1997).

Helping parents understand their role as their child's first and most impactful literacy model is one of teachers' most important tasks. In many of the following chapters, we will provide practical suggestions for providing resources for families and developing two-way communications with families.

Summary

In this chapter, we briefly compared the constructivist approaches to literacy learning (emergent literacy) with the new scientifically based reading research approach to literacy learning. We believe that the best literacy practices use strategies from both approaches. We firmly believe that teachers must use evidence (from research and from their children's performance) to guide their teaching.

In subsequent chapters, we provide many explanations of how to implement teaching strategies aimed at promoting different aspects of language and literacy development. In addition, the themes of respect for student diversity and instruction linked to assessment appear throughout the book. When appropriate, Special Features about the special needs of second-language learners are included. Further, given the importance of parents in young children's language and literacy development, we provide suggestions in several chapters on strategies teachers might use to work effectively with their children's parents.

To summarize the key points from this chapter, we return to the focus questions at the beginning of this chapter.

■ *How is the emergent literacy perspective different from the scientifically based reading research perspective on young children's early literacy learning?*

The emergent literacy perspective suggests that children learn about language and literacy by observing, exploring, and interacting with others. Children assume the role of apprentice—mimicking, absorbing, and adapting the words and literacy activities used by more knowledgeable others. As they engage in social interactions, children integrate new experiences with prior knowledge, constructing and testing hypotheses to make meaning. They store this newly constructed knowledge in mental structures called schemas.

The scientifically based reading research perspective argues that children need to be explicitly taught those skills that the research literature has identified as predictive of later reading success. To date, 11 variables have been identified as predictive of later reading success. These 11 variables include *alphabet knowledge,* print knowledge, *oral language/vocabulary,* environmental print, invented spelling, listening comprehension, phonemic awareness, *phonological short-term memory,* rapid naming, *phonemic awareness,* visual memory, and *visual-perceptual* skills. Those skills in italics are those evidencing the highest correlation with school-age decoding.

A key difference between the two perspectives, then, is the early literacy practices recommended as appropriate—explicit instruction versus allowing the children to acquire the skills of literacy through multiple interactions with print and more knowledgeable others. Unfortunately, to date there are few research-based suggestions on early literacy instructional strategies and programs. What do appropriate instructional strategies look and sound like? Teachers of young children must ensure that inappropriate strategies do not creep into their teaching practices as they shift to teaching the skills identified as central to children's success as readers.

■ *What principles should guide early childhood teachers' teaching of language and literacy?*

Effective early childhood teachers:
- Provide children with a print-rich classroom environment
- Demonstrate and model literacy events
- Link literacy and play
- Encourage children to experiment with emergent forms of reading and writing
- Provide opportunities for children to use language and literacy for real purposes and audience
- Read to children daily and encourage them to read books on their own and provide instruction linked to their state's standards
- Use multiple forms of assessment to find out what children know and can do
- Respect and make accommodations for children's developmental, cultural, and linguistic diversity
- Recognize the importance of reflecting on their instructional decisions and build partnerships with parents

LINKING KNOWLEDGE TO PRACTICE

1. Go to your state's department of education website to bookmark your state's early literacy standards. Compare what your state expects preschool children to know with what a neighboring state expects preschoolers to know. Check the Council of Chief School Officers' website to determine if national birth-to-kindergarten standards have been written.

2. Observe an early childhood teacher in a nearby classroom. How does this teacher's language and literacy instruction match up with the teaching principles described in this chapter?

Go to the Topics Organization and Program Management and Family Literacy in the MyEducationLab (www.myeducationlab.com) for your course, where you can:

- Find learning outcomes for Organization and Program Management and Family Literacy along with the national standards that connect to these outcomes.
- Complete Assignments and Activities that can help you more deeply understand the chapter content.
- Examine challenging situations and cases presented in the IRIS Center Resources.

Go to the Topic A+RISE in the MyEducationLab (www.myeducationlab.com) for your course. A+RISE® Standards2Strategy™ is an innovative and interactive online resource that offers new teachers in grades K-12 just in time, research-based instructional strategies that:

- Meet the linguistic needs of ELLs as they learn content
- Differentiate instruction for all grades and abilities
- Offer reading and writing techniques, cooperative learning, use of linguistic and nonlinguistic representations, scaffolding, teacher modeling, higher order thinking, and alternative classroom ELL assessment
- Provide support to help teachers be effective through the integration of listening, speaking, reading, and writing along with the content curriculum
- Improve student achievement
- Are aligned to Common Core Elementary Language Arts standards (for the literacy strategies) and to English language proficiency standards in WIDA, Texas, California, and Florida.

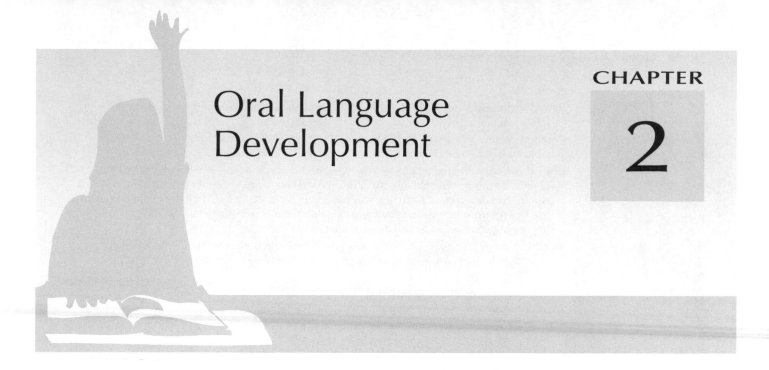

Oral Language Development

Perched in the shopping cart, 9-month-old Dawn babbles away to her mother. As they approach the checkout register, the clerk greets her mother. Dawn smiles, loudly says "Hi!" and waves her hand. The startled clerk smiles at Dawn and begins to talk to her. Dawn, obviously pleased with this attention, now babbles back to the clerk.

As this scenario reveals, the power of language is evident to even its youngest users. Dawn demonstrates that she knows how to use language to express—and realize—her desire to become a significant, communicating member in her world. By age 18 months, Dawn will have a vocabulary of dozens of words, and she will begin speaking in rule-governed, two-word sentences. By age 36 months, her vocabulary will number in the hundreds of words, and she will be using fully formed five- and six-word sentences.

Children's oral language development is remarkable. Lindfors (1987, p. 90) outlines the typical accomplishments of young language learners:

> Virtually every child, without special training, exposed to surface structures of language in many interaction contexts, builds for himself—in a short period of time and at an early stage in his cognitive development—a deep-level, abstract, and highly complex system of linguistic structure and use.

How does Dawn—and every other human child, for that matter—learn to communicate? How does this development occur so rapidly and without any seeming effort on the part of children or their parents? This question has fascinated scholars and parents for hundreds of years and is the subject of this chapter.

BEFORE READING THIS CHAPTER, THINK ABOUT . . .

- What were your first words? Although you probably do not recall uttering those words, maybe your parents or grandparents recollect your having spoken to them. Were your first words recorded someplace, or does your family rely on an oral tradition, telling the family stories orally?
- How do you think children acquire language? Is language development primarily a matter of genetics (an inborn ability to learn languages), the types of experiences and support children receive from their parents and other people, or a combination of these factors?
- When do children begin to express their thoughts orally? Why do some children develop language early while others experience language delays?
- Have you ever been in a situation where everyone around you used a language you don't know? How did you feel? How did you communicate with these speakers?

BOX 2.1
Definition of Terms

Behaviorist perspective: The view that language acquisition is a result of imitation and reinforcement.

Cerebral cortex: The largest part of the brain, composed of two hemispheres that are responsible for higher brain functions, including thought and language.

Critical period: A limited time in which an event can occur, a time in the early stages of a child's life during which it displays a heightened sensitivity to certain environmental stimuli and develops in particular ways due to experiences at this time. If the child does not receive the appropriate stimulus during this "critical period," it may be difficult, or even impossible, to develop some functions later in life.

Myelineation: A process in which the neurons of the brain become coated with a white substance known as myelin, which facilitates the transmission of sensory information and promotes learning.

Morpheme: The small unit of meaning in oral language. The word *cats* contains two morphemes: *cat* (name of a type of animal) and *s* (plural).

Nativist perspective: The view that language development is a result of an inborn capacity to learn language.

Neurobiological perspective: The view that language acquisition can be explained by studying the structural development of the brain.

Neuron: One of the impulse-conducting cells that make up the brain.

Otitis media: An inflammation of the inner part of the ear that can retard language acquisition.

Phoneme: The smallest unit of sound in a language. There are approximately 44 phonemes in English.

Pragmatic: Rule that affects how language is used in different social contexts.

Semantics: The part of language that assigns meaning to words and sentences.

Synapse: Connection between the neurons of the brain.

Syntax: Rules for arranging words into sentences.

Social-interactionist perspective: The view that language development is a result of both genetics and adult support.

Theory: A set of ideas that form an explanation that helps explain complex phenomena.

FOCUS QUESTIONS

- What are the major views on how children's language develops? Which aspects of language development does each view adequately explain?
- What are the major components of language?
- When does language development begin?
- How does the structural development of a child's brain affect language acquisition?
- What factors affect children's rate of language acquisition?
- How does children's acquisition of a second language compare with their first language acquisition? What should adults do to make it easier for children to learn English as a second language?

Perspectives on Children's Language Acquisition

Over the last 50 years, four main theories have been put forward to explain the process by which children learn to understand and speak a language: behaviorism, linguistic nativism, social interactionism, and the neurobiological perspective. Theories are propositions that help explain complex phenomena. The question that has long mystified scholars is whether a single theory can describe, in all situations, how humans learn to talk. Theories are also dynamic and fluid—they must continue to evolve as our understanding of human development, science, and the impact of social and cultural influences expand (Cromer, 1997; Schunk, 2003).

We shall consider each of these in turn. Before we do, it is important to recognize that they should not be seen simply as conflicting theories; rather, more researchers now believe that each theory may best describes the complex task of language learning more accurately at some ages and stages than others—replacing each other in a sequence (Golinkoff & Hirsh-Pasek, 1999). We present a brief description of each of these four perspectives in this chapter.

Behaviorist Perspective

The behaviorist view suggests that nurture—the way a child is taught or molded by parents and the environment—plays the dominant role in children's language development. Through the first half of the 20th century, this was the prevalent view. Researchers and teachers believed that all learning (language included) is the result of two basic processes—classical and operant conditioning (Skinner, 1957). Behaviorists attribute receptive language to associations that result from classical conditioning. For example, every time the baby is offered a bottle, the mother names the object, "Here's the bottle." After numerous repetitions with the adult presenting the action/object and phrase, the baby learns that the clear cylinder filled with food is called a bottle.

Behaviorists suggest that through operant conditioning, infants gradually learn expressive language by being rewarded for imitating the sounds and speech they hear. For instance, a baby spontaneously babbles and accidentally says or repeats the sound "mama." The mother responds joyfully, hugging and kissing the baby, saying "Yes, Mama!" The baby, given this reward, is reinforced and attempts to repeat the behavior. Once the behavior is repeated and rewarded often enough, the child connects the word sound to the object or event.

In the first few years of a child's life, when the child is learning to use her vocal apparatus (tongue, lips, palate and teeth) and to control the amount of airflow that produces the phonemes of our language, the behaviorist theory does explain these early language events. For instance, observe 15-month-old Bree learn to say her name:

Mom: Say *Bree*. (hyper articulating the word).

Bree: Eeee.

Mom: Brrrrrr eeeeee.

Bree: (Pouting her lips exactly like her mom) Brrrr.

Mom: Brrrr EEEEE.

Bree: Brrrr EEEEE. (smiles and claps her hands).

Mom: Good girl!

Likewise, when children, or adults for that matter, are first learning a second language, they will often work hard to articulate the sounds of the new language they are trying to master. Affirmation and reinforcement occurs when they are pleased when the word they articulate is actually matched to the object they are trying to name!

However, the behaviorist theory does have limitation. Language is based on a set of structures or rules, which could not be worked out simply by imitating individual utterances. For example, the mistakes made by young children reveal that they are not simply imitating but actively constructing rules. For example, a child who says "goed" instead of "went" is not copying an adult but rather *overapplying a grammatical rule*. The child has discovered that past-tense verbs are formed by adding a /ed/ sound to the base form. The "mistakes" occur because there are irregular verbs that do not behave in this way. Such forms are often referred to as intelligent mistakes or virtuous errors.

Nativist Perspective

The nativist view of learning and development, with its emphasis on nature, is at the opposite end of the continuum from the behaviorist perspective. According to the nativist view, a person's behavior and capabilities are largely predetermined. Nativists believe every child has an inborn capacity to learn language. If these theorists were using computer terminology, they would say that humans are hardwired for language. Noam Chomsky (1965) called this innate capacity a language acquisition device (LAD). Nativists posit that the LAD allows children to interpret phoneme patterns, word meanings, and the rules that govern language. For example, when children first begin to use past tenses, they often overgeneralize certain words, such as *drinked* for *drank* or *thinked* for *thought*. Because *drinked* and *thinked* are not words that children would hear adults say, these examples illustrate that children are using some type of internal rule system, not simple imitation, to govern their acquisition of language.

Nativists also believe that this innate language structure facilitates the child's own attempts to communicate, much the same way as the computer's wiring facilitates the use of a number of software programs. Nativists believe that language learning differs from all other human learning in that a child learns to communicate even without support from parents or caregivers. They view the environment's role in language acquisition as largely a function of activating the innate, physiologically based system. Environment, these theorists believe, is not the major force shaping a child's language development.

While recent advances in brain imaging techniques have left no doubt of the brain's hardwiring for language (see Special Feature 2.1, Imaging Techniques), there are issues with the nativist theory as well. Chomsky suggests that language development is innate and will develop naturally as the child grows. However, there is significant evidence for a critical period for language acquisition. This suggests that children who have not acquired language by the age of about 5 will never entirely catch up (Mayberry, Lock, & Kazmi, 2001; Newport, Bavelier, & Neville, 2001). The most famous example is that of Genie, discovered in 1970

SPECIAL FEATURE 2.1

Imaging Techniques

In the last three decades a number of new imaging techniques have been developed to obtain detailed information about the human body, especially how the brain functions. These imaging techniques use either magnetic energy, ultrasound, gamma rays, or X-rays to obtain a series of detailed pictures of areas inside the body (imaging); in all cases data from the imaging machines are interpreted by complex computer programs that are linked to the imaging machine.

- *Computed Axial Tomography (CAT):* This diagnostic technique uses hundreds of X-rays that are passed through the body at different angles to produce clear cross-sectional images, called slices, of the organ being examined. The computer organizes this information to provide detailed images. Developed in 1972, CT brain scanning revolutionized the diagnosis and treatments of tumors, abscesses, and hemorrhages in the brain, as well as strokes and head injuries, and all other areas of the body.
- *Positron Emission Tomography (PET):* Before performing the scan, patients are injected with radioactive isotopes. The isotopes travel through the bloodstream and demonstrate where the body's blood flow is most active. PET scans are particularly valuable for investigating the brain. They are used for detecting tumors, for locating the origin of epileptic activity within the brain, and for examining brain function in various mental illnesses. This technique has a serious drawback in

that it requires an injection of radioactive materials. While the dose is small, a person is not generally allowed to have more than one scan a year.
- *Magnetic Resonance Imaging (MRI):* Used primarily in medical settings to produce high quality images of the specific organs and/or entire systems inside of the human body, MRI provides an unparalleled view inside the human body without using X-rays or other radiation.
- *Functional Magnetic Resonance Imaging (fMRI):* is a relatively new imaging technology most often used to study the brain. Investigations in the fields of vision, language, motor function, memory, emotion, and pain have been greatly assisted by fMRI technology. fMRI can be used to map changes in the blood-oxygen flow, which allows for functional *mapping of the human brain*. *Consequently, an fMRI can provide high resolution, noninvasive reports of neural activity. For instance, fMRI allows us to see how speech is processed and when and how we receive visual information. This new ability to directly observe brain function opens an array of new opportunities to advance our understanding of brain organization, as well as a potential new technique for assessing neurological health and cognitive development.
- *Electroencephalography (EEG):* This technique measures the activation of the brain by measuring the electrical or magnetic field produced by the nervous system. This information is collected by having the patient wear a cap that has dozens of electrodes that touch the skull. Most information about young children is collected using this simple procedure.

at the age of 13. She had been severely neglected, brought up in isolation, and deprived of normal human contact. Of course, she was disturbed and underdeveloped in many ways. During subsequent attempts at rehabilitation, her caregivers tried to teach her to speak. Despite some success, mainly in learning vocabulary, she never became a fluent speaker, failing to acquire the grammatical competence of the average 5-year-old (Curtiss, 1977). Similarly, Jacqueline Sachs, Barbara Bard, and Marie L. Johnson (1981) published a study of a child known as Jim, the hearing son of deaf parents. Jim's parents wanted their son to learn speech rather than the sign language they used between themselves. He watched a lot of television and listened to the radio, therefore receiving frequent language input. However, his progress was limited until a speech therapist was enlisted to work with him. Simply being exposed to language was not enough. Without the associated interaction, it meant little to him.

Social-Interactionist Perspective

Social interactionists do not come down on either side of the nature versus nurture debate; rather, they acknowledge the influence of genetics and parental teaching. They share with behaviorists the belief that environment plays a central role in children's language development. Likewise, along with nativists, they believe that children possess an innate predisposition to learn language.

Interactionists such as Jerome Bruner (1983) suggest that adults support children's language through child-directed speech (or CDS) and also stress the child's own intentional participation in language learning in the construction of meaning. The social interactionist's point of view emphasizes the importance of the infant's verbal negotiations or "verbal bouts" (Golinkoff, 1983; Golinkoff & Hirsh-Pasek, 1999) with caregivers. These negotiations occur partly because mothers or other caretakers treat children's attempts at speech as meaningful and intentional (Piper, 1993). An example is shown by 11-month-old Dawn, standing by the garage door. Dawn is patting the door.

Dawn: "Bice!"
Mom: "Do you want ice?"
Dawn: (shaking her head) "Biiisse."
Mom: (opening the garage door) "Bise?"
Dawn: (pointing at the bike) "Bise."
Mom: "You want to go for a bike ride?"
Dawn: (raising her arms, nodding her head vigorously) "Bice!"

As Dawn's mother (and most mothers) begins to make sense of her child's speech, she also begins to understand her child's meaning and/or intent. Stephen Malloch and Colwyn Trevarthen (2010) studied these interactions between parents and babies who were too young to speak. They concluded that the turn-taking structure of conversation is developed through games and nonverbal communication long before actual words are uttered. Lev Vygotsky (1962) described this type of adult support, or scaffolding, as facilitating the child's language growth within the zone of proximal development, the distance between a child's current level of development and the level at which the child can function with adult assistance. In the preceding example, the mother's questions enabled Dawn to successfully communicate using a one-word sentence, something she could not have done on her own. Parents also support children's efforts to learn language by focusing the child's attention on objects in the immediate environment and labeling each object and its action.

Neurobiological Perspective

The psychologists, linguists, and anthropologists who developed the three preceding theories of language acquisition had to infer the origins of language and brain activity from careful, long-term observations of external behavior. Over the past two decades, technological innovations have enabled neuroscientists to study the brain at a cellular level. Brain imaging techniques are noninvasive procedures that allow researchers to graphically record and simultaneously display three-dimensional, color-enhanced images of a living brain as it processes information (look again at Special Feature 2.1, Imaging Techniques). These data provide researchers with a better way to understand the organization and functional operations of the brain. The research in this area has virtually exploded in the past decade. Hundreds of studies of how the brain develops, processes, organizes, connects, stores, and retrieves language have been conducted and have added greatly to our understanding of human language.

According to this new perspective, the capacity to learn language begins with brain cells called neurons. Neurons emerge during the early phases of fetal development, growing at the fantastic rate of 250,000 per minute (Edelman, 1995). As neurons multiply, they follow a complex genetic blueprint that causes the brain to develop distinct but interdependent systems—brain stem and limbic system, cerebellum and cerebral cortex (MacLean, 1978). New brain-imaging technology has allowed scientists to locate specific areas in the brain that are dedicated to hearing, speaking, and interpreting language. Thus, the nativist linguistic theory of language acquisition is, in part, correct—the human brain has dedicated structures for language, and infant brains are born capable of speaking any of the 3,000-plus human languages (Kuhl, 1993, 1999; Gopnik, Meltzoff, & Kuhl, 2001). However, infants are not disposed to speak any particular language, nor are they born language proficient. The language that a child learns is dependent on the language that the child hears spoken in the home (Sylwester, 1995; Gopnik, Meltzoff, & Kuhl, 2001).

The recent discoveries in neurobiology support elements of the nativist, behaviorist, and social-interactionist views of language development. These biological findings reveal that language learning is a reciprocal dialogue between genetics (nature) and environment (nurture). Clearly, infants are born with key brain areas genetically dedicated to language functions. Yet, for children to learn the language of their culture, it is necessary that they have consistent, frequent opportunities to interact with a persistent caregiver who models the language with the child. Likewise, neuroscientists agree that a child's language capacity is dependent on the quality of language input. Parents and caregivers who consistently engage in conversation with their infants actually help their children develop neural networks that lead to language fluency and proficiency (Werker & Yeung, 2005; Kuhl, Tsao, Liu, Zhang, & de Boer, 2001; Kotulak, 1997; Sprenger, 1999). In Figure 2.1, we summarize the major concepts of these four perspectives of language acquisition.

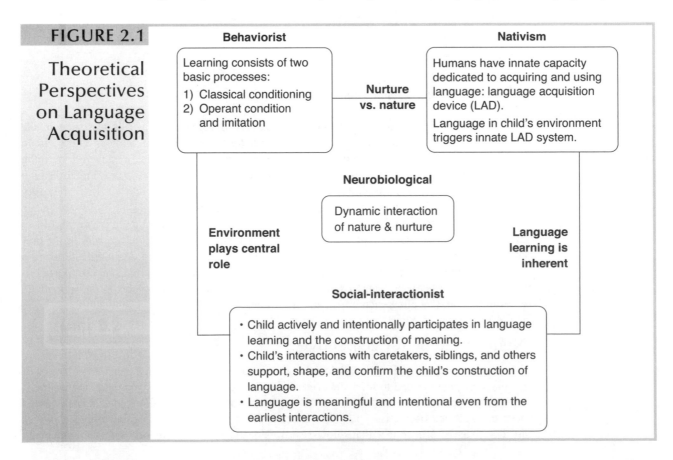

FIGURE 2.1

Theoretical Perspectives on Language Acquisition

Behaviorist

Learning consists of two basic processes:
1) Classical conditioning
2) Operant condition and imitation

Nurture vs. nature

Nativism

Humans have innate capacity dedicated to acquiring and using language: language acquisition device (LAD).

Language in child's environment triggers innate LAD system.

Neurobiological

Dynamic interaction of nature & nurture

Environment plays central role

Language learning is inherent

Social-interactionist

• Child actively and intentionally participates in language learning and the construction of meaning.
• Child's interactions with caretakers, siblings, and others support, shape, and confirm the child's construction of language.
• Language is meaningful and intentional even from the earliest interactions.

Linguistic Vocabulary Lesson

Linguistics is the study of language. To better understand the complexities of linguistic acquisition, we provide a brief discussion of the components of the linguistic structures of phonology, morphology, syntax, semantics, and pragmatics.

Phonology

The sound system of a particular language is its phonology, and the distinctive units of sound in a language are its phonemes. Individual phonemes are described according to how speakers modify the airstream they exhale to produce the particular sounds.

Phonological development begins when sounds of speech activate neural networks in the infant's brain. This process begins during the last three months of prenatal development as babies are able to hear intonation patterns from their mother's voice (Hetherington, Parke, & Otis, 2003; Shore, 1997).

Scientists have recently determined that because the mechanical aspects of the auditory system are in place prior to birth, the neural network that supports language acquisition has already started to develop. In fact, at birth babies demonstrate a preference for the phonemes, rhythms, and tonal patterns of their native language (Vouloumanos & Werker, 2007; Werker & Tees 2005). (See Special Feature 2.2, How Scientists Assess Infant Knowledge.)

However, language use begins in earnest when infants engage in verbal interactions with caregivers. These early interactions allow babies to clearly hear sounds of their native language(s) and observe how the mouth and tongue work to create these unique sounds. Simultaneously, as babies coo and babble, they gain motor control of their vocal and breathing apparatus. Interactions with caregivers allow babies an opportunity to listen, observe, and attempt to mimic sounds they hear and the mouth and tongue movements they see (Ramachandran, 2000). Through this process, babies begin to specialize in the sounds of their native language(s). The developmental window of opportunity (sometimes called the critical period) for mastering sound discrimination occurs within the first six months of an infant's life. By this time, babies' brains are already pruning out sensitivity to sounds that are not heard in their environment (Kuhl, 1993, 2000). This pruning is so efficient that children actually lose the ability to hear phonemes that are not used in their mother tongue. Children who consistently hear more than one language during this time may become native bi- or trilinguals, as they retain the ability to hear the subtle and discrete sounds (Werker & Byers-Heinlein, 2008).

SPECIAL FEATURE 2.2

How Scientists Assess Infant Knowledge

During the last 20 years developmental psychologists have developed creative ways to assess infants' knowledge. Developmental scientists have known for decades that infants are able to control their sucking movements long before they can control other motor movements, like reaching. Thus, developmental scientists exploit experimental methods that rely on infants' ability to control their sucking motions to assess what infants notice, perceive, and, in some cases, what they know. This experimental method is one way to assess human infant cognition.

For example, to assess newborn infants' recognition of their native versus an unfamiliar language, a researcher gives the infant a pacifier that is attached to a computer and can analyze the frequency and intensity of the infant's sucking. Over the years researchers have determined that infants suck harder and more frequently when they hear familiar voices, sounds, songs—this is called infant preference. An infant who hears an unfamiliar voice, sound, or song slows down his or her sucking response and reduces the intensity of sucking. This type of research has suggested several findings (Gopnik et al., 2001; Vouloumanos & Werker, 2007). Newborn infants recognize and prefer

- The sound of the human voice to all other sounds
- The sound of their mother's voice to all other female voices
- The cadence/tonal qualities of their native tongue(s)
- Familiar music they have heard frequently in the womb

Another important aspect of the English phonology is its prosody, or the stress and intonation patterns of the language. Stress refers to the force with which phonemes are articulated. Where the stress is placed may distinguish otherwise identical words (RECord [noun] versus reCORD [verb]). Intonation, on the other hand, refers to the pattern of stress and of rising and falling pitch that occurs within a sentence. These changes in intonation may shift the meaning of otherwise identical sentences:

IS she coming? (Is she or is she not coming?)

Is SHE coming? (Her, not anyone else)

Is she COMING? (Hurry up; it's about time)

Babies as young as four and five months begin to experiment with the pitch, tone, and volume of the sounds they make and often produce sounds that mimic the tonal and stress qualities of their parents' speech.

Morphology

As babies' phonological development progresses, they begin to make morphemes. Morphemes are the smallest unit of meaning in oral language. While it used to be thought that children didn't make word meaning to sound connections until around their first birthday, the science of infant language acquisition has learned a great deal more about how infants and toddlers develop language. For instance, scientists (Tincoff & Jusczyk, 1999) now report that the sounds that give parents such a thrill—*Mama, Dada*—actually mark the very beginning of human word comprehension. It is now believed that the origins of language—linking sound patterns with specific meanings—stem from discrete associations infants make, beginning with socially significant people, such as their parents, at 6 months of age. Real words are mixed with wordlike sounds (echolalia). As real words emerge, they can be categorized into the following:

Lexical: individual meaning carrying words, such as *cat, baby.*

Bound: units of sound that hold meaning (like *re, un*) but must be attached to other morphemes (*reorder, unbend*).

Derivational and inflectional: usually suffixes that change the class of the word; for example: noun to adjective—*dust* to *dusty;* verb to noun—*teaches* to *teacher.*

Compound: two lexical morphemes that together may form a unique meaning, such as *football* or *cowboy.*

Idiom: an expression whose meaning cannot be derived from its individual parts; for example, the saying "put your foot in your mouth" carries a very different meaning from the visual image it conjures up.

Syntax

Syntax refers to how morphemes, or words, are combined to form sentences or units of thought. In English, there are basically two different types of order, linear and hierarchical structure. Linear structure refers to the object-verb arrangement. For example, *Building falls on man* means something very different than *Man falls on building.* Hierarchical structure refers to how words are grouped together within a sentence to reveal the speaker's intent. However, different languages have unique and inherent rules that govern syntax. A speaker of English might say: *The long, sleek, black cat chased the tiny, frightened, gray mouse.* A language with syntactical rules that differ from English could state it this way: *Chasing the gray mouse, tiny and frightened, was the cat, long, sleek, and black.*

Shortly after their first birthdays, most children are able to convey their intentions with single words. Have you ever heard a young child use the powerful words *no* and *mine?* More complex, rule-driven communication usually emerges between the ages of 2 and 3, when children are able to construct sentences of two or more words.

Though children have prewired capacity for language rules (such as past tense), adult scaffolding or support plays a significant role in extending and expanding a child's language development. For instance, when Joe says *deenk,* his day care teacher can extend and clarify Joe's intentions: *Joe, do you want to drink milk or juice?* If Joe says *I drinked all the milk,* his teacher might tactfully expand his statement: *Yes, Joe, you drank all of your milk.* This type of subtle modeling is usually the most appropriate way to support children as they learn the conventional forms and complexities of their language. However, even when adults expand a child's speech, the child's own internal rule-governing system may resist modification until the child is developmentally ready to make the change (Gleason, 1967). The following interaction between a 4-year-old and an interested adult illustrates this phenomenon:

Child: My mom holded the baby and I kissed her.
Adult: Did you say your mom held the baby?
Child: Yes.
Adult: What did you say that she did?
Child: She holded the baby and I kisses her.
Adult: Did you say she held the baby?
Child: No. She holded the baby.

Semantics

"How would you differentiate among the following words that a blender manufacturer has printed under the row of buttons: stir, beat, puree, cream, chop, whip, crumb, mix, mince, grate, crush, blend, shred, grind, frappe, liquify?" (Lindfors, 1987; p. 47). Semantics deals with the subtle shades of meaning that language can convey. Variations in language meanings generally reflect the values and concerns of the culture. For instance, dozens of Arabic words may be dedicated to describing the camel's range of moods and behaviors. The Polynesian language has many words that define variations in the wind; likewise, Inuit languages include many words for snow.

Knowledge of word meaning is stored throughout the brain in a vast biological forest of interconnected neurons, dendrites, and synapses. Beyond culture, children's ongoing personal experience allows them to connect words and meaning. Because words are symbolic labels for objects, events, actions, and feelings, a child may initially call all four-legged animals *kitty.* However, after several firsthand encounters with kitties (with the support of adults who can help label and describe the event) a child will likely develop the concepts and vocabulary to discriminate kitties from doggies, kittens from cats, and eventually Persians from Siamese.

Pragmatics

Sitting in his bouncer, 2-month-old Marcus studies his mother's face as she talks to him. In a high-pitched voice, she exaggerates her words in a singsong manner: *Lookeee at Mommeeee. I see baabee Marceee looking at Mommeee.* Baby Marcus appears to mimic her mouth movements and responds to her conversations with smiles, wiggles, and very loud coos. After Marcus quiets, his mother knowingly responds to her baby's comments, *Yes, you're right, Mommeee does love her Marceee-Boy.*

When parent and child engage in singsong conversation of "parentese" and baby vocalizations, the basic conventions of turn-taking are learned, but rarely does the teacher or student realize that a lesson was being taught. Pragmatics deals with the conventions of becoming a competent language user. These include rules on how to engage successfully in conversation with others, such as how to initiate and sustain conversation, how to take turns, when and how to interrupt, how to use cues for indicating subject interest, and how to tactfully change subjects (Otto, 2006).

The social-interactionist perspective highlights the importance of infant verbal bouts with caregivers.

Pragmatics also refers to the uses of language (spoken and body) to communicate one's intent in real life. The message of a speaker's actual words may be heightened or may even convey the opposite meaning depending on the manner in which the words are delivered. This delivery may include inflection, facial expressions, or body gestures. Take, for example, this statement: *I'm having such a great time.* Imagine that the person who is saying this phrase is smiling easily and widely, with eyes making direct contact with the person with whom she is sharing her time. Now, picture the person saying *I'm having such a great time* while sneering and rolling her eyes (see Figure 2.2). Though the words are identical, the intent of the two speakers is obviously completely different. Further, pragmatics deals with an increasing conscious awareness of being able to accomplish goals through the use of language.

Children who are learning two languages simultaneously may also begin to exhibit the body languages that often accompany particular cultures. For example, 4-year-old Hasina Elizabeth speaks both Arabic (dad's language) and British-English (her mother's tongue). At her young

FIGURE 2.2

Language Is More Than Words Here

"I'm having such a great time."

"I'm having such a great time."

age, Hasina is fluent and responds back in the language she is prompted with including gestures and dialect. When her mother asks, "Do you want biscuits [the British word for *cookies*]," Hasina responds by straightening her back, lifting her chin, and saying a perfect, "Why, yes. Thank you!" All mannerisms would suggest a very proper British lady. The following morning when her dad asks the same question in Arabic, she responds by leaning in close to him and holding her hands out with a bold hand gesture; "Thank you very much," she replies. Though the words were nearly the same, her physical posture and facial expressions reflected the cultural mannerism that her parents model when they speak to her. Hence, we see that language is more than the words alone—instead it also includes nonverbal interactions and mannerisms (Mayberry & Nicoladis, 2000).

As children mature, they are also able to use social registers—or the ability to adapt their speech and mannerisms to accommodate different social situations. This level of communicative competence can be observed in children as young as 5 as they engage in pretend play. During dramatic play children may easily switch roles—baby to parent, student to teacher, customer to waiter—by using the vocabulary, mannerisms, and attitudes that convey the role they wish to play.

In reviewing these linguistic structures—phonology, morphology, syntax, semantic, and pragmatics—it seems amazing that children acquire these components naturally. Parents rarely teach these intricate conventions directly. Instead, children acquire these intricate communication skills by listening, imitating, practicing, observing, and interacting with supportive caregivers and peers.

Observing the Development of Children's Language

By the time they enter school, most children have mastered the basic structures of language and are fairly accomplished communicators. Though individual variations do occur, this rapid acquisition of language tends to follow a predictable sequence.

This progression will be illustrated by following Dawn from infancy through kindergarten. Dawn is the child of educational researchers. Her development is like that of almost every other normal child throughout the world, except that it was documented by her researcher-parents. Dawn's parents used a simple calendar-notation procedure to collect information about their children's language development. When Dawn's parents reviewed the datebook/calendar each morning, new words were recorded. Thus, it became quite easy to document Dawn's growth over time. When these busy parents had a reflective moment, they recorded their recollections (vignettes) of an event and dated it. Often, at family celebrations, a video camera was used to record the events of Dawn's use of language in great detail. Occasionally, videotapes also documented story times. By using the calendar vignettes and the videotapes, Dawn's parents were able to marvel at her growth and development.

In Dawn's five-year case study, we observe her language acquisition from a social-interactionist perspective and a *neurobiological view*. By intertwining the two views we can easily see how Dawn's language development is a dynamic interaction of her intentions, the physical coordination of her mouth and tongue, her neural development, and the support of her family members. This complex dance of nurture and nature reveals that Dawn's skills do not automatically develop at a certain point in brain maturation, but, by the same token, without a particular level of neural growth, Dawn would not be able to accomplish her goals.

Birth to One Month

During the first month of Dawn's life, most of her oral communication consisted of crying, crying, crying. The greatest challenge her parents faced was interpreting the subtle variations in her cries. It took about three weeks for them to understand that Dawn's intense, high-pitched cry meant she was hungry. Dawn's short, throaty, almost shouting cries indicated a change of diaper was necessary, while the whining, fussy cry, which occurred daily at about dinner time, meant she was tired.

At birth, the human brain is remarkably unfinished. Most of the 100 billion neurons, or brain cells, are not yet connected. In fact, there are only four regions of the brain that are fully functional at birth, including the brain stem, which controls respiration, reflexes, and heartbeat, and the cerebellum, which controls the newborn's balance and muscle tone. Likewise, infants' sensory skills are rudimentary; for instance, newborns can only see objects within 12 to 18 inches of their faces. Still, newborns are able to distinguish between faces and other objects and they recognize the sound of their parents' voices.

Two to Three Months

During the second to third months after Dawn's birth, she began to respond to her parents' voices. When spoken to, Dawn turned her head, focused her eyes on her mother or father, and appeared to listen and watch intensely. Her parents and grandparents also instinctively began using an exaggerated speech pattern called *parentese* (often called *baby talk*). Until recently, parents were cautioned against using baby talk or parentese with their infants because it was believed to foster immature forms of speech. However, recent studies have demonstrated that this slowed-down, high-pitched, exaggerated, repetitious speech actually seems to facilitate a child's language development because:

■ The rate and pitch of parentese perfectly matches the infants' auditory processing speed. As babies mature their brain eventually reaches normal speech rates.

■ Parentese also allows babies many opportunities to see and hear how sounds are made and, thus, to learn how to control their own vocal apparatus. As babies carefully observe parents, siblings, and other caregivers, they often mimic the tongue and mouth movements they see (Cowley, 1997; Field et al., 1982; Healy, 1994; Shore, 1997).

During the first three months of life, the number of neural synapses, or connections, increases 20 times to more than 1,000 trillion. These neural connections are developed through daily verbal and physical interactions that the infant shares with parents, siblings, and other caregivers. Daily routines such as feeding and bathing reinforce and strengthen particular synapses, while neural networks that are not stimulated will eventually wither away in a process called neural pruning.

Four to Six Months

During conversations with her parents, Dawn would often move her mouth, lips, and eyes, mimicking the facial movements of her parents. At the beginning of the fourth month, Dawn discovered her own voice. She delighted in the range of sounds she could make and sometimes chuckled at herself. At this point, Dawn (and most typically developing infants) could make almost all of the vowel and consonant sounds. She cooed and gurgled endlessly, joyfully experimenting with phonemic variations, pitch, and volume. When spoken to, she often began her own stream of conversation, called "sound play," which would parallel the adult speaker. At 6 months, Dawn was becoming an expert at imitating tone and inflection. For example, when her mother yelled at the cat for scratching the furniture Dawn used her own vocal skills to yell at the poor animal, too.

The cerebral cortex, the part of the brain that is responsible for thinking and problem solving, represents 70 percent of the brain and is divided into two hemispheres. Each hemisphere has four lobes—the parietal, occipital, temporal, and frontal. Each of these lobes has numerous folds, which mature at different rates as the chemicals that foster brain development are released in waves. This sequential development explains, in part, why there are optimum times for physical and cognitive development. For instance, when a baby is 3 or 4 months old, neural connections within the parietal lobe (object recognition and eye–hand coordination), the temporal lobe (hearing and language), and the visual cortex have begun to strengthen and fine-tune. This development allows babies' eyes to focus on objects that are more than two feet away from their faces. This new ability allows babies to recognize themselves in a mirror and begin to visually discern who's who. At this same time, babies begin to mimic the tongue and mouth movements they see. Babies also experiment with the range of new sounds they can make. These trills and coos are also bids for attention, as most babies have begun to make simple cause-and-effect associations, such as crying equals Momma's attention.

Six to Nine Months

During her sixth month, Dawn's muscle strength, balance, and coordination allowed her to have greater independent control over her environment as she mastered the fine art of crawling and stumble-walking around furniture. These physical accomplishments stimulated further cognitive development, as she now had the ability to explore the world under her own power.

At 7 months, Dawn's babbling increased dramatically. However, the sounds she produced now began to sound like words, which she would repeat over and over. This type of vocalizing is called "echolalia." Though "MmmaaaMmmaaa" and "Dddaaaddaaa" sounded like "Mama" and "DaDa," they were still not words with a cognitive connection or meaning.

In her eighth month, Dawn's babbling began to exhibit conversation-like tones and behaviors. This pattern of speech is called "vocables." While there were still no real words in her babble, Dawn's vocalizations were beginning to take on some of the conventions of adult conversation, such as turn-taking, eye contact, and recognizable gestures. These forms of prelanguage are playlike in nature, being done for their own sake rather than a deliberate use of language to communicate a need or accomplish a goal.

At approximately 9 months, Dawn first used real, goal-oriented language. As her father came home from work, she crawled to him shouting in an excited voice, "Dada, Dada," and held her arms up to him. Dawn's accurate labeling of her father and her use of body language that expressed desire to be picked up were deliberate actions that revealed that Dawn was using language to accomplish her objectives.

As a child matures, the actual number of neurons remains relatively stable. However, the human brain triples its birth weight within the first three years of a child's life. This change is caused as neurons are stimulated and synapse connections increase, as the message-receiving dendrite branches grow larger and heavier. In addition, the long axons over which sensory messages travel gradually develop a protective coating of a white, fatty substance called myelin. Myelin insulates the axons and makes the transmission of sensory information more efficient. Myelineation occurs at different times in different parts of the brain and this process seems to coincide with the emergence of various physical skills and cognitive abilities. For instance, the neuromuscular development during the first months of life is dramatic. Within the first six months, helpless infants develop the muscle tone and coordination that allows them to turn over at will. Babies develop a sense of balance and better eye–hand coordination as neural connections in the cerebellum and parietal lobe strengthen. This allows most 6-month-old babies to sit upright, with adult support, and successfully grasp objects within their reach. The ability to hold and inspect interesting items gives babies a lot to "talk" about.

Between 6 and 7 months, the brain has already created permanent neural networks that recognize the sounds of a child's native language(s) or dialect. Next, babies begin to distinguish syllables, which soon enables them to detect word boundaries. Prior to this, "doyouwantyourbottle?" was a pleasant tune, but was not explicit communication. After auditory boundaries become apparent, babies will hear distinct words, "Do / you / want / your / BOTTLE?" As sounds become words that are frequently used in context to label a specific object, the acquisition of word meaning begins. At this stage of development, babies usually recognize and have cognitive meaning for words such as bottle, momma, *and* daddy. *Their receptive or listening vocabulary grows rapidly, though it will take a few more months before their expressive or oral language catches up.*

From about the eighth to the ninth month, the hippocampus becomes fully functional. Located in the center of the brain, the hippocampus is part of the limbic system. The hippocampus helps to index and file memories and, as it matures, babies are able to form memories. For instance, babies can now remember that when they push the button on the busy box it will squeak. At this point, babies' ability to determine cause and effect and remember words greatly increases.

Nine to Twelve Months

Between age 9 months and her first birthday, Dawn's expressive (speaking) and receptive (listening and comprehending) vocabulary grew rapidly. She could understand and comply with dozens of simple requests, such as "Bring Mommy your shoes" or the favorite label-the-body game, "Where is Daddy's nose?" In addition, Dawn's command of nonverbal gestures and facial expressions were expanding from waving "bye-bye" to scowling and saying "no-no" when taking her medicine. In addition, holophrastic words began to emerge, in which one word carried the semantic burden for a whole sentence or phrase. For example, "keeths," while holding her plastic keys, purse, and sunglasses meant "I want to go for a ride," or "iith" meant "I want some ice." Dawn also used overgeneralized speech in which each word embraced many meanings. For instance, *doll* referred not only to her favorite baby doll but to everything in her toy box, and *jooth* stood for any type of liquid she drank.

> *At the end of the first year, the prefrontal cortex, the seat of forethought and logic, forms synapses at a rapid rate. In fact, by age 1, the full cortex consumes twice as much energy as an adult brain. This incredible pace continues during the child's first decade of life. The increased cognitive capacity and physical dexterity stimulates curiosity and exploration and a deep desire to understand how things work. Neural readiness, in combination with countless hours of sound play and verbal exchanges with loving caregivers, allows most children to begin speaking their first words.*

In Special Feature 2.3, Experience and the Developing Brain, Sandra Twardosz describes more about how the brain's expectation of certain stimulation helps with rapid brain development.

Twelve to Eighteen Months

At this time Dawn's vocabulary expanded quickly. Most of her words identified or labeled the people, pets, and objects that were familiar and meaningful to her. Clark's research (1983) suggests that young children between 1 and 6 will learn and remember approximately nine new words a day. This ability to relate new words to preexisting internalized concepts, then remember and use them after only one exposure, is called *fast mapping* (Carey, 1979).

Because chronological age is not a reliable indicator of language progression, linguists typically describe language development by noting the number of words used in a sentence, which is called "mean length of utterance" (MLU). At this point, Dawn was beginning to use two-word sentences such as "Kitty juuth." Linguists call these two- and three-word sentences "telegraphic speech" as they contain only the most necessary of words to convey meaning. However, these first sentences may have many interpretations; for instance, Dawn's sentence "Kitty, juuth" might mean "The kitty wants some milk," or "The kitty drank the milk," or even "The kitty stuck her head in my cup and drank my milk." Obviously the context in which the sentence was spoken helped her parents to better understand the intent or meaning of her communication.

> *By 18 months neural synapses have increased, strengthened, and are beginning to transmit information quite efficiently; hence, most toddlers begin to experience a language "explosion." Brain imaging technology clearly reveals that the full cortex is involved in processing language.*

Eighteen to Twenty-Four Months

Around age 18 months to 2 years, as Dawn began using sentences more frequently, the use of syntax became apparent. "No shoes" with a shoulder shrug meant she couldn't find her shoes, but "Shoes, no!" said with a shaking head, meant Dawn did not want to put on her shoes

> *At 2 years of age, most children have fully wired brains and nimble fingers and are sturdy on their feet. Though they are generally aware of cause and effect, they are still unable to foresee potential problems. In other words, children's physical abilities may exceed their common sense. By this time, most children are able to use language to communicate*

their needs and accomplish their goals. Increased neural activity, plus verbal expression and physical skill, also give rise to greater independence. At this time parents may hear the word "No!" quite often.

Biologically, the brain is fully functional by this time. The remainder of a child's language development relies on the experiences and opportunities the child has to hear and use language with more experienced language users.

Twenty-Four to Thirty-Six Months

Though Dawn's vocabulary grew, her phonemic competence did not always reflect adult standards. Many of her words were clearly pronounced (*kitty, baby*), while others were interesting phonemic attempts or approximations (*bise* for *bike, Papa* for *Grandpa, bawble* for *bottle*); others were her own construction (*NaNe* for *Grandma*). At this age, most children are unable to articulate perfectly the sounds of adult speech. Rather, they simplify the adult sounds to ones they can produce. Sometimes this means they pronounce the initial sound or syllable of a word (*whee* for *wheel*), and at other times they pronounce only the final sound or syllable (*ees* for *cheese*). Another common feature is temporary regression, meaning that they may pronounce a word or phrase quite clearly, then later produce a shortened, less mature version. This, too, is a normal language developmental phase for all children. Thus, it is important that parents accept their child's language and not become overly concerned with correcting their pronunciation.

Likewise, children's early attempts to use sentences need thoughtful support, not critical correction. Parents can best support their child's attempts to communicate through extensions and expansions. Extensions include responses that incorporate the essence of a child's sentence but transform it into a well-formed sentence. For example, when Dawn said, "ree stor-ee," her father responded, "Do you want me to read the storybook to you?" When parents and caregivers use extensions, they model appropriate grammar and fluent speech and actually help to extend a child's vocabulary.

When parents use expansions, they gently reshape the child's efforts to reflect grammatical appropriate content. For example, when Dawn said, "We goed to Diseelan," instead of correcting her ("We don't say *goed,* we say *went*") her mother expanded Dawn's language by initially confirming the intent of Dawn's statement while modeling the correct form, "Yes, we went to Disneyland."

The adaptations parents make when talking to young children such as slowing the rate of speech, using age-appropriate vocabulary, questioning and clarifying the child's statements, and extensions and expansions occurs in all cultures. These early interactions with children and the gradual and building support are called *parentese* or, more gender-specifically, *motherese* and *fatherese*. When parents use this form of support they are actually helping their children gain communicative competence and confidence (White, 1985). Between the ages of 2 and 3 years, Dawn's language had developed to the point where she could express her needs and describe her world to others quite well. In addition to using pronouns, she also began to produce grammatical inflections: *-ing,* plurals, the past tense, and the possessive.

Statements	Age
"I lub you, Mama."	2.0*
"Boot's crywing."	2.1
"Dawn's baby dawl."	2.2
"My books."	2.4
"Grover droppted the radio."	2.6
"Cookie monster shutted the door."	2.8
"She's not nice to me."	2.9
"Daddy's face got stickers, they scratch."	3.0

*Indicates age by years and months.

Dawn also loved finger plays such as the "Itsy, Bitsy Spider" and "Grandma's Glasses," poems such as "This Little Pig," and songs such as "Jingle Bells," "Yankee Doodle," and the "Alphabet Song." She was also beginning to count and echo-read with her parents when they read her favorite stories, like the "Three Little Pigs." Dawn would "huff and puff and blow your house down" as many times as her parents would read the story.

Three to Five Years

Dawn had become a proficient language user. She could make requests, "Please, may I have some more cake?" and demands, "I need this, now!" depending on her mood and motivation. She could seek assistance, "Can you tell me where the toys are?" and demonstrate concern, "What's the matter, Mama?" She sought information about her world, "Why is the moon round one time and just a grin sometimes?" She could carry on detailed conversations just as she did in the grocery store at 4.0 (4 years and 0 months):

Mom: Dawn, what juice did you want?

Dawn: Orange juice. But not the kind that has the little chewy stuff in it.

Mom: That is called pulp.

Dawn: Pulp—ick! I don't like it because it tasted badly.

Mom: Well, do you remember what kind has the pulp?

Dawn: You know, it comes in the orange can and has the picture of the bunny on it.

Mom: Well, there are several kinds in orange cans.

Dawn: Mom, I know that, cause orange juice is orange. But this one I don't like, at all, has a bunny on it.

Mom: Can you remember the name?

Dawn: Yeah, the writing words have A-B-C-O.

Mom: Oh, I know, the store's brand, ABCO.

Dawn: Yes, here it is. Now DON'T BUY IT!!

At the age of 4 to 5 years, Dawn began to engage in dramatic play, using her knowledge of common events in familiar settings such as the grocery store and the doctor's office to act out life scripts with other children. These dramas allowed Dawn and her peers the opportunity to use their language in many functional and imaginative ways. Her favorite script was the restaurant, as she always enjoyed being the waitress, describing the daily special to her customers, then pretending to write their orders.

Jim Johnson, Jim Christie, and Thomas Yawkey (1999) suggest that, during dramatic play, two types of communication can occur. First, *pretend communication* takes place when the child assumes a role and talks, in character, to other characters in the drama. The second type, *metacommunication,* occurs when the children stop the ongoing dramatic-play script and discuss the plot or character actions. The following is an example of metacommunication between Dawn and her friend Jennifer at age 5.6 years:

Dawn: Pretend you ordered pizza and I have to make it, okay?

Jennifer: Okay, but it should be cheese pizza, 'cause I like it best.

Dawn: Okay, I can use yellow strings (yarn) for the cheese.

Jennifer: Waitress, I want yellow cheese pizza, in a hurry. I'm hungry.

Dawn's language development, though completely normal, is also a human miracle. Language plays a central role in learning, and a child's success in school depends to very large degree on his or her ability to speak and listen. Dawn's case study also confirms the critical role of neurological growth and social interaction in language development.

What Is Normal Language Development?

While the process of learning to talk follows a predictable sequence, the age—or rate—at which children say their first word may vary widely from one child to another. Developmental guidelines provide descriptions of specific behaviors and delineate the age at which most children demonstrate this physical or cognitive skill. This type of information helps parents and physicians anticipate normal physical and cognitive growth. While physical maturation is easy

SPECIAL FEATURE 2.3

Experience and the Developing Brain

Sandra Twardosz

Brain development continues, not only during infancy and childhood, but throughout the life span, as life experiences affect the structure and function of the brain.

You will recall that the brain is not finished at birth and that the child's experiences—his or her interactions with family and the environment—play a major role in its further development. This is part of what we mean when we say that the brain is plastic; it can be changed by experience. However, not all of brain development is guided by experience. Much of what occurs before birth, for example, is genetically regulated and protected from minor variations in the environment; it is organized ahead of experience (Black, 2003; Marcus, 2003). Nerve cells (neurons) are born; migrate to precise locations, such as the frontal cortex or cerebellum; and take on their appropriate functions. These complex processes are guided primarily by gene expression; in other words, the genes provide an explicit blueprint of instruction for the construction of the brain. The result is that the infant enters the world with an unfinished brain but one that is human, individually unique, and set up to use experience to develop throughout life (Marcus, 2003).

Although billions of neurons have been produced and have migrated to specific locations during prenatal development, most of the connections or synapses among the neurons develop after birth. Neuroscientists who study the way the brains of animals and humans change across the life span believe that experience plays a role in the development of those connections in at least two major ways, experience-expectant and experience-dependent development. Experience-expectant development is associated with sensitive periods, times when the brain is more responsive to a certain type of experience than it will be later; experience-dependent development refers to the way experience is incorporated into brain structure and function throughout life (Bruer & Greenough, 2001; Greenough, Black, & Wallace, 1987).

Experience-expectant development occurs when the brain produces an overabundance of synapses at specific times in preparation for the stimulation that children will almost certainly have simply because they are human beings growing up in typical human environments. For example, almost all children are exposed to touch, sights, sounds, language, and parental care; the brain anticipates those experiences by producing an overabundance of connections and allowing experience to shape and prune them. Seeing patterned light or hearing the sounds of language help to select and organize the connections that will survive in the brain; those that are not selected by experience die, an essential part of the process that allows the brain to function normally and efficiently (Greenough & Black, 1999).

The overproduction and pruning of synapses does not occur simultaneously in all areas of the brain. For example, these processes occur in the visual and auditory areas of the cerebral cortex before they occur in areas devoted to language. The pruning of synapses in areas of the prefrontal cortex that control higher cognitive functions and self-regulation is not finished until midadolescence (Huttenlocher, 1999; Thompson & Nelson, 2001). Thus, different parts of the brain will be most responsive to experience at different times, and the earlier development of some areas may provide the basis for the development of others (Greenough & Black, 1999).

Periods of overproduction and pruning of connections mark the times when the brain is particularly sensitive to certain types of experience; if that experience is not available, or if sensory organs are not functioning properly, normal development may not occur even if the experience is available later. The child's developing visual system, for example, requires that both eyes send clear images to the brain and be pointed in the same direction for visual acuity and binocular vision to develop. This is because the visual cortex "expects" this type of information about the world to organize and prune the connections that have been produced in anticipation of this experience. Infants born with cataracts that cloud their vision or whose eyes are misaligned must have these conditions corrected very early in infancy if normal development of the visual cortex, and thus normal vision, is to occur (Tychsen, 2001).

Some aspects of language development also appear to operate in an experience-expectant manner. For example, before the age of 12 months, infants can discriminate among the phonetic units of all human languages; by the time they are a year old, however, they have lost that ability and resemble adults in being able to discriminate only among the sounds of the languages they have been hearing. As a result of being exposed to those specific sounds, the brain may have altered its structure, and this new structure interferes with learning the phonetic distinctions of a second language (Kuhl, 1999). Similarly, children who have been deprived of the opportunity to develop attachments with caregivers during infancy sometimes face difficulties with subsequent social development. The brain may be particularly responsive during infancy to the "expected" experiences provided to infants as they are protected and nurtured (Thompson, 2001).

Experience-expectant development predominates during infancy and early childhood and even extends into adolescence. However, it is not the only way in which experience shapes the brain. There is another mechanism that begins at birth and continues throughout life in which experience exerts its effect on brain connections in a different way.

Experience-dependent development occurs when new synapses are formed or existing synapses are modified in response to the experiences of the individual.

(continued on next page)

Connections are produced when they are needed rather than being produced in advance, and these new or modified synapses are then available to help with future learning. The ability to change in response to experience is a type of plasticity that the brain retains throughout life and that allows individuals to store information that is unique to them as a member of a specific culture, community, and family. These unique experiences are acquired through exploration of the environment, play, social interaction, or specific teaching (Black, 2003; Bruer & Greenough, 2001; Greenough et al., 1987).

As the individual matures beyond infancy, more brain development is likely to be experience dependent (e.g., Black, 2003), and this concept is probably more relevant for describing how children acquire vocabulary and literacy skills and how teachers learn new strategies for teaching them. Some evidence indicates that the mature brain does respond in this way to

experience. For example, Jacobs, Schall, and Scheibel (1993) found that there was greater dendritic branching in Wernicke's area (a part of the brain involved with processing language) in the brains of adults with higher levels of education.

The concepts of experience-expectant and experience-dependent development can help us think about how experience may be affecting the brain as we observe, interact with, and teach children and as we struggle with and enjoy learning as adults. However, we must be cautious with this information too. Despite the enormous advances that have been made in recent years, the study of the brain, particularly the human brain, is in its infancy. Thus, information from developmental neuroscience must be viewed as a supplement to the understanding we have about teaching and learning from other disciplines such as developmental psychology and education.

to observe, cognitive development is less obvious. Fortunately, children's language development provides one indication that their cognitive abilities are developing normally. In Table 2.1, we present the average ages for language acquisition. While most children demonstrate language skills well within the normal age range, some do not. If a child's language is delayed more than two months past the upper age limits, caregivers should seek medical guidance, as delays may indicate problems (Copeland & Gleason, 1993; Shevell, 2005) Early identification of potential problems leads to appropriate intervention.

TABLE 2.1   Typical Language Development

About 90 percent of children will develop the following language skills by the ages indicated. If a child does not demonstrate these behaviors by these ages, it is important for parents to seek medical guidance.

Age In Months

0–3	■ Majority of communication consists of crying, as larynx has not yet descended
	■ Turns head to the direction of the family's voices
	■ Is startled by loud or surprising sounds
3–6	■ Begins to make cooing sounds to solicit attention from caregivers
	■ Makes "raspberry" sounds
	■ Begins to play with voice
	■ Observes caregiver's face when being spoken to; often shapes mouth in a similar manner
6	■ Vocalization with intonation
	■ Responds to his or her name
	■ Responds to human voices without visual cues by turning head and eyes
	■ Responds appropriately to friendly and angry tones
12	■ Uses one or more words with meaning (this may be a fragment of a word)
	■ Understands simple instructions, especially if vocal or physical cues are given
	■ Practices inflection
	■ Is aware of the social value of speech

18	■ Has vocabulary of approximately 5–20 words
	■ Vocabulary made up chiefly of nouns
	■ Some echolalia (repeating a word or phrase over and over)
	■ Much jargon with emotional content
	■ Is able to follow simple commands

24	■ Can name a number of objects common to his or her surroundings
	■ Is able to use at least two prepositions, such as *in, on, under*
	■ Combines words into a short sentence—largely noun-verb combinations
	■ Approximately 2/3 of what child says should be understandable
	■ Vocabulary of approximately 150–300 words
	■ Rhythm, fluency often poor and volume, pitch of voice not yet well controlled
	■ Can use pronouns such as *I, me, you*
	■ *My* and *mine* are beginning to emerge
	■ Responds to such commands as "show me your eyes (nose, mouth, hair)"

36	■ Is using some plurals and past tenses—"We played a lot"
	■ Handles three-word sentences easily—"I want candy"
	■ Has approximately 900–1,000 words in vocabulary
	■ About 90% of what child says can be understood
	■ Verbs begin to predominate, such as "let's go, let's run, let's climb, let's play"
	■ Understands most simple questions dealing with his or her environment and activities
	■ Relates his or her experiences so that they can be followed with reason
	■ Able to reason out such questions as "What do you do when you are hungry?"
	■ Should be able to give his or her sex, name, age

48	■ Knows names of familiar animals
	■ Names common objects in picture books or magazines
	■ Knows one or more colors and common shapes
	■ Can repeat 4 digits when they are given slowly
	■ Can usually repeat words of four syllables
	■ Demonstrates understanding of *over* and *under*
	■ Often engages in make-believe
	■ Extensive verbalization as he or she carries out activities
	■ Understands such concepts as *longer* and *larger* when a contrast is presented
	■ Much repetition of words, phrases, syllables, and even sounds

60	■ Can use many descriptive words spontaneously—both adjectives and adverbs
	■ Knows common opposites: *big-little*, *hard-soft*, *heavy-light*, and the like
	■ Speech should be completely intelligible, in spite of articulation problems
	■ Should be able to define common objects in terms of use (hat, shoe, chair)
	■ Should be able to follow three commands given without interruptions
	■ Can use simple time concepts: morning, night, tomorrow, yesterday, today
	■ Speech on the whole should be grammatically correct

72	■ Speech should be completely intelligible and socially useful
	■ Should be able to tell a rather connected story about a picture, seeing relationships between objects and happenings
	■ Can recall a story or a favorite video
	■ Should be able to repeat sentences as long as nine words
	■ Can describe favorite pastimes, meals, books, friends
	■ Should use fairly long sentences and some compound and some complex sentences

While helpful, developmental guidelines are not perfect. To determine norms, data must be collected on specific populations. In most cases these data were collected on middle-income Caucasian children born in modern industrial-technological societies. Because this sample does not represent the world's population, the upper and lower age limits of these "universal" norms must be interpreted carefully (Cannella, 2002).

Factors Contributing to Variations in Rate of Language Acquisition

Because the critical period for language development occurs within the first 36 months of a child's life, significant language delay may indicate specific medical or cognitive problems. Beyond medical problems, there are several factors that could modify the rate of normal language production. We review these factors in the following discussion.

Gender Differences

Are there differences in the rate and ways that boys and girls develop language fluency and proficiency? This question reflects another facet of the ongoing nature versus nurture debate. Observational research consistently reveals that a majority of girls talk earlier and talk more than the majority of boys. It is also true that the majority of late talkers are young boys (Healy, 1997; Kalb & Namuth, 1997). However, it is difficult to determine whether differences in the rate of language acquisition are biological or if biological differences are exaggerated by social influences. There is evidence for both views. For example, neural-biological research offers graphic images that illustrate how men's and women's brains process language somewhat differently (Corballis, 1991; Moir & Jessel, 1991). Though this research appears to support nature as the dominant factor in language differences, it is also important to consider how powerful a role nurture plays. Experimental research consistently documents differential treatment of infants based on gender. In other words, men and women tend to cuddle, coo at, and engage in lengthy face-to-face conversations with baby girls. Yet, with baby boys, adults are likely to exhibit "jiggling and bouncing" behaviors but are not as likely to engage in sustained face-to-face verbal interactions. Perhaps girls talk earlier and talk more because they receive more language stimulation (Huttenlocher, 1991).

Socioeconomic Level

Numerous studies have long documented the differences in the rate of language acquisition and the level of language proficiency between low and middle socioeconomic families (Hart & Risley, 1995; Morisset, 1995; Walker, Greenwood, Hart, & Carta, 1994). These studies found that children, especially males, from low-income homes were usually somewhat slower to use expressive language than children from middle-income homes. These findings likely reflect social-class differences both in language use in general and in parent–child interaction patterns. For example, Betty Hart and Todd Risley (1995) estimate that, by age 4, children from professional families have had a cumulative total of 50 million words addressed to them, whereas children from welfare families have been exposed to only 13 million words. The children from professional families have had more than three times the linguistic input than welfare families' children; this gives them a tremendous advantage in language acquisition.

Results of long-term observations of middle-income and lower-income families concluded that all mothers spent a great deal of time nurturing their infants (e.g., touching, hugging, kissing, and holding), but that there were differences in the way mothers verbally interacted with their children. Middle-income mothers spent a great deal more time initiating verbal interactions and usually responded to and praised their infants' vocal efforts. Middle-income mothers were also more likely to imitate their infants' vocalizations. These verbal interactions stimulate neural-synapse networks that foster expressive and receptive language. It is still unclear why lower-income mothers do not engage their children in verbal interactions at the same level as middle-income mothers. The authors of these studies speculate that this may be a reflection of social-class differences in language use in general.

Cultural Influences

The rate of language acquisition may be somewhat different for children of different cultures. Because spoken language is a reflection of the culture from which it emerges, it is necessary to consider the needs verbal language serves in the culture. Communication may be accomplished in other meaningful ways (González, Oviedo, & O'Brien de Ramirez, 2001; Bhavnagri & Gonzalez-Mena, 1997). Janet Gonzalez-Mena (1997, p. 70) offers this example:

> The emphasizing or de-emphasizing the verbal starts from the beginning with the way babies are treated. Babies carried around much of the time get good at sending messages nonverbally— through changing body positions or tensing up or relaxing muscles. They are encouraged to communicate this way when their caregivers pick up the messages they send. They don't need to depend on words at an early age. Babies who are physically apart from their caregivers learn the benefits of verbal communication. If the babies are on the floor in the infant playpen or in the other room at home, they need to learn to use their voices to get attention. Changing position or tensing muscles goes unperceived by the distant adult.

Likewise, some cultures do not view babies' vocal attempts as meaningful communication. Shirley Brice Heath (1983) describes a community in which infants' early vocalizations are virtually ignored and adults do not generally address much of their talk directly to infants. Many cultures emphasize receptive language, and children listen as adults speak.

Medical Concerns

Beyond gender, socioeconomic, and culture differences, other reasons that children's language may be delayed include temporary medical problems and congenital complications. Estimates of hearing impairments vary considerably, with one widely accepted figure of 5 percent representing the portion of young children with hearing levels outside the normal range. Detection and diagnosis of hearing impairment have become very sophisticated. It is possible to detect the presence of hearing loss and evaluate its severity in a newborn child. There are four types of hearing loss:

- Conductive hearing losses are caused by diseases or obstructions in the outer or middle ear and can usually be helped with a hearing aid.
- Sensorineural losses result from damage to the sensory hair cells of the inner ear or the nerves that supply it and may not respond to the use of a hearing aid.
- Mixed hearing losses are those in which the problem occurs both in the outer or middle ear and in the inner ear.
- A central hearing loss results from damage to the nerves or brain.

In Special Feature 2.4, "She Just Stopped Talking," we provide an example of one of the most common childhood problems—otitis media—that, left unattended, could cause significant language delays and speech distortion and ultimately difficulty in learning to read and write.

SPECIAL FEATURE 2.4

She Just Stopped Talking

On her first birthday, Tiffany mimic-sang "Hap Birffaay meee" over and over. She said "Sank oo" when she received her birthday gifts and "Bye, seeoo" when her guests left. Later that summer, after a bad bout with an ear infection, Tiffany's mother noticed she was turning up the volume on the television when she watched *Sesame Street*. A few days later, after several restless nights, Tiffany became very fussy and irritable and began tugging on her ear. Her parents again took her to the doctor, who diagnosed another ear infection. After a ten-day treatment of antibiotics, Tiffany appeared to be fine, except that she seemed to talk less and less.

About a month later, the situation worsened. Tiffany would not respond to her mother's speech unless she was looking directly at her mother. At that point Tiffany had, for the most part, stopped talking.

Tiffany's story is all too common. She was suffering from otitis media with effusion. (See Special Feature 2.5, Otitis Media.)

Otitis Media

Otitis media (OM) is often called a middle ear infection. Three out of four children experience otitis media by the time they are 3 years old. In fact, ear infections are the most common illnesses in babies and young children, accounting for approximately 2 million physician visits annually.

OM infections are usually a result of a malfunction of the Eustachian tube, a canal that links the middle ear with the throat area. The Eustachian tube helps to equalize the pressure between the outer ear and the middle ear. When this tube is not working properly, it prevents normal drainage of fluid from the middle ear, causing a buildup of fluid behind the eardrum. When this fluid cannot drain, it allows for the growth of bacteria and viruses in the ear that can lead to acute otitis media. There are two different types of otitis media:

- **acute otitis media:** the middle ear infection occurs abruptly, causing swelling and redness. Fluid and mucus become trapped inside the ear, causing the child to have a fever, often extreme ear pain, and hearing loss.
- **otitis media with effusion:** fluid (effusion) and mucus continue to accumulate in the middle ear after an initial infection subsides. The child may experience a feeling of fullness in the ear and hearing loss. There may be little or no pain associated with this condition, but it can contribute to hearing loss.

The symptoms of otitis media with effusion usually appear during or after a cold or respiratory infection. Because fluid can collect in the middle ear (behind the eardrum) without causing pain, children with otitis media may not complain. The following is a list of possible symptoms; any one of these symptoms could indicate that a child has otitis media with effusion:

- rubbing or pulling at the ears
- cessation of babbling and singing
- turning up the television or radio volume much louder than usual
- frequently need to have directions and information repeated
- unclear speech
- use of gestures rather than speech
- talking very loudly
- delayed speech and language development.

Because language development is at its peak in the first three years of life, even a temporary hearing loss during this time interferes with speech articulation and language learning. Otitis media causes temporary loss of hearing when the fluid pushes against the eardrum. The pressure prevents the eardrum from vibrating, so sound waves cannot move to the inner ear, and the child's hearing is greatly distorted or muffled. Consequently, final consonant sounds and word endings are often unheard, and words blend into one another. Because one of the main reasons people talk is to communicate, a child who cannot understand what is said becomes frustrated and easily distracted. This type of hearing loss may continue for up to six weeks after the ear infection has healed.

Children who have acute OM are often treated by antibiotics (though this has become somewhat controversial in the medical profession) and with medication for pain. However, if fluid remains in the ear(s) for longer than three months (indicating otitis media with effusion), the child's physician often suggests that small tubes be placed in the ear(s). This surgical procedure, called myringotomy, involves making a small opening in the eardrum to drain the fluid and relieve the pressure from the middle ear. A small tube is placed in the opening of the eardrum to ventilate the middle ear and to prevent fluid from accumulating. The child's hearing is restored after the fluid is drained. The tubes usually fall out on their own after 6 to 12 months.

When Tiffany's parents realized that she had stopped speaking, their pediatrician referred them to a medical specialist called an otolaryngologist (ear, nose, and throat specialist). The doctor was pleased that Tiffany's parents had written down new words she used on the family calendar. As the doctor reviewed the calendar, it became apparent that Tiffany's normal language development had virtually stopped. He did not seem surprised when her parents mentioned that she had also stopped babbling and singing and that she no longer danced when music was played. Because Tiffany's pediatrician had already tried three months of antibiotics to control the infection with no success, the specialist suggested surgically placing bilateral vent tubes in the eardrum to drain the fluid from the middle ear. When the fluid is drained, the eardrum can then vibrate freely once again and normal hearing may be restored.

After a brief operation (approximately 30 minutes), 18-month-old Tiffany began to speak once again. Though her hearing was restored, the doctor suggested that Tiffany and her parents visit a speech therapist to help her fully regain her language.

Within a year, Tiffany's development was progressing normally, and by age three, the surgically implanted tubes naturally fell out of her eardrums.

Congenital Language Disorders

For most children, learning to communicate is a natural, predictable developmental progression. Unfortunately, some children have congenital language disorders that impair their ability to learn language or use it effectively. The origin of these disorders may be physical or neurological. Examples of physical problems include malformation of the structures in the inner ear or a poorly formed palate. Neurological problems could include dysfunction in the brain's ability to perceive or interpret the sounds of language.

Though the symptoms of various language disorders may appear similar, effective treatment may differ significantly, depending on the cause of the problem. For example, articulation problems caused by a physical malformation of the palate might require reconstructive surgery, while articulation problems caused by hearing impairment might require a combination of auditory amplification and speech therapy. Two of the most common symptoms of congenital language disorders are disfluency and pronunciation.

DISFLUENCY. Children with fluency disorders have difficulty speaking rapidly and continuously. They may speak with an abnormal rate—too fast or too slow; in either case, their speech is often incomprehensible and unclearly articulated. The rhythm of their speech may also be severely affected. Stuttering is the most common form of this disorder. Many children may have temporary fluency disruptions or stuttering problems as they are learning to express themselves in sentences. Children who are making a transition to a second language may also experience brief stuttering episodes. It is important for parents or teachers to be patient and supportive, as it may take time to distinguish normal developmental or temporary lapses in fluency from a true pathology. Stuttering may have multiple origins and may vary from child to child. Regardless of cause, recently developed treatment protocols have been effective in helping stutterers (Dodd & Bradford, 2000).

PRONUNCIATION. Articulation disorders comprise a wide range of problems and may have an equally broad array of causes. Minor misarticulations in the preschool years are usually developmental and will generally improve as the child matures (See Special Feature 2.6, Typical Pronunciation Development). Occasionally, as children lose their baby teeth, they may experience temporary challenges in articulation. However, articulation problems that seriously impede a child's ability to communicate needs and intentions must be diagnosed. Causes of such problems may include malformation of the mouth, tongue, or palate; partial loss of hearing due to a disorder in the inner ear; serious brain trauma; or a temporary hearing loss due to an ear infection (Copeland & Gleason, 1993; Forrest, 2002).

Family Focus: Developing Language Over Time

How do parents engage young children in language? Table 2.2 includes simple suggestions that will help enrich parent–child verbal interactions.

SPECIAL FEATURE 2.6

Typical Pronunciation Development

Three-year-old Annie points to a picture of an elephant and says, *"Yes, that's a ella-pant."* Two-year-old Briar sees her favorite TV show and shouts, *"It's da Giggles [Wiggles]!"* Two-and-a-half-year-old Robbie asks his grandma, *"Gigi, can I have some tandy [candy]?"*

Parents both delight in and worry about these darling mispronunciations, which are a normal part of the language development process. Most mispronunciations are usually caused by a combination of children mishearing sounds and misarticulation of new words. Most of these mispronunciations self-correct with maturation. The following list provides speech-language pathologists' terms for specific mispronunciations, examples of the articulation error, and the typical age these mispronunciations disappear.

It is important to remember that some children may simply show delayed language development; this may mean that a child is gaining control over speaking mechanisms at a slower rate than same-age peers or has had limited opportunity to hear speech or interact with others. Children who are learning a second language may also appear to have articulation difficulties when they attempt to use their second language. As Luisa Araújo explains in the following section, anyone learning a new phonemic system will experience some difficulty in expressing new sound combinations. "Bilingual children should be assessed in their native language and referred for therapy only if an articulation disorder is present in that language" (Piper, 1993, p. 193). Caregivers and teachers need to be careful not to confuse the normal course of second-language acquisition with speech disorders.

Speech pathologists' term	Example	Age of maturation
Context-sensitive voicing	Cup=gup	3.0
Final devoicing	bed=bet	3.0
Final consonant deletion	boat=bow	3.3
Velar fronting	car=tar	3.6
Consonant harmony	kittycat=tittytat	3.9
Weak syllable deletion	elephant=effant	4.0
Cluster reduction	spoon=boon	4.0
Gliding of liquids	leg=weg	5.0

Strategies for Teaching English Language Learners: Learning Two Languages

Luisa Araújo

Do you know any families who are raising children who speak a home language other than English or who speak both English and the caregivers' native language? In this chapter you have learned that the input, or the kind of linguistic information children are exposed to from an early age, influences their language development. You have learned that children have a natural instinct to learn language, that there are predictable stages of language development, and that parents support children's efforts to learn language in specific ways. In situations where children are learning English as a second language (ESL), caregivers' responses to children's

vocalizations and conversational bouts are as important as in first language (L1) situations. Valuing communicative interactions and expanding on children's language initiatives optimize language learning (Fennell, Byers-Heinlein & Werker, 2007; Kuhl, 2004).

Young children who learn two languages from birth to the age of 5 experience what experts call simultaneous bilingualism (Bialystok, 1991). When they learn a second language (L2) after the age of 5 they experience sequential bilingualism. Decades of research have shown that bilingual children do not experience any cognitive or language impairments as a result of learning two languages (August & Hakuta, 1997). They are quite capable of maintaining the two language systems separately and of communicating effectively in both. Interestingly, neurolinguistic findings indicate that when 5-year-old bilingual children retell a story in their two languages they activate the same brain area, regardless of the language in which they did the retelling (Kim, Relkin, Lee, & Hirsch, 1997). Bilingual adults who have learned a second language after the age of 7, on the other hand, activate different brain areas depending on whether they did the retelling in their first or second language. This tells us that children who acquire a second language before the age of 5 behave like native speakers because indeed they are (Sakai, 2005). They process the two languages in the same brain area at the same time that they are able to keep them separate.

At times, however, children may engage in *code switching,* the alternate use of two languages from sentence to sentence or even within the same sentence. Code switching is a rule-governed language behavior also used by adult bilinguals (Grosjean, 1982; Lessow-Hurley, 2000). It can be used to emphasize a point, to express ethnic solidarity, and to fill a lexical need. For example, a Spanish/English speaker may reiterate the same message in the two languages to emphasize an order: "Get up now. Levántate!"

A bilingual child who has been exposed to two languages from birth may show this linguistic sophistication in school in addition to the ability to converse with ease in two languages. Parents and teachers may even witness with awe how easily children are able to translate adequately from one language to another depending on the need to address speakers who speak only one language or the other.

Recent estimates tell us that in 2010 over 30 percent of all school-age children will come from homes in which the primary language is not English (Census Bureau, 2001). These children will acquire the second language—English—in the school setting (sequential bilingualism) and the majority of these English language learners (ELL) are Spanish speakers (Goldenberg, 2008). English language learners are individuals who are learning English. The term is usually used in education to refer to students who are acquiring English as a Second Language (ESL). The term ELL is now preferred over limited-English-proficient (LEP) as it highlights accomplishments rather than deficits. Most ELL children attend English-only language classrooms. Some attend first-language classrooms where only their L1 is used or bilingual programs where both English and the home language are used (Tabors, 1998).

English language learners progress through a series of levels of English proficiency. In English-only early childhood settings, a specific sequence explains second-language development: home language use, preproduction, early production, and speech emergence (Goldenberg, 2008; Tabors, 1998). First, young children may speak their home language because they have not yet discovered that a different language is used in the new setting. During the preproduction phase, children are taking in the new language and go through what is called the "silent period," which may take anywhere from one to three months (Krashen, 1981; Saville-Troike, 1988). Children may understand most of the discourse addressed to them in the second language

but are unable to speak it. In the third phase, students are capable of saying one- or two-word utterances. In the fourth phase, speech emerges, and children are able to produce longer phrases and sentences. In considering these levels we must bear in mind that they reflect general trends and that there is variation from child to child. Also, these levels explain only the English oral development of ELLs. In looking at literacy proficiency, including progression in reading and writing, additional developmental levels need to be considered.

Lindfords (1987) and Tabors and Snow (1994) have documented how social interactions assist young children in negotiating meaning while their oral English proficiency increases. Following the "silent period" children begin to use formulaic expressions they memorize and that assist them in communicating with others. They may say "Don't do that," "Wanna play?" to maintain and initiate interactions with other children. When they begin using one- or two-word utterances and longer sentences, their telegraphic discourse may be marked by the ungrammaticality that characterizes the speech of younger monolingual children. For example, in creatively constructing new sentences they may overgeneralize plural formation (foot-foots) and past tense rules for regular verbs (eat-eated). This indicates that children are actively constructing language, using words according to morphological and syntactic rules to form sentences. First and foremost, young children try to figure out how to use the language they know to meet their social needs (Wong-Fillmore, 1991a). Their desire to interact with other children, to play, and to make friends is what drives language learning.

Preschool ELL children have been observed to employ a variety of strategies to learn the second language (Tabors, 1998). Some will repeat to themselves, in a very low voice, the new language they hear. Other will attempt to communicate on early exposure by using gestures, mimes, and cries. In fact, it seems that personality traits and the characteristics of the social setting interact to create learning opportunities. A willingness to communicate and take risks in a nonthreatening social context invites communicative interactions that foster language development. For example, a second-language learner may communicate by saying "Dog run" to mean that the dog is running. A teacher who promotes the kind of interactions that facilitate language development will provide a scaffold by saying, "Yes, the dog is running." As Goldenberg (2008) states, "Students who are beginning English speakers will need a great deal of support, sometimes known as 'scaffolding' for learning tasks that require knowledge of English. For example, at the very beginning levels, teachers will have to speak slowly, with clear vocabulary and diction, and use pictures, objects, and movements to illustrate the content being taught. They should expect students to respond either nonverbally (e.g. pointing or signalling) or in one or two-word utterances" (p. 23).

Early childhood educators can help young ELL children by having a set of daily routines and by

(continued on next page)

(continued)

providing access to activities that are not highly demanding in terms of communication (Tabors, 1998). Daily routines help children predict events and thus learn expected language behaviours. Activities built around a housekeeping area, a sandbox with toys, or a block area engages children in play without the added pressure of having to communicate in specific ways. In addition, teachers should use lots of nonverbal communication or combine gestures with talk, keep the message simple, talk about the here and now, emphasize the important words in sentences, and repeat key words in a sentence. This will help children learn new vocabulary as will the regular reading of picture books because the pictures carry the message.

Indeed, storybook reading provides an authentic linguistic *input* that is easy to understand because it is contextually embedded (pictures). Moreover, it seems that language learning can be optimized when teachers explain the vocabulary using gestures, synonyms, and examples. A recent preschool study shows how

explaining new vocabulary helped Portuguese children—speaking children learn vocabulary from storybook reading (Collins, 2005). Vocabulary learning is a crucial component of literacy instruction because vocabulary building in the early years is associated with good reading performance in third grade (Sénéchal, Ouellette & Rodney, 2006).

Young ELL children need to feel increasingly able to communicate and to feel socially accepted. Teachers may use a buddy system, whereby an outgoing English-speaking child is paired with an ELL child, to help second-language children feel more affectively connected and socially accepted. Similarly, teachers should show children that their home language is socially accepted and valued. As their English proficiency increases, it is easy for children to lose their native language (Wong-Fillmore, 1991b). Asking parents to come to the classroom and share their language and culture will affirm that bilingualism is an asset and not a limitation.

TABLE 2.2   Strategies for Supporting Children's Language Development

Birth to Six Months	Six to Eighteen Months	Eighteen Months to Three Years
Use "parentese" intentionally to stimulate and extend infant's attention span. Talk frequently at close proximity to the infant's face. At about three to four months the child will begin to babble back. Engage in these two-way conversations!		
Describe actions and objects that are encountered in the daily routine (while dressing, changing, feeding, shopping, cleaning, preparing meals, etc.).	Continue to talk frequently all day long, describing actions and objects that are encountered in daily routines.	Talk frequently all day long, but now ask the child questions and wait for the child to respond. Engage in two-way conversations as often as possible.
Modulate voice and vary intonation to match levels of enthusiasm, emotion, meaning.	Use words to describe your feeling(s). *Mom is so happy!*	Use words to describe your feelings and ask child to use words to describe his or her feelings.
Talk face-to-face at a distance where infant can clearly see the adult's mouth and facial expressions as he or she speaks.	Talk face-to-face at a distance where child can clearly see the adult's mouth and facial expressions as he or she speaks.	Talk face-to-face at a distance where the child can clearly see the adult's mouth and facial expressions as he or she speaks.
Use a second language naturalistically if parent is bilingual.	Use a second language naturalistically if parent is bilingual.	Use a second language naturalistically if parent is bilingual.
Introduce songs and music at different times throughout the day and sing simple songs.	Continue to sing songs and engage in finger plays.	Encourage children to sing songs and sing along with them. Children love to sing with their families.

Hold child and read plastic, board, or cloth books on a daily basis to share new words and/or to repeat reading familiar books that the child enjoys.	Parent and child may co-hold the books several times a daily (five to ten minutes only). Child may begin to "read" along. Use your finger to point to the words as you read in order to share new words and/or to repeat reading familiar books that the child enjoys.
Deliberately point out and label simple attributes of objects (smooth, rough, hot, big, square, round, blue, red, striped, wet, etc.).	Ask the child to describe the attributes of objects. Reinforce his or her descriptions and add to the descriptions.
Deliberately point out objects that are the same, or different (e.g., smooth/round, hot/cold, big/little, up/down, over/under, open/shut, wet/dry).	Ask the child to tell you how objects are the same or different.
Read rhyming stories, songs, or finger plays with rhyming words with the child frequently.	Read rhyming stories or plays with rhyming words with the child frequently, pointing out how/where words sound alike and sound different.
	Play simple word games (e.g., the opposites game, complete the rhyme/complete the song phrase, etc.).

Summary

Children's acquisition of oral language is truly remarkable. By the time they enter kindergarten, most children have mastered the basic structures and components of their native language, all without much stress or effort. How did the information contained in this chapter compare with what you were able to discover about your own first words and early language learning? Which of the four perspectives described in this chapter comes closest to your view about children's language development?

To summarize the key points about oral language development, we return to the guiding questions at the beginning of this chapter:

■ *What are the major views on how children's language develops? Which aspects of language development does each view adequately explain?*

Four theories have been used to explain how children acquire language. The behaviorist perspective emphasizes the important role of reinforcement in helping children learn the sounds, words, and rules of language. This view handily explains the imitative aspects of initial language learning. Nativists stress the importance of children's inborn capacity to learn language and suggest that a portion of the brain is dedicated to language learning. Nativist theory explains how children "invent" their own two- and three-word grammars and overgeneralize rules for past tense ("He goed to the store") and plural ("I saw two mouses today!"). The social-interactionist perspective emphasizes the importance of both environmental factors and children's innate predisposition to make sense out of language and use it for practical purposes. According to this view, children learn about language by using it in social situations. The social-interactionist view highlights the role of parental support in language acquisition. Finally, new technology has allowed scientists to observe how the brain perceives, interprets, and expresses language. These developments have led to a new perspective of children's language learning, the neurobiological view, which complements the three earlier views on language development. This perspective explains how the structural development of the brain is related to language acquisition. It helps explain why children's experiences during infancy have such a crucial effect on later language learning.

■ *What are the major components of language?*

The major components of language are (1) phonology—the sounds that make up a language; (2) morphology—the meaning bearing units of language, including words and affixes; (3) syntax—the rules for ordering words into sentences; (4) semantics—the shades of meaning that words convey; and (5) pragmatics—the social rules that enable language to accomplish real-life purposes.

■ *How does the structure of an infant's brain develop? How does this structural development affect language acquisition?*

At birth, the human brain is remarkably unfinished. Most of the 100 billion neurons or brain cells are not yet connected. During the first month of life, the number of neural synapses or connections increase 20 times to more than 1,000 trillion. As a child matures, the actual number of neurons remains stable; however, the number of synapse connections increase, and the message-receiving dendrite branches grow larger and heavier. At age 1, the full cortex consumes twice as much energy as an adult brain. This neural readiness, in combination with countless hours of sound play and verbal exchanges with loving caregivers, allows most children to begin speaking their first words at this age.

By 18 months, neural synapses have increased and strengthened and are beginning to transmit information efficiently. Hence, most toddlers begin to experience a language explosion, particularly in the areas of vocabulary and syntax. During this time, children are able to learn as many as 12 words a day. Thus, the neurobiological perspective reveals how the rapid development of the brain during the first few years of life makes it possible for children to acquire language so quickly and efficiently. This perspective also explains why the first 36 months are a critical period for language development.

■ *What factors affect children's rate of language acquisition?*

Although language development follows a predictable sequence, the rate at which children acquire language varies tremendously. Gender, socioeconomic level, and cultural influences all can affect the rate of language acquisition. A child's language learning can also be impeded by illnesses, such as otitis media, and by a variety of congenital problems of a physical and/or neurological nature. Parents and caregivers are cautioned to seek a medical diagnosis if language development is significantly delayed, as early identification and treatment can often avoid irreparable disruption of the language acquisition process.

■ *How does children's acquisition of a second language compare with their first language acquisition? What should adults do to make it easier for children to learn English as a second language?*

In many ways, second-language acquisition in young children is similar to their acquisition of their first language. In learning a new language, children engage in the creative construction of the rules of the new language, and this creative construction occurs within the context of multiple social interactions as children use the new language with others.

Adults working with second-language learners need to focus both on making themselves understood by children and encouraging these children to use their new language. Adults need to focus on the learners' communicative intentions, not on the conventionality of their utterances. Children should be encouraged but not forced to use the new language, and children should not be belittled for hesitancy in trying it. Adults need to recognize that children are learning English even if they are not responding verbally. Adults need to encourage other children who are native speakers of English to have patience with ESL learners and to assist them in their learning. Finally, adults should value the native languages that children bring to school with them and encourage them to continue to use their native languages.

LINKING KNOWLEDGE TO PRACTICE

1. Interview a parent and an early childhood teacher regarding how they believe children learn language. Consider which theory of language acquisition best matches each interviewee's beliefs.
2. Interview a school nurse or health care aide about the numbers of children she or he sees who are affected by illnesses and congenital problems. From the health care worker's

perspective, what effect do these medical problems have on children? How often should children be screened for auditory acuity? If a family has limited financial recourses, what agencies can provide medical services?

3. Observe a second-language learner in a preschool or day care setting. Does the second-language learner comprehend some of the talk that is going on in the classroom? How does the child communicate with other children? How does the teacher support the child's second-language acquisition? Are other children helping? Does the second-language learner have any opportunities to use his or her native language?

Go to the Topics Oral Language Development, English Language Learners, and At Risk and Struggling Readers in the MyEducationLab (www.myeducationlab.com) for your course, where you can:

- Find learning outcomes for Oral Language Development, English Language Learners, and At Risk and Struggling Readers along with the national standards that connect to these outcomes.
- Complete Assignments and Activities that can help you more deeply understand the chapter content.
- Examine challenging situations and cases presented in the IRIS Center Resources.

Go to the Topic A+RISE in the MyEducationLab (www.myeducationlab.com) for your course. A+RISE® Standards2Strategy™ is an innovative and interactive online resource that offers new teachers in grades K-12 just in time, research-based instructional strategies that:

- Meet the linguistic needs of ELLs as they learn content
- Differentiate instruction for all grades and abilities
- Offer reading and writing techniques, cooperative learning, use of linguistic and nonlinguistic representations, scaffolding, teacher modeling, higher order thinking, and alternative classroom ELL assessment
- Provide support to help teachers be effective through the integration of listening, speaking, reading, and writing along with the content curriculum
- Improve student achievement
- Are aligned to Common Core Elementary Language Arts standards (for the literacy strategies) and to English language proficiency standards in WIDA, Texas, California, and Florida.

Family Literacy and Language Development

Snuggled next to her mother, 1-year-old Tiffany is listening to one of her best-loved bedtime stories, Goodnight Moon, *by Margaret Wise Brown (1947).*

> *Pointing to the picture, Tiffany says, "Mamma, da mousey."*
> *"That's right, Tiffany," says her mother, who resumes reading:*

A few moments later, Tiffany, touches the pictures of the bunny mother sitting in the rocking chair, says, "Dat's like Nane Gammaw."

> *Her mother replies, "Yes, Tiffany, she looks like Grandma."*
> *Throughout the story, Tiffany comments on the illustrations. As her mother finishes the last line, a very sleepy Tiffany yawns, "Ganight, Mamma."*

If you experienced moments like Tiffany's, you are indeed fortunate. Her mother's gentle support encouraged her language while the storybook reading provides a simple but effective blueprint for learning to read. Research demonstrates that a family's role in a child's language and literacy development is directly related to the child's communicative competence (Hart & Risley, 1995), positive attitudes toward reading and writing, initial literacy achievement (e.g., Christian et al., 1998; Epstein, 1986; Nord, Lennon, Liu, & Chandler, 2000), and it also appears to have an extended impact on high school achievement (Enz, 1992; Enz & Searfoss, 1995).

In recent years, researchers have made great progress in expanding our understanding of early language and literacy development. We now know that children acquire written language in much the same way that they learn oral language. Both are social, constructive processes. With oral language, children listen to the language that surrounds them, detect patterns and regularities, and make up their own rules for speech. Children then try out and refine these rules as they engage in everyday activities with others. Similarly, with written language, children observe the print that surrounds them and watch their parents and others use reading and writing to get things done in daily life. They then construct their own concepts and rules about literacy, and they try out those ideas in social situations. With experience, these child-constructed versions of reading and writing become increasingly similar to conventional adult forms.

In this chapter, we describe how children's knowledge of print develops and the role families play this ongoing process. For children living in a culture that values literacy, the process of learning to read and write begins very early, often before their first birthdays! This chapter also discusses the role families play in the development of a child's language acquisition. This chapter presents two case studies: Tiffany, a monolingual English speaker, and Alicia, a child who is learning English. Finally, we will describe strategies teachers can use to inform parents of all cultures and other primary caregivers about the critical role they play in their child's language and literacy development and how parents and teachers can work together to enhance language and reading and writing opportunities in the home.

BEFORE READING THIS CHAPTER, THINK ABOUT . . .

- Your early literacy experiences. Do you remember precious moments snuggling with a special person and sharing a book? Do you remember talking with an adult who provided you with many experiences and the words to describe these experiences? Do you remember an adult helping you read words in your environment?
- How you learned to read and write. Do you remember reading and writing at home before going to school? Do you remember having lots of books in your home? What were your favorite books as a young child?
- Do you remember having access to paper and pencils? Were you an early reader—that is, did you learn to read without any formal instruction from an adult?

FOCUS QUESTIONS

- How do reading and writing develop?
- What home factors affect young children's literacy development?
- How can parents best facilitate language development?
- What does emergent literacy look like in a language other than English?

Home Literacy Experiences

Interest in emergent literacy began with studies of early readers, children who learned to read before they entered kindergarten. This research led to investigations of what preschool-age children typically learn about print. At the same time, researchers began to investigate children's home literacy experiences, seeking to discover the factors that promote early literacy acquisition.

Early studies on home literacy learning focused on umbrella characteristics such as family income and parents' levels of education (Sulzby & Teale, 1991). Results revealed positive relationships between these variables and reading achievement in the early grades. For example, children from middle-income families tend to be better readers than those from low-income families. Unfortunately, such findings do little to explain how these variables directly affect children's literacy growth.

BOX 3.1 Definitions of Terms	**Early literacy:** A broad term that refers to the reading and writing behaviors that children engage in from birth to age 5 **Emergent literacy:** A view of literacy development suggesting children learn literacy by constructing, testing, and refining their own hypotheses about print **Emergent reading:** Forms of reading children use as they move toward conventional reading **Emergent writing:** Forms of writing children use as they move toward conventional writing **Scaffolding:** Temporary assistance that parents and teachers give to children to enable them to do things that they cannot do on their own

More recent studies have narrowed their focus and have attempted to describe the actual literacy-related experiences that children have at home. These home literacy studies have identified several factors that appear to have important roles in early literacy acquisition. These factors are described in the sections that follow.

Access to Print and Books

To learn about literacy, young children must have opportunities to see lots of print and must have easy access to books. Plentiful home supplies of children's books have been found to be associated with early reading (Durkin, 1966; Nord et al., 2000), interest in literature (Morrow, 1983), and positive orientation toward schooling (Feitelson & Goldstein, 1986).

Because of the literate nature of our society, all children are surrounded by large amounts of environmental print. For example, they see print on product containers (Cheerios, Pepsi), street signs (Stop), and store signs (McDonald's, Pizza Hut). Differences do occur, however, in children's exposure to books and other forms of reading materials. Bill Teale's (1986) descriptive study of the home environments of 24 low-income preschoolers revealed that, while some of the homes had ample supplies of children's books, other homes contained none. Some 25 years later, a readiness study conducted with over 1,100 Arizona kindergarteners and their parents, from a wide range of socioeconomic backgrounds, revealed similar findings. This study also found the number of books in the home was correlated with the children's level of alphabet recognition and concepts of print (Yaden, Enz, & Perry, 2010). This is not to suggest that all children from low-income families lack exposure to reading materials at home. However, those children who do not have access to books at home are at a great disadvantage in acquiring literacy.

Adult Demonstrations of Literacy Behavior

Children also need to observe their parents, other adults, or older siblings using literacy in everyday situations (Smith, 1988). When children see their family members use print for various purposes—writing shopping lists, paying bills, looking up programs in the television listings, and writing notes to each other—they begin to learn about the practical uses of written language and to understand why reading and writing are activities worth doing. If their parents happen to model reading for pleasure, so much the better. These children see literature as a source of entertainment. Children's exposure to these types of functional and recreational literacy demonstrations has been found to vary greatly (Enz & Foley, 2009).

Supportive Adults

Early readers tend to have parents who are very supportive of their early attempts at literacy (Morrow, 1983). While these parents rarely attempt to directly teach their children how to read and write, they do support literacy growth by doing such things as (1) answering their children's questions about print; (2) pointing out letters and words in the environment; (3) reading storybooks frequently; (4) making regular visits to the local library; (5) providing children with a wide variety of experiences such as trips to stores, parks, and museums; and (6) initiating functional literacy activities (such as suggesting that a child write a letter to grandmother or help make a shopping list).

The amount of such support that children receive during the preschool years varies greatly from family to family, and these differences have been found to have a considerable effect on children's literacy learning during kindergarten and the elementary grades (Grinder, Longoria-Saenz, Askov, & Aldemir, 2005).

Independent Engagements with Literacy

Young children need to get their hands on literacy materials and to have opportunities to engage in early forms of reading and writing. This exploration and experimentation allows children to try out and perfect their growing concepts about the functions, forms, and conventions of written language.

FIGURE 3.1

Ben's Post-it note: "Gone to soccer practice. Be back at 4."

Independent engagements with literacy often take place in connection with play. Don Holdaway (1979) has described how, as soon as young children become familiar with a storybook through repetitive read-aloud experiences, they will begin to play with the books and pretend to read them. He believes that this type of readinglike play is one of the most important factors promoting early literacy acquisition.

Young children also incorporate writing into their play. Sometimes this play writing is exploratory in nature, with children experimenting with different letter forms and shapes. At other times, emergent writing occurs in the context of make-believe play. Figure 3.1 is an example of this type of play-related writing. Four-year-old Ben was engaging in dramatic play in the housekeeping center. He wrote a Post-it Note message to another child, who was acting out the role of his mother, informing her that he was at soccer practice.

Young children also use literacy in functional, nonplay situations. An excellent example is Glenda Bissex's (1980) account of how her 4-year-old son Paul, after failing to get her attention by verbal means, used a stamp set to write "RUDF" (Are you deaf?). He also attempted to secure his privacy by putting the sign "DO NOT DSTRB GNYS AT WRK" ("Do not disturb—Genius at work") on his door.

Opportunities to engage in these types of independent engagements with literacy depend on access to books and writing materials. As mentioned previously, research on children's home environments indicates that there are wide discrepancies in the availability of children's books and other reading materials. Similar differences also exist in the availability of writing materials. Teale's (1986) descriptive study of the home environments of low-income preschoolers revealed that only 4 of 24 children had easy access to paper and writing instruments. He noted that these particular children engaged in far more emergent writing than did the other subjects in the study.

Storybook Reading

Storybook reading is undoubtedly the most studied aspect of home literacy. Quantitative studies have attempted to establish the importance and value of parents' reading to their children. A recent meta-analysis of 29 studies spanning more than three decades indicated that parent–preschooler storybook reading was positively related to outcomes such as language growth, early literacy, and reading achievement (Bus, van Ijzendoorn, & Pellegrini, 1995).

Reading storybooks

Other studies have attempted to describe and analyze what actually takes place during storybook-reading episodes and to identify the mechanisms through which storybook reading facilitates literacy growth (e.g., Altwerger, Diehl-Faxon, & Dockstader-Anderson, 1985; Heath, 1982; Holdaway, 1979; Sénéchal & LeFevre, 2002; Snow & Ninio, 1986; Yaden, Smolkin, & Conlon, 1989). These studies have shown that parent–child storybook reading is an ideal context for children to receive all of the previously mentioned factors that promote literacy acquisition:

1. Storybook reading provides children with access to enjoyable children's books, building positive attitudes about books, and reading (Nord et al., 2000).
2. During storybook reading, parents present children with a model of skilled reading. Children see how books are handled, and they hear the distinctive intonation patterns that are used in oral reading (Askov, Grinder, & Kassab, 2005).
3. Parents provide support that enables young children to take an active part in storybook reading. Early storybook-reading sessions tend to be routinized, with the parent first focusing the child's attention on a picture and then asking the child to label the picture. If the child does so, the parent gives positive or negative feedback about the accuracy of the label. If the child does not volunteer a label, the parent provides the correct label (Snow & Ninio, 1986). As children's abilities grow, parents up the ante, shifting more of the responsibility to the children and expecting them to participate in more advanced ways.
4. Storybook reading encourages independent engagements with literacy by familiarizing children with stories and encouraging them to attempt to read the stories on their own (Holdaway, 1979; Sulzby, 1985a).

Other researchers have studied how cultural factors affect the way parents mediate storybook reading for their children. Shirley Brice Heath (1982) found that middle-class parents tended to help their children link book information with other experiences.

For example, John Langstaff's popular predictable book *Oh, A-Hunting We Will Go* (1974, Macmillan) contains the word *pram*. To help the child understand the term *pram*, a middle-class parent might say, "The pram looks just like your sister's baby carriage." Working-class parents, on the other hand, had a tendency to not extend book information beyond its original context and would simply define the word *pram* for the child. Researchers speculate that these differences in story-reading style may have a considerable effect on children's early language and literacy acquisition (Christian et al., 1998; Enz & Foley, 2009; Griffin & Morrison, 1997; Morrow, 1988; Sulzby & Teale, 1991).

Case Studies

In the following sections we present two case studies of early literacy development. Tiffany, a native English-speaking child, is the subject of the first case study. The second study describes Alicia's literacy acquisition. Alicia is a native speaker of Spanish, and English is her second language. There are many interesting similarities and differences in the early literacy acquisition of these two girls.

Tiffany

Tiffany's parents began reading to her soon after birth, and by age 1 year, she was actively participating in storybook-reading sessions. Now, more than two years later, 30-month-old Tiffany has begun to attempt to read on her own. The story begins in her bedroom, where she was looking at Richard Scarry's *Best Word Book Ever* (1980, Western Publishing Company) with her sister Dawn. Though her house has many children's books, this book was one of her favorites. Tiffany delighted in labeling the pictures and describing the actions of the Bunny family as they engage in familiar, everyday situations. As Tiffany pointed to the pictures of Nicki Bunny going to the doctor for a checkup, both she and Dawn laughed at the animals who are all dressed up in clothing: "Nicki Bunny wears shoes!" While attempting to read this text, Tiffany displayed many aspects of her concepts about print, including book handling and turning pages (starting at the front of the book and progressing to the back), as well as an appreciation of storybook reading.

On the way to the grocery story several months later, Tiffany's family passed a McDonald's sign. Thirty-three-month-old Tiffany shouted with gleeful recognition, "Donald's—ummm, eat burgers." Tiffany, like most children brought up in a literate culture, had already begun to recognize that her world is full of environmental print. Though Tiffany's reading of the McDonald's sign came more from interpreting the color and shape of the logo than from differentiating letters, it demonstrated her understanding that print carries meaning—another important developmental milestone.

Tiffany was also beginning to demonstrate an understanding that writing, as well as oral language, communicates meaning. Waiting with her mother in the bank, 36-month-old Tiffany took a handful of bank forms. While her mother talked to the bank manager, Tiffany occupied herself by using a pen to fill out the many forms. Her writing contained many squiggly lines and some picturelike forms. When Tiffany's mother asked her what she had written, Tiffany replied, "I write, 'Tiffy can buy money'"(see Figure 3.2). At this stage, it is typical for

FIGURE 3.2

Tiffany (age 36 months) writes a note using drawing and scribbles: "Tiffy can buy money."

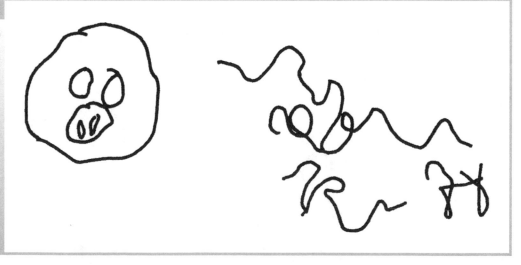

children's writing to include both pictographs (pictures that represent writing) and scribble writing. Notice that her scribbling has the appearance of an adult's English cursive writing.

Sitting on her Daddy's lap, 42-month-old Tiffany was reading him the story of Maurice Sendak's *Where the Wild Things Are* (1988, Scholastic)

> *This bad boy in the wolf pajamas is mean to his mommy.*
> *He runs away 'cause he is mad.*
> *He gets in a boat, like "rubba a dub" [Tiffany's bathtub toy boat]*
> *Then he meets some big bad chicken monsters and yells at them.*
> *They make him the King, 'cause he yelled so loud!!!*
> *Then he goed home 'cause he wanted to eat.*

The story she told consisted of her interpretations of the text's illustrations, and she used a storytelling tone as she held the book and turned the pages. As explained earlier, this behavior is indicative of Elizabeth Sulzby's category of emergent reading, "attending to pictures, forming oral stories" (Sulzby & Barnhart, 1990). Though Tiffany's oral retelling of the story was fairly accurate, her father noted that she did not include the monster refrain—"and they rolled their terrible eyes, gnashed their terrible teeth, and showed their terrible claws!" Her omission of this salient part of the story was probably caused by the fact that, during this stage of emergent reading, story retelling is guided by the illustrations rather than by the words in the text. As the pictures did not explicitly detail this refrain, Tiffany lacked the visual cues that would have triggered the recitation of this phrase.

At age 4 years, Tiffany continued to refine her understanding of the many functions of print. Sitting at her child-sized table in her pretend play house with her best friend Becca, Tiffany pondered over a piece of paper with her pencil in her mouth:

Tiffany: What do you think the babies will eat?

Becca: Baby food, Tiff.

Tiffany: I know that! What kind of baby food?

Becca: Oh, I think the orange stuff, but not the green.

Tiffany: [Now writing this information down] Okay. What else?

Becca: You need to write down cat food and take the coupons.

Tiffany: [Pulling out a bunch of coupons from her drawer, she sorts through them until she finds the Purina Cat Chow coupon.] Yeah, that coupon says "free cat food."

Tiffany had now begun to produce letterlike forms (see Figure 3.3). Though she continued to use pictographs, Tiffany could distinguish print from pictures. Pointing to the drawing she said, "This is a picture of baby food." She went on to describe her letterlike forms with the comment, "This says buy peaches and diapers."

This episode also reveals that Tiffany was continuing to expand her environmental print vocabulary. In fact, she was becoming quite adept at recognizing dozens of product names. This ability was fostered by parental praise and encouragement each time Tiffany joined her parents as a member of the grocery-shopping expedition.

FIGURE 3.3

Tiffany (age 48 months) writes a shopping list.

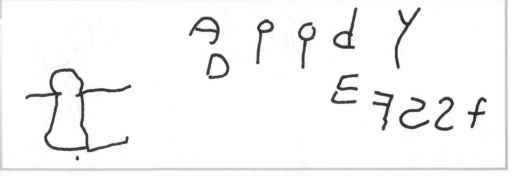

At age 4 years, Tiffany started preschool. One of the first academic activities her preschool teachers undertook was helping the children to recognize and print their own name. As is often the case, Tiffany's first attempts to print her name were somewhat frustrating. Though she was quite accomplished at making letterlike forms, trying to reproduce specific letters in a specified sequence was definitely a challenge. At that time, Tiffany received a chalkboard from her grandparents. The new writing implement seemed to inspire her to practice more frequently, and soon Tiffany had mastered the fine art of printing her name.

Along with printing her name, Tiffany, as well as most of her preschool classmates, was becoming interested in naming and printing the alphabet. This interest was sparked by her teachers through direct, developmentally appropriate instruction. Prior to her preschool experience, Tiffany only casually watched the Sesame Street letter segments, paying attention instead to the social drama of the Sesame Street characters. However, between the ages of 4 and 5 years, Tiffany became an astute alphabet hunter—shouting with great authority the names of the letters as they flashed across the television screen. Tiffany sang the alphabet song, read alphabet books, did alphabet puzzles and alphabet dot-to-dot worksheets, and molded clay letters. She diligently wrote alphabet symbols with every type of writing tool imaginable—markers, pens, pencils, and water paints and paint brushes. She wrote her letters on every surface conceivable, including her bedroom walls! Her all-time favorite alphabet activity was writing her letters with soap crayons on the bathtub/shower wall.

Tiffany's new proficiency with letter formation resulted in the production of many strings of random capital and lowercase letters or, using Sulzby's (1990) terminology, strings of nonphonetic letter strings. Notice that though Tiffany knew many upper- and lowercase letters, she was not yet forming words or clustering her letters in wordlike units. (See Figure 3.4).

Soon after Tiffany entered preschool, she became interested in joining her sister Dawn (age 7) in playing school. During these dramatic play sessions, Tiffany would listen to Dawn as she read basal texts and their favorite literature. In the role of teacher, Dawn would ask factual questions during and after reading storybooks to Tiffany. For example, after reading Maurice Sendak's *Where the Wild Things Are* (1984, Harper & Row), Dawn asked, "What did the monsters say to Max? What did Max say to the monsters?" Dawn would model writing letters on the chalkboard and then ask Tiffany to copy what she had written. Tiffany did her best to reproduce the words that Dawn wrote. Every so often, Tiffany would run out to her mom and proclaim, "Look it! What it say?"

FIGURE 3.4

Tiffany (age 54 months) writes a stream of random letters

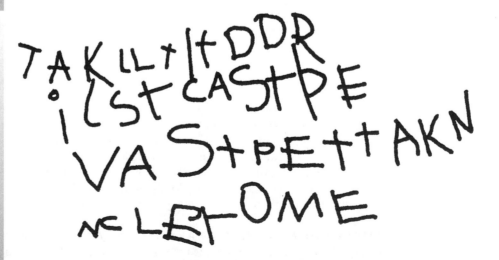

FIGURE 3.5

Tiffany (age 60 months) uses invented spelling in her journal.

Later in the year, when Dawn was at school, Tiffany would play school by herself, only this time she was the teacher. Dressed in a long white pleated skirt, heels, and jacket, she looked like Ms. O'Bannon, her sister's second grade teacher. She would "read" stories to her teddy bear and to rows of doll students, and she would use her ruler to point to alphabet cards posted on the wall. She would ask Teddy to pay attention and ask Annie (a doll) to tell her what the letters said. It is interesting to note that, when Tiffany pretended to be the teacher, her writing became more conventional. She carefully wrote her letters as she practiced saying the phrases that Dawn had used earlier: "Start at the top, draw a flat-hat top, then find the middle and draw a straight line. Now you see, you have a *T*."

Sitting in her miniature rocker holding her beloved baby doll Ramalda, 4 1/2-year-old Tiffany began reading another favorite story, *Old Hat, New Hat* by Stan and Jan Berenstain (1976, Random House). Pointing to the pictures, Tiffany recited the story line, "new hat, new hat, new hat" and "too feathery, too scratchy," then the rousing finale, "just right, just right, just right!" Tiffany's recitation involved following the pictures and recalling the phrases she had heard and repeated with her parents virtually dozens of times. At this point in her development, her storybook reading was beginning to sound like reading as she imitated the expression and phrasing her parents used when they read this story to her.

When Tiffany began kindergarten at age 5 years, she could recognize most alphabet letters. During her kindergarten year, Tiffany learned that each alphabet letter made a specific sound, but some alphabet letters made two or three sounds. For Tiffany, this phonics knowledge was an exciting step toward literacy. She reveled in baking Big Bird's brown banana bread with butter and studying the scientific qualities of bubbles and bouncing balls billions of times.

Her teacher, Ms. C., also modeled the writing process at the end of each day. She began by asking the children to summarize what they had learned that day, and as the children volunteered ideas, she would write their statements. While Ms. C. wrote, she would ask, "Who knows what letter Baby Bear starts with? What other sounds do you hear?" This type of informal modeling provided the spark that ignited Tiffany's reading-writing connection. This very sensitive teacher also had the kindergarten children write in their journals at their own developmental level. The writing sample illustrates one of Tiffany's first invented-spelling journal entries (see Figure 3.5). At this point, she was beginning to separate her words.

Alicia

Irene Serna and Sarah Hudelson present a second case study of early literacy. This case study features Alicia, who came from a home in which Spanish was the primary language. When she entered kindergarten, Alicia was speaking Spanish but was only partially proficient in oral English. She attended a bilingual kindergarten in which she learned to read and write in Spanish and then transfer what she had learned to English literacy. It is interesting to compare Alicia's acquisition of reading and writing in Spanish with Tiffany's literacy development in English. As you will see, there are many interesting parallels.

ALICIA'S HOME LANGUAGE AND LITERACY. Spanish was the dominant language in Alicia's home. Her mother reported that Alicia had requested that books be read to her since she was 4 years old. In addition, Alicia had been eager to engage in writing within family

Alicia's Early Literacy Development in Spanish

Irene Serna and Sarah Hudelson

As Tiffany's case study illustrates, young children begin to read and write English by engaging in daily literacy activities with family members and teachers.

These adults support early literacy by creating opportunities for reading and writing and by responding to children's requests for assistance. What does early literacy look like in a language other than English? Alicia is a Spanish-speaking kindergartner that Serna and Hudelson came to know through their research. She provides a good example of how children construct their literacy in Spanish.

activities. At home, Alicia helped produce shopping lists, notes, and cards sent to family members. Of course, these were written in Spanish. Clearly, Alicia came from a very literate home environment that featured frequent storybook reading, many opportunities to write in connection with daily activities, and adults who supported her early attempts at reading and writing. In this regard, Alicia's early literacy development was quite similar to Tiffany's and that of other English-speaking children who come from supportive home environments. There was one significant difference—Alicia reported that her mother and grandmother frequently told her *cuentos* (folk tales) and family stories. Thus, storytelling (oral literacy) was also a strong part of Alicia's home literacy experiences; for more information see Special Feature 3.1, The Home Literacy Experiences of Nonmainstream Children.

ALICIA'S LITERACY DEVELOPMENT IN KINDERGARTEN. Though Alicia participated in a bilingual Head Start program as a 4-year-old, when she entered kindergarten, her score on an oral language proficiency test identified her as limited-English proficient.

SPECIAL FEATURE 3.1

The Home Literacy Experiences of Nonmainstream Children

The majority of the research on the home literacy experiences of young children has been conducted in white, middle-class homes. In recent years, however, increasing attention is being given to the home literacy experiences of nonmainstream children—children from low-income and ethnically diverse families. The findings are mixed and show a complex picture of these children's early experiences with language and literacy.

On the one hand, some studies have shown that many poor families have had difficulty providing their children with the rich types of language and literacy experiences that middle-income families typically provide (Vernon-Feagons, Hammer, Miccio, & Manlove, 2001). The Hart and Risley (1995) study, described in detail in Chapter 2, reported that low-income mothers used fewer words and a more restricted vocabulary in conversations with their children. Other studies suggest that many low-income children may have less experience with rhyming activity (Fernandez-Fein & Baker, 1997) and are less

likely to visit public libraries (Baker, Serpell, & Sonnenschein, 1995).

Other studies have documented a wide range of home literacy environments and practices within nonmainstream families (Purcell-Gates, 1995; Taylor & Dorsey-Gaines, 1988; Teale, 1986). For example, Purcell-Gates's study of 20 low-income families of differing ethnic backgrounds revealed great variability in the literacy experiences of children. The total number of literacy events in the low-income homes ranged from 0.17 to 5.07 per hour, meaning that some children had opportunities to experience more than 25 times the amount of literacy than other children! Similarly, Teale's study of low-income children in San Diego, California, revealed that the average number of minutes per hour that children engaged in literacy activities ranged from 3.6 to 34.72, almost a tenfold difference. While on average the home literacy experiences of low-income children may not be as rich as those of the average middle-class children, some nonmainstream children do have frequent interactions with print.

Vernon-Feagans, Miccio, Manlove, and Hammer, (2001) point out a shortcoming of research on nonmainstream children's home literacy environments: "Most studies of poverty have generally measured

(continued on next page)

environmental factors in the home at the exclusion of measuring health and the larger discrimination in the larger society." For example, they cite Vernon-Feagans's (1996) study of rural African American children in the Piedmont area of North Carolina. This study found that, within this group of children, those with early nutritional deficits were at much greater risk of having problems acquiring literacy. Larger societal factors also enter the picture. Neuman and Celano (2001), for example, found that low-income families had much more restricted access to public libraries and places to buy books. In addition, the school libraries in low-income neighborhoods had fewer books per child, lower-quality books, less-qualified librarians, and fewer computers. So limited access to literacy materials and good places to read, caused by societal inequities, may be contributing factors to many low-income children's "at-risk" status.

Two-thirds of the children in her bilingual kindergarten program spoke English, and one-third spoke Spanish. Alicia used both languages to socialize with her peers. However, she primarily used Spanish to explain her thinking, to narrate stories, and to express herself personally. At the beginning of kindergarten, Alicia discussed only books that were read aloud in Spanish. By the latter half of the year, she was discussing books read in both languages. This was particularly helpful to the monolingual children because Alicia could interpret books and communications in English or Spanish. Alicia's role in the classroom became that of translator. Thus, while her one year of Head Start was not sufficient time for Alicia to develop oral proficiency in English, the second year of bilingual programming in kindergarten did allow her to develop bilingual abilities.

WRITING. Beginning in October of her kindergarten year, Alicia was asked to write in a journal for 45 minutes daily. Throughout the year, she also drew and wrote in learning logs to record information from study in thematic units. She contributed to group language experience charts, which summarized findings from the children's thematic studies. In her earliest journal entries, Alicia wrote a patterned and familiar phrase in English, "I love my mom." A November entry demonstrated that Alicia had moved from producing a patterned phrase to creating a label for her picture: *"Mi papalote"* ("my kite"). In November, Alicia also wrote her first sentence describing a picture, *"Yo ciro mi babe Martinsito"* ("I love my baby Martincito"), using both invented (*ciro* for *quiero*) and conventional spelling. She also wrote additional patterned sentences, *"Mi Nana bonita come sopa Mi mami bonita come sopa"* ("My pretty grandmother eats soup. My pretty mother eats soup."). In December, Alicia repeated phrases to write two lines of text describing her picture, *"Los colores del arco iris son bonitos Colores del arco ids"* ("The colors of the rainbow are pretty. The colors of the rainbow"). Her writing did not become more expressive until February when she wrote about playing in the pile of snow that had been trucked to the school (see Figure 3.6).

This February sample demonstrates that Alicia's invented spellings included most sounds in each syllable, that the vowels were standardized, and that she confused some of the consonants. Though she put spaces between most words, conventional word separation was not used consistently.

In April, Alicia wrote a personal narrative about her little cousin Martincito, primarily describing how she cared for and played with him. Figure 3.7 contains two of the ten sentences she wrote in this personal narrative. Written over a three-week period, Alicia's personal narrative illustrates that her invented spellings were very close approximations of standard Spanish spellings. Alicia also separated words more consistently. Syntactically, all of her sentences were complete, and all grammatical inflections were correct. By the end of kindergarten, Alicia was the classroom's most fluent writer in Spanish. As a result, other children often asked her to write their personal narratives.

READING. From September through February, Alicia retold stories from familiar, predictable picture books using some of the story language in Spanish and some in English. In March, her first story was typed for publication (in Spanish). Alicia read this text for the first time

FIGURE 3.6

Alicia's February writing sample.

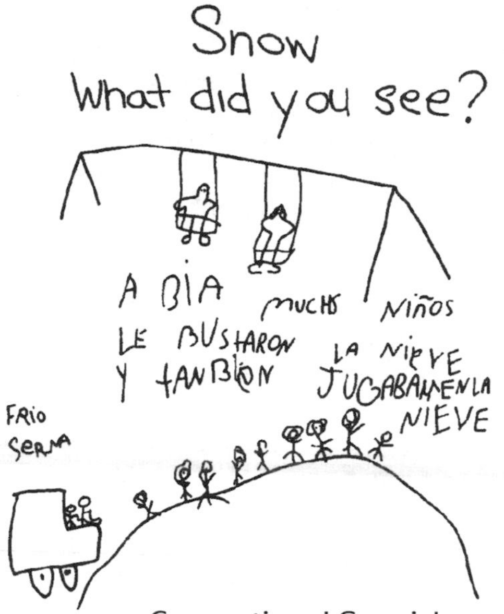

Alicia's spelling	Conventional Spanish spelling	English translation
A bia muchs niños	Habían muchos niños	There were many children
le bustaron la nieve	Les gustaron la nieve	They like the snow
y tanbien	Y también	And also
jugaban en la nieve	jugaban en la nieve	they played in the snow

FIGURE 3.7

Alicia's April writing sample.

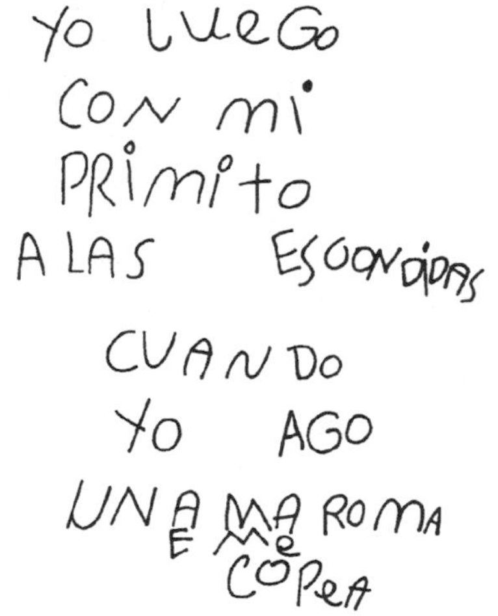

Alicia's spelling	Conventional Spanish spelling	English translation
Yo juego	Yo juego	I play
con mi	con mi	with my
primito	primita	little cousin
alas escondidas	a las escondidas	hide-and-seek
Cuando	Cuando	When
Yo ago	yo hago	I make
una ma roma	una moroma	a somersault
e me copea	el me copea	he copies me

using letter–sound cues and a phonetic decoding strategy (i.e., she tried to sound out the words). While this initial reading was not very smooth, Alicia practiced reading the words until she could reread her own story fluently. From March to the end of the year, Alicia used this same strategy with familiar, predictable books in Spanish. Initially, each book was read using the phonetic decoding strategy, focusing on sounding out unfamiliar words. Subsequently, she reread the text until she could read it fluently. Alicia chose to read books that had plain print, with only one or two lines of text per page. She rejected books with too many words or italic print. By the end of May, Alicia read the Spanish versions of Maurice Sendak's *Where the Wild Things Are* (1988, Harper & Row) and Robert Kraus's *Herman the Helper* (1974, Windmill), familiar and unfamiliar texts, respectively. She made a few mistakes, primarily grammatical. She did not correct these mistakes, but they were rather minor and did not change the meaning of the story. Alicia read more effectively, using multiple cues (letter–sound, meaning, and grammatical) as well as illustrations to decode unfamiliar words. Alicia also demonstrated that she was reading to construct the meaning of each text because she was able to retell each story accurately. By the end of kindergarten, Alicia had become a fluent writer and reader in Spanish. She was able to use sophisticated invented spellings that were very close approximations of standard Spanish spellings, and she could compose coherent narrative stories. Alicia learned to read in Spanish through reading both her own writing and familiar, predictable books. By April, Alicia was reading picture books fluently and independently. She was able to use multiple cuing systems and reading strategies in Spanish.

Home Talk: A Natural Context For Learning And Using Language

Four-year-old Evan, from Arizona, was visiting his grandmother in Vermont during the Christmas holiday. Upon opening the drapes one morning, he viewed snow-covered trees and fields. Evan gasped, "Grammie, who spilled all the sugar?" His grandmother responded, "Evan, that's very clever. It sure looks like sugar. Actually, it's snow."

Clearly, Evan's unfamiliarity with snow didn't prevent him from drawing a clever comparison. His grandmother responded by first showing appreciation for Evan's deduction and then providing the correct word, *snow*. Evan had a great opportunity to learn about the qualities of snow through conversations with his parents, grandparents, and older sister as they played together in the snow. During these adventures, they offered appropriate words for and information about all the new sights, sounds, tastes, smells, and feelings. By the end of the week, Evan knew the difference between wet and powder snow. He made snow angels, helped build a snowman and snow fort, engaged in a snowball war, and had an exhilarating ride on a sled. The new experiences he shared with older and more snow-experienced language users allowed Evan to build new vocabulary and cognitive understandings.

Evan's family helped him understand and label his new experience with snow. Their language support was natural and was guided by Evan's constant questions "Why doesn't this snow make a snowball? Why can't I make an angel on this snow?" Evan's learning while he played was nothing new or extraordinary; he has received language support from his parents and sibling from the moment he was born. His parents and older sister intuitively supported his attempts to communicate. When Evan was an infant his parents, like most parents, naturally used parentese. That is, they talked to him in higher pitched tones, at slower rate of speech, and with exaggerated pronunciation and lots of repetition of phrases. Parentese helped Evan hear the sounds and words of his native language. Between the ages of 18 months and 3 years, as Evan's communicative competence grew, his family intuitively adjusted their verbal responses so that he could easily learn new vocabulary and grammatical structures. When Evan pointed to objects and asked "de dat?" his family would offer the name of the object immediately and provide additional information (see Special Feature 3.2, Shared Visual Attention).

Evan's family and most adults automatically support children's language development. This type of scaffolding (described in Chapter 2, Table 2.2: How Parents Can Scaffold Young Children Language) is a prime example of Vygotsky's (1978) zone of proximal development, in which adults help children engage in activities that they could not do on their own. Through

SPECIAL FEATURE 3.2

Shared Visual Attention

Wha dat? asked 15-month-old Briar, while pointing her finger at an elephant at the zoo. Her mother pointed to the elephant also and replied, *That's an elephant, Briar. Isn't he big!*

This scene, though quite common, is extraordinary. Young children across the world point and through various means ask parents/caregivers to label objects in their environment and typically most adults (or older siblings) oblige. Psychologists call this human event *shared visual attention;* it appears to be necessary for children to develop vocabulary (Camaioni, Perucchini, Bellagamba, & Colonnesi, 2004; Flom, Deák, Phill, & Pick, 2003; Namy & Waxman, 2000;).

In research studies conducted by Amanda Woodward (2002) and her colleague, young children were tested in two conditions. In both conditions, researchers introduced an unknown object and gave the object a nonsense name. In the first condition, the researcher and child shared a joint visual gaze at the object while the researcher labeled the object. In the second condition, the same child was introduced to another new object, but the researcher looked away while labeling the object. Later in the day the child was asked to locate the objects from a group of similar objects. Results showed that children were quickly able to correctly identify and locate objects that were introduced in the first condition (joint visual gaze) but had difficulty identifying objects that were introduced in the second condition. These findings suggest that children need the support of others in highly specific ways to learn new vocabulary. In other words the child and adult need to share a visual "embrace" when the object is labeled.

---

ongoing interactions with his parents, sister, and other caregivers, Evan (and most children) quickly learn basic conversation skills (Danst, Lowe, & Bartholomew, 1990; Manning-Kratcoski & Bobkoff-Katz, 1998; Norris & Hoffman, 1990). By age 3, Evan, like most children, had learned to take turns, back-channel (use fillers like "uh-huh" to keep conversations going), be polite, and make appropriate responses (Menyuk, 1988). He knew how to engage in conversations with adults and his peers.

In fact, the most important component of learning language is actually engaging children, even infants, in conversational bouts. In Chapter 2 we discussed how families provide the rich social context necessary for children's language development. The thousands of hours of parent–child interactions from the moment of birth through the preschool years provide the foundations for language. As children acquire language, they are able to share with others what they feel, think, believe, and want. Although most children begin to use their expressive vocabulary in the second year of life, research has long documented that children differ in their ability to learn and use new words (Smith & Dickinson, 1994). In an effort to understand what accounts for these differences, researchers Betty Hart and Todd Risley (1995) documented parent and child interactions during the first three years of children's lives.

Their research team observed 44 families from different socioeconomic and ethnic backgrounds one hour each month for two-and-a-half years. Their data revealed vast differences in the amount of language spoken to children. Children from homes that received welfare assistance heard, on average, 616 words an hour; children from working-class families heard 1,251 words an hour; and children from professional homes heard 2,153 words per hour. If one thinks of words as dollars, the children from these different socioeconomic homes would have significantly disparate bank accounts. Further, this long-term study revealed that early language differences had a lasting effect on children's subsequent language accomplishments both at age 3 and at age 9. In other words, talk between adults and children early in life makes a significant difference. To look at an example of how this language difference begins to multiply, observe the following language of three parents when interacting with their babies when preparing to eat a meal.

> *Mom 1:* Okay, Crystal, let's eat.
>
> *Mom 2:* Okay, Paulie, it's time to eat our lunch. Let's see what we are having? Yes, let's have carrots.

> ***Mom 3:*** Okay, Teryl, it's lunchtime. Are you hungry? Mommy is so hungry! Let's see what we have in the refrigerator today. What is this? It's orange. Could it be peaches? Could it be apricots? Let's see! See the picture on the jar? That right, it's carrots.

The amount of words spoken during these simple interactions clearly illustrates how children can have vastly different experiences in hearing language.

Encouraging Personal Narratives

Evan's family played a vital role in helping him interpret, label, and recall his new experiences with snow. Back in Arizona, Evan had many stories to tell his teacher and playmates at preschool. For the next several months, each time he spoke with his grandparents, he relived his snow-day tales. The stories, or personal narratives, that Evan told helped him make sense of this new experience, broadened his vocabulary, and reinforced his expressive language skills. Likewise, each time Evan told the story about how the snowball he threw at his sister knocked off the snowman's nose and made his dad laugh, he deepened his memory of the event.

Children's personal narratives are a window into their thinking. Their language also reveals how they use current knowledge to interpret new experiences. Evan's first interpretation of a snowy field was to relate it to a recent incident with a broken sugar bowl. These verbal expressions of new mental constructions can be both fascinating and humorous. Likewise, children's personal narratives offer insight into their language development and overall intellectual, social, and emotional growth.

Though children instinctively know how to put experiences, feelings, and ideas into story form, parents and caregivers can encourage their children's language development by offering many storytelling opportunities and attentively listening while children share their accounts of events (Canizares, 1997). Though nothing can replace quiet and private time to listen to children, many working parents report that they use the time in the car, bus, or subway going to and from day care and/or errands to listen carefully to their children.

Children often share what they know or have learned in story form. This is because the human brain functions narratively—for most of us it is much easier to understand and remember concepts when we are given information in story form rather than as a collection of facts. Because the human brain retains information more efficiently in story form, parents can explain new information using stories (Sprenger, 1999). For example, when 5-year-old Tiffany wanted to know how to tie her shoelaces, her daddy told her the following story:

> *Once upon a time, there were two silly snakes [the shoelaces] who decided to wrestle. They twisted around each other and tied themselves together very tightly [first tie]. The snakes became scared and tried to curl away from each other [the loops]. But the snakes tripped and fell over each other and tied together.*

As discussed in Chapter 2, most children develop language within normal developmental guidelines. However, that is not the case for all children. Some children experience language delays or significant articulation difficulties. Special Feature 3.3, Supporting Children Who Experience Language Delay or Speech Challenges offers suggestions for parents and teachers on how to support children who experience language delays.

Reading Storybooks

In addition to providing a foundation for literacy, research reveals a connection between the amount of time adults spend reading storybooks to children and the level of children's oral language development. The stories, pictures, and accompanying adult-to-child interactions (think

SPECIAL FEATURE 3.3

Supporting Children Who Experience Language Delay or Speech Challenges

Kathy Eustace

I teach in an inclusion preschool of 4-year-olds. Each year nearly half my students exhibit some type of speech production challenge. As their teacher I see one of my roles as being a language facilitator for *all* my students. Whether the child is classified as typically developing or exhibits a speech production disorder or presents evidence of language delay, each is merely at a specific stage of development. My job is the same for all students: to assess their current level of ability, support mastery at this stage, and then help them learn the skills necessary to move on to the next stage. The most common challenges I see when I work with children include articulation disorders, fluency disorders, and language delay.

Articulation disorders account for the majority of all speech production difficulties in young children. These generally involve the mispronunciations of the *s, r, l, th,* and *sh* sounds. The child either:

- omits the sound completely (e.g., *alt* for *salt*),
- substitutes one sound for another consistently (e.g., *wabbit* for *rabbit*), or
- distorts or does not produce the sounds precisely (e.g., *Eidabeth* for *Elizabeth*).

Nearly all children experience some level of misarticulation while they are learning to speak, and most children correct through normal development. Speech therapy is usually necessary only if the misarticulations prohibit others from understanding the child's verbal communication or if the problem persists and becomes embarrassing for the child.

Fluency disorders occur when the normal rate of speech "flow" is atypical. Stuttering is one form of fluency disorder. Stuttering occurs when repetitions of sounds interrupt the child's flow of speech, for example, *ppppp please*. Cluttering is another form of disfluency. Cluttering involves excessively fast speech in which word boundaries are often obscured or garbled, for example, *Idonwnnagotoleep* for *I don't want to go to sleep*. Once again, nearly all children occasionally stutter and/or clutter when they are excited or tired. Disfluency disorders are not considered problematic unless they are constant and prevent a child from communicating his or her intentions.

Language delay is diagnosed when children have difficulty understanding a communicated message or expressing their thoughts verbally as contrasted to a developmental standard. For example, a 2-year-old who responds in one- or two-word sentences is developmentally normal, but a 4-year-old who responds only in one- or two-word sentences would be classified as language delayed.

Language delays may be exhibited as a primary condition caused by temporary health concerns such as colds or ear infections. Other more serious causes of language delay also include language-impoverished home environments or damage to the areas of the brain that process language. Language delays also occur as secondary symptoms to other physical conditions such as mental retardation, autism, cleft palate, or cerebral palsy.

While there are many reasons children many not acquire the typical language skills expected for their age, the cause is less important than the treatment. For example, a child may exhibit language delays due to mental retardation, or a child with normal intelligence may not have acquired normal language due to temporary hearing loss or an environment that was not verbally interactive. Regardless of the circumstance, the instructional goal is to increase the production of verbal communication, and therefore the treatment is nearly identical.

When I plan activities for my inclusive class, I plan language opportunities that would be appropriate for a range of abilities, from the typically developing child to the children who exhibit speech production challenges to language delays. I also facilitate student participation based on the ability level of each child, always keeping the child's individual goals in mind. The activities are open ended and designed to elicit responses at all four levels. The following examples are based on a discussion I had with my class after we had read *Little Cloud* by Eric Carle (1996, Scholastic).

- *Level 1* involves an indication that the child has a receptive understanding of a new concept, in this case, clouds. At this level I merely ask the child to demonstrate his or her understanding of the new concept by pointing to a visual representation of the concept. *Where are the clouds in this picture, Jamie?*
- *Level 2* asks a child to use a one-word response to communicate. This one word may help me gauge a child's receptive understanding or a linguistic concept, or it may include a targeted speech sound that is typically mispronounced by this child. For example, *On this page what did Little Cloud turn into? Gustavo? Yes, that is right, RRRRabbit.*
- *Level 3* involves a multiword response from a child whose goal it is to increase his or her mean length of utterance or who is working on syntax. *Can you tell me three or four things that Little Cloud changes into? Sarafina?*
- *Level 4* involves helping children make inferences or comparisons. This level of response gives children an opportunity to elaborate their thoughts and to work on the aspect of their language that is in question. *How are sheep and clouds alike? Who helped Little Cloud make the rain?*

shared visual attention—look again at Special Feature 3.2) facilitate language use and increase expressive and receptive vocabulary (Brooks & Meltzoff, 2005). Further, children who have been read to frequently are better able to retell stories than children who have had few opportunities to engage in story time (Barrentine, 1996; Durkin, 1966). Caregivers may also encourage discussion and comprehension by asking open-ended questions about the story. Children often relate to the characters and story lines, and, when encouraged, they reveal interesting views. The following conversation occurred when Dominique was 4 years old, after a reading of *Goldilocks and the Three Bears:*

> *Mom:* What part of the story did you like the best?
>
> *Dominique:* When Goldilocks kept messing up baby bear's stuff.
>
> *Mom:* Who did you like best in the story?
>
> *Dominique:* Baby bear.
>
> *Mom:* Why?
>
> *Dominique:* 'Cause baby bear is like me. All of his stuff is wrecked up by Goldilocks, like Sheritta [her 18-month-old sister] messes up mine.

Notice that Dominique's mother asked open-ended opinion questions and accepted her child's responses. This type of question encourages oral responses and children's personal interpretation of the story. Adults should refrain from asking interrogation or detail questions, such as, "What did Goldilocks say when she tasted the second bowl of porridge?" Detail questions tend to make story time avoidable, not enjoyable.

As children snuggle in a parent's lap or beside their parent in a chair or bed, story time creates a comforting, private time to talk together and learn new vocabulary. However, in today's culturally, linguistically, and socioeconomically diverse society, teachers may find that some of their students' parents are unsure how to successfully engage their children in story time. Special Feature 3.4, Language Development via Storybook Reading, offers a model teachers may wish to share with parents.

Closed-ended questions usually only require a single-word answer—"yes" or "no"—or require the "right answer." Open-ended questions, on the other hand, have no right or wrong answers and encourage children to talk more and to use richer language.

SPECIAL FEATURE 3.4

Language Development via Storybook Reading

In recent years, studies have revealed that home literacy experiences, or the lack of them, profoundly influence children's later literacy development and language development. However, storybook reading is not an instinct. Knowing how to interact with children and storybooks takes time and practice. One simple approach that significantly increases a child's involvement in the story time experience is called "Dialogic Reading." It involves parents asking questions (See Table 3.1, Closed- and Open-Ended Questions) about the stories as they read, such as asking children to describe what they are seeing on the page. Parents are also encouraged to label objects and add descriptive information.

The following scene illustrates the Dialogic Reading approach. Dad is reading Jane Manning's *Who Stole the Cookies from the Cookie Jar?* (2001, Harper Festival) to 3-year-old Jasper. Before Dad even reads begins the story, he asks Jasper about the cover illustration.

> *Dad:* Jasper, who is on the cover?
>
> *Jasper:* Doggie, kitty, piggy, rabbit, and mouse.
>
> *Dad:* Look, Jasper. Do you see that the book is shaped like our cookie jar?
>
> *Jasper:* Daddy, see the cookies, they are chocolate chip!
>
> *Dad:* Your favorite. Jasper, the title of this book is *Who Stole the Cookies from the Cookie Jar?* Who do you think stole the cookies?
>
> *Jasper:* I think Piggy or Cookie Monster.

SPECIAL FEATURE 3.4 *(continued)*

The reading and conversation about this 12-page storybook lasted more than a half hour with Jasper deeply engaged with describing the richly detailed illustrations and guessing who had stolen the cookies.

In addition to dialogic reading, there are other simple and enjoyable strategies parents can use to help their children get the most from storytime:

- Read the same books again and again. Children learn new things each time they hear a story and look at the pictures.
- Ask children to find and label objects. This helps to keep them involved in the story.
- Ask open-ended questions. Asking questions like "What do you think will happen next?" or "What was your favorite part of the story?" encourages children to share their feelings and opinions. Table 3.1 provides several examples of open-ended questions.
- Expand your child's answers. Adding to your child's responses encourages him or her to interact with you and keeps him or her involved.
- Read with enthusiasm. Taking on the voices of the three little pigs and the wolf is fun and exciting and brings the story to life.
- Encourage children to act out the story. Storybook dramas are excellent for language development and are also a great deal of fun. (See Chapter 6 for more information.)

TABLE 3.1	This set of questions refers to Maurice Sendak's *Where the Wild Things Are*

Close-Ended Questions	Open-Ended Questions
Did you like Max?	What did you think about Max?
Why did Max get into trouble?	How did you feel when Max's mother sent him to bed?
Were the wild things monsters?	Tell me about the wild things. What did they look like?
What did Max do to the wild things?	Why did Max stare at the wild things?
Did you like the story?	What part of the story did you like best?

Remember to ask questions before, during, and after the story as this helps to maintain child involvement. However storybook reading is not the only time parents can engage children in conversation. Television and movies also provide great opportunities for building vocabulary and comprehension. Special Feature 3.5, Television as a Language Tool, provides guidance on how this medium can be used effectively.

SPECIAL FEATURE 3.5

Television as a Language Tool

Television has been a major influence in family life in almost all U.S. households since the 1950s. In the 1980s the availability of video rentals and inexpensive video players, video movies, and video storybooks and cartoons increased the range of options for young children. Currently cable and interactive electronic games have added yet another dimension to television watching. In the 21st century it has been estimated that 99 percent of U.S. homes have at least one television set, and most U.S. homes report multiple TVs, with children learning to use remote tuners before they have mastered dining utensils (Schnabel, 2009). In addition, the TV is usually in the part of the home where most family interactions occur (Miller, 1997). Sadly, the average child between 2 and 5 years of age will spend 27 hours a week viewing television programming. Anything that occupies children for so many hours a week deserves careful consideration.

(continued on next page)

SPECIAL FEATURE 3.5 *(continued)*

Time. Research regarding the amount of time young children watch TV and the effect of viewing on later academic success is inconclusive, though the data clearly suggest that watching for many hours per day or week has a negative effect on children's academic performance. Susan Neuman (1988) suggests that more than four hours of TV viewing a day has a negative effect on children's reading achievement. Likewise, Angela Clarke and Beth Kurtz-Costes's (1997) study of low-socioeconomic African American preschool children shows that children who watched the most television (between 30 and 55 hours per week) exhibited poorer academic skills than their peers who watched fewer than 25 hours per week. On the other hand, moderate amounts of TV viewing may be beneficial. The Center for the Study of Reading landmark report, "Becoming a Nation of Readers," suggests that there is actually a positive link between watching up to 10 hours of television a week and reading achievement (Rice, Huston, Truglio, & Wright, 1990). Clarke and Kurtz-Costes (1997) suggest that the variation in researchers' findings may be due in part to the home climate. They suggest that who watches TV with young children and how TV is watched may have a greater effect on children's learning than simply the amount of TV viewing.

Choosing Programming for Children. Selecting appropriate children's programming has become more challenging in recent years. In addition to regular public access, cable service may offer as many as 100 options to choose from each hour of the day. And while there are a number of proven classics—such as *Sesame Street* and *Reading Rainbow*,—children's programs change from year to year. One way parents can determine the quality of children's programming is through considering children's needs. Diane Levin and Nancy Carlsson-Paige (1994) created a list of children's developmental needs and suggested program criteria to accommodate these concerns.

Active Viewing. Children are extremely impressionable, and television's visual imagery is a powerful force in their lives. Therefore, it is important for parents to help guide and mediate the viewing process.

Susan Miller (1997) suggests a number of ways parents and caregivers may interact with children as they view television:

- *Watch television together:* Help children interpret what is seen on the screen.
- *Talk about the programs:* Conversations initiated by television programming offer opportunities to discuss a wide variety of issues.
- *Observe children's reactions:* Ask children to label or describe their feelings.
- *Foster critical thinking:* Ask children what they think about a program. Would they have handled the problem differently? Did they agree with the character's actions?
- *Extend viewing activities:* Children are often motivated to learn more about a topic or activity once television has sparked their interest.

In short, while the television can be a powerful tool in children's learning, careful consideration of how much, what, and how children view TV programs is needed.

Special Note Regarding Electronic Media and Infants and Toddlers

The last ten years have seen the introduction of television shows and educational videos designed specifically for infants and young toddlers. While research suggests that 3- to 5-year-old children *can* learn words and other concepts from educational shows such as *Sesame Street* and *Barney* (e.g., Anderson, Huston, Linebarger, Wright, 2002), it is less clear whether there are any benefits for children any younger than that, even when assessing only those shows designed specifically for infants. For example, one study found that watching supposedly "educational" shows designed for infants predicted lower vocabulary scores for infants aged 8 to 16 months; furthermore, the more hours the infant watched, the lower the vocabulary score was likely to be (Zimmerman, Christakis, & Meltzoff, 2007). It appears that for very young children the importance of face-to-face interactions and storybook engagements can't be underestimated.

Family Focus: Parent Workshops

Helping parents become successful language and literacy models is one of a teacher's most important tasks. Over the last quarter-century research on children's literacy development has consistently found a strong connection between parent/caregiver modeling of literacy practices on children's school readiness and ultimate school success. These findings are true for all children but particularly for children whose families are socially or economically disadvantaged (Comer & Haynes, 1991; Morrow, 1988; Nord et al., 2000; Reaney, Denton, & West, 2002). Knowing what is appropriate language and literacy is a first step and Table 3.2: Age-Appropriate Support Activities: Birth to Age Five offers explicit examples of typically literacy development

TABLE 3.2		Age-Appropriate Support Activities: Birth to Age Five		
Months		**Speaking/Listening**	**Receptive/Reading**	**Expressive/Writing**
0-6	CD	Babbling, extensive sound play		
	PS	Talk to baby. Sing to baby. Make direct eye contact with baby when speaking. Use parentese.		
6-12	CD	echolalia, vocables, first words.	Is able to listen to short stories. Wants to handle books.	
	PS	Label objects. Scaffold child's language efforts.	Provide cloth and cardboard books. Read to your child.	
12-24	CD	Begins to use words/gestures Responds to simple requests.	Begins to recognize environmental print/logos.	Begins to use writing implements to make marks.
	PS	Listen and actively respond Read stories. Engage in frequent conversations.	Confirm print recognition. "Yes, that is a coke." Read to your child.	Offer chalk/chalkboard, paper/crayons.
24-36	CD	Uses simple sentences, adds new words rapidly, and experiments with inflection.	Attends to pictures, describes picture, then begins to form oral stories reflecting pictures.	Know print has meaning meaning and serves practical uses. Makes scribble marks.
	PS	Engage child in complex conversations frequently. Listen to child.	Read, read, read to your child. Ask child to label characters and objects.	Provide access to many types of writing implements/paper,
36-48	CD	Proficient language user.	Attends to pictures. Repeats familiar story phrases.	Print recognition—may write letter-like units, and nonphonetic letter-like strings.
	PS	Engages in dramatic play. Likes to learn songs Serve as coplayer in dramas. Teach new songs. Ask child questions to encourage two-way dialogue.	Reread familiar stories. Ask open-ended questions.	Model writing process. Demonstrate your interest in your child's writing efforts.
48-60	CD	Uses language to obtain and share information.	May begin to recognize individual words.	Conventional writing emerges as letter-sound relationship develops.
	PS	Offer logical explanations. Listen and respond thoughtfully and thoroughly.	Shared reading. Frequent visits to library and expand home library. Demonstrate your enjoyment of reading.	Begin to write notes to child. Read your child's writing encourage the effort.

CD – child's development

PS – parental support

Collin (1992, p. 2) refers to the parents' nurturing role in their child's literacy development as "planting the seeds of literacy." And while almost all parents want to plant these seeds, many are unsure of the best way to begin. Similarly, most parents and other primary caregivers vastly underestimate the importance of their role in helping children become competent language users (McNeal, 1999). Fortunately, one highly effective strategy for involving and directly informing parents of preschool and kindergarten students about how to support their children's language and literacy learning is through parent workshops; see Special Feature 3.6, Leaps and Bounds: A Learning Opportunity for the Entire Family, as an example. The purpose of the workshops is to share explicit information about the children's development and the class curriculum and to provide practical suggestions that parents may use at home to support their child's learning (Brown, 1994; Rhodes, Enz, & LaCount, 2006).

SPECIAL FEATURE 3.6

Leaps and Bounds: A Learning Opportunity for the Entire Family

Michelle Rhodes and Marilyn La Count

Research studies conducted over the past 25 years consistently demonstrate that children who have parents that help prepare them for school by engaging in reading, math, and social activities are highly successful in school (Henderson & Berla, 1994; Ramey & Ramey, 1999; Snow et al., 1998). Because research consistently demonstrates that parents have the greatest influence on children's school readiness, it is important to get them involved in their child's learning (Enz, 2003; Epstein, 1996).

Promoting school readiness through strengthening partnerships with parents is a complex but worthy task. When schools acknowledge the relevance of the child home culture as a legitimate learning environment, they can develop a supportive environment for learning through meaningful activities that both involve and empower families (Ramey & Ramey, 1999; Snow et al., 1998).

The mission of the Leaps and Bounds program is to provide high needs communities with a research-based program that provides generally Spanish speaking parents and family members with practical knowledge necessary to prepare their children for kindergarten. The family-friendly activities use common, home-related items to promote logical mathematic knowledge, language-literacy development, and social competence.

In the "World as a Classroom" workshop series, parents, family members, and their children attend four 75-minute workshops, in which they engaged in activities demonstrated by program facilitators (often preschool or kindergarten teachers at the school site) and college student interns. The four workshops include

- *Workshops #1 and #2—Learning around the House:* Activities focus around learning in and around the house including the kitchen, bathroom, and family room. Activities will also focus on learning with music, art, and play. Parents will learn to teach their child through everyday activities in their environment. (See Appendix 1 – Learning Activity for Leaps and Bounds.)
- *Workshops #3 and #4—Learning in the Environment:* Activities focus around family outings in the familiar environment (i.e., baseball game, grocery store, going out to eat, going to the park, and so on). Activities are focused around learning with music in the environment and riding in the car or bus or walking through their community.

One of the most important features of the workshops is the time parents, children, and facilitators spend together brainstorming about how families can extend these simple learning activities at home. Through active participation and open social interaction, this program provides parents and family members with the support and confidence necessary to be their child's first teacher. By simply providing parents and family members with knowledge and support in using inexpensive and immediately accessible resources, parents spend increased amounts of time with their children and are better able to fulfill their role as their child's first teacher. Programs like Leaps and Bounds can increase parental involvement at home and lead to increased learning and performance in school.

To begin, the teacher should design a "Needs Assessment Survey" to determine parents' special interests and needs. In Figure 3.8, we provide an example of a survey that covers possible workshop topics, meeting times, and child-care needs.

After the survey has been returned and the results tallied, the early childhood teacher should publish and "advertise" the schedule of workshops. We recommend the teacher select the "top" two or three topics and identify the time(s) and day(s) listed as convenient for most of the parents. Generally the most convenient meeting place is the classroom or the school's or center's multipurpose room. Scout troops, parent volunteers, or older students may provide child care. Teachers should be sure to have parents confirm their participation in the workshop (see Figure 3.9). This will allow the teacher to prepare sufficient materials and secure appropriate child-care arrangements. Send reminders the day before the workshop. Don't be surprised if only a few parents attend initially. Parent workshops may be a new concept, and it might take a little time for parents to become comfortable with this approach to parent/teacher interactions.

FIGURE 3.8

Needs Assessment
Survey

Dear Parents,

Did you know you are your child's first and most important teacher? One of my responsibilities as a teacher is to work and share all my teaching colleagues for the benefit of the special student we share—your child. I would like to conduct several workshops this year, and I need to know what topics you are most interested in learning about. Please complete the survey and have your child return it by _____.
Place "X" by topics you would like to attend.

__ Storytelling Techniques   __ Linking Play and Literacy

__ Writers Workshop   __ Kitchen Math and Science

__ Rainy Day Fun   __ Learning Motivation

__ Other _____

_____

What is the most convenient day? What time is the most convenient for you to attend a workshop?

__ Monday   __ Tuesday   __ 9:00am   __ 4:00pm   __ 7:00pm

__ Wednesday   __ Thursday

__ Friday   __ Saturday

Would I use a child-care service if one was provided?

__ Yes—list number of children needing care __ .

__ No.

Teachers must *prepare* for a parent workshop. They need adequate supplies. They may need to organize the room. They need to set up refreshments. (Parent/Teacher Organizations or center budgets can often reimburse teachers for refreshments.) Teachers need to prepare name tags, double-check child-care arrangements, develop an evaluation form for the workshop, and create a detailed lesson plan!

There are several points for teachers to remember when running a parent workshop. First, the workshop should begin promptly. Secondly, start with a get-acquainted activity to put people at ease and begin the workshop on a relaxed, positive note. Thirdly, remember that parents should not be lectured to; instead, they should experience hands-on, highly engaging activities. After the parents have engaged in the activity, provide brief, specific information about the theory underlying the process. Most importantly, remember to *smile*. When the teacher has a good time, the parents will also! Finally, have parents complete the workshop evaluation form; this will help to continually refine the quality of the workshops (see Figure 3.10).

FIGURE 3.9

Workshop Confirmation Letter

Dear Parents:

The topics that most most of you wanted to learn more about were:
Writing Workshop, Kitchen Math and Science, and Rainy Day Fun!

The times that were convenient for most of you were:
Wednesdays at 7:00 p.m. and Saturdays at 9:00 a.m.

I have used this information to create a schedule of workshops for the Fall semester.
Please fill out the personal information and put an X by the workshops you plan to
attend. All workshops will be in my classroom. Refreshments will be served. Dress
comfortably as we might be getting messy. Children will be cared for in the cafeteria by
the Girl Scouts and their leaders.

_____

Name _____   Phone _____

Number of children needing child care _____

___ Writers Workshop—Wednesday, October 2, 7:00–8:30 p.m.
___ Kitchen Math and Science—Saturday, November 4, 9:00–10:30 a.m.
___ Rainy Day Fun—Wednesday, November 9, 7:00–8:30 p.m.

Summary

In this chapter, we discussed how children's knowledge of print develops and the critical role families play in this ongoing process. This chapter also continued to discuss the role families play in the development of a child's language acquisition. These social, constructive processes are observed by children who continue to try out their newly developed knowledge and skills. Children continue to refine their understanding of print and language through interacting with their caregivers and parents. To summarize the key points about facilitating oral language learning, we return to the guiding questions at the beginning of this chapter:

■ *What are emergent writing and emergent reading?*

According to the emergent literacy view, the literacy learning process shares much in common with the oral language development process. Literacy acquisition, like oral language development, begins early. For many children, literacy development begins in

FIGURE 3.10

Workshop Evaluation
Form

Workshop Name _____ Date _____

List two activities you enjoyed or learned the most about.

1.

2.

List any information that was not useful to you.

The workshop was (mark all that apply):

___ clear ___ confusing ___ enjoyable ___ boring
___ too short ___ too long ___ informative

Any other comments?

Thanks for attending!

infancy when caregivers read storybooks to children and children begin to notice print in the environment. Literacy learning is an active, constructive process. By observing print and having stories read to them, young children discover patterns and create their own early versions of reading and writing that initially have little resemblance to conventional forms; the story they read may be quite different from the one in the book, and their writing may look like drawing or scribbles. As children have opportunities to use these early forms of literacy in meaningful social situations and as they interact with adults who draw their attention to the features and functions of print, their constructions become increasingly similar to conventional reading and writing.

■ *What home factors affect young children's literacy development?*

Several factors have been identified as having important roles in early literacy acquisition. These include

1. opportunities to see lots of print and have easy access to books;
2. opportunities to observe adults using literacy in everyday situations;

3. adults who support children's literacy development by answering children's questions, pointing to letters, taking the children to the library, providing children with a wide variety of experiences, and initiating functional literacy activities;
4. literacy materials that support children's engagement in early forms of reading and writing; and
5. experiences with adults who share books with children.

■ *How can parents best facilitate their children's oral language development?*

Parents can promote their children's oral language by scaffolding their language, encouraging them to tell personal narratives about their experiences, reading stories to them on a regular basis, and monitoring their children's TV viewing and encouraging active viewing.

■ *What does early literacy look like in a language other than English?*

Children learn the dominant language of their home. When these homes—be they English speaking, Spanish speaking, or Arabic speaking—provide a literate model, typically the young children who live in them are eager to engage in talking, writing, and reading in the home's dominant language. So early literacy across languages looks quite similar. Some cultures and families place emphasis on oral storytelling in addition to reading and writing. Adults in these homes share stories with their young literacy learners and with each other. Of course, children from families whose dominant language is one other than English will enter school using the language that works for them in their home environment. A quality program that supports these children's emergence as readers and writers is important.

LINKING KNOWLEDGE TO PRACTICE

1. Read a storybook with a child 3 years of age or older. Ask the child to point to where you should begin reading. Does the child know that you will read the print, not the pictures? After you have read the story to the child, ask the child to read the story to you. What form of emergent reading does the child use to read the story (e.g., attending to pictures, forming oral stories; attending to pictures, forming written stories; attending to print)? Compare your findings with those gathered by your colleagues.
2. Plan a parent workshop that will help parents become effective storybook readers. Present your workshop plan to the class.

Go to the Topics Family Literacy, English Language Learners, and At Risk and Struggling Readers in the MyEducationLab (www.myeducationlab.com) for your course, where you can:

- Find learning outcomes for Family Literacy, English Language Learners, and At Risk and Struggling Readers along with the national standards that connect to these outcomes.
- Complete Assignments and Activities that can help you more deeply understand the chapter content.
- Examine challenging situations and cases presented in the IRIS Center Resources.

Go to the Topic A+RISE in the MyEducationLab (www.myeducationlab.com) for your course. A+RISE® Standards2Strategy™ is an innovative and interactive online resource that offers new teachers in grades K-12 just in time, research-based instructional strategies that:

- Meet the linguistic needs of ELLs as they learn content
- Differentiate instruction for all grades and abilities
- Offer reading and writing techniques, cooperative learning, use of linguistic and nonlinguistic representations, scaffolding, teacher modeling, higher order thinking, and alternative classroom ELL assessment
- Provide support to help teachers be effective through the integration of listening, speaking, reading, and writing along with the content curriculum
- Improve student achievement
- Are aligned to Common Core Elementary Language Arts standards (for the literacy strategies) and to English language proficiency standards in WIDA, Texas, California, and Florida.

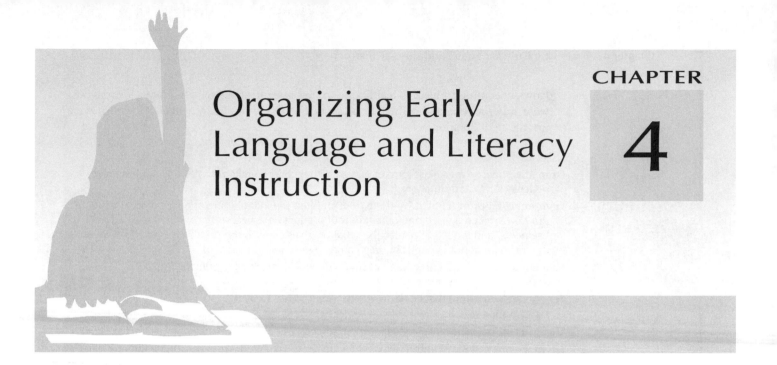

Organizing Early Language and Literacy Instruction

When you enter Mrs. Altamirano's preschool classroom, you immediately notice that the room is attractive, filled with meaningful print, and divided into distinct areas, each with a different focus. There is a comfortable library center that is stocked with large numbers of high-quality children's books. Nearby is a writing center, equipped with many different things to write with and to write on. Across the room is a literacy-enriched play center. This week it is set up as a doctor's office and contains a number of medical-related reading and writing materials (patient folders, prescription pads, wall signs, appointment books, and the like). In addition, the walls of the room are covered with meaningful print, including functional print (helper charts, storage labels), many samples of student writing, and charts with teacher dictation. You also notice that there is a smooth rhythm to the daily schedule, as children transition from large group circle time to tables for small group instruction. Later, the children have opportunities to work independently at centers, engaging in activities that are related to content that has been taught in large and small groups. Little time is wasted going from one activity to another, and often these transitions include brief activities that help children practice and reinforce skills learned in the curriculum.

Mrs. Altamirano knows how to effectively organize early literacy instruction. She provides her children with a literacy-rich classroom environment that supports children's early reading and writing development. In addition, she manages time effectively by establishing a daily schedule that provides children with opportunities to learn language and literacy skills in large group, small group, and center-based settings. The children transition smoothly between these instructional settings, wasting little time going from one activity to another. This type of effective classroom management and organization is a key element of effective teaching (Foley, 2010). When instruction runs smoothly and is supported by the environment and schedule, teachers can focus their attention on instruction rather than on controlling children's behavior.

In this chapter, we focus on these two key elements of instructional organization. First, we discuss how teachers can set up well arranged, literacy-rich classroom environments that provide ideal settings for learning to read and write. Then we discuss how the daily schedule can be organized to maximize literacy learning.

BEFORE READING THIS CHAPTER, THINK ABOUT . . .

- How everyday settings like grocery stores, banks, libraries, and doctor offices affect your behavior.
- Environmental print you remember from your childhood. Could you spot a McDonald's a mile away? Did your favorite toy or snack food have a special logo or trademark?

■ How scheduling influences learning. Can you remember instructional presentations that were way too long and boring? Sessions that were too brief and rushed? Ones that were just the right duration?

BOX 4.1 **Definition of Terms**	**Dramatic play:** An advanced form of play in which children take on roles and act out make-believe stories and situations **Environmental print (EP):** The real-life print children see in the home or community, including print on food containers and other kinds of product boxes, store signs, road signs, advertisements, and the like. Because the situation gives clues to the print's meaning, EP is often the first type of print young children can recognize and understand. **Functional literacy activities:** Reading and writing activities that accomplish real-life purposes, such as writing lists and reading directions **Functional print:** Print that guides everyday classroom activity (e.g., labels, lists, directions, sign-up sheets) **Library center:** Special area in the classroom stocked with books and materials related to reading **Literacy-enriched play centers:** Play centers that are enhanced with appropriate theme-related literacy materials **Writing center:** Special area in the classroom stocked with writing materials and tools

FOCUS QUESTIONS

■ How can teachers arrange the classroom's physical environment to support children's language and literacy learning?

■ How can teachers set up a well-designed library center?

■ Why is a writing center an important area in the preschool classroom? Why is it also important to have writing materials available in other centers?

■ How can dramatic play centers be set up to encourage young children's literacy development?

■ What are functional literacy activities, and how can teachers use these activities in a preschool or kindergarten classroom?

■ How can the daily schedule support language and literacy learning?

Why Classroom Environments Are Important

Ecological psychology attempts to explain how human behavior is influenced by the surrounding environment (Barker, 1978). The environment is viewed as a set of behavior settings that shape how we act and behave. Each setting—a movie theater, grocery store, gym, library—contains a set of choices and constraints that dictate how one behaves in that particular setting. According to ecological psychologists, settings tend to coerce or nudge people to act in predictable ways (Gump, 1989).

Classrooms are one such behavioral setting. How a classroom is arranged and the materials it contains can have a tremendous effect on children's behavior and learning. When classrooms are effectively arranged and contain lots of meaningful print, language, and literacy opportunities, children's literacy learning is promoted (Neuman & Roskos, 2007). Mrs. Altamirano's classroom in the opening vignette to this chapter is a good example of this type of setting. The classroom environment functions as additional "teacher," providing children with many rich learning opportunities.

Unfortunately, these types of supportive classroom environments are somewhat rare. Lea McGee (2007) reports that, while most early childhood educators believe they have print- and language-rich classrooms, in reality these teachers provide children with only the basic level of environmental support. She used the ELLCO (Early Language and Literacy Classroom Observation) Toolkit (Smith & Dickinson, 2002), which has a possible 41 points, to evaluate preschool classroom environments. The ELLCO checklist is divided into five categories: Book Area, Book Selection, Book Use, Writing Materials, and Writing around the Room. Raters assign points for the presence of specific items within each category. For example, in the Book

Use category, raters assign points for the number of books in the science area, in the dramatic play area, in the block area, in other areas of the classroom, and for the presence of a place for children to listen to recorded books or stories. McGee found that most of the preschool classrooms that she observed received scores between 10 and 22, only one-third to one-half of the possible points. Most teachers had library centers with an adequate number of books, but these books did not include the diversity of genres or difficulty levels needed to match the ability and interests of typical preschoolers. Few had well-equipped writing centers, reading and writing materials throughout other centers, or a print-enriched dramatic play area. So environmental enrichment is an area that many early childhood teachers need to address.

Designing a Print-Rich Classroom Environment

Several basic principals guide the design of a literacy-rich classroom environment. A well-designed classroom is shown in Figure 4.1. This classroom demonstrates five basic elements of classroom design:

▪ *Carve the large classroom space into well-defined areas*: Notice how the classroom in Figure 4.1 is divided into small, well-defined activity areas. Small, clearly defined areas encourage more interaction and sustained activity than do large areas. In addition, smaller areas accommodate fewer children, which leads to a quieter classroom and fewer behavior problems. Classroom areas or "centers," as they often are called, can be clearly defined with movable furniture (such as bookshelves, cupboards, tables, boxes), screens, and large plants (real, if possible, but if not, artificial will do). Typically, these centers are designed around each content area. Hence, classrooms have a science center, a mathematics center, a library center, a writing center, a dramatic play center, and so forth. To assist children's understanding of the purposes of the areas, each area should be clearly labeled with a sign mounted near the children's eye level. With young children, an appropriate picture or symbol should accompany the written label.

▪ *Gather appropriate resources to support the children's learning:* Typically, the materials needed to support children's engagement in activities are housed in the various centers. Each item should have a designated storage place. This designation helps children to find

FIGURE 4.1

Well-Designed Classroom

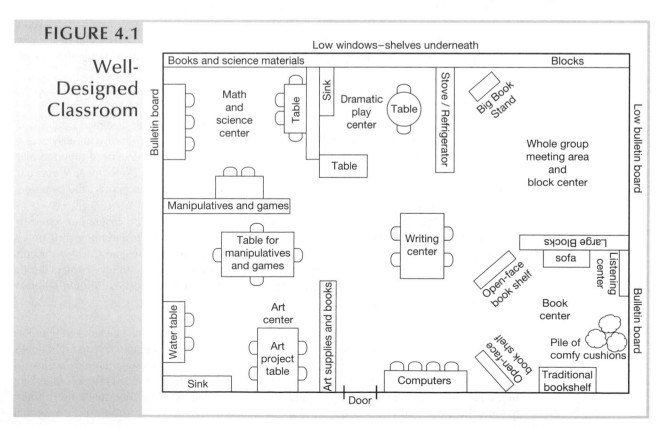

the materials with ease and to replace the materials for the next child's use. This means that each center needs shelves, tables, or boxes for the materials, with the designated spot for each material clearly labeled. Within each center, the method of exhibiting the materials should be considered. For example, blocks of like sizes, like shapes, or like materials should be grouped together in the block center (sometimes called the construction site). The labels might read: *long, rectangular, wooden blocks*; or *small, square, wooden blocks;* or *red Lego blocks*. Pictures of each kind of block by the words will support the youngest children's reading. Similarly, paper in the writing center can be grouped by color, kind, and size. Labels might include those for publishing paper, rough-draft paper, stationery, and cards.

■ *Place similar or related centers near each other:* In the classroom depicted in Figure 4.1, the library or book center and the writing center are placed close to each other. These two centers belong together because they both encourage children's development and use of literacy. In fact, some educators combine these centers into a literacy center because their focus is children's literacy development. The two areas both involve complementary activities that involve low levels of noise and physical activity. In another example, the art and water table are adjacent to each other. Both centers involve messy, rather noisy activities.

■ *Make Literacy Materials a Part of the Fabric of Each Center:* In the classroom in Figure 4.1, the science center has many science books in it; so does the block area. By including books, writing tools, posters with print, magazines, and other relevant materials in each center, each center's potential for developing children's literacy is enhanced. Putting literacy materials in the various centers supports children's literacy development and is an important way for teachers to enhance children's literacy learning. By enriching all centers, children read, write, speak, listen, and observe to learn.

In environments like classroom in Figure 4.1, children are immersed in literacy learning in every center. Such environments support children's natural literacy experimentation throughout the entire day. Because these environments are rich with print (e.g., books, magazines, posters, functional signs, writing paper and tools), young children can engage in meaningful explorations of speaking, listening, reading, and writing in real-life situations. They read the *"Open"* sign, and they know what it means. They record their observations in their learning log to help them remember what they saw. They are readers and writers because their teachers have provided them with multiple opportunities to interact with the written word.

In the sections that follow, we describe how teachers can set up a supportive classroom environment by designing effective library centers, writing centers, and literacy-enriched dramatic play centers and by supplying their classrooms with environmental and functional print.

The Classroom Library Center

A key feature of a classroom for young children is a well-stocked, well-designed library center. Classroom libraries promote independent reading by providing children with easy access to books and a comfortable place for browsing and reading. Children have been found to read more books in classrooms with libraries than in ones without libraries (Morrow & Weinstein, 1982). As Stephen Krashen (1987, p. 2) has pointed out, this finding supports "the common-sense view that children read more when there are more books around."

However, the mere presence of a classroom library is not enough to ensure heavy use by young children. The library must contain an ample supply of appropriate and interesting books for children to read. Design features are also important. Lesley Morrow and Carol Weinstein (1982) found that children did not choose to use "barren and uninviting" library corners during center time. However, when the design features of centers were improved, children's library usage increased dramatically.

BOOKS. To attract and hold children's interest, a classroom library must be stocked with lots of good books to read. Experts recommend that classroom libraries contain five to eight books per child (Morrow, 2005; Neuman & Roskos, 2007). According to these guidelines, a class of 20 children would require 100 to 160 books. These books should be divided into a core collection and one or more revolving collections. The core collection should be made up of high-quality literature that remains constant and available all year. These should be books that

A well-designed library center invites children to read books.

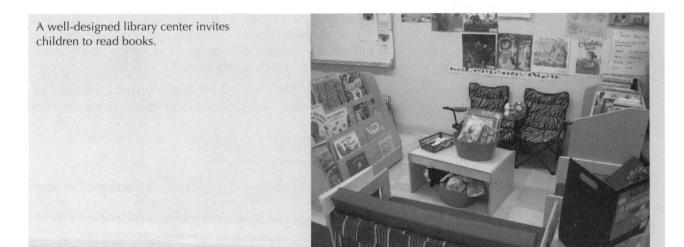

appeal to most of the children in class and that most children will enjoy reading on more than one occasion. Lesley Morrow (2009) also recommends that the books be color coded according to type. For example, all animal books could be identified with blue dots on their spines so they can be clustered together on a shelf marked *Animals*. Each category would be distinguished by a different color.

Revolving collections change every few weeks to match children's current interests and topics being studied in class. For example, if several children become hooked on an author, such as Tomie de Paola or Maurice Sendak, collections of the author's books could be brought into the library to capitalize on this interest. If the class were studying seeds and plants, then picture storybooks and informational books relating to these topics could be added. When student interest shifts to a new author or when a new topic is under investigation, the old sets of revolving books are replaced with new ones.

Quality and variety are also of utmost importance in selecting books for the classroom library (Fractor, Woodruff, Martinez, & Teale, 1993). To motivate voluntary reading and to instill positive attitudes toward written texts, books must catch children's attention, hold their interest, and captivate their imaginations. Only high-quality literature will achieve these goals.

PHYSICAL CHARACTERISTICS. A number of physical features have been identified that make libraries attractive to children and that promote book reading (Morrow, 2009; Morrow, Freitag, & Gambrell, 2009; Neuman & Roskos, 2007):

■ *Partitions:* Bookshelves, screens, large plants, or other barriers set the library center apart from the rest of the classroom. This gives children a sense of privacy and provides a cozy, quiet setting for reading.

■ *Ample space:* There should be enough room for at least five or six children to use the library at one time.

■ *Comfortable furnishings:* The more comfortable the library area, the more likely it is that children will use it. Soft carpeting, chairs, old sofas, bean bags, and a rocking chair all help create a comfortable atmosphere for reading.

■ *Open-faced and traditional shelves:* Traditional shelves display books with their spines out, whereas open-faced shelves display the covers of books. Open-faced shelves are very effective in attracting children's attention to specific books. Researchers have found that when both types of shelves are used, kindergartners chose more than 90 percent of their books from the open-faced displays (Fractor et al., 1993). Traditional shelves are also useful because they can hold many more books than open-faced shelves. Many teachers rotate books between traditional and open-faced shelves, advertising different books each week.

■ *Book-related displays and props:* Posters (available from such sources as the Children's Book Council, 67 Irving Place, New York, NY 10003; the American Library Association, 50 East

Huron Street, Chicago, IL 60611; and the International Reading Association, 800 Barksdale Road, Newark, DE 19711), puppets, flannel boards with cutout figures of story characters, and stuffed animals encourage children to engage in emergent reading and to act out favorite stories. Stuffed animals also are useful as listeners or babies for children to read to.

■ *Labels for the center:* Like cordoning off the area from the classroom space, symbolic cues help define the space and identify appropriate activities for young children. Using both print, "Library Corner," and symbols associated with the library—book jackets, a photograph of a child looking at a book—help even the youngest child read the label for the corner.

To this list, Miriam Smith and David Dickinson (2002) add:

■ *Listening center:* This center is typically located on a table large enough for four to six children to gather around a cassette or CD player, put on headphones, and listen to taped stories. The teacher provides multiple copies of the book on tape or CD so that children can turn the pages of the book as they listen to the story unfold.

Remember, the better designed the library corner, the more use children will make of it—that is, more children will choose to participate in book reading and literature-related activities during free-choice periods. Therefore, a classroom library corner that is voluntarily used by few children is suspected to be a poorly designed center. What might an enticing library corner look like? We provide a drawing of a possible library corner for an early childhood classroom in Figure 4.2.

FIGURE 4.2 Library Center

The Writing Center

A writing center is a special area in the classroom that is stocked with materials that invite children to write (see Figure 4.3). Judy Schickedanz and Renee Casbergue (2009) recommend that writing centers contain a variety of writing implements such as markers, pencils, and pens and paper of different sizes, textures, and colors. These materials provide an environmental press to engage in writing activities. In addition, teachers can provide a social stimulus for writing by providing a table and at least two chairs in the writing center. Children want to share their writing with peers, to know what their peers are writing, to ask for assistance with the construction of their text. "Morning. How do you spell 'mororornnn-nnninggg'?"

GATHER THE NEEDED MATERIALS. In addition to a table and chairs, teachers stock the writing center with materials that invite children to write, to play with writing materials. Such materials include but are not limited to the following:

- Many different kinds of paper (e.g., lined theme paper, typical story paper, discarded computer or office letterhead paper with one side clean, lots of unlined paper, paper cut into different shapes to suggest writing about particular topics, paper folded and made into blank books, stationery and envelopes, cards);
- Various writing tools (e.g., pencils, markers—be certain to purchase the kind that can withstand the kind of pressure young children exert as they write—crayons, felt-tip pens, a computer or computers with a word-processing program);
- Writing folders for storage of each child's writing efforts;
- An alphabet chart at the children's eye level and in easy view from all chairs; and
- A box or file drawer in which to store the file folders.

Notice that oversized (fat) pencils and special primary-lined paper were not recommended as the only paper and pencils to be provided. For young children, Miriam Martinez and Bill Teale (1987) recommend unlined paper because it does not signal how writing is supposed to be done. Children are freer to use the emergent forms of writing—pictures used as writing, scribble writing, letterlike forms, and so on—that do not fit on the lines of traditional lined writing paper or story paper (e.g., top half blank, bottom half lined).

In addition to these required items, many teachers include the following items in their classroom writing center:

- A bulletin board for displaying such items as samples of the children's writing, examples of different forms of writing (e.g., thank-you notes, letters, postcards, stories), writing-related messages (e.g., "Here's our grocery list"), messages about writing (e.g., "Look at this! Shawn's sister published a story in the newspaper"), and the children's writing;
- Posters showing people engaged in writing;
- Clipboards for children who want to write someplace other than at the table;
- Mailboxes (one for each child, the teacher, the principal or center director, and other appropriate persons, as determined by the children) to encourage note and letter writing;
- Alphabet strips on the writing table so that the children have a model readily available when they begin to attempt to link their knowledge of letter sounds with their knowledge of letter formations;
- Blank books made by placing two or three pieces of blank paper between two sheets of colored construction paper and stapled on one side, often cut in a shape that corresponds with the topic being studied (e.g., butterflies or trees when studying the environment, hearts when studying the body);
- Card sets of special words (e.g., words relating to the topic being studied, classmate names, common words) made by writing a word on an index card and (when possible) attaching a picture of the word, punching a hole in the corner, and using a silver ring to hold the card set together;
- Dry-erase boards or magic slates;
- Letter stamps and letter pads; and
- Plastic, wooden, and/or magnetic letters and letter templates.

Mailboxes can be made in various ways. For example, they might be made from the large tin food cans available from the cafeteria. Kindergarten teacher Debbie Czapiga, a clever seamstress, made mailboxes for each child by sewing pockets of discarded jeans onto a colorful, stiff piece of fabric. She then attached the strip of fabric to the bottom of the chalkboard and labeled each pocket with a child's name.

Most teachers introduce the materials to the children gradually; that is, they do not place all these materials in the writing center on the first day of school, which young children would find overwhelming. They make the writing center new and exciting over the year by regularly adding new materials and tools.

ARRANGE THE MATERIALS. With so many different materials in the writing center, keeping the supplies orderly and replenishing them can be time consuming. Some teachers label the places where the various tools and paper belong in the writing center; this helps all the children know where to return used materials and it helps a child "clerk" know how to straighten the center at cleanup time. Further, labeling the places where the items belong permits a quick inventory of missing and needed items. Figure 4.3 provides an illustration of a well-equipped, well-arranged writing center.

COMPUTERS AND WORD PROCESSING. A growing number of early childhood classrooms have computers in the writing center. Teachers in these classrooms are indeed fortunate! So are the children in these classrooms. Doug Clements and Julie Sarama (2003) summarized the research on young children and technology. In the language and reading area, they report that computers facilitate increased language use (children talk more to peers when they are at the computer than at other activities). Software programs can help children develop prereading skills also. In writing, children "using word processors write more, have fewer fine motor control problems, [and] worry less about making mistakes. Young children cooperatively plan, revise, and discuss spelling, punctuation, spacing, and text meaning and style" (pp. 36–37). Notice the two chairs in front of each computer. This arrangement encourages increased talk between peers. Technology expert Patricia Scott highly recommends the following software packages for their user-friendly qualities; that is, young children can easily use them to write: *Orly's Draw-a-Story, Claris for Kids,* and *The Writing Center* (the new

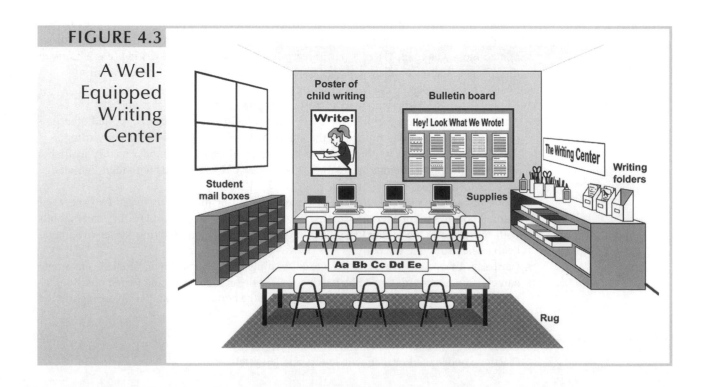

FIGURE 4.3

A Well-Equipped Writing Center

and improved version). Some older favorites include *Kid Works 2* (Davidson), *Storybook Weaver* (MECC), *Wiggins in Storybook Land,* and *The Incredible Writing Machine* (The Learning Company).

Marilyn Cochran-Smith, Jessica Kahn, and Cynthia Paris (1986) point out that all writers, regardless of age, require time at the computer when their attention is focused on learning word-processing skills. For example, Bev Winston, a kindergarten teacher, introduced her young students to word processing during the school's orientation days, those days that precede the first full day of school. Then she watched her children as they played with word processing during their free-play time and provided instruction as each child needed it. Word processing is a tool to preserve children's important first writings. It is important for teachers to keep this in mind. Young children need time to experiment with this tool just as children need time to experiment with pencils, pens, markers, and so forth.

WRITING MATERIALS IN OTHER CENTERS. Earlier we suggested that every center in the classroom should be literacy enriched. Every center should have print materials (e.g., books, magazines, pamphlets) connected with the topic under investigation available for the children's use. In addition, every center should include props to support the children's writing explorations (e.g., paper and writing implements). Miriam Smith and David Dickinson's (2002) Literacy Environment Checklist asks, "Are there writing tools in the dramatic play and block area? Are there props that prompt children to write in the dramatic play and block area?" When classrooms are assessed with the ELLCO Toolkit, they earn points when the rater responds with a *yes* to these questions.

When every center has writing tools, children can use writing to achieve a variety of purposes and practice using the form of writing (linear scribble, phonics-based spellings) that serves their need at the moment. In the science center, for example, teachers should provide forms to encourage children's recording of their scientific observations. Addie, a delightful 4-year-old, was studying the life cycle of the butterfly when we met her. Because paper and writing tools were available, she recorded her discovery (see Figure 4.4). (After we requested a copy of her

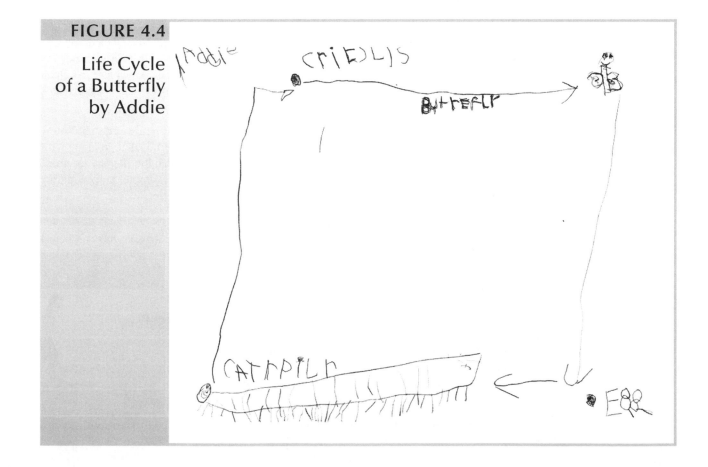

FIGURE 4.4

Life Cycle of a Butterfly by Addie

writing for publication in this book, she made poster copies of her discovery for every person in her neighborhood.) Writing tools in the library center encourage children to use books as models for their writing. When blue paper and writing tools were available in the block center, children made "blueprints" of the building they intended to construct, labeling the rooms. The blueprints that lined the walls of the block center during the construction unit provided a model for the children's drawing and writing. Using paper in the math center, children in Eileen Feldgus and Isabel Cardonick's (1999, p. 72) classrooms made bar graphs to illustrate their classmates' answer to a question (e.g., "Have you ever had a cast?"), wrote their observations of different objects' weight, and recorded their guesses of how many objects were in a jar. (Chapter 6 in their book contains numerous suggestions for engaging children in writing across the curriculum.) Clearly, putting writing tools at children's fingertips allowed them to use those tools for multiple purposes.

Literacy-Enriched Play Centers

Dramatic play occurs when children take on roles and use make-believe transformations to act out situations and play episodes. For example, several children might adopt the roles of family members and pretend to prepare dinner, or they may become superheroes who are engaged in fantastic adventures. This type of play—also called sociodramatic, make-believe, pretend, or imaginative play—reaches its peak between the ages of four and seven (Johnson, Christie, & Wardle, 2005).

As will be explained in Chapter 5, dramatic play is an idea context for developing children's oral language. This advanced form of play can also offer a context in which children can have meaningful, authentic interactions with reading and writing (Roskos & Christie, 2000, 2007a). The following vignette, which involves 4-year-old preschoolers, illustrates dramatic play's literacy learning potential:

> With some teacher assistance, Noah and several friends are getting ready to take a make-believe plane trip. The elevated loft in the classroom has been equipped with chairs and has become the plane, and a nearby theme center has been turned into a ticket office. Noah goes into the ticket office, picks up a marker, and begins making scribbles on several small pieces of paper. The teacher passes by with some luggage for the trip. Noah says, "Here Kurt! Here are some tickets." The teacher responds, "Oh great. Frequent flyer plan!" Noah then makes one more ticket for himself, using the same scribblelike script. The teacher distributes the tickets to several children, explaining that they will need these tickets to get on board the plane. As Noah leaves the center, he scribbles on a wall sign. When asked what he has written, Noah explains that he wanted to let people know that he would be gone for a while.

To provide these types of rich interactions with print, dramatic play areas need to be "literacy enriched"—stocked with an abundance of reading and writing materials that go along with each area's play theme. The goal is to make these play centers resemble the literacy environments that children encounter at home and in their communities. For example, a pizza parlor center can be equipped the following props:

- Cardboard pizza crusts (large circles)
- Felt pizza ingredients (tomato sauce [large red circles the same size as the cardboard crusts], pepperoni, black olives, onions, and the like)
- Pencils, pens, markers
- Note pads for taking orders
- Menus
- Wall signs ("Place Your Order Here," "Pay Here," "Shirts and Shoes Required")
- Employee name tags
- Environmental print—pizza boxes with company name and logo
- Cookbooks
- Bank checks, money, and credit cards
- Newspaper ads and discount coupons

These props invite children to incorporate familiar pizza-restaurant-based literacy routines into their play.

The most obvious benefit of linking literacy and play is that play can provide motivation for literacy learning. When children incorporate literacy into their play, they begin to view reading and writing as enjoyable skills that are desirable to master.

A second benefit is that adding print-related props to play areas results in significant increases in the amount of literacy activity during play (Roskos, Christie, Widman, & Holding, 2010). This provides children with valuable practice with emergent reading and writing. As young children have repeated exposure to print props, opportunities arise for developing alphabet and sight word recognition. Some children may learn to recognize the letter *p* because it is the first letter in *pizza*. Others may learn to recognize entire words such as *pepperoni, menu,* and *cheese*. Research has shown that children learn to recognize environmental print in play settings (Neuman & Roskos, 1993; Vukelich, 1994).

In addition, literacy-enriched play settings provide children with opportunities to learn important concepts about print. The pizza parlor setting contains many examples of the functional uses of print. Print is used to convey information on menus and pizza boxes. Signs such as "Place Your Order Here" and "The Line Starts Here" illustrate the regulatory function of print. Pizza parlors also are associated with literacy routines—sets of reading and writing actions that are ordinary practices of a culture (Neuman & Roskos, 1997). These routines demonstrate the instrumental functions of print and present opportunities for children to use emergent forms of writing and reading. Customers can read or pretend to read menus while placing orders. Waiters and counter clerks can use notepads to write down orders that will later be used by the chefs to determine which types of pizzas to bake. Chefs can consult cookbooks for information on how to prepare pizzas. Once the pizzas are baked, customers can use discount coupons from the newspaper to reduce the cost of their meals and pay their bill by writing checks.

Opportunities also exist to learn comprehension skills. Neuman and Roskos (1997) have detailed how playing in print-enriched settings can lead children to develop several types of strategic knowledge that have a role in comprehending text. In a pizza parlor setting, children have opportunities to:

▪ *Seek information:* A child might ask a playmate about the identity of a word on the pizza menu.
▪ *Check to see if guesses and hypotheses are correct:* A child might ask the teacher, "Is this how you spell *pizza?*"
▪ *Self-correct errors:* While writing the word *pizza* on a sign, a child might exclaim, "Oops, *pizza* has two *z*'s!"

Checking and correcting are self-regulatory mechanisms that build a base for cognitive monitoring during reading.

The literacy-enriched play setting strategy is easy to implement. Teachers simply add theme-related reading and writing materials to the dramatic play center (see Table 4.1). The literacy-learning potential of the dramatic play area is further strengthened when the center's theme is linked with the rest of the academic curriculum (Roskos & Christie, 2007b). This "networking" of play and the curriculum can provide opportunities for children to practice and consolidate skills and concepts taught in large and small group instruction.

Jim Christie (2008) describes how preschool teacher Mrs. Lemos connected dramatic play with a published curriculum to teach early literacy skills to the English language learners in her classroom in San Luis, Arizona. The curriculum was organized into thematic units centering on sets of children's books. Mrs. Lemos's class was studying building and construction. The curriculum has identified approximately 20 target words that are to be directly taught to children, including the names of tools (*hammer, saw, safety goggles, tape measure, nails*) and construction equipment (*dump truck, backhoe, crane*). On this particular day, Mrs. Lemos was teaching the "target" tool words. She began circle time with the shared reading of a rhyme poster. While the primary function of the poster was to teach rhyme identification, Mrs. Lemos instead focused the children's attention on the two tool words in the rhyme. She had children make a hand motion when *hammer* is mentioned and use their fingers to show how small the *tiny little nails* are. Next, Mrs. Lemos did a shared reading of a big book about building a dog house. This informational book had very few text words but contains several photographs that

TABLE 4.1

Literacy Props for Dramatic Play Centers

Home Center	Business Office
Pencils, pens, markers	Pencils, pens, markers
Note pads	Note pads
Post-it notes	Telephone message forms
Baby-sitter instruction forms	Calendar
Telephone book	Typewriter
Telephone message pads	Order forms
Message board	Stationery, envelopes, stamps
Children's books	File folders
Magazines, newspapers	Wall signs
Cookbooks, recipe box	
Product containers from children's homes	
Junk mail	

Restaurant	Post Office
Pencils	Pencils, pens, markers
Note pads	Stationery and envelopes
Menus	Stamps
Wall signs ("Pay Here")	Mailboxes
Bank checks	Address labels
Cookbooks	Wall signs ("Line Starts Here")
Product containers	

Grocery Store	Veterinarian's Office
Pencils, pens, markers	Pencils, pens, markers
Note pads	Appointment book
Bank checks	Wall signs ("Receptionist")
Wall signs ("Supermarket")	Labels with pets' names
Shelf labels for store areas ("Meat")	Patient charts
Product containers	Prescription forms
	Magazines (in waiting room)

Airport/Airplane	Library
Pencils, pens, markers	Pencils
Tickets	Books
Bank checks	Shelf labels for books
Luggage tags	("ABCs," "Animals")
Magazines (on-board plane)	Wall signs ("Quiet!")
Air sickness bags with printed instructions	Library cards
Maps	Checkout cards for books
Signs ("Baggage Claim Area")	

include pictures of tools. Even though the tools are not mentioned in the text, Mrs. Lemos paused to discuss them. She first asked, "What kind of tools will they need to build the dog-house?" As she read each page, she pointed to each of the tools in the illustrations and asks, "Does anyone know the name of this tool?" After the story was read, children went to center time. Mrs. Lemos arranged the environment to provide additional opportunity to encounter and use tool words. Several regular-sized copies of the doghouse book were placed in the classroom library for independent or partner reading. There were blackline masters of tools for the children to color and label in the art center. Finally, the dramatic play center contained a cardboard frame that resembled a doghouse and toy replicas of all of the tools mentioned in the doghouse book: plastic hammers, nails (actually wooden golf tees), measuring tape, safety goggles, and a toy circular saw. Two girls and a boy spent a half hour playing together, pretending to build a doghouse. In this play, the names of tools were used numerous times, and the children helped each other learn how to properly use each tool. For example, one of the girls reminded the boy to put on his safety goggles when using the saw!

Environmental and Functional Print

As Isaac enters his kindergarten classroom, he and his classmates collect laminated helper necklaces from their name pockets on the attendance chart. Each necklace has a tag listing a classroom task. Isaac "reads" his tag—Errand Runner. He checks the nearby Helper Board where all the duties for each task have been described in both words and pictures. Today he will run any errands his teacher may have, such as taking the attendance count to the center's office. Yesterday, Isaac was Pencil Sharpener, which involved gathering and sharpening pencils. He hopes to be Pet Feeder tomorrow.

As we explained in Chapter 3, children's home literacy experiences are often functional in nature. Children watch their parents and older siblings use reading and writing to accomplish real-life purposes. They often join in these activities (e.g., reading food labels and signs in the environment).

It is important for teachers to provide opportunities for children to continue to learn about functional qualities of reading and writing. In the preceding vignette, note how the helper necklaces in Isaac's classroom provide the same type of functional literacy experiences that children have at home. The print on the helper necklaces serves a real purpose and assists with everyday activities (classroom chores). The surrounding context—the chores that are done on a daily basis in the classroom—makes it easy for Isaac to recognize and understand the print on the necklaces.

Functional literacy activity provides opportunities for children at different stages in their literacy development to learn new skills and concepts. For example, if Isaac is just beginning to learn about the meaning and functions of print, the helper necklaces provide an opportunity to learn that print can inform him about his assigned chores and help him remember these chores. If he has already acquired this basic concept, the necklaces provide opportunities to learn about the structure of print. For example, he may eventually learn to recognize some of the printed words on the necklaces (*runner, pencil, pet*) or to figure out some related letter–sound relationships (the letter *p* represents the sound that *pencil* and *pet* begin with).

In the sections that follow, we describe two types of print that can provide children with functional literacy activities: (1) environmental print that exists in everyday life outside of school and (2) functional print that is connected with classroom activities.

ENVIRONMENTAL PRINT. At home and in their neighborhoods, young children are surrounded by print that serves real-life functions: labels on cereal boxes and soft drink cans, road signs, billboards, and restaurant menus. This type of print is referred to as environmental print (EP). Because the situation gives clues to the print's meaning, EP is often the first type of print that young children can recognize and understand.

The educational benefits of EP are very controversial. On the one hand, proponents of emergent literacy believe that EP is a valuable instructional resource (Prior and Gerard, 2004). Other researchers with a bent toward the scientifically based reading research (SBRR) point of view (discussed in Chapter 1) have argued that EP is of little instructional importance. For example, Ehri and Roberts (2006) found evidence that children did not focus on the alphabet letters in EP. Rather, children tended to focus on more visually salient cues such as color and logo designs. This led Ehri and Roberts (2006, p. 121) to conclude that "even though children may be able to read environmental print, this capability does not appear to promote letter learning."

Our position is that, because EP is so meaningful and easy to read, it should be available in all preschool and kindergarten classrooms. For this print to promote alphabet knowledge and phonics, teachers need to draw children's attention to letters that occur in EP. We recommend the following EP strategies:

- *EP board:* The teacher asks children to bring from home examples of EP that they can read. Selected pieces are displayed on a bulletin board titled "Print I Can Read." For example, the board might contain empty, clean product containers (cereal boxes, milk cartons, candy wrappers, toy boxes), menus for local fast-food restaurants, shopping bags with store logos, illustrated store coupons, and so on. Children work in small groups to try to figure out the meaning of all the pieces of EP on the board.

- *EP alphabet chart:* The teacher places pieces of chart paper around the room for every letter of the alphabet. Each day, children bring to class product labels they can "read." During circle time, these labels are read and attached to the correct chart. For example, the Kix (cereal) label would go on the *K k* page. Then the group reads the labels on all the charts, starting with the *A a* page. After several months, when most of the chart pages are full, the teacher can bundle the charts together in alphabetical order and make a "I Can Read Print" big book.

- *EP folders:* Selected pieces of EP can be attached to file folders to make EP books (Anderson & Markle, 1985). For example, a pizza book could be made by pasting or laminating the product logos from pizza advertisements, coupons, and delivery containers onto the inside surfaces of a file folder. Children can decorate the front cover with pizza-related illustrations. Other book possibilities include toothpaste, cookies, milk, cereal, and soft drinks. These EP folders should be placed in the classroom library so that children can show off to their friends how well they can read this type of contextualized print.

- *EP walks:* This strategy involves taking a class for a walk in the neighborhood surrounding the school (Orellana & Hernández, 1999). Before leaving, the children are told to be on the lookout for EP. As examples of EP are encountered during the walk, they are pointed out by the teacher or by the children. After the children return to the classroom, they draw pictures of the print they could read on the walk. The pictures are put into a group book, which the teacher reads aloud to the class, focusing their attention on the letters in this print. The children can then take turns reading EP items in the book.

- *Individual EP booklets:* This approach involves using magazine coupons or advertisements that feature products children are familiar with to make personalized "I Can Read" books. Children sort through the ads or coupons, select the products they recognize, and then use glue sticks to secure the coupons to premade construction paper booklets. The children can share their booklets with each other and take them home to read to family members.

- *Sociodramatic play:* As we explained earlier in this chapter, environmental print can be used as props in children's dramatic play. For example, empty product boxes such as cereal containers and milk cartons can be used in the kitchen area of housekeeping or home centers. As children act out home-related themes such as making dinner, they will have opportunities to attempt to read the print on the containers. Teachers should draw children's attention to the letters in this play-related print.

FUNCTIONAL PRINT. Unlike environmental print that is found in the world outside of school, functional classroom print is connected with everyday school activities. This print is practical as well as educational. The helper necklace in the opening vignette helps children remember their assigned chores, making the classroom run more smoothly. Simultaneously, the necklaces offer opportunities for children to learn about the functions and structure of print. As with all functional print, the context helps children discover the meaning of the print and learn concepts about print (Strickland & Schickedanz, 2009).

In the sections that follow, we describe the major types of functional print that are commonly found in preschool and kindergarten classrooms: labels, lists, directions, schedules, calendars, messages, sign-in and sign-up lists, and inventory lists:

TRADE SECRETS

4.1

Head Start teachers Gloria Cortez and Mayela Daniels use labels with children's names to designate where children hang their backpacks. They have placed labels with each child's name (in large computer font) and their pictures above the pegs where backpacks are stored. To get some educational mileage out of this functional print, Mrs. Cortez and Mrs. Daniels decided to turn this display into a timeline of children's progress in learning to write their names.

Every two months, the children write their name on a small piece of paper, and the teacher dates it. These samples of name writing are placed above their typed name and picture, in chronological order. This provides a concrete record of each child's writing development. It is quite motivating for the children to see their progress. Because the hooks are right next to the front door, the children's parents also get to enjoy this "portfolio on a wall."

■ *Labels:* As illustrated by the helper necklaces in the vignette at the beginning of this section, labels may be used to delineate tasks that students are assigned to complete, such as line leader, pencil sharpener, pet feeder, or paper passer. Labels can also be used to help organize the classroom. For example, cubbies can be labeled with children's names so that students know where their belongings are stored. Containers can be labeled to designate their contents, and labels can be used on shelves to indicate where materials are to be stored. Labels can also be used for designating different areas of the classroom (library, home center, blocks, games, art), informing children about the types of activities that are supposed to take place in each location. Finally, labels can be used to convey information. For example, teachers often use labels to identify objects in displays (e.g., types of seashells) and pictures ("This is a . . ."). Trade Secrets 4.1 describes how one teacher uses labels with children's names for two purposes: to organize their backpacks and to provide a record of their progress in learning to write their names.

■ *Lists:* Lists have a variety of practical classroom uses. Attendance charts can be constructed by placing each child's picture and name above a pocket. The children sign in by finding their name card in a box and by matching it with their name on the chart. After the children become familiar with their printed names, the pictures can be removed.

The teacher can use a second set of name tags to post jobs on a helper chart. This chart, which is an alternative to the helper necklaces described at the beginning of this chapter, contains a description of jobs needing to be done and display pockets that hold the children's name cards (see Figure 4.5). When attendance and helper charts are used on a daily basis, children quickly learn to recognize their own names and the names of their classmates.

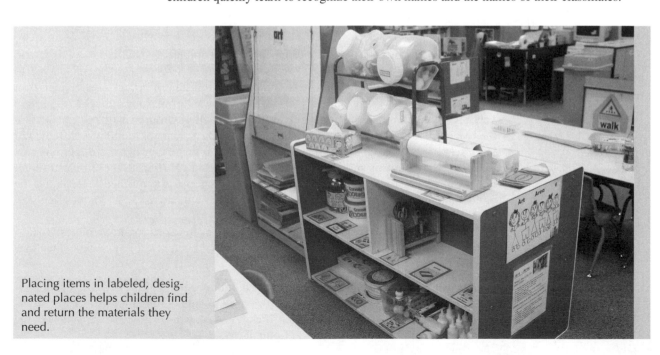

Placing items in labeled, designated places helps children find and return the materials they need.

FIGURE 4.5

Helper Chart

■ *Directions:* Instructions can be posted for using equipment such as CD players and computers. Classroom rules (e.g., "We walk in our classroom") can be displayed to remind children of appropriate behavior. In addition, children can create their own personal directives. For example, a child may place a "Look, don't touch!" sign on a newly completed art project or block structure. At first, children will need help from the teacher or from peers in reading these types of directions. Soon, however, they will learn to use the surrounding context to help them remember what the directions say. Teachers can help this process by constantly referring children to these posted directions. For example, if a child is running in the classroom, the teacher could direct the child's attention to the "We walk in our classroom" sign and ask, "What does that sign say?"

Directions can also include recipes for cooking or directions for art activities. The directions can be put on wall charts. Even very young children can follow simple directions that use both words and pictures.

■ *Schedules:* A daily schedule can be presented at the beginning of class to prepare children for upcoming activities. Pictures can be used to help children remember the different segments of the day (see Figure 4.6). If children ask what is going to happen next, the teacher can help them use the chart to figure it out.

FIGURE 4.6

Daily
Schedule

FIGURE 4.6 Daily Schedule

SCHEDULE

9:00	Opening
9:10	Free-choice time
10:00	Circle time
10:30	Snack
10:45	Outdoor play
11:30	Go home

■ *Calendars:* A monthly calendar can be set up at the beginning of each month and used for marking children's birthdays, parties, and other special events (such as field trips, classroom visitors, or when a student's dog had puppies). The teacher can encourage the children to use the calendar to determine how many more days until a special event takes place and to record events of importance to them.

■ *Messages:* Often, unforeseen events change the day's plans. It's raining, so there can be no outdoor playtime. Instead of just telling children, some teachers write a message. For example:

> Circle time will be first thing this morning.
> We have a special visitor!
> She will share her cookies with us.

Because these messages inform children about activities that directly affect their day, even the youngest children quickly learn to pay close attention to these notices.

■ *Sign-In and Sign-Up Lists:* Children can write their names on lists for a variety of functional purposes. For example, kindergarten teacher Bobbi Fisher (1995) writes the date and day at the top of a large 9- by 18-inch piece of drawing paper and has her children write their names on the paper each morning when they first arrive in the classroom. Ms. Fisher and her assistant teacher also sign the list. During circle time, the list is read to the class as a means of taking attendance and to build a sense of community. As the children become familiar with each other's printed names, they take over the activity.

She periodically uses this sign-in procedure to assess the children's emerging writing abilities.

Lists can also be used to sign up for popular classroom centers and playground equipment. Judith Schickedanz (1986) describes how teachers at the Boston University laboratory preschool had children sign up on lists to use popular centers such as the block and dramatic play areas. A child who does not get a chance to use the area on a given day is first in line to use it the next day. Sign-up sheets are also used to get turns using tricycles on the playground.

Children should be encouraged to use emergent forms of writing. If a child's writing is completely illegible, the teacher may need to write the child's name conventionally next to the child's personal script. The teacher can explain, "This is how I write your name." Once the child's name is recognizable, this scaffold can be discontinued.

■ *Inventory Lists:* Lists can also be used to create inventories of the supplies in different classroom areas. Susan Neuman and Kathy Roskos (2007) give an example of a chart that contains an inventory of the supplies in the art area. The list contains a picture and the name of each item, as well as the quantity of each item available. The sign informs children that there are eight paintbrushes, twelve pairs of scissors, lots of paper, and so on. During cleanup, children can use this information to make sure the center is ready for future use.

Organizing the Classroom's Daily Schedule: Using Time Wisely

Effective early literacy instruction requires more than a print-rich environment, age-appropriate instruction, and opportunities for meaningful reading and writing experiences. The daily schedule needs to be established that will allow children to have the optimal amount of time to take advantage of these learning opportunity—not too little or not too much. In addition, transitions need to be streamlined so that little time is wasted moving from one activity and another (Vukelich & Christie, 2009).

A sample half-day preschool schedule is provided in Table 4.2. In establishing this schedule, the teacher has followed several principles:

■ Balance quiet times with noisier times, and sitting and listening time with movement time;
■ Provide large chunks of time for individual and small-group investigations and shorter amounts of time for whole-group activities;
■ Recognize children's need for time to work together as a whole group, to work with peers in small groups, and to work independently; and
■ Value having children choose and make decisions about how to structure their personal time.

TABLE 4.2 A Sample Half-Day Preschool Schedule		
	8:00–8:30	Children arrive, sign in, use library center materials while waiting for group time to begin
	8:30–9:00	Whole-group morning gathering, morning messages, discussion of the topic being studied, overview of the day
	9:00–10:00	Activity time in literacy-enriched play settings; teacher works with small groups of children on literacy activities suited to their needs
	10:00–10:20	Clean-up and snack
	10:20–10:45	Shared storybook reading (done in small groups led by teacher and assistant teacher)
	10:45–11:15	Outdoor play
	11:15–11:45	Songs, poems, movement
	11:45–12:00	Review of the day and preparation for going home

TABLE 4.3		
A Sample Full-Day Preschool Schedule	8:00–8:30	Children arrive, sign in, use library center materials while waiting for group time to begin
	8:30–9:00	Whole-group morning gathering, morning messages, discussion of the topic being studied, overview of the day
	9:00–10:00	Activity time in literacy-enriched play settings; teacher works with small groups of children on literacy activities suited to their needs
	10:00–10:20	Clean-up and snack
	10:20–10:45	Shared storybook reading in small groups (teacher and assistant teacher)
	10:45–11:15	Outdoor play
	11:15–11:45	Whole-group: Songs, poems, movement
	11:45–12:15	Lunch
	12:15–12:40	Storybook reading in small groups
	12:40–1:40	Outdoor play
	1:40–2:10	Activity time in literacy-enriched settings; teacher works with small groups on math- and science-related activities
	2:10–2:40	Whole-group circle time that focuses on summarizing the day's activities, predicts tomorrow's activities, and reviews stories read in group times
	2:40–3:00	Preparation for going home

A growing number of preschool children attend full-day programs, like Head Start and day care. In addition, a growing number of states are implementing full-day kindergarten programs; in some states full-day kindergarten is mandated, while in others it is optional or being piloted in only some districts. Dixie Winters, Carol Saylor, and Carol Phillips (2003) investigated the benefits of full-day kindergarten and discovered that the research on the effects of full-day kindergarten on children's social development and academic achievement is positive, particularly for children from low-income backgrounds. Of course, the caveat is *when implemented with a high-quality curriculum and appropriate teaching practices.* Teachers respond positively to the full-day model. They report that the pace is more relaxed, less tiring, and less stressful for the children. They have a greater sense of accomplishment because they are able to accelerate all the children's language and literacy skills. Parents, too, respond positively. For working parents, a full-day program means that their children are ensured a level of quality care for a major portion of the day, and they experience fewer day care issues. Also, they report that the teachers know their children better and that their children's early literacy skills are greatly enhanced. So what might a full-day schedule for young children look like? See Table 4.3.

Through the use of these principles, these teachers demonstrate their recognition of children's need for diversity and variety in their daily activities. They also recognize children's need for predictability and a not-so-hidden structure to each day—a rhythm.

How firmly should teachers hold to a time schedule? Carol Wien and Susan Kirby-Smith (1998) suggest that teachers consider having an order of events but allowing the children to dictate the timing of the changes in activities. Kirby-Smith worked with two teachers of toddlers (age 18 to 30 months) to test the idea of letting children's interests dictate the length of activities. After an initial period when the teachers experienced frustration and a period when the children were very happy, the teachers came to see that allowing the children's rhythm to control the timing allowed the children to focus. The teachers discovered that children preferred (1) being greeted on arrival and helped to make an activity choice; (2) having a long free-play period with snack and toileting naturally occurring without interrupting the whole group's play; (3) having a short circle time with music and action after the long free-play period; and (4) ending the morning with outdoor play time. Now the toddlers "co-own" the curriculum.

What Happens during Whole-Group Time?

Some teachers call whole-group sessions meeting time or circle time. It is during these times that the children and their teacher come together, typically in a carpeted area of the classroom. During the first whole- group time of the day, teachers usually take attendance; make announcements; with kindergarten and older children, recite the pledge of allegiance to the flag; check the date on the calendar; report on the news of the day; and discuss plans for the day. Other whole-group sessions are used for introducing and discussing the integrated unit being studied; for the teacher to read literature aloud; for teacher presentation of a lesson on a writing or reading strategy; for singing songs; for the choral reading of poems; and for bringing closure to the day.

Whole-group instruction is efficient because the teacher can provide instruction to the entire class at same time. It also builds a sense of classroom community, giving children common experiences that bond them together into a learning community. However, to meet the developmental characteristics of 3- and 4-year-old children, whole-group instruction should be fast-paced, brief in duration, and engaging. Thirty minutes is usually the maximum length for an effective large-group session with 4-year-olds. Three-year-olds and less mature 4-year-olds do best with 20-minute sessions. Some teachers schedule 30-minute large-group sessions but arrange for the assistant teacher to pull out younger or less mature children after about 10 to 15 minutes. These children are then given small-group instruction, while the rest of the class finishes up the large-group time.

Of course, these recommendations are only approximate, and the optimal length of whole-group sessions is also influenced by content. If children are very interested and engaged in a whole group lesson, longer time periods are appropriate. Children's attention spans are remarkably long when they are engaged in an activity of interest to them! On the other hand, Neuman and Roskos (2005) describe a classroom situation in which preschool children had to endure a 45-minute circle time in which each child in the class had to come up to the alphabet frieze and point out the first two letters in his or her name, compare all the letters in the names of the days of the week, and then count up to 30. The children quickly became disengaged and listless. This was caused by a combination of rote, uninteresting skill-and-drill content, and too much time. Such lengthy bouts of large-group teaching are not recommended, as they are counterproductive and almost always lead to behavior problems.

What Happens during Small-Group Activity Time?

Increasingly, early childhood teachers are recognizing the need to pull small groups of children together for explicit instruction on the language and literacy skills. Small groups enable all children to actively engage in an activity and have a chance to talk. The smaller the group, the more each child gets to participate. In addition, small groups enable teachers to focus lessons on skills that specific children need to learn. Large-group instruction, on the other hand, is usually a compromise, teaching skills that many but not all of the children need.

According to McGee (2007), preschool teachers typically organize small groups in two ways: (a) having a separate small-group instruction period in which the class is split into several groups, with the teacher working with one group and the assistant teacher working with another; and (b) embedding small-group instruction in center time, pulling out a small number of children for intensive instruction while the rest of the class works and plays in centers.

In an example of the "splitting up" strategy, teachers in the Miami/Dade County Early Learning Coalition Early Reading First project in Florida divided their children into three groups for small-group instruction. For 30 minutes each day, the children rotated among the three literacy activities (spending 10 minutes in each small-group activity). The classroom teacher engaged in a dialogic reading activity with six children; the classroom assistant engaged in a print awareness activity with another group of six children; and a third group of children played independently with literacy-related materials. Every 10 minutes, the children moved to a new activity. In this way, the teachers were able to work with a small group of children explicitly teaching using SBRR-supported strategies. Some days the children with similar literacy needs were grouped together. Other days, the teacher intentionally created small groups of children with differing literacy needs.

The Mohave Desert Early Literacy Coalition Early Reading First project in Bullhead City, Arizona, modified the entire daily schedule to split preschool classes into smaller groups. Each class was divided into two groups based on the children's language and literacy abilities. All children attended the morning session, Monday through Friday. During the afternoon session, half of the children in each class attended afternoon sessions on Mondays and Wednesday, and half attended on Tuesdays and Thursdays. This split schedule allowed afternoon "whole-group" instruction to be delivered to groups of approximately 10 children, increasing participation and interaction opportunities. This split schedule also allowed the teacher and assistant to divide children into even smaller groups of four to five children for instruction that targets each group's specific needs, as identified by continual progress monitoring with curriculum-based measures.

The other common grouping strategy is for the teacher to pull a very small group of two to five children aside during center time for more intensive instruction. This "concentrated" instruction is often referred to as Tier 2 instruction, and it is intended for children who are not responding well to regular Tier 1 curriculum. Because this very-small-group instruction occurs during center time, it preempts the teacher's ability to interact with children while they engage in center activities, and McGee (2007) recommends that teachers teach only one such group per day. As she points out, "The conversations that you have with children as they play in centers are important for children's language development, and you don't want to lose those opportunities" (McGee, 2005, p. 125). David Dickinson (2010) agrees with McGee. Some years ago he gathered data on teachers' interactions with their preschool children. Later he studied the relationship between different kinds of teachers' interactions he had observed and the children's reading performance when they were in fourth grade. He discovered that the frequency and quality of the teachers' talk with the children during center time was critically important to the children's later reading achievement.

What Happens during Center or Activity Time?

Preschool and kindergarten classrooms are commonly divided into activity areas, or learning centers, with each area having its own particular set of materials and activities. In center-based classrooms, children interact with focused sets of materials and help each other build their own knowledge and skills. The teacher's role is to set up the environment, observe as children interact with the materials, supply help and guidance when needed, and occasionally introduce new activities for each center. If centers are set up properly and if an effective management system is established, the classroom environment does much of the "teaching"!

Typically, the children's curiosity will be aroused or their focus will be directed during the whole-group meetings. During center time, the children can act on their interests. During these times, the children might move freely about the classroom, selecting the area or center of interest to them. They might write in the writing center, read books in the cozy corner library, build structures in the block or construction center, or investigate and record their observations in the science center. It is important for teachers to provide children with time to engage in activities of their choice and to plan the use of their time.

Centers offer an ideal opportunity for children to practice and perfect literacy skills. For example, if the teacher has read the big book, *Tabby Tiger Taxi Driver* by Joy Cowley (Wright Group/McGraw Hill, 2001) to children during large-group time, children can extend their knowledge of taxis and transportation-related concepts and vocabulary during center time. Children playing in the taxi-theme dramatic play center can hail taxis, drive to various destinations, pay their fares, and receive receipts from the driver. The children also can "read" maps and "drive" cars along pretend roads in the block center. In the writing center, they can make license plates and signs for use in the taxi play center. They can read books on transportation in the library center.

During these free-choice times, the children might work with a small group of peers to answer questions of shared interest. In other instances, groups might form spontaneously; those five children who are interested in playing in the dramatic play area come together for play and stay until they are tired of playing in the center.

It is important for teachers to actively engage in learning with their children during these free-choice times. This is not the time for teachers to work at completing administrative tasks. It is the time to read a book with a child or two, take a child's dictation, happen on a child at just that moment when she or he needs instruction, or play with the children in dramatic play area.

Center periods are typically 40 to 60 minutes in length. Why the long block of time for activity time and the shorter block of time for whole-group time? Young children need a generous uninterrupted block of time for play. It takes considerable time for them to plan their play with their peers, to negotiate roles with each other, and to carry out their play ideas. Children generally require from 30 minutes to an hour to develop and act out a single play scenario (Christie & Wardle, 1992). The best play scenarios evolve over several days, with children resuming and extending their play each day.

Transitions

Transitions are the times during the daily schedule when children move from one activity to another. These transition times commonly include arriving at the beginning of the day; moving between large-group, small-group, and center activities; preparing for outdoor play, meals, and/or nap time; and getting ready to go home (Hemmeter, Ostrosky, Artman, & Kinder, 2008). There are several reasons that teachers should pay close attention to these transition periods. First, research has shown the preschoolers typically spend as much as 20 to 35 percent of their time in these transitions (Wilder, Chen, Atwell, Pritchard, & Weinstein, 2006), so transitions take up a big chunk of the daily schedule. Second, transitions often lead to challenging behaviors, particularly if transitions are too numerous, too lengthy, or inadequately planned (Hemmeter et al., 2008).

Ostrosky, Jung, and Hemmeter (2008) recommend the following strategies to support smooth transitions:

▧ Provide verbal ("Okay, it's almost time for clean up") and nonverbal (turning on a special lamp to indicate clean up time) reminders before transitions start.
▧ Allow children to move individually from one area to another without having to wait for the whole group to get ready (after children have finished their snack, they can get a library book and read it while waiting for small-group instruction to start).
▧ Provide positive feedback when children follow transition routines ("I like how you all started to clean up when I turned on the lamp").
▧ Teach peers to help children who have a difficult time with transitions (e.g., transition buddies).

We also recommend making transition activities educational and engaging. Transitions can provide a perfect opportunity for children to practice language and literacy skills. Teachers in the Mohave Desert Coalition Early Reading First project in Bullhead City, Arizona, have children say a "password" when entering the classroom after outdoor play. This password is a theme-related vocabulary word on a poster or picture/word card. During a transportation unit, the passwords were the names of different kind of motor vehicles. During a construction unit, the passwords were the names of tools. In another example, teachers could have each child quickly point to a letter on the Word Wall when transitioning from large group to center activities.

These activities are done at a brisk pace so that no child needs to wait more than two or three minutes to get a turn. Of course, if children have difficulty doing the task, this presents an excellent opportunity for some teacher scaffolding.

Strategies for Teaching English Language Learners: Modifying the Classroom Environment

Myae Han

Imagine yourself in a subway station trying to find a way to get to another station. Add a little more imagination; you are in a foreign country, and everything is labeled in a language you cannot read. How would you find your way?

This may be how new immigrant children feel when they enter the classroom in the United States for the first time. Fortunately, most preschool classrooms are filled with hands-on materials and activities for the children's engagement. Teachers can modify their classroom environment to make easy access for English language learners (ELLs). An environment that thoughtfully accommodates the cultural and linguistic needs of children helps smooth ELL children's adjustment and transition from home to school. Such environments also support ELL children's language and literacy development. The following are several strategies to make the classroom environment more welcoming for ELL children:

- Include pictures and words in each ELL child's first language when labeling classroom areas and objects.
- Display a daily schedule with pictures, such as story time, snack time, cleanup, hand washing, and so on. This gives a general sense of daily structure.
- Display children's names with pictures and verbalize them as often as possible. Have other English-speaking children say the names of ELL children. This supports positive peer relationship. Peer partners are very helpful in a classroom with a diverse population. Researchers have found that peer tutoring has a positive impact for both English-speaking and ELL children (Hirschler, 1994).
- Have ample play materials that children can play with without assistance. Teachers should ensure

that they are providing places in the classroom where ELL children can feel comfortable, competent, and occupied.
- Early in the school year, it is desirable to stick with a strict routine to minimize the ELL children's confusion. This helps the ELL children to adjust in the classroom and feel more secure sooner.
- Include a picture dictionary in the classroom library.

Most preschool classrooms provide a free-choice time during the day. Researchers found that lengthy play periods (at least 45 to 60 minutes) can promote children's self-expression and self-direction (Isenberg & Jalongo, 1993). Children become self-directed learners when they know that they have enough time during the school day to complete the learning activities they have chosen. Free-play time is also less stressful than structured group time for ELL children, a well as a time when the classroom adults can provide individual support to the ELL children within the context of joyful activities.

What can teachers do to support ELLs during free-play time? Tabors (1997) recommends two strategies: running commentary and context-embedded language. Running commentary is a strategy called "talking while doing." When teachers use this strategy, they explain their actions or others' actions as an activity unfolds. For example, a teacher might say, *"I'm getting some writing paper from the shelf here, and I'll need a Magic Marker from the writing tools box. I'm writing a note to myself to remember to get popcorn for the children tomorrow. I write 'p-o-p-c-o-r-n' [saying each letter as she writes it]."* Context-embedded language is language related to the immediate situation, particularly in the course of sociodramatic play. In child-initiated activities, the child creates a context first, and then the teacher follows the child's action verbally so that the teacher's language is more meaningful to children. For example, Martinec and De'Zebbra are building in the block corner. The teacher says, *"De'Zebbra is putting one block down. Martinec is putting one block on top of De'Zebbra's block. De'Zebbra is putting one block on top of Martinec's block."* The teacher continues this description of the children's actions in this context until she says, *"Look! Martinec and De'Zebbra built a tall tower!"*

Strategies for Children With Special Needs: Adjusting the Daily Schedule

Karen Burstein and Tanis Bryan

The majority of children with special needs have difficulties in language, reading, and written

expression. Research indicates that these problems stem from deficits in short-term memory, lack of self-awareness and self-monitoring strategies, lack of mediational strategies, and inability to transfer and generalize learned material to new or novel situations. Hence, many students with special needs may have difficulty in classroom settings that use a high degree of implicit teaching of literacy. These students typically can benefit from explicit instruction. Here are some general teaching strategies

(continued on next page)

(continued)

that teachers can use to support students with special needs:

- Establish a daily routine on which the student with special needs can depend.
- Allocate more time for tasks to be completed by students with special needs.
- Structure transitions between activities, and provide supervision and guidance for quick changes in activities.
- Adapt the physical arrangement of the room to provide a quiet space free of visual and auditory distractions.
- Plan time for one-on-one instruction at some point in the day.
- Use task analysis to break learning tasks into components.

- Recognize the different learning styles of all students, and prepare materials in different ways—for example, as manipulatives, audio recordings, visual displays, and the like.
- Try cross-ability or reciprocal peer tutoring for practice of learned material.
- Consistently implement behavior change programs.
- Encourage all students to respect and include students with special needs in their academic and play activities.
- Establish a routine means of communication with parents.
- Locate strategies that help parents select materials that are developmentally and educationally appropriate for their students.

Summary

In this chapter, we discussed two key elements of instructional organization: planning the classroom environment and scheduling time for instruction. First, we examined how teachers can set up well-arranged, literacy-rich classroom environments that provide ideal settings for learning to read and write. Then we discussed how the daily schedule can be organized to maximize literacy learning.

■ *How can teachers arrange the classroom's physical environment and daily schedule to support children's language and literacy learning?*

Teachers can create a classroom environment that supports language and literacy learning by (1) carving classroom space into small, well-defined areas; (2) gathering appropriate resources to support the children's learning; (3) placing similar or related centers near each other; (4) making literacy materials part of the fabric of each center; and (5) creating an aesthetically pleasing environment.

The daily schedule should also support the integrated curriculum. Large chunks of time are necessary for individual and small-group investigations and shorter amounts of time for whole-group activities. Quiet times during which children sit and listen should be balanced with active times. The schedule should also feature flexibility, so that children have the freedom to pursue their interests, and predictability, so that there is a rhythm to the day.

■ *How can teachers set up a well-designed library center?*

A well-stocked and managed classroom library should be a key feature of every early childhood classroom. To encourage young children to engage in book reading in this area, the classroom library must be well-designed with partitions, ample space, comfortable furnishings, open-faced and traditional bookshelves, and book-related props and displays. Teachers will know quickly if their classroom library meets the well-designed criteria; inviting classroom libraries are heavily used by the children.

■ *Why is a writing center an important area in the preschool classroom? Why is it also important to have writing materials available in other centers?*

A writing center is that area of the classroom where the teacher has stocked materials (different kinds of papers, various writing tools, alphabet reference charts, computers, samples of children's writing) that invite children to write. Concentrating all these writing supplies and aids in one area encourages children to engage in emergent writing. When every center has writing tools, children can use writing to achieve a variety of purposes and practice using the form of writing (linear scribble, phonics-based spellings) that serves their need at the moment. Making writing materials available in other centers will encourage even more writing. When every center has writing tools, children can use writing to achieve a variety of purposes and practice using the form of writing (linear scribble, phonics-based spellings) that serves their need at the moment.

■ *How can dramatic play centers be used to encourage young children's literacy development?*

Literacy-enriched play centers can provide an ideal context for children to have meaningful, authentic interactions with print. The teacher simply needs to place theme-related reading and writing in the dramatic play area. For example, if the center is set up as a restaurant, the teacher and children can add wall signs, menus, pencils, and note pads to jot down customer orders. This type of literacy-enriched dramatic play can offer children of all ages and abilities multiple low-risk opportunities to explore and experiment with emergent reading and writing.

■ *What are functional literacy activities, and how can teachers use these activities in a preschool or kindergarten classroom?*

Functional print (labels, lists, directions, and schedules) is ideal for beginning readers because the surrounding context helps explain its meaning. This contextualized print is easy for young children to read and helps them view themselves as real readers. In addition, functional literacy activities help develop the concept that reading and writing have practical significance and can be used to get things done in everyday life. This realization makes print more salient to children and provides important motivation for learning to read and write. Functional print also presents opportunities for children to learn to recognize letters and words in a highly meaningful context.

■ *How can the daily schedule support language and literacy learning?*

A wonderful environment without blocks of time to use it is worthless. Large chunks of time are necessary for individual and small-group investigations and shorter amounts of time for whole-group activities. Quiet times during which children sit and listen should be balanced with active times. The schedule should also feature flexibility, so that children have the freedom to pursue their interests, and predictability, so that there is a rhythm to the day.

LINKING KNOWLEDGE TO PRACTICE

1. Observe a library center in an early childhood classroom, and evaluate its book holdings and design features. Are there a large number and wide variety of books available for the children to read? Are any basic types of books missing? Does the library center contain partitions, ample space, comfortable furnishings, open-face and traditional bookshelves, and book-related props and displays? Is there a writing center nearby?
2. Visit a classroom set up for 3-year-olds and a classroom set up for 5-year-olds in an early childhood center. Draw a diagram of each classroom's writing center and make a list of the writing materials the teacher has provided. Compare the materials in these classrooms' writing centers with the list of recommended materials on pages 77–78. Describe the differences between the writing center set up for 3-year-olds and that set up for 5-year-olds. Observe the classrooms' teachers as they interact with the children in the writing center. Describe what they talk about with the children.
3. Visit a preschool or kindergarten classroom, and record the different types of functional literacy activities and the ways they are used in the classroom. How did the children respond to or use functional print within the classroom? Did the teacher refer to the functional print?
4. With a partner, design plans for a literacy-enriched play center. Select a setting appropriate for a group of children. Describe how this center might be created in a classroom. What literacy props could be placed in the play center? What functional uses of print

might be used to convey information? What literacy routines might children use in this center? What roles might children and teacher play? How might you scaffold children's play and literacy knowledge in this play center?

5. Visit a preschool or kindergarten classroom, and make copy of the daily schedule. Evaluate the schedule in terms of the criteria discussed in this chapter.

Go to the Topics Organization and Program Management, English Language Learners, and At Risk and Struggling Readers in the MyEducationLab (www.myeducationlab.com) for your course, where you can:

- Find learning outcomes for Organization and Program Management, English Language Learners, and At Risk and Struggling Readers along with the national standards that connect to these outcomes.

- Complete Assignments and Activities that can help you more deeply understand the chapter content.

- Examine challenging situations and cases presented in the IRIS Center Resources.

Go to the Topic A+RISE in the MyEducationLab (www.myeducationlab.com) for your course. A+RISE® Standards2Strategy™ is an innovative and interactive online resource that offers new teachers in grades K-12 just in time, research-based instructional strategies that:

- Meet the linguistic needs of ELLs as they learn content

- Differentiate instruction for all grades and abilities

- Offer reading and writing techniques, cooperative learning, use of linguistic and nonlinguistic representations, scaffolding, teacher modeling, higher order thinking, and alternative classroom ELL assessment

- Provide support to help teachers be effective through the integration of listening, speaking, reading, and writing along with the content curriculum

- Improve student achievement

- Are aligned to Common Core Elementary Language Arts standards (for the literacy strategies) and to English language proficiency standards in WIDA, Texas, California, and Florida.

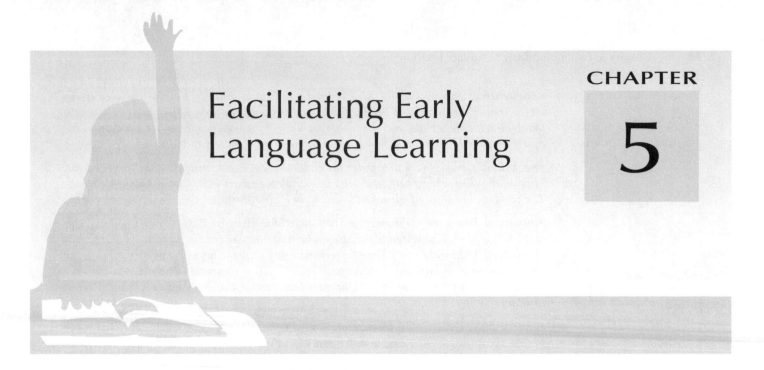

Facilitating Early Language Learning

Ms. V. is working with predominantly English-speaking kindergarten children from lower socioeconomic homes. Most of these children are able to share their wants and needs and express their feelings, but Ms. V. has noticed that most of the children have limited vocabularies. Her purpose is to help them build expressive vocabulary—to be able to use new words in their speech. The following scenario describes Ms. V.'s explicit vocabulary activities beginning with a game she plays with the children once or twice a week. She usually plans her target words to extend a storybook or a social studies or science lesson. Ms. V. begins by explicitly introducing new vocabulary words to the children the minute they enter the classroom today:

■ ***Morning greeting:*** *"Martine, you are clever," whispers Ms. V. into Martine's ear. Moving to Jorge, she again whispers, "Jorge, you are so smart." Kevin is next; Ms. V. whispers, "Kevin, you are so bright." And she repeats the procedure with several more children, as the class assembles for group time.*

■ ***Group time:*** *Ms. V. continues to extend the new words* clever, smart, *and* bright *during group time. She tells the class, "I whispered a word to many of you this morning as you came in the door. But I didn't use exactly the same word. So listen closely! If I told you that you were clever, please stand up!" Four children stand. "Great. This is the word* clever" *(holding a word card that will later go on the vocabulary word wall). "If I told you that you were smart, stand up! If I told you that you were bright, stand up!" She asks the children to repeat the words on the card as she points to them on the chalkboard. Then she asks the children, "What do you think is the meaning of these words? Turn to your neighbor and tell him or her what* smart *means. Can some of you share your ideas? Do you agree?* Smart *means knowing a lot of things? Okay, what does* clever *mean? Tell another partner." Children begin to offer their ideas; Ms. V. listens and nods. She says, "Jason and Gabby think* clever *also means someone knows a lot of stuff but might be sort of tricky. What do the rest of you think?" Now the children discuss* bright. *Two young ladies, Hannah and Emma, suggest* bright *may have something to do with knowing a lot of stuff, but it also means really colorful, like Rainbow Brite dolls. Ms V. takes a large piece of construction paper and asks the children whether they can agree that* bright, clever, *and* smart *all mean knowing a lot. The children agree, and she writes this common definition on the paper and then puts the three words below. She asks the children if there are any other words they can think of that also mean knowing a lot of stuff. Connor suggests* brilliant. *"Ron said that Hermione [in the Harry Potter books and movies] is brilliant when she had a really good idea." Ms. V. congratulates Connor on being very clever! Ms. V. adds* brilliant *to the list. She reminds the students that today they are going to try to use their new words and listen to see if Ms. V. uses them.*

◼ *Activity time: During centers, Ms. V. roams the room and catches the children being clever, smart, brilliant, and bright. Each time she uses the words the children repeat it loudly. Each time a child uses the word (correctly) in a sentence the other children in the center clap. Using these new words is exciting and immediately reinforced.*

◼ *Snack time: During snack time today the children's comments are full of the target words. This snack will make us brilliant! Milk is a drink for smart kids. Clever kids eat carrots. The children are pleased when Ms. V. claps for their efforts.*

◼ *Story time: Today the children hear* The Gingerbread Boy *by P. Galdon (Houghton Mifflin, 1975). After Ms. V. reads the story, she asks the children to describe the different characters. Elija suggests, "The Gingerbread Boy thought he was smart, but really he wasn't because he kept teasing everyone else." Ariel comments, "The fox was clever—smart and tricky—because he caught the Gingerbread Boy." Gabby exclaims, "Wow, brilliant!"*

◼ *Outdoor play: On the playground Tony is heard shouting, "I'm the smartest"; under her breath Kara responds by saying to her teacher, "No, he's just fast; that doesn't mean he knows a lot."*

Ms. V.'s clever use of words was brilliant, don't you think? A few moments of preparation and a great deal of determination are helping her bright young students become even smarter.

Research has consistently shown that oral vocabulary is a strong predictor of elementary-grade reading comprehension (Dickinson & Tabors, 2001) and that the strength of this relationship increases progressively from grade 1 to grade 7 (Snow, 2002). Other aspects of young children's oral language, including listening comprehension and grammar, also have important roles in later literacy achievement (National Early Literacy Panel, 2008).

Chapter 2 discussed how infants and toddlers learn their native language through complex social interactions with parents, siblings, and other caregivers. These individuals are essentially a child's first and most important teachers. Chapter 3 explains how, throughout the preschool years, the family plays a significant role in helping children begin to learn about print and become accomplished language users. We examined the talk that goes on in homes and described ways parents can support and enrich language development.

However, a child's family is not the only source of language stimulation. Preschool teachers also play a crucial role promoting language development, particularly in the case of children who are not exposed to rich language at home. In their extensive home-school study of young children's oral language environments, Patton Tabors, Catherine Snow, and David Dickson (2001, p. 326) found that "excellent preschools can compensate for homes that offer well below average access to language and literacy support." Note that this applies to *excellent* preschools—schools where teachers expose children to rich language models and opportunities (Casbergue, McGee & Bedford, 2008).

In this chapter, we examine the ways teachers can provide children with both direct vocabulary lessons and language learning activities. Strategies include explicit vocabulary instruction throughout the day but particularly during storybook readings and content instruction. We will also discuss more embedded language activities such as rich teacher discourse, reciprocal conversation, classroom activities that encourage language use, and activities that focus children's attention on language.

BEFORE READING THIS CHAPTER, THINK ABOUT . . .

◼ The conversations that took place in your classroom when you were in school. Were they mainly teacher-centered exchanges in which you and your classmates responded to questions asked by the teacher, or did you have the opportunity to engage in two-way conversations with the teacher and other children?

◼ Sharing or show-and-tell. What did you like about this activity? What, if anything, did you not like about it?

- The make-believe play you engaged in when you were a child. What were some of the favorite roles and themes that you acted out during this play?
- How was vocabulary taught by your teachers? Did they use picture cards, real objects, workbooks, dictionaries, or other methods to teach you the meaning of new words?

FOCUS QUESTIONS

- What are effective, explicit approaches to teach vocabulary?
- What is the initiation, response, evaluation (IRE) pattern of class talk? What problems are associated with this type of discourse? How can teachers provide students with more stimulating conversations in the classroom?
- How do group activities, learning centers, and dramatic play promote oral language acquisition?
- What can teachers do to promote language-rich dramatic play?
- How can sharing or show-and-tell be turned into a valuable oral language activity?
- How should teachers teach new vocabulary words?
- What can teachers do to optimize oral language experiences for bilingual and second-language learners?
- How can teachers encourage parents to extend language development at home?

While children vary widely in their ability to use and respond to language young children should be able to successfully demonstrate the skills listed in Table 5.1, Language Skills. If children are not demonstrating these skills, then professional assessment is recommended.

Explicit Vocabulary Instruction

The word *vocabulary* refers to children's knowledge of word meanings. While vocabulary acquisition is one of the key components of oral language development, it also plays an important role in reading comprehension and academic success as children matriculate through school (Chris & Wang, 2010). Researchers Steven Stahl and William Nagy state it most persuasively in their 2006 text, *Teaching Word Meaning:*

> A person who knows more words can speak, and even think, more precisely about the world. A person who knows the terms *scarlet* and *crimson* and *azure* and *indigo* can think about colors in a different way than a person who is limited to red and blue . . . words divide the world, the more words we have, the more complex ways we can think about the world. (p. 5)

BOX 5.1	
Definition of Terms	**Active listening:** The listener combines the information provided by the speaker with his or her own prior knowledge to construct personal meaning.
	Dramatic play: An advanced form of play in which children take on roles and act out make-believe stories and situations.
	Initiation, response, evaluation (IRE): A pattern of classroom talk in which the teacher asks a question, a student answers, and the teacher either accepts or rejects that answer and then goes on to ask another question.
	Metalinguistic awareness: The ability to attend to language forms in and of themselves. For example, a child may notice that two words rhyme with each other.
	Metaplay language: Comments about play itself ("I'll be the mommy, and you be the baby").
	Pretend language: Comments that are appropriate for the roles that children have taken in dramatic play. For example, a child pretending to be a baby might say "Waah! Waah!"
	Vocabulary: Children's knowledge of word meanings.

TABLE 5.1 Typical Language Skills

Speaking and Communicating Preschool Through Kindergarten

- Demonstrates increasing ability to attend to and understand conversations, stories, songs, and poems
- Shows progress in understanding and following simple and multiple step directions
- Understands an increasingly complex and varied vocabulary
- Participates in conversations with peers and adults about topics and texts being studied
- Listens to others and take turns speaking
- Asks questions to get information, seek help, or clarify something that is not understood
- Describes familiar people, places, things, and events and, with prompting, provides additional details
- Understands and uses question words (e.g., who, what, where, when, why, how) in discussions
- Forms regular plural nouns when speaking
- For non-English-speaking children, progresses in listening to and understanding English
- Develops increasing abilities to understand and use language to communicate information, experiences, ideas, feelings, opinions, needs, questions and for other varied purposes
- Progresses in abilities to initiate and respond appropriately in conversation and discussion
- Uses an increasingly complex and varied spoken vocabulary
- Progresses in clarity of pronunciation and toward speaking in sentences
- Uses common affixes/suffixes in English (un, re, dis / ly, ing, ness)
- Uses common adjectives
- For non-English-speaking children, progresses in speaking English

---

Research has shown that the size of children's vocabulary at age 3 is strongly associated with reading comprehension at the end of third grade (Hart & Risley, 2003). Sadly, research also consistently suggests that the size of children's vocabulary also appears to be correlated to their socioeconomic status (Degarmo, Forgatch & Martinez, 1999; Hoff, 2003; Linver, Brooks-Gunn, & Kohen, 2002). Fortunately, research has also shown that vocabulary growth is promoted through direct instruction of targeted words and by arranging experiences so that children encounter these targeted words frequently in different contexts (Beck, McKeown, & Kucan, 2002; McCardle & Chhabra, 2004).

Vocabulary learning can promoted through direct instruction of word meanings (Biemiller, 2001) and through incidental learning from contexts that provide rich verbal opportunities (Biemiller, 2001; Roskos, Tabors, & Lenhart, 2009; Weizman & Snow, 2001). Early childhood teachers have traditionally used incidental approaches to provide vocabulary instruction, looking for "teachable moments" during storybook reading and classroom conversations to build children's knowledge of word meanings. What is new in SBRR programs is that vocabulary instruction is intentional and preplanned, as well as incidental.

A research synthesis of effective vocabulary strategies in preschool and primary classrooms (Chris & Wang, 2010; Silverman & Dibara-Crandell, 2010) suggests the following:

1. Provide purposeful exposure to new words; teachers should decide in advance to teach selected words to children, using both high-utility root words (Biemiller & Slonim, 2001) and "rare words" (Hirsch, 2003). High-utility root words refer to uninflected words that occur with high frequency in oral language. These words are useful to know, because of they can be used to create many related words (*move > moved, moveable, remove,* and so on). Rare words refer to specialized vocabulary needed for development of domain knowledge in content areas (e.g., *excavate, backhoe, scoop, blueprint, plaster,* and the like).

2. Intentionally teach word meaning. Select words that are important for comprehension and useful in everyday interaction (Beck et al., 2002; Biemiller & Boote, 2006). There are several effective approaches to teaching word meaning, described in Table 5.2, Approaches to Defining Words.

3. Teach word learning strategies. For young children to develop the mental tools to infer word meanings from context, they need to be taught how. This is best accomplished when the teacher models through a think-aloud. Think back to Mrs. Lemos's preschool class as they learned about the tools of construction. When she paused to discuss the tools for construction, she asked the children to use prior knowledge from other texts they had been reading about building. This strategy encourages children to make text to text connections (Wasik & Bond, 2001).

4. Offer opportunities to use newly learned words. Often, these targeted words are connected to other parts of the academic curriculum—an ongoing thematic unit, books that are being read, field trips, and the like. These vocabulary-curriculum connections provide opportunities for children to encounter the targeted words repeatedly in a short period of time—a crucial factor in word learning (Siegler, 2005; Stahl, 2003). The vignette of vocabulary instruction in Special Feature 1.1 in Chapter 1 is an excellent example of this type of integrated teaching.

Given the important role of vocabulary in early and later literacy development and that many children from low-income families tend to lag far behind their middle-class peers in learning new words (Hart & Risley, 1995), one would expect that vocabulary be a high instructional priority in preschool, kindergarten, and the middle grades. Unfortunately, this is not the case. Susan Neuman and Julie Dwyer (2009) report that vocabulary instruction is "missing in

TABLE 5.2 Approaches to Defining Words

Illustration/Model	*"perched."*
Teacher uses visual support such as a picture, gesture, or example.	"There were *grumblings* in the hen house." Teacher demonstrates a scowling face and asks the children what they feel when they make a face like that.
Analyze	*"cuisine"*
Teacher prompts children to analyze how words are related by comparing and contrasting, attending to multiple meanings, and providing synonyms and antonyms.	The story has been about the new foods the animals are cooking, so the teacher asks, "Could we put the word *food* in for *cuisine*? Would it mean the same thing?" *"scents"* Are scents something you see or smell?
Embed/Define	*"succulent"*
Teacher provides the definition of the word in the context that it appears.	That means delicious and tasty.
Contextualize/Extend	*"Fiesta!"*
Teacher guides the children to apply word knowledge by using the word in a new context other than the one in which the word appeared.	Would you like to have a fiesta? When have we had a fiesta in class? Have you had a fiesta for your birthday?

Story: *Chicks and Salsa* by A. Reynolds. New York: Bloomsbury Publishing, 2005. Words from the story.

Adapted from Silverman, R., & Dibara-Crandell, J. (2010). Vocabulary practices in prekindergarten and kindergarten classrooms. *Reading Research Quarterly* 45(3), 318–340. Doi.org/10.1598/RRQ.45.3.3

action" in early education. They cite research by Beck and McKoewn (2007) and the research synthesis by the National Reading Panel (2000) as showing that very little explicit, intentional teaching of vocabulary occurs in prekindergarten, kindergarten, and the primary grades. In addition, Neuman and Dwyer found that the major commercially published early literacy curriculums do a mediocre job of systematically teaching vocabulary.

Day care, preschool, and kindergarten teachers must consistently work to enhance children's language development. Fortunately, the school day offers numerous opportunities for both direct instruction and incidental oral interactions. However, teachers of young children must be diligent and mindful to create vocabulary learning moments. Kathy Roskos, Patton Tabors, and Lisa Lenhart (2009) suggest that teachers who are also playful, planful, and purposeful are successful in helping children to develop oral language competence and simultaneously expand their vocabulary. These efforts can be extended throughout the day, as Ms. V demonstrated in the opening vignette. Her playful, planful, and purposeful introduction of new vocabulary also was reinforced intentionally throughout the day as she employed classroom routines to reinforce new vocabulary instruction.

Teacher Discourse

Every school day offers dozens of possibilities for verbal interactions (Dickinson, Darrow & Tinubu, 2008; Smith & Dickinson, 1994). Unfortunately, research indicates that these opportunities are often overlooked in traditional transmission-oriented classrooms. A synthesis of these studies has shown that in many classrooms the teacher dominates the language environment, which does little to promote the children's oral language growth (Cazden, 1988; Howard, Shaughnessy, Sanger, & Hux, 1998; Justice, 2002; Wells, 1986). For example, in some classrooms:

- Teachers spend most of the time talking *to* rather than talking *with* children.
- Teachers dominate discussions by controlling how a topic is developed and who gets to talk.
- Children spend most of their time listening to teachers.
- When children do talk, it is usually to give a response to a question posed by the teacher.
- Teachers tend to ask testlike, closed-ended questions that have one correct answer (that the teacher already knows).

The typical pattern of classroom discourse is characterized by teacher initiation, student response, and teacher evaluation. In this *initiation, response, evaluation* (IRE) pattern, the teacher asks a question, a student answers, and the teacher either accepts or rejects that answer and goes on to ask another question (Galda, Cullinan, & Strickland, 1993). For example, before the following discussion, the kindergarten children had listened to *The Three Little Pigs:*

> *Teacher:* What material did the pigs use to build their first house?
>
> *Bobbie:* They used sticks.
>
> *Teacher:* Yes. That is correct, the pigs used sticks for the first house. What did the pigs use to build the third house?
>
> *Manuel:* They used cement.
>
> *Teacher:* No. Who remembers what the book says? Jon?
>
> *Jon:* Bricks.
>
> *Teacher:* Yes. The pigs used bricks.

Notice how the teacher's questions are not real questions; rather, they test whether these young students recalled specific details of the story. Notice also that these children have no opportunity to construct their own meaning of the story by combining text information with their prior knowledge. For example, Manuel's answer, *cement,* suggests that Manuel was making inferences based on prior experience. The teacher's negative response to Manuel's comment probably communicates to him that it is incorrect to make inferences when reading. This response sends a message to students that one should recall exactly what is said in the text. Finally, notice that there is absolutely no interaction from student to student. The turn-taking pattern is teacher–student–teacher–student.

These types of IRE interactions are sometimes appropriate because teachers do need to get specific points across to students (Genishi & Dyson, 1984). Problems ensue, however, if this is the only type of talk that is taking place in the classroom. IRE discussions do not provide the type of language input and feedback that "advance children's knowledge of language structure and use" (Menyuk, 1988, p. 105). In addition, these teacher-dominated exchanges do not allow students to negotiate and build meaning through dialogue (Hansen, 1998).

What can early childhood teachers do to provide children with more stimulating experiences with language? We offer four recommendations:

1. Engage students in reciprocal discussions and conversations.
2. Provide ample opportunities for activity-centered language that invite (and, at times, require) students to use language to get things done.
3. Provide language-centered activities that focus students' attention on specific aspects of language.
4. Provide direct, systematic vocabulary instruction.

In the sections that follow, we present guidelines for implementing each of these recommendations.

Reciprocal Discussions and Conversations

Teachers' verbal interaction styles set the general tone for classroom language environments. The worst-case scenario occurs when a teacher insists on absolute silence except during teacher-led initiation, response, evaluation discussions. Such environments definitely limit continued oral language development. Other teachers provide ideal language environments by engaging students in genuine conversations, conducting stimulating reciprocal discussions, and allowing children to converse with each other at a moderate volume during classroom learning activities, using "inside voices" (soft voices that do not disrupt classroom learning).

Teachers have many opportunities to talk with students throughout the school day, ranging from one-to-one conversations to whole-group discussions. Following is an example of an effective conversation between Ms. E., a preschool teacher, and Roberto, age 4:

Roberto: See my new backpack, Teacher?

Ms. E.: What a neat backpack, Roberto. Show it to me.

Roberto: It has six zippers. See? The pouches hold different stuff. Isn't it neat?

Ms. E.: I like the different-size pouches. Look, this one is just right for a water bottle.

Roberto: Yeah. The arm straps are great too. See, I can make 'em longer.

Ms. E.: Yes [nods and smiles]. It fits your arms perfectly. Where did you get this nifty backpack?

Roberto: We got it at the mall.

Ms. E.: What store in the mall?

Roberto: The one that has all the camping stuff.

Ms. E.: The Camping Plus store?

Roberto: Yeah. That's the one.

Notice how Ms. E. allowed Roberto to take the lead by listening carefully to what he said and by responding to his previous statements. She let him do most of talking, using back channeling (nodding and smiling) to keep the conversation going. Ms. E. asked only three questions, and they were genuine: She wanted to know where Roberto purchased the backpack.

Reciprocal conversations are not restricted to one-to-one situations. Teachers can also engage children in genuine discussions pertaining to ongoing instructional activities. Cory Hansen (1998) gives an example of group discussion of George MacDonald's 1872 classic, *The Princess and the Goblin* (Puffin Books). The chapter book is being discussed by a group of kindergarten students in Chris Boyd's classroom.

Previously in the story, the grandmother had given the princess a gift of a glowing ring from which a thread would lead her to comfort if she were frightened.

The princess assumed it would lead her to her grandmother, but one night it led her deep into a cave and stopped at a heap of stones. The chapter ("Irene's Clue") ends with the princess bursting into tears at the foot of the rocks. Curdie, the fearless miner's son, was missing:

Joseph: I think that Curdie's on the other side of the rocks.

Mrs. B.: Where'd you get the clue for that?

Anna: Because the strings led her to the mountain. That means it was close to Curdie because Curdie lived by the mountain.

Kim: Maybe Curdie's on the other side of the stones!

Jamal: I think her grandmother was a goblin since she could have went through the rocks.

Jordan: I know. Maybe—when she was falling asleep on the other side—but how could the goblins be that fast?

Anna: Because they're magic.

Richard: I know how Curdie got to the other side.

Chorus: Children begin to talk in small groups simultaneously.

Joseph: Maybe Curdie's in the heap of stones.

Mrs. B.: What makes you say that?

Joseph: Because in the last chapter—"Curdie's Clue"—it said they piled the rock—a big stone in the mouth of the cave.

Kim: The grandmother said the ring always led to the grandmother's bedroom so she . . .

Anna: No it didn't. It said, "This will take me to you—wherever it takes you, you go." And the grandmother said, "Wherever it takes you, you will go."

Mrs. B.: Can you think of any reason why the princess should go to the cave?

Joseph: Because it said, "You must not doubt the string."

Adam: The grandmother said the thread would lead to her but it ended up leading her to Curdie.

Alondra: I think the grandmother knows about Curdie.

Kim: It's because her grandmother wanted her to save Curdie!

Anna: That was the clue.

Jamal: To get Curdie out cuz she know about him.

Joseph: Yeah. (Hansen, 1998, pp. 172–173)

Here, Mrs. B. let the students take the lead by listening closely to what they said and responding to their comments. Her questions were genuine (she did not know what the children's responses would be) and were open-ended in nature ("What makes you say that?"). By welcoming the children's viewpoints, she encouraged them to bring their personal interpretations to the story. Also notice that the children talked to each other; they engaged in real conversations. The teacher facilitated this child–child turn-taking pattern by encouraging the students to respond to other's ideas.

Ms. E.'s and Mrs. B.'s effective use of reciprocal questions allowed students to engage in authentic discussion with the teacher and each other. Obviously, the way a teacher interacts with children influences the way children communicate. Therefore, it is important for teachers to reflect on the quality of their conversations and discussions with students of all ages.

As teachers work with the students in their classrooms it is important to remember that many children do not speak academic or "standard" English. Teachers must be sensitive and respectful to the wide range of dialects they hear, always remembering that the language of the child's home must be valued even as teachers help children learn a more academic vocabulary. Special Feature 5.1 offers some guidance for teachers in understanding and supporting language variation.

SPECIAL FEATURE 5.1

Understanding and Supporting Language Variation

Welcome to my home. Please, do come in.
Hey yaw'l. Jes come rite-on in ta mah plaaace.
Dude, catch the crib. Wanna crash?

As you read the sentences above, did you begin to form mental images about the speakers? Did you make predictions about their ages, places of origins, and social status? If you did, then you are not alone; the study of dialects offers a fascinating look at how the language we use is linked to our social identity. Likewise, the study of dialects often provides the most vivid illustration of how language changes over time (Hazen, 2001).

Many people believe that there is only one correct form of English, what is often called Standard English. According to this view, the phrase *My sister is not home* will always be preferred to the phrase *My sister ain't home*. Linguists, however, suggest that what is appropriate language depends on the situation. In many contexts, *My sister ain't home* is more acceptable. This wording, called Rhetorically Correct English, suggests that what is "correct" varies and is governed by the speaker's intention, the audience, and the context (Crystal, 1995; Demo, 2000).

Unfortunately, dialect discrimination is widely tolerated in the United States. Many people believe that there is only one kind of appropriate English that all children should learn and that all teachers should be required to teach. Today, however, even this long-held view is being challenged. In the mid-1990s, the Oakland, California, school board proposed that Ebonics be accepted as a school language. The outcry against this idea was national: The frequent response was the only Standard English should be taught in schools. When educator-linguist Lisa Delpit (1997, p. 6) was asked if she was for or against Ebonics her answer was complex:

My answer must be neither. I can be neither for Ebonics nor against Ebonics any more than I can be for or against air. It exists. It is the language spoken by many of our African-American children. It is the language they heard as their mothers nursed them and changed their diapers and played peek-a-boo with them. It is the language through which they first encountered love, nurturance and joy. On the other hand, most teachers of those African-American children who have been least well-served by the educational system believe that their students' chances will be further hampered if they do not learn Standard English. In the stratified society in which we live, they are absolutely correct.

As Delpit suggests, no matter how accepting teachers may be of a child's home language in the classroom, a child's dialect may serve as a source of discrimination as he or she matures. So what is the role of the teacher? According to Lily Wong-Fillmore and Catherine Snow (2000, p. 20): "Teachers must provide children the support needed to master the English required for academic development and for jobs when they have completed school. However, this process does not work when the language spoken by the children—the language of their families and primary communities—is disrespected in school."

In summary, teachers need to teach children the dialect of school and work. To accomplish this goal, teachers need to provide the same type of scaffolding parents used when children were first learning to talk (Manning-Kratcoski & Bobkoff-Katz, 1998). Teachers must extend and expand children's language in a respectful manner, for example, as a simple expansion:

CHILD: That ain't right
TEACHER: I agree, this isn't right.

Notice how the teacher recasts the child's effort in Standard English. Notice also that the teacher does not emphasize the correct form but uses it naturally. When adults use expansions, they introduce and help children build new vocabulary.

Contexts That Encourage Language Use

What students say and do is greatly influenced by where they are and what is around them. For example, as Evan played in the snow, he learned snow-related vocabulary with his family. Teachers must create dynamic learning environments that are contexts for language development. In other words, the curriculum must give children something to talk about. In the following section, we describe how teachers might use group activities, learning centers, and dramatic play to expand students' learning and opportunities to use language.

GROUP ACTIVITIES. Teachers can support language by involving children with group activities that encourage, and at times necessitate, verbal interaction. What sort of activities would require children to talk? As Celia Genishi (1987) points out, "Almost every object or activity presents an opportunity for talk when teachers allow it to" (p. 99). Likewise, researchers Susan

Burns, Peg Griffin, and Catherine Snow suggest that "sociodramatic play activities give children a chance to develop language and literacy skills, a deeper understanding of narrative, and their own personal responses to stories," (1999, p. 72). In the following vignette, we provide an illustration of a whole-group activity that required a rather large group of multilingual 4-year-old children to reveal and assert needs and wants and connect with themselves and others.

The young students have been learning about manners and balanced meals. As part of a culminating activity, the entire room has been transformed into a restaurant. Twelve little tables are draped with tablecloths, and on each table sits a vase of flowers. Today, the teachers are waitresses, and a few parents have volunteered to cook real food. The children must choose between the Panda Café (spaghetti, meatballs, garlic toast, juice or milk) or the Café Mexico (burrito, chips, salsa, juice or milk). Each café has a menu with words and pictures. The children must select the specific items they wish to eat and give their orders to the waitress. The waitress takes the children's orders on an order form and gives the order form to the cooks. The cooks fill the orders exactly as the children request. Then, the waitress returns with the food and the order form and asks the children to review the order.

> *Teacher:* What café would you like, sir?
>
> *Roberto:* [Points to menu.]
>
> *Teacher:* Which café? You must tell me.
>
> *Roberto:* The Café Mexico.
>
> *Teacher:* Right this way, sir. Here is your menu. Take a moment to decide what you want to eat. I'll be right back to take your order.
>
> *Roberto:* [Looks over the menu and shares his choices with his friend by pointing to the items he wants.]
>
> *Teacher:* OK, sir. What would you like?
>
> *Roberto:* [Points to the items on the menu.]
>
> *Teacher:* Please, sir. You will have to tell me.
>
> *Roberto:* [Hesitates for a few seconds.] I want the burrito and chips and juice.
>
> *Teacher:* Do you want salsa? [She leans over so he can see her mark the items on the order form.]
>
> *Roberto:* No. [Firmly.]

Notice how the teachers organized this activity so that the children had to verbally express their needs multiple times throughout the restaurant adventure. In addition, the children had many opportunities to see how print is used in real life. Teachers, however, are not the only valuable source of language input. Children can also gain valuable oral language practice from talking with peers who are not as skilled as adults in initiating and maintaining conversations. To encourage peer-to-peer interactions, these teachers also created a miniature version of the restaurant in a dramatic play learning center. In this center, Roberto and his classmates will be able to play restaurant together for a few weeks.

As teachers of children observe their students in a variety of learning situations that require the children to use their language skills, they will often notice some who are having difficulty with the production of speech. Good teachers know that children with speech challenges and language delays should receive specialized support, as explained in the section on helping children with special needs at the end of this chapter.

LEARNING CENTERS. Because children's learning and language is greatly influenced by their environment, good teachers guide children's language development through the deliberate structuring of the classroom environment. For example, the teachers in the previous vignette created a restaurant to encourage talk about food, ordering meals, taking orders, cooking meals, and the like. Later, as the children interacted together in the restaurant dramatic play center, they continued to help each other build and reinforce their knowledge of restaurants. In learning center classrooms, the teacher's role is to set up the environment, observe as children interact with the materials, supply help and guidance when needed, and engage in conversations with the children around the materials and the children's use in their learning. A good deal of the teacher's effort is expended on the setting-up or preparation phase. Centers are created when the teacher carves the classroom space into defined areas. Readers seeking more information on establishing centers will find *The Creative Curriculum for Early Childhood Education* (Dodge & Colker, 2010) a useful resource. This book presents detailed, easy-to-follow instructions for setting up popular interest areas (centers). It also contains practical tips on schedules, routines, and other aspects of classroom management, plus good suggestions for encouraging parental involvement.

DRAMATIC PLAY. Another context for activity-centered language is *dramatic play*. Dramatic play occurs when children take on roles and use make-believe transformations to act out situations and play episodes. For example, several children might adopt the roles of family members and pretend to prepare dinner, or they may become superheroes who are engaged in fantastic adventures. This type of play—also called sociodramatic, make-believe, pretend, or imaginative play—reaches its peak between the ages of 4 and 7.

Although to some dramatic play appears simple and frivolous at first glance, close inspection reveals that it is quite complex and places heavy linguistic demands on children (Burns et al., 1999; Fessler, 1998). In fact, Jerome Bruner (1983, p. 65) reported that "the most complicated grammatical and pragmatic forms of language appear first in play activity." When children work together to act out stories, they face formidable language challenges. They not only need to use language to act out their dramas, but they must also use language to organize the play and keep it going. Before starting, they must recruit other players, assign roles, decide on the make-believe identities of objects (e.g., that a block of wood will be used as if it were a telephone), and plan the story line. Once started, language must be used to act out the story, keep the dramatization heading in the right direction (e.g., be sure that everyone is doing things appropriate to their role), and reenergize the play if it is becoming repetitive and boring.

To accomplish these tasks, children must use two different types of language: (1) *pretend language* that is appropriate for their roles and (2) *metaplay language* about the play itself. Children switch between their pretend roles and their real identities when making these two types of comments. For example, if children are acting out the roles of parents (Child 1 is the mother, and Child 2 is the father), the following dialogue might occur:

> *Child 1:* Daddy, set the table while I get supper ready.
> *Child 2:* Okay. [Puts some building blocks on the table.]
> *Child 1:* No, don't do that! Use the real forks and spoons in the cupboard. Not blocks, for goodness sake!

Notice how Child 1 switches from her make-believe role to her real life identity in order to manage the play and to reprimand Child 2 for doing something that did not fit with the dramatization.

To take full advantage of dramatic play's potential as a medium for language development, attention needs to be given to three factors: (1) the settings in which play occurs, (2) the amount of time allocated for play activities, and (3) the type of teacher involvement in play episodes.

It is important to remember that children play best at what they already know. Therefore, dramatic play settings need to be familiar to children and consistent with their culture (Neuman, 1995). For example, the domestic play themes, such as parents caring for a baby or a family eating a meal, are very popular with young children because these are the roles and activities with which they are most familiar. For this reason, we recommend that preschool and kindergarten classrooms contain a housekeeping dramatic play center equipped with props that remind children of their own homes. Not only do such centers encourage dramatic play, but they also provide a context in which children can display the types of literacy activities they have observed at home.

The range of children's play themes and related literacy activities can be greatly expanded by the addition of a theme center to the classroom. These centers have props and furniture that suggest specific settings that are familiar to children, such as a veterinarian's office, restaurant, bank, post office, ice cream parlor, fast-food restaurant, and grocery store. (Table 4.1 contains lists of literacy materials that can be used in a variety of theme centers.) For example, a veterinarian's

Dramatic play is an ideal medium for promoting oral language development

office might be divided into two areas: a waiting room with a table for a receptionist and chairs for patients and an examination room with another table, chairs, and a variety of medical props (doctor's kit, scales, and the like). Stuffed animals can be provided as patients. Theme-related literacy materials—appointment book, patient folders, prescription forms, wall signs, and so on—should also be included to encourage children to reenact the literacy activities they have observed in these settings. Children will use their knowledge of visits to the doctor to engage in play with their peers. The following scenario illustrates how three preschoolers verbalize their knowledge of what occurs at the animal hospital:

> *Sergio:* [The vet is looking at the clipboard.] It says here that Ruffy is sick with worms.
>
> *Marie:* [Owner of a toy kitty named Ruffy.] Yep, uh huh. I think she ate bad worms.
>
> *Sergio:* That means we gotta operate and give Ruffy big horse pills for those worms.
>
> *Joy:* [The nurse.] Okay, sign here. [Hands Marie a big stack of papers.] Sign 'em all. Then we'll operate. But you gotta stay out in the people room. You could faint if you stay in here.

Chari Woodard (1984), a teacher who has had considerable success with theme centers in her university's laboratory preschool, recommends that one theme center be introduced at a time and left for several weeks. Then the center can be transformed into another theme. She also advises locating these centers near the permanent housekeeping center so that children can integrate the theme center activities with their domestic play. Children acting as parents for dolls, pets, or peers in the housekeeping area might, for example, take a sick baby to the doctor theme center for an examination. Or children might weld or examine cars in the classroom garage (Hall & Robinson, 1995). Woodard found that children, particularly boys, began engaging in more dramatic play when the theme centers were introduced.

Dramatic play requires providing a considerable amount of time for children to plan and initiate. If play periods are short, then children have to stop their dramatizations right after they have started. When that happens frequently, children tend to switch to less advanced forms of play, such as functional (motor) play or simple construction activity, which can be completed in brief sessions.

Research has shown that preschoolers are much more likely to engage in rich, sustained dramatic play during 30-minute play periods than during shorter 15-minute sessions (Christie, Johnsen, & Peckover, 1988). Our experience indicates that even longer periods are needed. For example, Billie Enz and Jim Christie (1997) spent a semester observing a preschool classroom that had 40-minute play periods. Very often, the 4-year-olds had just finished preparing for a dramatization when it was time to clean up. Fortunately, the teachers were flexible and often let the children have an extra 10 to 15 minutes to act out their dramas. We recommend that center time last for at least 60 minutes whenever possible.

For many years, it was believed that teachers should just set the stage and not get directly involved in children's play activities. This hands-off stance toward play has been seriously challenged by a growing body of research that suggests that classroom play can be enriched through teacher participation. Teacher involvement has been found to assist nonplayers to begin to engage in dramatic play, to help more proficient players enrich and extend their dramatizations, and to encourage children to incorporate literacy into their play episodes (Enz & Christie, 1997; Roskos & Neuman, 1993). Teachers, however, need to use caution because overzealous or inappropriate forms of involvement can interfere with ongoing play and can sometimes cause children to quit playing altogether (Enz & Christie, 1997).

The simplest and least intrusive type of teacher involvement in play is observation. By watching children as they play, teachers demonstrate that they are interested in the children's play and that play is a valuable, worthwhile activity. Observation alone can lead to more sustained play. Jerome Bruner (1980) reported that preschoolers' play episodes lasted roughly twice as long when a teacher was nearby and observing than when children played completely on their own. In addition, the children were more likely to move toward more elaborate forms of play when an adult was looking on.

Observation can also provide clues about when more direct forms of teacher involvement in play are appropriate. A teacher may find that, despite conducive play settings, some children rarely engage in dramatic play. Or the teacher may notice that there is an opportunity to extend or enrich an ongoing play episode, perhaps by introducing some new element or problem for children to solve (Hall, 1999). Both situations call for active teacher involvement.

Chapter 4 describes three roles that are ideal for initiating and extending dramatic play: the stage manager role, in which the teacher supplies props and offers ideas to enrich play; the coplayer role, in which the teacher actually takes on a role and joins in the children's play; and the play leader who stimulates play by introducing, in a role, some type of problem to be resolved. (For more information about these roles and other roles that teachers can adopt during play, see Jones and Reynolds, 1992.)

In addition to promoting language acquisition, dramatic play encourages children to help each other learn academic skills and content (Christie & Stone, 1999; Hansen, 1998), make friends, and develop important social skills (Garvey, 1977). Peer-to-peer interaction is particularly important for the growing numbers of students who are learning English as a second language and need help with more basic aspects of oral language (Fessler, 1998). For these reasons, dramatic play centers need to be a prominent feature in early childhood classrooms.

Language-Centered Activities for Children

Beyond creating contexts that encourage language and facilitate verbal interactions, teachers can also provide activities that focus specifically on language. Read-alouds, sharing, storytelling, and language play all fall into this category. (Teacher read-alouds is the subject of an entire section in Chapter 6.) Storybook reading can be an ideal context for promoting attentive listening and oral discussion skills. We discuss the remaining four language-centered activities below.

SHARING. Sharing, or show-and-tell, is a strategy designed to promote students' speaking and listening abilities. Traditionally, sharing has been a whole-class activity in which one child after another gets up, takes center stage, and talks about something of her or his own choosing, often some object brought from home (Gallas, 1992). Children in the audience are expected to listen quietly and not participate.

In this traditional format, sharing is not a very productive language experience for the child who is speaking or for those who are listening. The large group size can intimidate the speaker and reduce participation because only a small percentage of students get to share on a given day. If many students share, it becomes a very drawn-out, boring affair. The lack of participation on the part of the audience leads to poor listening behavior. Listening is an active, constructive process in which listeners combine information provided by a speaker with their own prior knowledge to build personal meaning. Mary Jalongo (1995) relates a teacher's definition of listening that captures the essences of *active listening:* "It is hearing and making and shaping what you heard—along with your own ideas—into usable pieces of knowledge" (p. 14). The passive role of the audience in traditional sharing works against this process.

With two modifications, sharing can be transformed into a very worthwhile language activity. First, group size should be "small enough to reduce shyness, encourage interaction, permit listeners to examine the object, and afford everyone a long enough turn without tiring the group" (Moffett & Wagner, 1983, p. 84). Groups of three to six students are ideal for this purpose. Second, listeners should be encouraged to participate by asking questions of the child who is sharing. "Let the sharer/teller begin as she will. When she has said all that initially occurs to her, encourage the audience by solicitation and example to ask natural questions" (Moffett and Wagner, 1983, p. 84). The teacher's role is to model questioning that encourages elaboration and clarification ("When did you get?" "What happened next?" "What's that for?"). After asking one or two questions, teachers should pause and encourage the audience to participate. Prompts such as "Does anyone have questions for Suzy?" may sometimes be needed to get the process started. Once children realize that it is acceptable for them to participate, prompting will no longer be necessary.

This peer questioning stimulates active listening by giving the audience a reason to listen to the child who is sharing. Children know that to ask relevant questions they are going to have to listen very carefully to what the sharer has to say. The child who is sharing benefits as well. Children can be encouraged to elaborate their brief utterances or organize their content more effectively and to state it more clearly (Moffett & Wagner, 1983).

We suggest that teachers can add variety to sharing by occasionally giving it a special focus. For instance, they can ask students (and share these ideas with parents) to bring in an item that:

■ Has a good story behind it, which encourages narrative discourse.
■ They made or grew, which facilitates explanation or description.
■ Works in a funny or interesting way, which fosters expositive communication.

STORYTELLING. Telling stories to children is also very worthwhile. The direct connection between the teller and audience promotes enjoyment and active listening. Marie Clay (1989, p. 24) describes some of the values of storytelling:

> Storytelling is more direct than story reading. Facial expressions, gestures, intonations, the length of pauses, and the interactions with the children's responses create a more direct contact with the audience, dramatic in effect. The meaning can be closer to the children's own experiences because the teller can change the words, add a little explanation, or translate loosely into a local experience.

The first stories that children tell usually involve real-life experiences: They relate something that has happened to them. Sharing can be an ideal context to allow children to tell these types of stories in the classroom. Small-group, interactive sharing provides feedback that enables children to tell clearer, better-organized stories about personal experiences (Canizares, 1997).

Some children need assistance in broadening the range of their storytelling to imaginative, fictional stories. The following suggestions can help with this task:

■ Open up the sharing period to include fantasy stories. Once teachers begin permitting their children to tell "fictional" stories, the children may begin sharing imaginative, creative stories that feature language that is much richer than that used in their show-and-tell sharing (Gallas, 1992).

- Encourage children to retell the stories contained in their favorite storybooks. Books remove the burden of creating an original story to tell. Story retelling has other benefits for children, including enhanced oral fluency and expression and improved story comprehension (Morrow, 1985).
- Have children make up words for the stories in wordless picture books, such as *Pancakes for Breakfast* by Tomie dePaola (Harcourt, Brace, Jovanovich, 1978). Here again, the book is providing the content for the child's story.
- Link storytelling with play and writing. Vivian Paley (1990) has developed a strategy in which children come to a story table and dictate a story that the teacher writes down. During this dictation, the teacher asks the children to clarify any parts of the story that are unclear or difficult to understand. The teacher reads the story plays to the class. Finally, children serve as directors and invite classmates to join in acting out their stories. Children enjoy watching their stories dramatized, motivating them to create additional imaginative stories.

LANGUAGE PLAY. In addition to using language in their dramatic play, children also play with language. This intentional "messing around" with language begins as soon as children have passed through the babbling stage and have begun to make words (Garvey, 1977). This play involves the phonological, syntactic, and semantic aspects of language. By age 2, language play becomes quite sophisticated. Ruth Weir (1962) placed a tape recorder in her 2 1/2-year-old son Anthony's crib and turned it on after he had been placed in his crib for the evening. During this presleep time, Anthony engaged in an extensive amount of systematic language play. He experimented with speech sounds ("Babette Back here Wet"), substituted words of the same grammatical category ("What color. What color blanket. What color mop. What color glass"), and replaced nouns with appropriate pronouns ("Take the monkey. Take it" and "Stop it. Stop the ball. Stop it"). These monologues constituted play because language was being manipulated for its own sake rather than being used to communicate.

Young children also make attempts at humor, playing with semantic aspects of language. Kornei Chukovsky (1976) explains that "hardly has the child comprehended with certainty which objects go together and which do not, when he begins to listen happily to verses of absurdity" (p. 601). This play, in turn, leads children to make up their own nonsense. Chukovsky uses his 2-year-old daughter as an example. Shortly after she had learned that dogs say "bow wow" and cats say "miaow," she approached him and said, "Daddy, 'oggie—miaow!" and laughed. It was his daughter's first joke!

Children gain valuable practice while engaging in these types of language play. They also begin to acquire *metalinguistic awareness,* the ability to attend to language forms as objects in and of themselves. Courtney Cazden (1976) explains that when language is used for its normal function—to communicate meaning—language forms become transparent. We "hear through them" to get the intended message (p. 603). When children play with language, the situation is reversed. The focus is on the language, on the grammatical rules and semantic relationships they are manipulating.

The type of language play children engage in is also age related (Geller, 1982). At age 3, children like to repeat traditional rhymes ("Mary had a little lamb"). They eventually begin to make up their own nonsense rhymes, playing with sound patterns ("Shama sheema / Mash day n' push day"). By ages 5 and 6, children delight in verbal nonsense ("I saw Superman flying out there!") and chanting games ("Cinderella, dressed in yellow / Went upstairs to kiss her fellow / How many kisses did she get? / 1, 2, 3, 4, 5"), which are forms themselves rather than meaning. Children become aware of the sounds "Teddy bear, Teddy bear, turn around, Teddy bear, Teddy bear, touch the ground" (Cole, 1989).

The obvious educational implication is that language play should be encouraged and supported at school (Cazden, 1976). We recommend that teachers try three things to stimulate their students to play with language:

1. Create a fun and caring climate that allows play to flourish.
2. Model language by sharing stories, jokes, songs, fingerplays
3. Listen carefully when children share their stories with you.

SONGS AND FINGER PLAYS. Sitting on the floor with a small group of preschoolers, Ms. K. begins:

Where is Thumbkin?

Where is Thumbkin?

Here I am! Here I am!

How are you today, sir?

Very well, I thank you.

Run away, Run away.

The 3-and 4-year-old children quickly join in and immediately start the finger movements that accompany this familiar song. Very young children love to sing. The human fondness for a catchy tune and a snappy, clever rhyme begins early. Beginning in infancy and continuing on throughout their childhood, children experiment with their voices and the sounds that they can make. In Special Feature 5.2, we describe children's musical development from infancy through kindergarten. Singing encourages risk-free language play, especially for children who are learning a second language (Freeman & Freeman, 1994; Jackman, 1997). Singing songs in a new language allows children to make safe mistakes as they experiment with the new phonemic system, in a similar way as toddlers may begin to sing jingles they hear on the television long before they can actually speak in full sentences. As noted in a report by Catherine Snow and her colleagues (1998), singing songs is an important literacy activity.

Therefore, teachers of young children would be wise to build in singing as part of their language arts curriculum (Collins, 1997). In particular, children enjoy songs that offer repetition and chorus, such as "Polly Put the Kettle On," "Mary Had a Little Lamb," and "Here We Go Round the Mulberry Bush"; provide repeated words or phrases that can be treated like an echo, such as "Miss Mary Mack" and "She'll Be Comin' Round the Mountain"; require sound effects or animal noises, such as "If You're Happy and You Know It" and "Old MacDonald Had a Farm"; tell a story, such as "Hush, Little Baby," "Humpty Dumpty," and "Little Bo Peep"; and ask questions, such as "Where Is Thumbkin?" and "Do You Know the Muffin Man?" In addition to singing, many songs or poems include finger plays. Do you recall the "Itsy-Bitsy Spider" and how your fingers became the spider that climbed up the waterspout? Children's minds are fully engaged when they act out the words of a song or poem with their fingers (Collins, 1997).

SPECIAL FEATURE 5.2

Musical Development from Infancy through Kindergarten

Age 0 to 9 months
- Begins to listen attentively to musical sounds; is calmed by human voices. Starts vocalization, appearing to imitate what he or she hears.

Age 9 months to 2 years
- Begins to respond to music with clear repetitive movements. Interested in every kind of sound; begins to discriminate among sounds and may begin to approximate pitches. Most attracted to music that is strongly rhythmic.

Age 2 to 3 years
- Creates spontaneous songs, sings parts of familiar songs; recognizes instruments and responds more

enthusiastically to certain songs. Strong physical response to music.

Age 3 to 4 years
- Continues to gain voice control; likes songs that play with language; and enjoys making music with a group as well as alone. Concepts such as high and low, loud and soft are beginning to be formed. Likes physical activity with music.

Age 4 to 6 years
- Sings complete songs from memory; is gaining pitch control and rhythmic accuracy. Loves language play and rhyming words. Attention span increases for listening to recorded music.

Adapted from Mitzie Collins, 1997. Children and Music. In B. Farber (Ed.), *The Parents' and Teachers' Guide to Helping Young Children Learn.* Cutchogue, NY: Preschool Publication.

Strategies for Teaching English Language Learners: Helping Children Develop Conversational and Academic Language Skills

Luisa Araújo

Second-language acquisition research shows that there are several variables affecting language learning (Lessow-Hurley, 2000). As we discussed in Chapter 2, the effect of age is well documented, and there is general agreement that younger is better. Neurolinguistic findings indicate that children who acquire a second language before the age of 5 behave like native speakers, while children who learn a second language after puberty tend to speak a second language with an accent (Pinker, 1995; Sakai, 2005). However, second-language proficiency entails the mastery of other language aspects related to semantics, syntax, and pragmatics. Indeed, children between the ages of 5 and 12 may have a cognitive advantage over younger children because they are more mature and they already know a first language. This may make them especially apt at figuring out how to learn the language needed for school. Similarly, many adults become proficient in a second language, even though they may have an accent when they speak.

Jim Cummins (1994) proposes two complementary notions to describe second-language development in a school setting. Children need to develop *Basic Interpersonal Communicative Skills (BICS)* and *Cognitive Academic Language Proficiency (CALP)* to communicate effectively and to perform academic tasks. BICS is the ability to communicate fluently in a second language, for example, the ability to talk about personal experiences, likes, and dislikes. CALP entails effective performance of cognitively demanding academic tasks that involve processing decontextualized language. For example, the ability to solve a math story problem requires the understanding of CALP. Conversational fluency in BICS is often acquired to a functional level within about two years of initial exposure to the second language. However, children may take five to seven years to catch up to native speakers in academic aspects of the second language (Collier, 1987; Cummins, 1994; Thomas and Collier, 1997). Students, who arrive in the United States with a few years of schooling in their primary language reach grade-level performance after five years (Lessow-Hurley, 2000).

As Claude Goldenberg states (2008),

> Academic English—the type of language that is essential for school success—is particularly difficult to master because it is generally not used outside of the classroom and it draws on new vocabulary, more complex sentence structures, and rhetorical forms not typically encountered in non-academic settings. Knowing conversational English undoubtedly helps in learning academic English, but the latter is clearly a more challenging task that requires more time. (p. 13)

Several states, such as California, use ELL developmental levels in their state Language Arts Standards to place students in a language proficiency continuum. These levels range from beginning to advanced, with two or three intermediate levels, and may have separate language behavior descriptors according to oral language comprehension and production, reading and writing. It is quite common for ELL children to take longer to move from intermediate to advanced levels than to move from a beginning level to an intermediate one (Goldenberg, 2008). Again, this is because it takes time to achieve full command of the language to perform academic tasks.

Failure to take into account the BICS/CALP (conversational/academic) distinction may result in discriminatory psychological assessment of bilingual students and premature exit from language support programs (Cummins, 1994). These programs are designed to assist learners in developing the conversational and academic skills necessary for their success in mainstream classrooms. English as a second language (ESL) support programs are usually pull-out programs where children work on developing conversational skills and knowledge of academic content. The pull-outs are done on a daily basis or a few times a week for about an hour each day, and the students work with a teacher specialized in ESL methodologies.

ESL instruction optimizes language learning through the use of comprehensible *input* and contextualization. According to Krashen (1981), comprehensible *input* is modified language that is provided by the teacher. ESL teachers make sure that they present language that is only a little beyond a child's capabilities. In addition, they work on increasing children's academic proficiency by providing contextual cues for the understanding of cognitively demanding tasks. When teaching the Civil War, an ESL teacher might use a map of the United States and show cause-and-effect relationships using a diagram with arrows. Visual reinforcements could also include props, pictures, films, demonstrations, and hands-on activities. Other strategies that help support English Language students include:

- Slow but natural levels of speech
- Clear enunciation
- Short, simple sentences
- Repetition and paraphrasing
- Controlled vocabulary and idioms

The use of these strategies in addition to frequent comprehension checks will ensure that students who do not know the second language very well do not fall behind academically; the strategies can also be used by regular classroom teachers. In fact, ESL teachers and regular classroom teachers should plan together and devise instructional strategies that maximize language learning (Lessow-Hurley, 2000). Although there is no doubt that these modifications optimize language learning, it is also true that "good instruction for students in general

(continued on next page)

(continued)

tends to be good instruction for English Language Learners in particular" (Goldenberg, 2008, p. 17).

Supporting English language learning in English-only settings entails providing good instruction in general, making modifications where necessary and teaching ESL as a separate subject at a distinct time during the day. ESL teachers, because they work with small groups of ELL children, can spend more time on oral English and can be more focused on their use of instructional time. Effective strategies in these complementary teaching/learning situations should comprise the following (Goldenberg, 2008, p. 20):

- Graphic organizers that make content and the relationships among concepts and different lesson elements visually explicit;
- Additional time and opportunities for practice, either during the school day, after school, or for homework;
- Redundant key information, e.g., visual cues, pictures, and physical gestures about the lesson content and classroom procedures;
- Identifying, highlighting, and clarifying difficult words and passages within texts to facilitate comprehension, and more generally greatly emphasizing vocabulary development;

- Helping students consolidate text knowledge by having the teacher, other students, and ELLs themselves summarize and paraphrase;
- Giving students extra practice in reading words, sentences, and stories to build automaticity and fluency;
- Providing opportunities for extended interactions with teacher and peers;
- Adjusting instruction (teacher vocabulary, rate of speech, sentence complexity, and expectations for student language production) according to students' oral English proficiency; and
- Targeting both content and English language objectives in every lesson.

It is also ideal to help ELL learners become aware of what they already know in their first language so that they can apply this knowledge in their second language. For example, students should be able to identify cognate words like *elefante* and *elephant* because this can assist them in spelling and in developing comprehension skills (Goldenberg, 2008).

From pp. 147-148, and 156 of Chapter 7, "Improving Achievement for English Language Learners" by C. Goldenberg from *Educating the Other America* (2008), edited by S. Neuman. Copyright © 2008 Paul H. Brookes Publishing Co., Inc., Baltimore, MD. Adapted by permission.

Many preschool and kindergarten teachers write the songs the children love to sing on chart paper or purchase the big book format of these beloved songs. As the children sing, the teacher uses a pointer to underline each word. The follow-the-bouncing-ball approach to teaching reading is quite effective with some children (Segal & Adcock, 1986). Singing is a wonderful way for children to play with and enjoy language.

Strategies for Children with Special Needs: Speech Delays

Karen Burstein and Tanis Bryan

When children come to school, they are expected to be able to communicate. Language is the ability to communicate using symbols; it includes comprehension of both oral and written expression. Speech is one component of oral expression. Many young children come to school with delays in speech and language (comprehension and expression). Speech problems such as misarticulations and dysfluencies are frequently seen in young children with and without special needs. Less obvious are problems understanding others' speech. Fortunately, the majority of children with language problems are able to successfully participate in all aspects of general education with a few modifications to the environment or curriculum.

Frequently, children with language problems receive special education services from a speech and language pathologist. However, the classroom teacher also has important roles to fulfill: (1) monitoring chil-

dren's comprehension of instructions and classroom activities and (2) providing opportunities for oral language practice and interaction with peers and adults.

The following are strategies that classroom teachers can use to help promote speech development in children with oral language delays:

- Collaborate with the speech and language pathologist in selecting activities, materials, and games that promote language development.
- Model appropriate grammar, rhythm, tone, and syntax.
- Keep directions simple, brief, and to the point.
- For students who have difficulty expressing themselves, do not rely solely on open-ended questions.
- Use yes or no questions that are easier to answer.
- When students with speech problems speak, give them your full attention and ensure that other students do the same.
- Errors should not be criticized. Pay attention to the content of the child's message. Do not call attention to misarticulations, especially dysfluencies, as the problem may become more serious if attention is called to it (Lewis & Doorlag, 1999).

- Children who stutter may have improved speech quality if alternate styles of communication are used, such as whispering, singing in a higher or lower pitch, or choral reading.
- Give children with special needs multiple opportunities across the day to converse with you.
- Encourage parents to routinely engage in conversations using children's new words, experiences, and relationships.

Special strategies are also needed to help language-delayed children learn the meanings of new words (receptive vocabulary) and be able to use these new words to communicate effectively.

- Teach vocabulary in all subjects: math, science, social studies, health, and so on.
- Assess the child's prior knowledge before introducing a new topic.
- Have the student develop a word book of new words for practice. Pair these words with pictures.
- Encourage children to ask about words they do not understand. Pair these new words with concepts already known.

- Have the students paraphrase new words they are acquiring.
- Use physical demonstrations of words, such as verbs and prepositions, that are difficult to explain. Show children the meanings of these words.
- Have the students physically demonstrate the meanings of words.
- Use manipulatives that children can handle to teach new words.
- Give multiple examples of word meanings.
- Teach students to use picture dictionaries to locate unfamiliar words.
- Keep parents informed of these special strategies and urge them to continue their use outside of school.

For children with more severe special needs, secure the services of a specialist in augmentative communication. These individuals have specific skills in communication boards, electronic communication devices, and computer voice synthesis. For more information about this special area, contact the Assistive Technology On-Line website at www.asel.udel.edu, sponsored by the DuPont Hospital for Children and the University of Delaware.

Family Focus: Sharing the Fun and the Language Learning

What did you learn today? Is a common question parents ask their young children. Many times children answer with a shrug or a comment about who traded a cookie at lunch! To improve communication and help parents support learning and language at home, teachers need to help by weekly newsletters. This type of frequent communication help build classroom community and offer parents effective ways to continue learning opportunities at home.

While traditionally newsletters have been printed on paper, with the growing number of homes that have computers and Internet access, some teachers now publish their classroom newsletters on a classroom website or share through a listserve. Of course, teachers must check with their children's parents to learn which homes have access to these services.

Because consistent communication helps create a sense of community, the authors strongly recommend weekly, or at minimum, bimonthly notes. Frequent communications allow teachers the opportunity to

- Provide a bond between school and home experiences,
- Share the new vocabulary
- Extend parents' understanding of the curriculum,
- Encourage parents to reinforce and enrich children's learning, and

- Strengthen the working partnership between parents and teacher.

Weekly notes are typically one page in length and generally include (1) information about upcoming events; (2) items about children's achievements; (3) explanations about the curriculum that help parents understand how children learn to read and write; (4) practical and developmentally appropriate suggestions for working with children; and (5) recognition of parents who have helped support classroom learning—for example, parents who accompanied the class on a field trip (Enz, Kortman & Honaker, 2008; Gelfer, 1991).

It is important for informal weekly notes to be reader friendly and brief and to suggest successful activities for parents and children to do together. These suggestions typically are well received if they are stated in a positive, proactive manner—for example, "Reading to your child just ten minutes a day helps your child become a better reader," instead of "Your child will not learn to read unless you read to her or him."

Figure 5.1 is a sample of a weekly newsletter. Observe how Mrs. Martin reviews the previous week's activities and reviews the new vocabulary the children are learning. Notice also how she takes the opportunity to thank parents who have provided supplies or support. Next, she describes the focus of this week's curriculum and provides suggestions that will help parents reinforce this information at home. Notice how Mrs. Martin uses friendly, everyday language to introduce and explain new concepts and suggests realistic, content-appropriate literacy activities that encourage parents to become involved in classroom learning.

(continued on next page)

(continued)

FIGURE 5.1

Weekly Newsletter

Dear Parents,

As you know , this month we are meeting community helpers. Last week our field trip to the hospital was exciting, and we learned even more about how doctors and nurses serve our community! Have your child read you the story he or she wrote and illustrated about what we learned on our hospital journey. One of the most exciting stops in the hospital was the baby nursery. All of the children were interested in their own first stay at the hospital. Perhaps you will be able to share your memories about the special event. Some new hospital words we learned included:

- Ambulance and emergency room
- Neonatal—newborn
- Stethoscope—a tool that doctors and nurses use to listen to our hearts and chests

We now have a hospital play center in our classroom complete with an emergency room and cardboard ambulance, right beside our neonatal unit with our newborn babies. Our doctors and nurses are using their stethoscopes to listen carefully to our hearts.

A big thank you to Mrs. Delgato and Mrs. Cruz for being chaperones and helping us visit the hospital last week.

This week and next we will be learning about fire safety at home and at school. We will draw and label a map of our school and practice following the fire safety exit. We will review and practice appropriate behavior during a fire drill. We will learn to listen (no talking), follow the teacher's directions, walk (no running), and leave all our possessions behind.

Because you and your family are so important, I am asking you to work with child to draw and label a map of your home and design the best fire exit from your home. We will place all of our maps on the board to review all our fire safety concepts and new vocabulary that includes:

- Fire alarm
- Extinguish—to put out the fire
- Extinguisher—the tool to put out a fire
- Oxygen—what a fire needs to burn
- Suffocate—a way to put a fire out by taking away the oxygen

This week we will also visit our local fire station. Attached to this note is the permission slip that will need to be signed and returned by Monday. Because this is a walking field trip I will need at least four parent volunteers. Please check the box and send me your phone number if you can help us out.

This week we will be reading more about fire safety and fire fighters. We have several books that you might like to check out, including:

> No Dragons for Tea: Fire Safety for Kids (and Dragons) by J. Pendziwol
> Firefighters A To Z by C. L. Demarest
> Out and About at the Fire Station by Muriel L. Dubois

If you have experiences with First Safety, please let me know. You can be an expert speaker for our classroom.

Have a wonderful week! Mrs. Martin

Summary

This chapter described ways that teachers can provide young children with stimulating oral language experiences that promote active listening and more precise, sophisticated speech. How did your own at school compare with those described in this chapter? Did you recall other types of beneficial oral language activities that were not covered?

To summarize the key points about facilitating oral language learning, we return to the guiding questions at the beginning of this chapter:

■ *What are effective, explicit approaches to teach vocabulary directly?*

   a. Provide purposeful exposure to new words—teachers should decide in advance to teach selected words to children, using high-utility root words
   b. Intentionally teach word meaning. Select words that important for comprehension and useful in everyday interaction.
   c. Teach word learning strategies. For young children to develop the mental tools to infer word meanings from context, they need to be taught how. This is best accomplished when the teacher models through a think-aloud.
   d. Offer opportunities to use newly learned words. Often, these targeted words are connected to other parts of the academic curriculum.

■ *What is the initiation, response, evaluation (IRE) pattern of class talk? What problems are associated with this type of discourse? How can teachers provide students with more stimulating conversations in the classroom?*

   The IRE pattern of discourse occurs when the teacher asks a question, a student answers, and the teacher either accepts or rejects that answer and goes on to ask another question. These types of question-and-answer exchanges do not provide the type of language input and feedback needed to advance children's language skills. Teachers can provide richer oral language experiences for children by engaging them in reciprocal conversations and discussions: listening closely and responding to their comments; asking genuine, open-ended questions; welcoming the interjection of personal experiences; and encouraging child–child turn-taking interactions.

■ *How do group activities, learning centers, and dramatic play promote oral language acquisition?*

   These types of activities create language content (i.e., give children something to talk about). In addition, children must use language to participate successfully in these types of activity.

■ *What can teachers do to promote language-rich dramatic play?*

   Teachers can promote language-rich play by providing (1) settings equipped with theme-related, culturally relevant props; (2) scheduling lengthy play periods; and (3) being actively involved in children's play activities.

■ *How can sharing or show-and-tell be turned into a valuable oral language activity?*

   Traditional sharing involves having one child speak to the entire class. This activity can be transformed into a valuable oral language activity by limiting group size and encouraging children in the audience to participate actively by asking questions and making comments.

■ *What can teachers do to optimize oral language experiences for bilingual and second-language learners?*

   Supporting English language learning in English-only settings entails providing good instruction in general, making modifications where necessary (e.g., the use of comprehensible *input* and contextualization), and teaching ESL as a separate subject at a distinct time during the day.

LINKING KNOWLEDGE TO PRACTICE

1. Identify an expository text. Next, identify three target vocabulary words. How will you explicitly teach these words using strategies discussed in Table 5.1, Approaches to Defining Words?
2. Visit an early childhood classroom and observe children interacting in a dramatic play center. Notice the theme that the children are acting out and the roles that they are playing. Record examples of both meta-play language and pretend language.
3. Observe students engaging in a sharing (show-and-tell) activity. Describe the teacher's role and the students' behavior (both the speaker and the audience). Did this sharing time involve most of the students in active listening?
4. Based on a classroom experience, write a one-page weekly note for parents.
5. Write a "Dear Teacher" question-and-answer for inclusion in a preschool classroom's newsletter. Make a photocopy for everyone in your college class.

Go to the Topics Word Study, English Language Learners, and At Risk and Struggling Readers in the MyEducationLab (www.myeducationlab.com) for your course, where you can:

- Find learning outcomes for Word Study, English Language Learners, and At Risk and Struggling Readers along with the national standards that connect to these outcomes.
- Complete Assignments and Activities that can help you more deeply understand the chapter content.
- Examine challenging situations and cases presented in the IRIS Center Resources.

Go to the Topic A+RISE in the MyEducationLab (www.myeducationlab.com) for your course. A+RISE® Standards2Strategy™ is an innovative and interactive online resource that offers new teachers in grades K-12 just in time, research-based instructional strategies that:

- Meet the linguistic needs of ELLs as they learn content
- Differentiate instruction for all grades and abilities
- Offer reading and writing techniques, cooperative learning, use of linguistic and nonlinguistic representations, scaffolding, teacher modeling, higher order thinking, and alternative classroom ELL assessment
- Provide support to help teachers be effective through the integration of listening, speaking, reading, and writing along with the content curriculum
- Improve student achievement
- Are aligned to Common Core Elementary Language Arts standards (for the literacy strategies) and to English language proficiency standards in WIDA, Texas, California, and Florida

Sharing Good Books with Young Children

The 4-year-olds in Ms. Andrea Jackson's classroom are gathered together in the circle time area. They are ready for story time. Ms. Jackson begins by showing the children the back of the book. "Today I'm going to read you a story that is one of my favorites, Click, Clack, Moo: Cows That Type. *Am I ready to begin reading?" Several children respond, "You have to turn the book the other way." Ms. Jackson turns it upside down. "No! To the front!" Ms. Jackson responds, "You are so right! Here is the front of the book." She reads the title, pointing to each word. "Doreen Cronin is the author of this book. What is an author?" Germaine responds, "The author writes the story and the illustrator draws the pictures." Several children express their agreement with Germaine's explanation. Ms. Jackson confirms, "You are so right! Doreen Cronin wrote this story, and the pictures are by Betsy Lewin. Take a look at the picture on the front of this book. Tell me what you see." The children label the picture—cows, chicken, bird. Ms. Jackson labels the chicken as a hen and the bird as a duck. As Ms. Jackson predicted, none of the children label the typewriter. She reaches behind her, pulls the cover off an old typewriter, and places it on a stand so all the children can see it. "What is this?" she asks. Quintella responds, "An old computer." Ms. Jackson asks him to explain his thinking. He notes that it has a "keyboard a little like the [classroom's] computer." Ms. Jackson compliments him on his observation. She explains, "Before computers, people typed their messages on this machine. It's called a typewriter. Say that with me. Typewriter." She hits a couple of keys so that the children can hear the click and the clack. "I'll leave this typewriter out during center time so that you can try typing a message on a typewriter. [She puts special stress on the word.] We'll take a poll to see which you like best, a typewriter or a computer." She opens the book to the title page and rereads the title. She turns to the first page. "Now, this is a story about cows who like to do what?" The children respond, "Type." Ms. Jackson asks, "On what?" The children respond, "A typewriter!" Ms. Jackson asks, "So if this story is about cows, who might this man be?" She points to the picture of the farmer. The children respond, "A farmer!" Ms. Jackson asks, "Does he look happy or sad?" Anarundle thinks sad "because his mouth is upside down." Ms. Jackson expands, "His mouth is upside down. He is frowning." She reads the text. "So was Anarundle right? Is the farmer sad?" The children think so. "Why?" she asks. Germaine says, "Farmer Brown is not happy because the cows are typing and making noise." Ms. Jackson says, "Let's see." On each page, the children and the teacher talk about the text. The teacher explains unfamiliar words, like* strike, impatient, furious, ultimatum, *and* diving board. *They figure out that Farmer Brown is probably really unhappy when the cows type a note telling him that they won't give him milk and another note that the hens won't give him eggs unless they get the electric blankets they requested. "He's getting madder and madder." They talk about why Farmer Brown typed his note to cows and hens. "What do you think he hoped would happen?" They talk about how Farmer Brown's problem with the cows and hens was solved. They talk about how Farmer Brown probably felt when he heard the ducks typing "click, clack, quack." They talk about whether or not the ducks had a good idea. "Would they get their diving board?" Ms. Jackson asks. As Ms. Jackson turns the last page, a wordless page, she asks the children, "What do you think the ducks might be saying?" De'Zebbra responds, "Hooray! We got our diving board!" As Ms. Jackson closes the book, she asks, "Have you ever written a note or letter asking for something? Did you get what you wanted?" Ms. Jackson elaborates. "Yesterday, I wrote a note to your families asking them if they could send in celery and cream cheese for our cooking activity tomorrow. Look at that shelf over there. Did my note work? Did I get what I wanted?" These 4-year-olds struggle to share examples from their experiences. Ms. Jackson says, "I put some special note-writing paper in the writing center today. Maybe you want to write someone about something you want or need. Maybe you want to type your note on the typewriter that I'll put in the writing center. [Later in the day, Ms. Jackson receives the following typed message: I ned nu mrkrz. (I need new markers.) The next day she brings in new markers, reads the child's message, and shows the children the new markers. Guess what happened that day during center time.]*

As early as 1908, Edmond Huey wrote about children's acquisition of reading and noted that "the key to it all lies in the parents reading aloud to and with the child" (p. 332). Today, after decades of research on the teaching of reading, we continue to agree with Huey. More recently Susan Neuman, Carol Copple, and Sue Bredekamp (1998) summarized what many educators believe and research supports: "The single most important activity for building [children's] understandings and skills essential for reading success appears to be *reading aloud to children*" (p. 5). Even more recently, reading to children has been characterized as "a cornerstone of literacy development and classroom practice" (Brabham & Lynch-Brown, 2002, p. 465). This single act—parents' and teachers' reading aloud to children—has received more research attention than any other aspect of young children's literacy development.

What do we know about the benefits of parents' or other adults' reading aloud to young children? Come peek in on one of Aslan's storybook-reading events with his father, Martie. The reading begins with Martie inviting 24-month-old Aslan to pick "a book for Daddy to read." Aslan knows exactly which book he wants his daddy to read; the family just built the best snowman in the neighborhood in the front yard—and Aslan's Daddy and Aslan snuggle together in a corner of the sofa. Already *Aslan knows that books are enjoyable;* he even has favorites. [He even knows that he was named after one of his brother's favorite characters in one of his favorite books. Do you know which storybook?] Daddy waits for Aslan to settle in and to hand him the book, which Aslan does, cover up and spine to the left. Already *Aslan knows how to hold the book and knows that it needs to be held in a certain way to open*—skills Marie Clay (1985) would call important concepts about print. Aslan says, "Read the title, Daddy." His daddy reads the title and the author, "The title of this book is ____, and the author is ____. *Aslan already knows that books have titles*—another concept about print. He and his daddy turn to the first page of the story. His daddy reads, and Aslan focuses on the page and listens. *He knows what his father will do (read and talk), and he knows what he should do (listen and talk).* Sometimes Martie says, "What's this?" as he points to a picture in the book. Aslan is excellent at labeling the pictures. When he isn't sure, Martie says, "It's a ____, isn't it?" *Aslan increases his vocabulary as he labels pictures in books* and as he hears words read aloud in the context of a story. He and his daddy read and talk their way through the book. Martie wonders aloud what the main character might be thinking, if Aslan agrees with the decisions the main character is making, and so forth. Often he invites Aslan to compare the book's snowman to the "best snowman in the neighborhood in our front yard." *Aslan is learning that what he can make connections between what is read to him and his life.* Most important of all, it is clear that storybook reading is very important for children's language and literacy development. *Aslan is learning to love books.*

This chapter is about how to share books with young children. We begin by providing resources teachers might use to assist in the selection of quality books and explaining how teachers can effectively read stories to young children. Then we describe a variety of activities teachers might use to enrich and extend children's responses to books. We end with descriptions of storybook reading with English language learners and special needs children and of how to involve parents and their children in storybook reading events.

BEFORE READING THIS CHAPTER, THINK ABOUT . . .

- The favorite books from your childhood. Did you have one or two favorite books that you liked to have your parents, siblings, or other adults read to you or a favorite book that you liked to read on your own?
- When your teachers read stories to you in school. Does any one teacher stand out as being particularly skilled at storybook reading? If so, why?

FOCUS QUESTIONS

- Where might teachers look for advice on storybooks to share with their young learners?
- What are the characteristics of effective adult storybook reading?
- What are some of the ways children can respond to and extend the stories that they have been read?
- What special considerations are needed when sharing literature with English language learners and special needs children?
- How might teachers provide their children's families with easy access to books and guidance in how to read to their children?

The Selection of Books to Share with Young Children

The careful selection of quality picture storybooks can play an important role in young children's development. There are numerous resource books available to guide teachers' storybook selections (e.g., Glazer & Giorgis, 2008; Huck, Kiefer, Hepler, Hickman, 2004). In addition to book resources, we suggest the Internet. One of our favorite websites is the American Library Association's *Great Web Sites for Kids.* This site links readers to numerous other sites, each coded for its appropriateness for preschool children (*www.ala.org/gwstemplate.cfm?section= greatwebsites&template=/cfapps/gws/default.cfm*). Another excellent Internet resource is the Children's Book Council website. In the "Booklists" section, for example, readers will find a list of recommended books for children age 0 to 3 and thematic annotated reading lists for all ages, which are updated bimonthly (*www.cbcbooks.org*). A third resource, the Cooperative Children's Book Center, has created bibliographies and lists of recommended books on a wide range of themes and topics. This website has a special section for early childhood care providers. (See *www.education.wisc.edu/ccbc/areyoua/careprovider.asp.*) Further, most trade book publishers have individual websites that showcase their authors' books. Several of these sites have an advanced search feature that allows searches by title, author, illustrator, subject, or age group. Several of the websites referenced here sort their book recommendations by age (e.g., age 0 to 3, 3 to 5). This is very helpful to teachers because children of different ages, or stages

BOX 6.1 **Definition of Terms**	**Author study:** Teacher reads a set of books by one author and invites children to discuss and compare the books
	Creative dramatics: Children act out a story with no printed script or memorized lines
	Decontextualized language: Language that is removed from everyday tangible and familiar experiences within the immediate context; no supports from the immediate environment to help get the point across
	Interactive reading: Important interactions that occur between adults and children during storybook reading
	Read-aloud (shared reading): Adult (parent, teacher) and child reading and talking about a book or an adult reading and talking about a book to a group of children
	Shared big-book reading: Teacher reading of an enlarged book—a book different from the typical book read to children in size only—to a group of children

Reading by Ages and Stages

Dawn Foley, Monique Davis, and Billie J. Enz

Certain types of books are better for young children at different ages and stages.

BIRTH TO ONE YEAR

High Contrasting Colors (Black/White/Red) (Birth to 6 Months)

Studies have shown that babies prefer these colors in the early weeks of life up until 6 months of age. Their vision is not fully developed, and they respond best to bold contrasting colors and graphics.

> *White on Black.* Hoban, T. (1993). New York: Greenwillow Books.
> *Black on White.* Hoban, T. (1993). New York: Greenwillow Books.
> *What Is That?* Hoban, T. (1994). New York: Greenwillow Books.
> *Who Are They?* Hoban, T. (1994). New York: Greenwillow Books.
> *Baby Animals Black and White.* Tildes, P. (1998). Watertown, MA: Charlesbridge Publishing.

Colors (5 Months to 1 Year)

Babies gain visual perception much more quickly than was once believed. It is important to select books with a single object on each page so as to not overstimulate children. Children less than 18 months old often have difficulty understanding complicated illustrations that adults recognize instantly. Books with one color image are the best.

> *Spot Looks at Colors.* Hill, E. (1986). New York: Putnam Publishing Group.
> *Red, Blue, Yellow Shoe.* Hoban, T. (1986). New York: Greenwillow Books.
> *Brown Bear, Brown Bear.* Carle, E. (1992). New York: Henry Holt & Company LLC.
> *I Love Colors.* Miller, M. (1999). New York: Little Simon.
> *Happy Colors.* Weeks, S. (2001). New York: Reader's Digest Children's Books.
> *Little Blue and Little Yellow.* Lionni, L. (1995). New York: Mulberry Books.

Textured Books

These books encourage babies to reach out and touch the pages. Shared reading, then, becomes an enjoyable tactile experience. Texture also allows babies to use their sensory exploratory approach to learning about the objects around them.

> *Touch and Feel: Baby Animals.* (1999). New York: Dorling Kindersley Publishing.
> *Touch and Feel: Kitten.* (1999). New York: Dorling Kindersley Publishing.
> *Touch and Feel: Puppy.* (1999). New York: Dorling Kindersley Publishing.
> *That's Not My Teddy.* Watt, F., & Wells, R. (1999). London: Usborne Publishing Ltd.
> *That's Not My Puppy.* Watt, F., & Wells, R. (1999). London: Usborne Publishing Ltd.
> *Kipper's Sticky Paws.* Inkpen, M. (2001). London: Hodder Children's Books.
> *Touch and Feel: Pets.* (2001). New York: Dorling Kindersley Publishing.
> *Night, Night Baby.* Birkinshaw, M. (2002). London: Ladybird Books.

Object Labeling (Familiar and Environmental) with Texture

Babies are beginning to learn and explore their world. Object labeling allows them to get to know their environment. These kinds of books encourage the readers to point to and name the objects in the book.

> *Touch and Feel: Home.* (1998). New York: Dorling Kindersley Publishing.
> *Touch and Feel: Clothes.* (1998). New York: Dorling Kindersley Publishing.
> *Match Shapes with Me.* Hood, S. (1999). New York: Reader's Digest Children's Books.
> *Baby Faces.* Miller, M. (1998). New York: Little Simon.
> *Touch and Feel: Shapes.* (2000). New York: Dorling Kindersley Publishing.
> *Buster's Bedtime.* Campbell, R. (2000). London: Campbell Books.
> *Touch and Feel: Bedtime.* (2001). New York: Dorling Kindersley Publishing.
> *The Going to Bed Book.* Boynton, S. (1995). New York: Little Simon.
> *Froggy Gets Dressed.* London, J. (1992). New York: Scholastic.

ONE TO TWO YEARS

Interactive/Lift the Flap Books

These kinds of books encourage babies to reach out and touch the pages. Again, they experience and enjoy reading as a tactile experience. Texture also allows babies to build on their sensory exploratory approach to learning about the objects around them.

> *Where Is Baby's Belly Button?* Katz, K. (2000). New York: Little Simon.
> *Fit-A-Shape: Shapes.* (2000). Philadelphia, PA: Running Press.
> *Fit-A-Shape: Food.* (2001). Philadelphia, PA: Running Press.

Where's My Fuzzy Blanket? Carter, N. (2001).
New York: Scholastic Paperbacks.
Where Is Baby's Mommy? Katz, K. (2001).
New York: Little Simon.
Fit-A-Shape: Clothes. (2001). Philadelphia, PA:
Running Press.
The Wheels on the Bus. Stanley, M. (2002).
Bristol, PA: Baby's First Book Club.
Touch and Talk: Make Me Say Moo! Greig, E.
(2002). Bristol, PA: Sandvick Innovations.
Quack, Quack, Who's That? Noel, D. & Gallo-
way, R. (2002). London: Little Tiger Press.

Labeling Familiar People, Emotions, and Actions

These kinds of books encourage the reader to point to
and name the objects in the book. In addition, readers
can encourage the child to say the name of the objects
in the book.

Winnie the Pooh: Feelings. Smith, R. (2000).
New York: Random House Disney.
WOW! Babies. Gentieu, P. (2000). New York:
Crown Publishers.
Faces. Miglis, J. (2002). New York: Simon
Spotlight.
Feelings. Miglis, J. (2002). New York: Simon
Spotlight.
Where the Wild Things Are. Sendak, Maurice
(1988). New York: Harper Trophy.
*Alexander and the Terrible, Horrible, No Good,
Very Bad Day.* Viorst, J. (1987). New York:
Aladdin Library.
The Selfish Crocodile. Charles, F. & Terry, M.
(2000). New York: Scholastic.
*Glad Monster, Sad Monster: A Book about
Feelings.* Emberley, E. & Miranda, A. (1997).
New York: Scholastic.
No David! Shannon, D. (1998). New York:
Scholastic Trade.

Rhyme and Rhythm

Between 12 and 18 months, children discover that
words have meaning. With this in mind, book selections should stimulate the children's sight and hearing.
Books with rhymes are excellent because they introduce the children to sounds and syllables and to the
rhythm and rhyme of language.

Each Peach Pear Plum. Ahlberg, A. & Ahlberg, J.
(1978). London: Penguin Books Ltd.
Moo, Baa, La La La. Boynton, S. (1982).
New York: Little Simon.
Down by the Bay. Raffi & Westcott, N. B. (1990).
New York: Crown Publishers.
Five Little Ducks. Raffi (1999). New York: Crown
Publishers.
Five Little Monkeys Sitting in a Tree. Christelow, E.
(1993). St. Louis, MO: Clarion.

This Old Man. Jones, C. (1990). New York:
Houghton Mifflin Co.
The Itsy Bitsy Spider. Trapani, I. (1993).
Watertown, MA: Charlesbridge Publishing.
Find the Puppy. Cox, P. (2001). London: Usborne
Publishing Ltd.
Find the Kitten. Cox, P. (2001). Newton, MA: EDC
Publications.
Five Little Monkeys Jumping on the Bed. Christelow,
E. (1998). New York: Houghton Mifflin.

TWO TO THREE YEARS

Encourage Scribbling

Children who are encouraged to draw and scribble
"stories" at an early age will later learn to compose
more easily, more effectively, and with greater confidence than children who do not have this
encouragement.

Crayon World. Santomero, A. (1999). New York:
Simon Spotlight.
Figure Out Blue's Clues. Perello, J. (1999)
New York: Simon Spotlight.
Blue's Treasure Hunt Notebook. Santomero, A.
(1999). New York: Simon Spotlight.
*Harold's Fairy Tale: Further Adventures with the
Purple Crayon.* Johnson, C. (1994). New York:
Harper Trophy.
Harold's Trip to the Sky. Johnson, C. (1981).
New York: HarperCollins.
A Picture for Harold's Room. Johnson, C. (1985).
New York: Harper Trophy.
Harold and the Purple Crayon. Johnson, C. (1981).
New York: HarperCollins.
Get in Shape to Write. Bongiorno, P. (1998).
New York: Pen Notes.
Messages in the Mailbox: How to Write a Letter.
Leedy, L. (1994). New York: Holiday House.
*Let's Learn to Write Letters: A Wipe-It-Off Practice
Book.* Troll Books (1994). Memphis, TN: Troll
Association.
*Let's Learn to Write Numbers: A Wipe-It-Off Prac-
tice Book.* Troll Books (1994). Memphis, TN:
Troll Association.

Environmental Print

Children of this age are beginning to attend to print
in the environment. Readers might select books that
they "read" with the children. With the supportive surrounding context, many children can read many words
found in their environment (e.g., STOP, EXIT).

M & M's Counting Book. McGrath Barbieri, B.
(1994). Watertown, MA: Charlesbridge
Publishing.
The Pokéman Book of Colors. Muldrow, D.
(2000). New York: Golden Books Company.

(continued on next page)

SPECIAL FEATURE 6.1 *(continued)*

The Pokéman Counting Book. Muldrow, D. (1999). New York: Golden Books Company.

The Cheerios Play Book. Wade, L. (1998). New York: Little Simon.

The Cheerios Animal Play Book. Wade, L. (1999). New York: Simon and Schuster Merchandise.

Pepperidge Farm Goldfish Fun Book. McGrath, B.B. (2000). New York: Harper Festival.

Kellogg's Froot Loops! Counting Fun Book. McGrath, B.B. (2000). New York: Harper Festival.

The Sun Maid Raisins Playbook. Weir, A. (1999). New York: Little Simon.

The Oreo Cookie Counting Book. Albee, S. (2000). New York: Little Simon.

Pepperidge Farm Goldfish Counting Fun Book. McGrath, B.B. (2000). New York: Harper Festival.

of development, need books with different features. In Special Feature 6.1, Billie Enz and two colleagues provide a few book suggestions for children from birth through age 3 based on developmental characteristics.

Certainly, teachers should share literature representative of various cultures. Again we recommend the Internet for the most up-to-date information on multicultural books. For example, *www.multiculturalchildrenslit.com/* is a website of annotated bibliographies organized by genre (e.g., realistic fiction, nonfiction, biography, fantasy) and culture (e.g., African American, Latino/Hispanic American, Korean American, Japanese American, Jewish American, Middle Eastern, Native American). Vietnamese American is a new addition to this website. A variety of sites can be found using descriptors "multicultural children's literature" with any of the major search engines (Google, Yahoo, Lycos, Excite, and so on).

Teachers should share all genres of literature with their young learners—narrative, informative, poetry. For over a decade, Nell Duke (2000) has encouraged teachers to expose their children to informative texts. Yet, when researchers (Pentimonti, Zucker, & Justice, in press; Yopp & Yopp, 2006) studied the read-aloud practices of preschool teachers they have discovered that only a small percentage (i.e., 5 percent) of the books the teachers they studied read were informative texts. Jill Pentimonti and her colleagues (2010) say that these findings are "troubling" (p. 657). Not reading informative texts denies young children the opportunity to become interested "as early as possible in topics commonly featured in informational texts, such as scientific and mathematical topics" (p. 657). A "balanced diet" of children's books, therefore, is very important (Teale, 2003, p. 127).

Fifteen-month-old Emma reads one of her favorite books.

Today, providing children with high-quality books in print is not enough. Linda Labbo (2005) reminds teachers that access to "just" books is no longer sufficient. Young children also should have access to "appropriately designed computer programs and Internet sites . . . [to] support [their] . . . engagement with ideas, words, and various genres of text" (Labbo, 2005, p. 288). Early childhood teachers should choose storybook software with a high degree of interactivity, allowing children control over such features as the pace of the presentation, the turning of the "page," and the reading of the text word by word or line by line.

Collectively, these sources are helpful in guiding teachers' selection of books to be shared with young children. Once appropriate selections have been made, the teacher's attention can shift to how to share storybooks with her young learners.

Sharing Literature with Children

Teachers can share literature with young children in several ways: by reading stories aloud, by engaging children in shared reading, and by encouraging them to respond to literature in a variety of ways.

Effective Story-Reading Strategies

In the earlier edition of this book, the following vignette introduced this chapter:

> The 4-year-olds in Ms. Jensen's class sit expectantly in a semicircle on the floor, waiting for one of their favorite activities—story time. They know that every day at this time their teacher will read them an interesting and entertaining story. "Today, I'm going to read you one of my all-time favorites, *Where the Wild Things Are* by Maurice Sendak. Look at the strange creatures on the cover! What do you think this story will be about?" After fielding several predictions and comments from the children, Ms. Jensen reads this classic story with expression and a sense of drama. The children listen raptly to each page as Max, the main character, takes a fantastic journey to an island populated with fierce monsters. The children like the way Max manages to take control of the huge beasts (symbols for adults?) and becomes king of the island, but they are also relieved when Max decides to give up his newly found power and return to the comforts of home. When the story is finished, Ms. Jensen invites the children to discuss the parts that they liked best and to tell what they would have done if they were in Max's place. She then shows the children some stick puppets that represent Max, his mother, and some of the monsters. She invites the children to reenact the story during free-choice activity time.

Compare Ms. Jensen's reading of *Where the Wild Things Are* to Ms. Jackson's reading of *Click, Clack, Moo: Cows That Type,* the vignette at the beginning of the chapter. Ms. Jensen just read the book to her children, which is beneficial. But Laura Justice and Khara Pence's (2005) review of the storybook-reading literature led them to recommend interactive reading behaviors. They suggest that interactive reading is much more effective in building children's skills than just reading books to children. For example, when teachers use interactive reading strategies they can track print as they read, comment on where they will begin reading, pause to ask questions and make comments, and provide child-friendly definitions for words that are unfamiliar to the children.

The verbal interaction between adult and child that occurs during story readings has a major influence on children's literacy development (Justice & Ezell, 2000; Wasik & Bond, 2001; Whitehurst et al., 1994). Getting children to talk about the text or think about what is going on in the story is central to children's literacy growth.

ADULT BEHAVIORS WHILE READING. The majority of researchers have concentrated on the human interactions during story reading. From this research, we learn about turn-taking in story reading. Through story reading, very young children are guided into the turn-taking pattern inherent in all conversation: the adult (in this research the adult is usually a parent) talks, then the child talks, then the adult talks, and so forth.

It is within this verbal exchange that the parent and child engage in negotiating the meaning of the story. Obviously, the adult's understanding exceeds the child's understanding of the text. Through scaffolding, the adult gently moves the child toward the adult's understanding of the text. The adult questions the child about the text's meaning. The child replies, and this reply gives the adult a cue. Based on the child's response, the adult adjusts the kind of support (the scaffold) provided. To aid the child's construction of the meaning, the adult behaves in three ways: (1) as a corespondent who shares experiences and relates the reading to personal experiences, (2) as an informer who provides information, and (3) as a monitor who questions and sets expectations for the reading session (Roser & Martinez, 1985).

Adults play these roles differently depending on the child's response and age:

■ With a baby or toddler (12 months or younger), the adult tends to do most of the talking. Mostly adults label the pictures. "Look, Licky, a train! Yup, that's a train—choo, choo!" Typically adults point as they label.

■ Between the ages of 12 and 15 months, adults tend to ask the child rhetorical questions (e.g., DeLoache, 1984): "And that's a kite. Isn't that a kite, Josh?" The questions function to reinforce the picture's label; the adult does not really expect the child to answer. The adult's playing of both roles, asking the question and giving the answer, provides the toddler with experience in the question–answer cycle before the child is required to participate verbally in the exchange.

■ Beginning around 15 months, the adult's expectations rise, and the child is expected to be a more active participant in the story reading. As the child acquires more facility with language, the adult expects the child to answer more of the questions posed. First, the adult asks the child to provide the label for the picture. The adult says things like "Look!" or "What's that?" or "It's a what?" If the child hesitates, the adult intervenes and provides the answer. When the child seems to be correct (Joseph says, "Pithee" in response to his father's query), the adult typically repeats the label or positively reinforces the toddler's response (Joseph's father says, "Yeah. These are peaches."). When the child shows competence at this task, the adult ups the ante, requesting perhaps a description, like asking for information about the color.

Researchers have discovered that this story-reading sequence (adult question, child response, adult feedback) is just like the typical interaction sequence between teacher and student in many classrooms (Mehan, 1979).

Hence these storybook readings also begin children's socialization into the response pattern typical of many classrooms. Researchers like Marilyn Cochran-Smith (1984) and Denny Taylor and Dorothy Strickland (1986) discovered that adults from all socioeconomic levels do the same thing when they introduce a child to a new concept in a book. They try to make the concept meaningful for the child by linking the text to the child's personal experiences. For example, Ann Mowery (1993, p. 46) describes how, when young Joseph and his father read *Wish for a Fish,* Joseph's father made numerous text-to-life connections: "That sure looks like where we go, doesn't it?" "See, that's a can of worms just like what we fish with." "That's a bobber just like ours." "That boy is waiting quietly for a fish. You usually play with the worms and throw rocks, don't you?"

When children approach about 3 years of age, adult story readers tend to increase the complexity of the questions. Now they question the child about the characters and the story's meaning—and they expect the child to raise questions about the characters and the story's meaning. It is this talk surrounding the reading that researchers judge to be the most valuable aspect of the storybook-reading activity for enhancing children's language development. David Dickinson and Miriam Smith's (1994) and Bill Teale and Miriam Martinez's (1996) careful analyses of the teacher/student book-reading interactions suggest that the best talk is the kind that invites children to reflect on the story content or language. The focus of teacher/student talk is: What are the important ideas in this story?

Recently researchers have learned that, in addition to the child's age, the book's genre, whether it is a fictional narrative with a problem with attempts to solve the problem and a solution or an expository text with information about a topic, affects how parents interact with their young children during a book sharing. When reading an expository text, parents of young children tend to read less and talk more. To help their children negotiate the meaning of the text, they tend to ask a greater number of more cognitively demanding questions; they ask questions that require their children to hypothesize, predict or explain. Further, the vocabulary used in expository texts tends to be more challenging than in narrative texts. Each of these adult book-reading behaviors has been shown by other researchers to have a positive effect on children's language and literacy growth. These findings led Lisa Price, Anne van Kleeck, and Carl Huberty (2009) to conclude that sharing this genre with young children and having adults support the children's ability to take information from the text add much to children's preschool language and literacy experiences.

CHILD BEHAVIORS DURING READING. What do children do when they are being read to by a caring adult? Several researchers (e.g., Baghban, 1984; Morrow, 1988) have studied young children's behavior, often their own children, during adult–child readings. These researchers tell us that even infants focus on the book. They make sounds even before they are speaking, as if they are imitating the reader's voice. They slap at the picture in the book. A little older child with some language facility begins to ask questions about the pictures. They play the "What's that?" game, pointing and asking "What's dat? What's dat? What's dat?" almost without pausing for an answer.

CULTURAL VARIATIONS IN STORY READING. Do children from nonmainstream families have similar early childhood home reading experiences? Shirley Brice Heath's answer to this question is no. In her classic book *Ways with Words* (1983), Heath provides a rich description of the literacy experiences of working-class African American, working-class Caucasian, and mainstream families in the Piedmont area of the Carolinas. From her research, Heath learned that the parents from mainstream families read to their children well into elementary school; use a wide variety of complex questioning strategies to develop their children's understanding of story, plot event sequence, and characterization; and look for ways to connect the text information to their children's experiences. Parents from the working-class Caucasian families also read to their children, but what they do while they read is different. They stress the sequence of the stories and ask children literal meaning questions ("What did the little boy do then?" "What's the hen's name?"). Further, they make few attempts to connect the events described in the books to their children's experiences. Finally, Heath learned that the African American families tell lots of stories, but reading is strictly for functional purposes. These families read forms, recipes, and the newspaper. They tend not to read books to their children. Of course, Heath's work cannot be generalized to all mainstream, Caucasian working-class, or African American families. As Teale (1987) notes, there is a great deal of variation among and within social and cultural groups. Teachers need to learn from their students' parents about the experiences their young children have had with books.

We believe that children who have had experiences with books and have experienced dialogic interactions with adults with books are advantaged over children who have no experiences with books and whose parents or early teachers have not shared books with them. Therefore, we strongly encourage teachers and parents of young children to read, read, read to their children—and to talk, talk, talk while reading about the important content, allowing children sufficient time to reflect on the content.

CLASSROOM READ-ALOUDS. When a parent and a child read together, they cuddle. Like 24-month-old Aslan, whom readers met at the beginning of this chapter, the child typically sits in the parent's lap or snuggles under the parent's arm. Many parents establish a bedtime reading ritual, cuddling with the child for a quiet reading time before the child goes to bed. Parents report enjoying this ritual as much as the child, and it establishes a mind-set that encourages the child to read before going to sleep when the child can read independently. Teachers of the very youngest children, infants, and toddlers should follow parents' lead and apply what is known about how parents read to infants and toddlers to their reading to their young students. The low teacher–child ratio recommended by the National Association for the Education of Young Children for infant (one adult to one infant) and toddler (one adult to four toddlers) programs helps permit this kind of adult–child interaction—though with toddlers, such one-on-one reading together requires some careful arranging (Bredekamp, 1989). We recommend that teachers create a daily reading ritual, perhaps just before nap time. Some day care centers connect with church groups or nearby residential facilities for elderly citizens for the explicit purpose of adults coming to the center just before nap time to read to the children. Now, like at home, every child can have a lap, a cuddle, and a "grandparent" all alone.

We are concerned when we hear infant and toddler teachers say, "Read to the kids in my classroom? You must be kidding!" We are even more concerned when we read that this response about reading to young children is not uncommon (Kupetz & Green, 1997).

Two former early childhood teachers, Barbara Kupetz and Elise Green, acknowledge that it takes organization and working together to structure the infants' and toddlers' day to include story reading. "Reading to infants and toddlers is certainly not a large-group activity. It can effectively occur only in very small groups or in one-to-one pairing" (p. 23). Like us, they recommend the center attempt to make appropriate extra-adult arrangements to ensure the inclusion of this important activity in infants' and toddlers' days.

The older the young child, the larger the permitted-by-law number of children in the group. The typical kindergarten class, for example, is often one teacher and 20 (unfortunately, sometimes even more) children. Teachers of these children are challenged to keep read-alouds enjoyable, pleasurable experiences. Of course, selecting age- and interest-appropriate books is important. Read-aloud experiences are one means to ensure that high-quality literature is accessible to all students, something that is especially important for children who have had few storybook experiences outside school.

The *how* of reading is also important. Now there are too many children for everyone to cuddle next to the adult reader. Yet physical comfort is important. Having a special carpeted area for reading to the group is important. Often this area is next to the library center. Nancy asks her young learners to sit in a semicircle. Patty asks her young learners to sit on the *X* marks she has made using masking tape on the carpet. Lolita asks her 3-year-olds to sit or lie wherever they like in the small carpeted area—as long as they can see the pictures. Each day a different child gets to snuggle with her. In each of these classrooms, the teacher sits at the edge of the circle or the carpet on a low chair, holding the picture book about at the children's eye level. The chair the teacher sits in to read from is a special chair, used both for teacher read-alouds and for the children to read their own writing to the class. Each teacher calls this chair *the author's chair*.

Nancy, Patty, and Lolita have mastered reading from the side. Thus the children can see the illustrations while the teacher reads. These teachers know the story they are about to read. They have carefully selected it and read it through, practicing how it will sound when read aloud, in advance. They know how to read it with excitement in their voices. They are careful not to overdramatize, yet they use pitch and stress to make the printed dialogue sound like conversation. They show that they enjoy the story.

The following suggestions for effective read-alouds are recommended by several groups of researchers based on their survey of research studies, reading methods textbooks, and books and articles about reading to children.

■ *Read to students every day:* Research done during the 1980s indicated that only 50 to 60 percent of teachers read aloud to their classes on a regular basis (Lapointe, 1986; Morrow, 1982). A more recent study by James Hoffman, Nancy Roser, and Jennifer Battle (1993) presents a much more positive picture. These researchers found that, on a given day, 84 percent of kindergarten teachers read to their classes.

■ *Select high-quality literature:* A key element to a successful read-aloud experience is the book that is being read. Find books that will appeal to the children's interest, evoke humor, stimulate critical thinking, stretch the imagination. Find books from multiple genres (fictional narratives, concept, poetry, informational/expository). Find books that include "diverse representation of characters and family structure, including people of differing race, gender, ability and language" (Smith, Brady, & Anastasopoulos, 2008, p. 26).

■ *Show the children the cover of the book:* Draw the children's attention to the illustration on the cover ("Look at the illustration on this book!"). Tell the children the title of the book, the author's name, and the illustrator's name. ("The title of this book is . . . The author is . . . The illustrator is . . . ") Tell the children that the author is the person who wrote the book and the illustrator is the person who drew the pictures. Later, ask the children what the author and the illustrator do. Draw your finger under the title, the author's name, and the illustrator's name as you read each. Remind the children that the title, author's name, and illustrator's name are always on the front of the book. Remember that these are new concepts for young children.

■ *Ask the children for their predictions about the story:* ("What do you think this story might be about?") Take a few of the children's predictions about the story's content. ("Let's read to see what this story is about.")

■ *Or provide a brief introduction to the story:* This can be accomplished in a number of ways. You might provide background information about the story ("This story is going to be about . . ."), connect the topic or theme of the story to the children's own experiences, draw the children's attention to familiar books written by the same author, draw the children's attention to the book's central characters, clarify vocabulary that might be outside the children's realm of experiences, and so on. Keep the introduction brief but sufficient to build the children's background knowledge, so there is ample reading time.

■ *Identify where and what you will read:* Two important concepts about print for young children to learn are that readers read the print on the pages, not the pictures, and where readers begin reading. Begin read-alouds by identifying where you will start reading and what you will read. Repeating this information often ("Now, I'll begin reading the words right here") weaves this important information into the read-aloud. Be sure to point to the first word on the page as you say where you will begin. Eventually the children will be able to tell you where to begin reading. After many exposures to this important concept, you might playfully ask, "Am I going to read the words or the pictures in this book?" "Where should I begin reading?"

■ *Read with expression and at a moderate rate:* When teachers read with enthusiasm and vary their voices to fit different characters and the ongoing dialogue, the story comes alive for children. It is also important to avoid reading too quickly. Jim Trelease (2006), a leading authority, claims that this is the most common mistake that adults make when reading aloud. He recommends reading slowly enough that children can enjoy the pictures and can make mental images of the story (not too slow and not too fast, just right). Miriam Smith, Joanne Brady, and Louise Anastasopoulos (2008) agree, adding that exemplary reading is characterized by "expressiveness and fluency, which supports children's understanding of the book, characters, and/or content" (p. 32).

■ *Read favorite books repeatedly:* Not every book you read has to be a book the children have never heard before. In fact, repeated readings of books can lead to enhanced comprehension and better postreading discussions (Martinez & Roser, 1985; Morrow, 1988) and increased likelihood that the children will retain the new vocabulary word, both expressive (words the children produce) and receptive (words the children understand) (Justice, 2002; Penno, Wilkinson, & Moore, 2002). In addition, reading a book three or more times increases the likelihood that young children will select that book during free-choice time and will try to reenact or read it on their own (Martinez & Teale, 1988). Of course, the benefits of repeated reading need to be balanced against the need to expose children to a wide variety of literature.

■ *Allow time for discussion after reading:* Good books arouse a variety of thoughts and emotions in children. Be sure to follow each read-aloud session with a good conversation, with questions and comments ("What part of the story did you like best?" "How did you feel when . . . ?" "Has anything like that ever happened to you?" "Who has something to say about the story?"). This type of open-ended question invites children to share their responses to the book that was read. After listening to a book read-aloud, children want to talk about the events, characters, parts they liked best, and so forth. As children and teacher talk about the book together, they construct a richer, deeper understanding of the book. Reader response theorists, like Louise Rosenblatt (1978), provide theoretical support for the importance of teachers' talking with children about shared books. Rosenblatt believes that, as children listen to stories, they are constructing meaning based on the previous experiences they bring to the text and their purpose for listening. Listeners focus on two kinds of information: remembering information (e.g., the story's main idea, the three main events) and connecting through personal images, ideas, feelings, and questions evoked while listening. Through good conversations about books, teachers and children can explore ideas of personal importance and thus can analyze and interpret the book. Teachers want to work toward being a member of the book circle, one of the discussants who takes turns talking with the children. When the teacher does ask questions, they are open-ended questions that encourage children to interpret, extend, and connect with the text. In Trade Secrets 6.1, Cory Hansen describes how Chris Boyd engages her kindergartners in discussions that help them jointly construct deeper meaning for the stories they are read. Chris's strategy lays the foundation for literature study groups in the primary grades.

■ *Read stories interactively; that is, encourage children to interact verbally with the text, peers, and the teacher during the book reading:* In interactive reading, teachers and children pose questions throughout their book reading to enhance the children's meaning construction and to show how one makes sense of text (Barrentine, 1996). Teachers encourage their students to offer spontaneous comments, to ask questions, to respond to others' questions, and to notice the forms and functions of print features (words, punctuation, letters) as the story unfolds. They use the during-reading book discussions to help children understand what to think about as a story unfolds. Interactive storybook reading provides an opportunity for children's engagement with the story. "Adult-child interactive storybook reading . . . is . . . one of the most potent and frequent contexts for . . . incidental language and literacy learning of young children" (Justice & Pence, 2005, p. 7).

But merely inviting children to talk during storybook reading is not sufficient. Various literacy experts and researchers have proposed interactive storybook reading strategies. For example, in their book *Scaffolding with Storybooks: A Guide for Enhancing Young Children's Language and Literacy Achievement*, Justice and Pence describe how to use specific storybooks and interactive storybook-reading strategies to assist children in developing print knowledge, word knowledge, phonological knowledge, alphabet knowledge, narrative knowledge, and world knowledge. The multiple examples of the "extratextual conversation" language (what does it really sound like when teachers engage in conversations with their students during storybook reading?) scaffold teachers new to interactive storybook-reading strategies as they work to change or develop their storybook-reading behavior from "just" reading to reading interactively.

Anne Gregory and Many Ann Cahill (2010) describe an interactive reading strategy used by a kindergarten teacher. This teacher taught her young learners how to use three hand signals to show how they were comprehending a story. They hold their hand in the shape of a *C* to indicate that they are making a connection to the story, a *V* to indicate that are picturing something in their mind, and wiggle a finger to indicate a question. While reading, the teacher periodically stops to ask the children to share their connections, mind pictures, and questions.

Grover Whitehurst and his colleagues (Whitehurst et al., 1988) call their interactive reading approach "dialogic reading." Dialogic reading is often used by teachers of young children. In Trade Secrets 6.2, Silvia Palenzuela describes how preschool teachers in several early childhood classrooms in the Miami, Florida, area are using this approach with their young children.

While each of these interactive reading strategies is different, all share the need for teachers to prepare for the read-aloud by reading the storybook ahead of time and considering which questions are important to ask the children to aid them in comprehending the story. Some of these questions will be literal (e.g., who, what, where, when, in what order), and some will be inferential (e.g., relate text to life experiences, predict outcomes, compare and contrast, determine cause and effect). If the story is a narrative one, some will focus on the story's structure (sometimes called the story grammar). That is, the teacher will draw the children's attention to story's setting, the main character, the story's problem, how the character attempts to solve the problem, and how the problem is solved. Such questions are key to supporting young children's development of story structure knowledge (Stevens, Van Meter, & Warcholak, 2010). All of these interactive reading approaches aim to help children comprehend the stories read to them. In addition, all of these approaches help children acquire the early reading standards deemed important for their success as readers. In Special Feature 6.2, we provide examples of typical standards like those used in various states and the common core standards.

TRADE SECRETS

6.1

Getting Children to Talk about a Story

Cory Hansen and Chris Boyd

I had the opportunity to observe in Chris Boyd's kindergarten classroom on the day she read De Paola's (1975) *Strega Nona,* a wonderful story of what happens when Big Anthony ignores good advice and overruns his town with pasta from the magic pasta pot. As Chris was reading the book, the carpet in front of her was scattered with children. Some were lying flat on their backs looking up at the ceiling; others were on their sides, only a finger wiggle away from good friends; and others were sitting up, cross-legged, their eyes never leaving the pages of the story. The last page of the story is wordless. Big Anthony's expression tells it all as he sits outside the house, his stomach swollen almost to bursting, with one last strand of pasta lingering on his fork. The children burst into laughter, and as Chris motioned with her index finger, they regrouped, calling out, "I think . . . , I think . . ." on their way to forming a large circle. And for the next half hour, that was what was talked about: what the children thought about the story.

The conversation began with what the children thought was going to happen and comparing it to what really did. Chris asked the children why they thought the way they did, and then the serious business of making meaning together began. (She gradually lowered herself down from the reading chair and joined in as one participant in this group talked about the story: the one with a copy of the text and the one writing comments into a notebook.) The kindergartners called on her only when they needed someone to reread part of the text to settle disputes. Chris did not enter the conversation unless the children lost sight of her one rule for talk about the story or unless an opportunity to seize a literary teachable moment emerged.

After the group examined Big Anthony's motives and explored connections from this story to their own lives, Chris and I had an opportunity to talk about how she structured and scaffolded meaningful talk about the story with young children. My first question was why the children were all over the room as she read. She explained that she offered the children the opportunity to "go to wherever they could do their best listening." In this way she felt she respected the children's choices and could hold them accountable if they acted in ways that did not show good listening by moving them to a different part of the room. By respecting their choices, focus was on listening and thinking rather than sitting or being still.

"So why," I was quick to ask, "do they form a sitting circle after the story?"

"Well, first, it is easier to hear what is being said if they are in a circle. I teach them to look at the person who is talking. I think it encourages them to listen carefully and think through what others are saying. As well, when they are all in a circle they begin to watch for nonverbal cues that show that another person has something to add or introduce to the conversation."

I noticed that the kinds of questions Chris asked her kindergartners during the talk were different than those I had heard in other classrooms. When the children were arguing about why Big Anthony didn't know to blow the three kisses, Chris's question to the group was, "Was there any clue that that might have been a problem for him?" Matthew was quick to suggest that Chris should read the part when Strega Nona was singing to the pot again. The children listened very carefully as Chris reread that part of the story and used the information from the book to settle their disagreement. While that particular part of the conversation was going on, Chris was writing hurriedly in her notebook. I asked her why she recorded what the children were saying as they talked about story.

"When I write down what they say, they see and feel the importance of their words. They know I value what they say and what they think is special enough to write down. It makes them realize how important talk about story really is. Also, I can bring the conversation back around to something a child said when everyone gets talking at once or if a soft-spoken or shy child makes a comment that may otherwise go unnoticed. Like when they were arguing about Big Anthony, Sara made a really smart comment about how the pot needed someone to be nice to it. Her comment was lost in the discussion, but later on, after the issue was settled, I could bring it up again and then the conversation started anew."

I wondered why Chris didn't just have the children raise their hands when they had something to say. She told me that even though it takes a long time and lots of patience to teach children to follow her one rule for talk about story—talk one at a time and talk to the whole group—they eventually learn more than just being polite. Chris found that if she had children raise their hands to talk, they just sat there, waving their arms, waiting to say what they wanted without listening to and considering what other people were saying or connecting their ideas to the book or the opinions of others. Even though it is loud and messy at times, the results are worth the effort.

The kindergartners in Chris Boyd's classroom obviously loved the chance to talk about the story with each other. They used talk about the story to learn more about how things worked in the world and, in the process, learned more about the world of story.

When teachers follow the preceding guidelines, they can help ensure that their story reading has the maximum impact on children's language and literacy learning.

Dialogic Reading

Silvia Palenzuela

Dialogic reading is a way to enhance emergent literacy with preschoolers. It's a conversation about books that focuses on teaching children new vocabulary and improving overall verbal fluency. Reading to children provides them with the opportunity to hear and learn new vocabulary, to hear the sound structure of words, and to see and understand the meaning of print and the structure of stories. It also provides them with firsthand experience of the pleasure of reading books.

The goal of dialogic reading is to develop the child's language skills through reading—to increase the child's number of words, length of sentences, complexity of responses, and ability to use decontextualized language.

How we read to children counts!

Children at the preschool age cannot read, and they need to "hear" the story before they can "say" anything about it. While reading the picture book, the adult has a conversation, a dialogue, with the child. In the context of reading the storybook, the adult models oral language and encourages the children to express their thoughts in words.

In dialogic reading, books are selected based on quality and richness of illustrations. Rhyme books and wordbooks are not proper choices for dialogic reading.

It is an active method. The child is highly engaged in the storytelling, and it is keyed to the child's interests, intrinsic motivation, curiosity, and motivation to explore and experiment with a variety of literacy materials. The adult allows the child to take the lead and follows the child's lead.

With continued practice in the dialogic reading method, the children will increase and strengthen their language skills.

DIALOGIC READING LEVEL 1

Goal: To encourage the children to talk during story time to increase their language skills. This is done by having the children name the pictures and gradually say more about them. Do not use yes-no or pointing questions.

How to Do It

1. Ask "what" questions:
   What's this?
   What is he pulling?
2. Follow answers with questions.
   Ask questions about an aspect of the object.
   What shape is this?
   What color is this?
   What's this part?

Ask questions about what the object is used for.
   What is it used for?
   Who is using it?
3. Repeat what the children say.
4. Scaffold the children by prompting and cuing.
   Have you seen something like this?
   Do you remember what it was called?
5. Praise and encourage.
6. Shadow the children's interests. When the children show an interest in something on one of the pages, get them to talk more about it. Then go back to the reading.
7. Have fun!

DIALOGIC READING LEVEL 2

Goals: To continue with "wh" questions as prompts and to add expansions and open-ended questions.

How to Do It

1. Add only one or two words to what the child says.
2. Be sure to repeat at least part of what the child says.
3. Give feedback . . . at least some of the time (e.g., "Right!")
4. Pause after an expansion to see if the child will repeat spontaneously.
5. Sometimes ask the child to repeat the expansion.
6. Stress the new word or words and speak slowly.
7. Ask open-ended questions.
   What's happening here?
   What do you see in this?
   Tell me more.
   What else do you see?

Examples

A. Child: "a mouse"
   Adult: "a mouse hiding"
B. Child: "boat"
   Adult: "big boat"
C. Child: "It on that."
   Adult: "Right, it's on the couch."
D. Child: "I sawed it."
   Adult: "You saw it, did you?"
E. Child: "It eating."
   Adult: "Good, the ladybug is eating."
F. Child: "turtle up there"
   Adult: "The turtle is hiding."

Other Ways to Get Children to Talk

1. Model what you want the children to say (e.g., make comments about the pictures using sentences at about the same level as the children's, and then pause).

TRADE SECRETS 6.2 *(continued)*

2. Say something that is incorrect, and pause to see if the children correct you.
3. Say part of a sentence, and have the children (or a child) fill in the last word.

DIALOGIC READING LEVEL 3

Goal: To focus on the use of new vocabulary while talking about the story plot or the children's personal experiences in order to:

- Reinforce vocabulary;
- Link the vocabulary with the story plot;
- Link the vocabulary with personal experience;
- Fain verbal fluency with new vocabulary.

Make sure the children can easily answer Level 1 and Level 2 questions before moving on to Level 3.

Use a book that is very familiar to the children. Always start a new book at Level 1.

How to Do It

1. Continue to repeat and expand what the children say.
2. Continue to use Level 1 and Level 2 questions as needed.
3. Continue to provide models, taking turns with the children.

Examples

A. Take turns with the child *telling the story*. The teacher can hold the book or the children can, whichever is easier. Provide help when needed with vocabulary words, but let the children direct the activity. Don't overcorrect, and don't be too concerned with the children getting the story "right." The focus is verbal fluency and use of new vocabulary. Variation: Have the children ask the questions.

B. Ask *recall questions* (refers to story plot or narrative).
Why was he sad?
Where are they?
What happened at the end?

C. Ask questions that refer to *personal experiences*.
Have you ever been to a farm?
Tell me about it.

D. Ask questions that relate to *sequence of events*.
What happened first?
What happened next?
What happened last?

E. Ask questions that relate to prediction.
What do you think will happen next?
What would you do?

F. Have the children act out the story. They can describe what they are doing as they do it or simply speak the lines. The children also can describe who they are, what they are wearing, and so on.

Here is an easy way to remember what to do. Just remember the word *car!*

*C*omment and wait.
*A*sk questions and wait.
*R*espond by adding a little more.

SPECIAL FEATURE 6.2

Typical Storybook Reading Standards

- Make predictions about what might happen in a story.
- Correctly identify characters, objects, and actions in a picture book as well as stories read aloud, and begin to comment about each.
- Ask and answer questions related to a story that has been read or told to him or her.
- Make up and/or retell stories.
- Retell key details and information drawn from the text.
- Explain the subject of the text or the problem the characters face.
- Ask and answer questions about characters and events that take place in the text.
- Retell the beginnings, middles, and endings of stories.
- Identify the feelings of characters and the reasons for their actions.
- Compare and contrast characters or events from different stories written by the same author or written about similar subjects.
- Identify the main topic and ideas in the text.
- Ask questions about unknown words.
- Relate pictures or illustrations to the words in the text.

SHARED BIG-BOOK READING. Teachers usually read picture books to their classes by holding the books so that the children can see the illustrations, pausing to elicit students' reactions to the stories or to ask story-related questions. This traditional whole-class read-aloud experience differs from parent–child storybook-reading interactions in a very important way: Most children can see only the pictures, not the print. To remedy this situation, Holdaway (1979) devised the shared-book experience, a strategy that uses enlarged print, repeated readings, and increased pupil participation to make whole-class storybook-reading sessions similar to parent–child reading experiences. Today the shared-book experience has become an important component of a quality early literacy program.

To use this strategy, the teacher first needs to select an appropriate book. Andrea Butler and Jan Turbill (1984) recommend stories that have (1) an absorbing, predictable story line; (2) a predictable structure, containing elements of rhyme, rhythm, and repetition; and (3) illustrations that enhance and support the text. These features make it easy for children to predict what is upcoming in the story and to read along with the teacher.

Once a book has been selected, an enlarged copy needs to be obtained. This can be done in several ways. The teacher can (1) rewrite the story on chart paper, using one-inch- or two-inch-tall letters and hand-drawn illustrations; (2) make color transparencies of the pages from the original picture book and use an overhead projector; or (3) acquire a commercially published big-book (about 24 to 26 inches) version of the story. Commercial big books are becoming increasingly available. Scholastic and McGraw-Hill/The Wright Group, for example, publish enlarged versions of a number of high-quality picture books. Initially, only picture storybooks were available in the big-book size. Today informational books also can be located in big-book size. These ready-made big books have the advantage of saving teachers time by eliminating the need to make enlarged texts. Understandably, they are expensive because they include large versions of the original illustrations.

Unlike when regular-size books are shared with children, big books permit all children to see the print. Teachers may take advantage of the enlarged print by drawing young children's attention to the print in the same ways that a parent draws a child's attention to the print in a regular-size book during a read-aloud. Laura Justice and her colleagues (2009) provide teachers with a simple "scientifically validated" technique to guide their instruction in print knowledge, a technique they found to successfully influence young children's print knowledge. The features of this technique include "asking questions about print (e.g., 'Do you see the letter *S* on this page?'), commenting about print (e.g., 'That words says *"Splash!"*'), and tracking one's finger along the text [or using a pointer to point to the words] while reading" (p. 68). When teachers do not draw children's attention to the print in books, children seldom (less than 5 percent of the time) focus on the print (Justice, Pullen, & Pence, 2008). Using a pointer to point to the words, teachers can invite the children to read along, particularly to the words in a familiar text or to the refrain in a book. As children "read" along with the teacher, they internalize the language of the story. They also learn about directionality (reading from left to right with return sweeps), one important print knowledge skill.

Through the use of big books, teachers can introduce children to other print knowledge skills: to the sequence of letter sounds in words; to the differences among letters, words, and sentences; to the spaces between words; to where to start reading on the page; to reading left to right; to return sweeps; to punctuation; to the order in which pages are read in a book. In addition, through the use of big books, teachers are able to further children's development of important concepts about books (e.g., the front and back of a book, the difference between print and pictures, that pictures on a page are related to what the print says, that readers read the print, where to begin reading, where the title is and what it is, what an author is, what an illustrator is). In essence, teachers can use big books to teach skills in context.

While teachers can use big books to teach a broad range of language and literacy skills, they cannot introduce all of the skills to their students during a single reading. Therefore, big books should be read to children multiple times, for instance, daily for a week. Various educators have designed daily procedures to guide teachers' big book reading. In Special Feature 6.3, we provide our version of a five-day big-book–reading strategy based on our reading of the literature on shared big-book reading.

SPECIAL FEATURE 6.3

Shared Big-Book Reading

DAY 1

Before Shared Reading

- Read the title, author, and illustrator. Point to each word as you read. Tell the children that the author is the person who wrote the book and the illustrator is the person who drew the pictures.
- Show the children the book's cover. Ask them to tell you what they think the story will be about. On chart paper, write a few words for each suggestion to help you and the children remember the predictions. Ask the children to explain their rationale for each prediction.
- Do a picture walk-through the book. That is, show each page to the children. Point to the characters and ask, "Who might this be?" Point to the key objects on each page and ask, "What is this? What might it be used for?" Ask the children to describe what they see happening on each page.
- Make connections to the children's prior knowledge or experiences. "Remember when we . . . ? Have you ever . . . ?"
- Introduce the children to vocabulary words that are key to their understanding the story.
- Build any necessary background knowledge.

DAY 2

Before Shared Reading

- Show the children the cover. "Does anyone remember the title of the book? the author? the illustrator?" Point as you read.
- Read the list of predictions the children made about the story.

During Shared Reading

- Show the children where you will begin reading, the direction you will read, and where you will go after you have read the first line. "Now, I'll begin reading right here. I'll read this line (draw your finger under the line), and then I'll return to here" (draw your finger back to the next line at the left-hand side of the page).
- Read the story. Pause on each page to ask questions, such as: "So what is happening so far in the story? Why do you think [insert character] said [insert what character said]? How do you think [insert character] is feeling now? What do you think is going to happen next? Why?" Encourage the children to ask questions and contribute their ideas about what is happening or is going to happen in the story.

After Shared Reading

- Compare what happened in the story with what the children thought would happen. Were any of their predictions accurate? Why or why not?
- Connect the story's content to their experiences. Ask questions such as: "Has anything like that ever happened to you?" Focus on the story's problem. Would they have solved the problem the way the main character did?

DAYS 3, 4, AND 5

Before Shared Reading

- Read the title of the story. Ask: "How many words are in the title? Count them with me." Read the author's name. Ask: "And what does the author of a story do?" Read the illustrator's name. Ask: "And what does the illustrator of a story do?"
- Prompt the children to retell the story by looking at the pictures. Ask questions to guide their retelling. (This should be a quick retelling.)

During Shared Reading

- Ask the children where you should begin reading.
- Invite the children to read the lines they know with you. Point to the words while you read. (Initially, the words they remember likely will be the repetitious words or sentences.) Compliment them on what fine readers they are!
- You might want to echo read. You read a line, and then the children read the same line. Point while you and they read, and compliment them on their reading.
- If this book's sentences end in rhyming words, focus on these words. Pause before you read the second word, allowing the children to fill in the missing word. Tell the children that ___ and ___ rhyme. Later, ask them what they just made.

After Shared Reading (*Do one of the following, a different one each day*)

- Return to the page or pages with a pair of rhyming words. Read the sentence or sentences again. Write the two words on chart paper. Can the children think of other rhyming words? Add these words to the words on the chart paper. (Nonsense words are acceptable; the focus is on rhyming.)
- Look for words that begin with the same letter. Read those two words, without pointing. Ask the children what they notice about those two words. Ask: "What letter makes that sound?" Say the sound slowly. Write the two words on chart paper. Can the children think of other words that begin with the same letter? Add their words to the chart paper.
- Hunt for a letter. Can the children, for example, find all of the letter *T*'s in the story? Mark each letter with a Post-it Note so that all of the *T*'s can be counted. (Initially the children will need a

(continued on next page)

model, a *T* on a card that can be moved under the letters on the page. Later they may be able to find the *T*'s without a model, and still later they may be able to find the *T*'s and the *t*'s.)
- Hunt for a particular word using a procedure like that above.
- Count the number of words in two of the sentences. Which sentence was longer?
- Select a sentence. Using a Post-it Note, cover all of a word but the first letter. Read the sentence. Can the children guess what the covered word is? How do they know? Can they think of any other word that would "fit" in the sentence? Write their word on a Post-it. Read the sentence with the new word.

- When the story includes several dialogues and action, provide props to support the children's dramatization of the story.
- Plan an art activity that connects with the book (e.g., a collage activity after reading a Leo Lionni book, a watercolor activity after reading *Dawn* by Uri Shulevitz [1987]).

FOLLOW-UP

Place the book in a prominent location in the library corner. Invite the children to read it to you, another adult, or a peer during center time. Perhaps they would like to play teacher with a group of friends.

Many of the packaged early childhood language and literacy programs (e.g., *Doors to Discovery,* published by McGraw-Hill/The Wright Group in 2002) not only include big books for shared-reading experiences but also include poems and songs on large colorful poster boards. The teacher's guide suggests that each poem be shared with the children, pointing to each word as the poem is read, several times over several days. After several readings, the children can "read" the poems themselves. Of course, teachers can use the posters in the same way they used the big books, to introduce the children to the conventions of print; to the sequence of letter sounds in words; to the differences among letters, words, and sentences; and so forth. And teachers also can make large posters using chart paper, Magic Markers, and their best manuscript penmanship. All of the children's favorite songs, poems, and finger plays can be written in large print.

Extending Literature

Interactive storybook readings and postreading discussions are not the only ways children can respond to books. Teachers also might use retelling as a tool to enhance children's comprehension of stories. In the following paragraphs, we describe how they can use dramatizations, puppetry, and flannel or felt boards to support children's retellings. Then we describe some activities—drawing, cooking, and writing—to extend stories' content.

First, a word about the importance of retellings: Inviting children to retell the story they have just listened to helps develop vocabulary, syntax, comprehension, and sense of story (Ritchie, James-Szanton, & Howes, 2002). Lesley Morrow, Elizabeth Freitag, and Linda Gambrell (2009) suggest that, with practice, retelling helps young children learn the text structure of a narrative story or an expository text. For example, when retelling a narrative story, children learn to begin with an introduction such as "once upon a time," describe the setting, identify the story details and sequence, change their voice to represent the various characters, and focus on the how the text is organized (e.g., cause/effect, problem/solution). When the text is an informative one, they suggest that retelling helps children "distinguish the main ideas from the supporting details" (p. 57). Retelling helps develop children's comprehension of storybook readings.

CREATIVE DRAMATICS. Creative dramatics is informal dramatizing with no printed script or memorized lines. Stories that are good for dramatizing need dialogue and action—characters who say and do something. Sometimes props are used; sometimes the children use their imaginations. For example, they can imagine the bears' bowls, chairs, and beds when acting out *The Three Bears* (Galdone, 1979) or the Troll's bridge when dramatizing *The Three Billy Goats Gruff* (Galdone, 1973). Sometimes the teacher reads the story, pausing for the players to pantomime and fill in the dialogue. For example, student teacher Syma reads that old favorite *Caps for Sale* (Slobodkina, 1947) to her young students. One child is the peddler; the other children, seated in their spots on the rug, are the monkeys. As she reads about the peddler's efforts to sell his caps, the child chosen to play the role of the peddler walks back and forth in front of her classmates, inviting the "monkeys" to buy a cap. The "peddler" does not say exactly what the peddler says in the book; this is acceptable. Syma moves on to the next page. Later, the children delight at shaking their fingers and then their hands at the "peddler" who wants his caps back from the "monkeys."

Karen Valentine has props stored in large see-through plastic bags in her classroom's library center for various old favorites. During free choice, Doug coerces three friends into playing *The Three Bears* with him. He puts on the yellow crepe-paper wig and assumes the role of Goldilocks and the narrator. One child puts on the Daddy Bear headgear (made of poster board), another child puts on the Momma Bear headgear, and a third child puts on the Baby Bear headgear. Doug lines up three chairs and gathers three bowls from the dramatic play center. He tells the story while his friends pantomime and speak. Doug often corrects their language because they are not saying exactly what he thinks they should say.

Such experiences promote many aspects of development by offering children an opportunity to take on the behaviors of others, to try out vocabulary and sentence structure perhaps unfamiliar to them, to play cooperatively with others, and to accept and give criticism.

PUPPETS. Many young children, particularly shy ones, can speak through the mouth of a puppet in ways they can not speak on their own. Puppets provide children with another means—for some children, a safer means—of dramatizing a good story. Again, stories with strong dialogue and distinctive characters who do something are best suited for dramatization with puppets, stories like "The Three Little Pigs," "The Three Bears," "The Three Billy Goats Gruff," "Little Red Riding Hood," and so forth.

Manufactured puppets are available from many sources; for example, most early childhood equipment catalogs and teacher stores include puppets for retelling children's favorites. Typically these are hand puppets (the kind that fit over the hand of the puppeteer). However, teachers can also construct their own puppets (Figure 6.1).

FELT OR FLANNEL BOARDS AND CHARACTERS. In Chapter 5, we share information about the importance of providing opportunities for children to tell stories in the early childhood classroom. Our focus here is literature that stimulates storytelling. Typically, this literature is a folktale or a fairy tale. Children are nudged to retell these stories by teachers who tell them first. Sadly, many teachers have yet to be converted to the art of storytelling. Their children are missing much, for a good story can take children into a different world, into another place, and perhaps into another time. An excellent website to support teachers as storytellers is Better Kid Care: Storytelling (*www.nncc.org/Literacy/better.storytell.html*). This website provides suggestions for stories to tell, how to prepare for storytelling, and four ways to tell a story.

Teachers can use several different kinds of visual aids to illustrate stories. Some might use stick puppets; some might draw with chalk while telling the story; others prefer to use a felt or flannel board with paper or cutouts made of interfacing fabric, for this is the most popular visual aid used in early childhood classrooms. (Interfacing fabric can be purchased in a store that sells materials for sewing. It is typically used to interface garments, to add stiffness to collars and cuffs.)

Books are available to reduce the time it takes for teachers to locate stories appropriate for telling and to make Pellon or paper characters. One of the authors' favorites is Doris Hicks and Sandy Mahaffey's (1997) *Flannelboard Classic Tales,* published by the American Library Association. This book contains the script for stories to tell and the patterns for the characters to accompany each story. For teachers with modest artistic talent, they are a must. Several commercial companies also provide "felt sets" of favorite preschool stories.

STORY DRAMA. Todd Wanerman (2010) has devised a special kind of retelling known as story drama that is ideal for 2- and 3-year-old preschoolers. A storybook is used as the script. The teacher begins with repeated readings of one of children's favorite storybooks Next, the teacher uses the storybook, reading the book while the children do the reenactment and add some of the dialogue on their own. He recommends that simple props be used so that the physical settings helps with the reenactment. During initial reenactments, the teacher takes on one of the roles and models how to act out part of the story. The teacher should also help children interact socially to negotiate roles, work together to build props, and so on. If several children want to have the same role, Wanerman recommends that children "share" the role and

FIGURE 6.1 Puppets

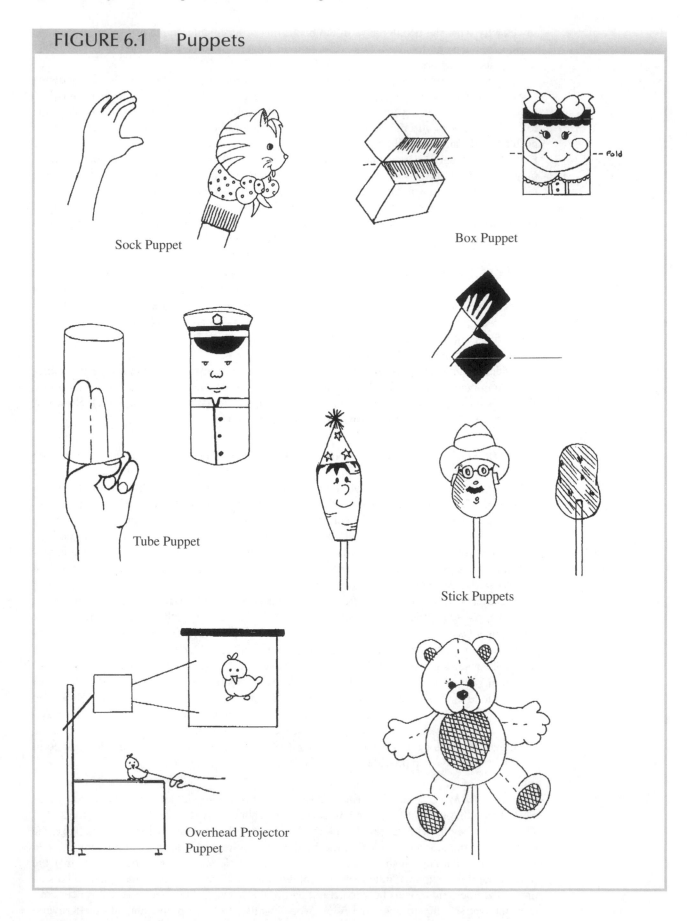

Sock Puppet

Box Puppet

Fold

Tube Puppet

Stick Puppets

Overhead Projector
Puppet

take turns playing the character. Finally, he suggests that teachers encourage children to experiment with their own variations of the story (e.g., make up a new ending).

Greta Fein, Alicia Ardila-Rey, and Lois Groth (2000) have developed a more sophisticated version of story drama that they call *shared enactment.* It combines story drama with shared writing, a strategy which is discussed in Chapter 8. During free-choice activity time, the teacher sits in the classroom writing center and encourages children to tell stories. The teacher writes down the children's words verbatim. When a child finishes with his or her story, the teacher asks if there is anything else that child wishes to add. Then the teacher reads the story back to make sure that it matches the child's intentions. The child decides whether he or she wishes to share the story with the group. If the child does, it is put in a special container called the story box. Later, during shared enactment time, the teacher reads the story to the class, and the story is dramatized. The story's author identifies the characters and selects peers to play the various roles. The teacher reads the story slowly so that the actors can engage in the described behavior and pauses so they can provide the dialogue.

Fein and her colleagues used the shared enactment procedure with a class of kindergartners twice a week for twelve weeks and found that it resulted in a substantial increase in narrative activity (story enactment and storytelling) during free play. The investigators noted that this brief intervention appeared to penetrate the daily life of the classroom and promised to make important contributions to the children's narrative development.

COOKING. Teachers of young children have long recognized the value of cooking activities as a component of their total program for young learners. In cooking, children experience math (e.g., measurement, counting, determining how much is needed so that everyone in the class gets a piece), reading (e.g., the recipe), social skills (e.g., following the recipe together, eating), health and safety habits (e.g., nutrition and preparing food), and eating the food they enjoyed making. As Betty Coody (1997, p. 141) notes, "Cooking makes the book memorable, and in turn, the story serves to make cooking in the classroom even more important."

Some books include a recipe for readers to test. For example, Tomie dePaola's (1978) *The Popcorn Book* suggests two ways popcorn might be made. What better incentive to try two approaches to making popcorn? The content of other books suggests appropriate cooking activities. For example, after hearing Russell Hoban's (1964) *Bread and Jam for Francis,* a natural response is for the children to try their hands at making jam sandwiches, and after hearing Ed Arno's (1970) *The Gingerbread Man,* a natural response is to make a gingerbread man. A rainy day presents a reason for reading at least two books followed by cooking: Listening to Maurice Sendak's (1962) *Chicken Soup with Rice* and making chicken soup with rice or listening to Julian Scheer's (1964) *Rain Makes Applesauce* and making applesauce. Many books can be stretched to connect with a related cooking activity. For example, an extension of Robert McCloskey's (1963) *Blueberries for Sal* might be the making of blueberry pancakes or blueberry muffins, and an extension of Ruth Krauss's (1945) *The Carrot Seed* might be the making of buttered carrots, carrot cake, or carrot bread.

ART PROJECTS. The central purpose of an art program for young children should be free expression. Teachers should offer children opportunities to be creative, to use their imaginations, to produce something original, and to be inventive. How the children do (the process) is far more important than what the children produce. Therefore, teachers of young children do not want to produce models that all children must copy or to tell children to "draw a picture of your favorite part of the story." Instead, teachers of young children should put materials out for children's exploration and creation. Within these boundaries, literature can serve as a stimulus for many creative art projects:

■ *Artist's media:* Many illustrators (e.g., Leo Lionni, Eric Carle, Ezra Jack Keats) use collage to illustrate children's books. Shirley Rigby, a collage artist and a teacher of 4-year-olds, follows the reading of *Inch by Inch* (Lionni, 1962) with a brief discussion of Lionni's choice of medium—collage—and then sends her young artists off to cut and tear shapes from many different materials so that they, too, can be collage artists.

Teachers can invite children to experience the media used by many different picture book artists. What better way for them to understand artists' techniques?

■ *Papier-mâché:* Perhaps the children have a favorite literary character: Curious George? Francis? By inflating a balloon or balloons, the teacher can craft a form for the children's creation of a replica of their literary favorite. By dipping newspaper strips into a bowl of wallpaper paste thinned to about the consistency of cream and applying the strips to the balloons until the balloons have about four layers of paper on them, the children can create the literary animal shape. When the paper is dry, the children can paint the figure with tempera paint. The teacher can add distinguishing features (e.g., eyes, mouth).

■ *Paint-on shapes:* Nadine Herman's 3-year-olds love Eric Carle's books, especially *The Very Hungry Caterpillar.* One day, Nadine cut butterfly shapes for the children to paint on at the easel, instead of using the regular-size easel paper. More children than ever chose to easel paint. The following day the children attached pipe cleaners to the painted butterfly shapes for antennae. Nadine made a paper replica of a *Buddleia* plant (the plant that attracts butterflies) in one corner of the room, and the children hung their butterflies on the plant. Later, when Nadine read *The Very Busy Spider* (Carle, 1984), the children wondered: Could they paint on spider paper? Nadine answered, "How about using chalk on black spider shapes?"

Strategies for Teaching English Language Learners: Storybook Time

Myae Han

Large-group story time is one of the most challenging times for teachers with English language learners (ELLs). Teachers worry that these children may not understand the story but still need to listen to storybook reading. The following are several suggestions for ways teachers might make storybook reading more successful for these children:

• Start with patterned books or predictable books. These books are highly repetitive and have simplified texts that make it easy for ELL children to become engaged with them. Gradually expand beyond predictable books to books consistent with the children's interests. When choosing books, consider the vocabulary, length, and cultural sensitivity.

• When children are not following the book's words, talk the story rather than reading it. Also consider the use of puppets or storytelling props to assist children's understanding of story. For example, one of the popular children's books *There Was an Old Lady Who Swallowed a Fly* (Taback, 1997) can be better understood with a prop of a big old lady. Before the story is read, say the names of the animals. As the story is read, attach the animal figures to the old lady's stomach.

• Keep storybook reading time short. Don't make storybook reading time a patience contest. If the book is too long, it is fine to stop in the middle and finish it at a later time.

• Consider small group book reading. Instead of having one large group story time, teachers can have small group story time with different groups of children during free-choice time or by splitting the group into two groups and having the teacher read to one group while the classroom assistant reads to the other group. When grouping children, flexible grouping (mixing ELL children with English-speaking children) is recommended. However, depending on the type of book, the content and level of difficulty, the teachers may consider grouping only the ELL children together on some occasions.

• Read the same storybook again and again—at least three or four times. Children get more information each time they listen to the story. It is also important to remember to focus on different aspects of the story each time the book is read. For example, during each reading focus on different vocabulary, words, predictions of what will happen next, comprehension questions, or alphabet letters.

• To teach vocabulary, select appropriate words from the storybook, provide child-friendly explanations of the selected words, and use these words during classroom activities as well as during the readings to ensure word learning.

• When possible, follow Theresa Roberts's (2008) suggestion, and invite the parents to read the storybook at home to their children prior to the teacher's reading of the storybook in the classroom. Roberts discovered that it made no difference if the parents' home reading of the storybooks was in English or the child's primary language. Both resulted in children learning significantly more English vocabulary words than when the children heard only the teacher's reading of the storybook in English in the classroom. Of course, the teacher will need to be resourceful to obtain the storybooks in the children's primary language.

Strategies for Teaching Children With Special Needs: Reading Storybooks with Children with Disabilities

Laura M. Justice

All children can benefit from and enjoy being read storybooks, including children who have significant disabilities. The disabilities to which I am referring include intellectual disability (as occurs often in Down syndrome), autism, cerebral palsy, severe hearing loss, and blindness. Unfortunately, it seems that children with these types of disabilities may have less access to and experience with storybooks than children who are developing typically. This might occur because other needs of the child take precedence, such as developing self-help skills or basic communicative repertoires. It may also occur because parents and other professionals underestimate the capacity of the child to appreciate shared-reading experiences and to benefit from these. Finally, it is also the case that some children with disabilities may find it difficult to engage in shared-reading experiences in the same way that other children might; they might have gross-motor challenges that make turning pages or otherwise manipulating the book difficult, and they might have language-processing difficulties that compromise their comprehension and verbal contributions. Nonetheless, despite all of these issues, participating in reading experiences is not only a basic activity that all children can enjoy and learn from, but it supports the child's development of important language and literacy skills in a way that few other activities can.

Two issues of special importance when sharing books with young children with disabilities include: (a) promoting the child's active engagement in the shared-reading experience, and (b) promoting the communicative- and linguistic-richness of the activity. Regarding the former, children greatly benefit from being active participants in reading experiences, as this promotes not only their enjoyment of and motivation toward the activity but also the learning that takes place. One can promote the child's active engagement in a number of ways, such as:

- Allow the child to select the book being read (even if it's one that has been read repeatedly!).
- Allow the child to pick where the reading takes place (e.g., on the floor, at a table, in your lap) and how the participants are positioned.
- Allow the child to hold the book and turn the pages, even if some pages are skipped.
- Allow the child to set the pace of the reading activity.
- Accept any form of participation (if a child wants to make a sound with each page turning, see this as a form of participation).
- Encourage the child to participate in any manipulative aspects of the book, such as lifting flaps or touching textures.
- Encourage the child to point to or comment on any aspects of the pictures that he or she finds interesting (you can do this by pausing or commenting yourself).

In general, all of these suggestions are similar in that the child is given some control over the activity. By exercising control over aspects of the reading experience—including what is read and the pace at which the interaction takes place—the child's motivation toward and engagement in the activity will be supported.

Another important aspect of storybook reading with special needs children is promoting the communicative and linguistic richness of the book-reading experience. Children can learn a great deal from storybook-reading experiences, such as how conversation involves a give-and-take (turn-taking), the meanings of interesting words, and even common grammatical structures. This learning can be boosted by a variety of adult interactive strategies, such as:

- Repeating what the child says verbatim (e.g., if the child says "That is a cow," you can repeat "That is a cow").
- Naming interesting features of illustrations—including both perceptual features of the page (e.g., "That's Thomas") and conceptual features (e.g., "He looks really angry").
- Waiting expectantly for the child to comment or participate (e.g., on turning a page, simply sit and wait to see if the child has a contribution to make).
- Pointing out, with enthusiasm, interesting words or concepts (e.g., "Wow, I can't believe the size of the cake!").
- Praising the child's contributions (e.g., "You know a lot about this book!").

Oftentimes, adults dominate book-reading experiences both physically (holding the book, turning the pages) and communicatively (asking lots of questions, not waiting for the child to respond). For children with disabilities—like all young children—allowing the child to be a more active and involved participant can promote not only the child's positive motivation toward literacy experiences but also the developmental benefits of this activity.

Family Focus: Sharing Instructional Materials and Offering Guidance

Preschool teachers frequently recommend that parents read to their young children (Becker & Epstein, 1982). Unfortunately, many parents face great financial hardships and cannot provide a large number of quality reading materials in their homes. Nor do they have time for or easy access to public libraries. Further, parents may not know how to encourage and engage their children's interest in reading (Richgels & Wold, 1998). To help parents to fulfill their role as partners in literacy programs, it is vital for teachers to work with these families to offer easy access to books of all kinds (Brock & Dodd, 1994) and guidance in how to use them (McGee & Richgels, 1996).

Classroom Lending Library. Susan Neuman's 1999 study examined the effect of flooding more than 330 child care centers with storybooks. The results of her study confirm that children who have access to high-quality storybooks and teachers who are trained to support children's storybook interactions score significantly higher on several early reading achievement measures than children who have not experienced high-quality storybooks and trained teachers. In other words, it is critically important for young children to have easy access to high-quality storybooks and expository text. Further, it is essential that parents and child care providers know how to support a child's early interactions with print. Though most public schools possess libraries, children generally are restricted to borrowing only one or two books a week. Some child care centers use public libraries with similar restrictions. While this may be appropriate for older children who can read chapter books, this quantity is insufficient for young children who are learning how to read. Young children should have the opportunity to have at least one new book an evening. One way to ensure early literacy development at home and foster the home–school connection is through a classroom lending library. A classroom lending library allows children to check out a new book each day, thus ensuring that all parents have an opportunity to read to their child frequently.

The acquisition of quality books for daily checkout is the first step in establishing a classroom lending library. Because the children will exchange their book each day, all a teacher needs to begin a library is one book per child. Managing the classroom lending library requires that all books contain a library pocket and identification card. The teacher needs to create a classroom library checkout chart. When a child borrows a book, the teacher simply removes the book's identification card and replaces it in her or his name pocket on the classroom checkout chart. The teacher can easily see what book each child has checked out at a glance. The rules that accompany the classroom lending library are simple. A child may borrow one book each day. When the book is returned, the child may check out another. Teaching the children to manage the checkout routine is easy. When the children enter the classroom in the morning, they return their books to the library by removing the book's identification card from their name pocket. They place the identification card back in the book's library pocket, and they place the book back on the shelf. The children may select new books anytime throughout the day.

Book Bags. Yet another way to encourage family participation and successfully engage and guide parents' literacy interactions with their children is through book bags (Barbour, 1998–1999). Book bags may be checked out of the classroom lending library for a week at a time. Book bags contain a collection of high-quality books and offer informal, interactive activities for extending children's language and literacy acquisition. When designing the bags, teachers need to consider their children's developmental stages, interests and experiences, and literacy levels. The book bags (nylon gym bags) typically contain three or four books and activities inspired by a specific theme (see Figure 6.2 for sample book bag themes). In addition, each bag contains two response journals (one for the child and one for the parent). Each bag also contains an inventory that helps parents and children keep track of and return materials assigned to each bag.

Teachers typically initiate the program by sending home a letter describing the program. In addition to the introductory letter, each family also receives a contract. The terms of the contract are simple: Parents promise to spend time regularly reading to their children; children promise to spend time with the books and activities and treat each bag with care; and teachers promise to instill a love of reading in children and to manage the program. All three participants sign the contract.

The book bag project has been highly successful in many teachers' classrooms. The book bags supply parents the appropriate materials and explicit guidance, which in turn empower and motivate them to become teachers of their own children, encourage them to provide supportive home learning environments, and expand their knowledge of how to interact with their children.

WRITING. Tabby Tiger is very popular with the Lambson Head Start Center children in New Castle, Delaware. He is the central character in several books the teachers read to the children. Because of the children's attachment to this storybook character, the Center's family liaison purchased a small stuffed animal that looks like Tabby Tiger and a spiral-bound journal notebook for each classroom. Each night a different child takes Tabby and the journal home. The child's "homework" assignment is to have fun with Tabby and to write about Tabby's adventure in the journal. As the center serves 3- and 4-year-old children, the children's parents or

FIGURE 6.2   Sample Book Bag Themes

Counting Theme
Hillanbrand, W. (1997). *Counting Crocodiles.* Orlando: FL: Harcourt Brace.
Kirk, D. (1994). *Miss Spider's Tea Party.* New York: Scholastic.
Barbieri-McGrath, B. (1998). *Hershey's Counting Board Book.* Wellesley, MA: Corporate Board Book.

Alphabet Theme
Wilbur, R. (1997). *The Disappearing Alphabet.* New York: Scholastic.
Alexander, M. (1994). *A You're Adorable.* New York: Scholastic.
Martin, B., & Archambault, J. (1989). *Chicka Chicka Boom Boom* New York: Simon & Schuster Children's Publishing.

Rhyming Books
Goldston, B. (1998). *The Beastly Feast.* New York: Scholastic.
Slate, J. (1996). *Miss Bindergarten Gets Ready for Kindergarten.* New York: Scholastic.
Wood, A. (1992). *Silly Sally.* Orlando: FL: Harcourt Brace.
Degen, B. (1996). *Jesse Bear, What Will You Wear?* New York: Simon & Schuster Children's Publishing.
London, J. (1997). *Froggy Gets Dressed.* New York: Viking Children's Press.
Regan, D. (1998). *What Will I Do If I Can't Tie My Shoe?* New York: Scholastic.

older siblings do most of the writing, though often the children add a few words in their personal script. In six months, no classroom has lost a Tabby Tiger. No child has failed to return to the center the following day without Tabby Tiger. He has had a few memorable adventures that concerned him, like a few swishes in the washing machine and a ride on the back of a family's dog.

AUTHOR STUDY. Ellen Booth-Church (1998) suggests that an author study is a great way to invite children to take an insider's look at the art and craft of writing and illustrating children's books. Each week or month, a different author holds center stage. Through discussion and careful analysis, the children come to understand the themes, characters, rhythm, story patterns, and structure used by different authors. Invite children to discuss and compare the books written by Ezra Jack Keats or Denise Fleming or Leo Lionni. Church describes how a group of kindergarten children discovered that Denise Fleming usually writes about animals and that there are rhythmic similarities between the text and the title of *In the Small, Small Pond* (1993) and *In the Tall, Tall Grass* (1991). Inspired, the children wrote their own book—*In the Big, Big Kindergarten.* Soon they moved on to comparing two authors. They learned that Leo Lionni usually uses collage (tearing paper into small pieces) and Denise Fleming does not. Both authors usually write about animals. Fleming uses short rhymes and phrases, and Lionni uses detailed stories.

Summary

To summarize the key points about selecting and sharing literature with young children, we return to the guiding questions at the beginning of this chapter:

■ *Where might teachers look for advice on storybooks to share with their young learners?*
  There are numerous book and Internet resources to assist teachers in selecting high-quality books to read to their students. Search engines are useful tools to facilitate this search. Remember to read storybooks from each of the genres of literature.

■ *What are the characteristics of effective adult storybook reading?*
  What adults say—the verbal interaction between adult (parent or teacher) and child—during story readings has a major influence on children's literacy development. During storybook readings, children learn about the turn taking inherent in all

conversation. The adult helps the child negotiate the meaning of the text, assisting by relating the content to personal experiences, providing information, asking questions, and setting expectations. Who talks the most and the content of the talk varies with the age of the child.

Specific read-aloud strategies have been recommended for use in early childhood classrooms. These include reading aloud every day, select high-quality literature, showing and discussing the cover of the book before reading, asking children to make predictions about the story, providing a brief introduction, identifying where and what you will read, reading with expression at a moderate rate, reading stories interactively, reading some stories repeatedly, and allowing time for discussion during and after reading.

Shared reading is also recognized as a critically important practice in quality early childhood literacy programs because big books permit all children to see the print, something not possible when teachers read aloud a regular-size book. By using big books, teachers can introduce children to the conventions of print and the concepts about books.

■ *What are some of the ways children can respond to and extend the stories that they have been read?*

Interactive storybook readings and postreading discussions are not the only ways that children can respond to books. Children can also engage in dramatizing a story, in retelling the story using puppets and a felt or flannel board and characters, in participating in a cooking experience, in creating an art project, in writing, or in studying an author's art and craft of writing.

■ *What special considerations are needed when sharing literature with English language learners and special needs children?*

Myae Han makes several suggestions aimed at ensuring that large-group storybook reading is successful for all children, including English language learners. She suggests starting with patterned or predictable books; "talking" the book, rather than reading it, when the children seem to be struggling to comprehend the story; keeping the storybook reading times short; perhaps reading to small groups of children rather than to the children in a large group; and reading the same book three or four times. She also recommends encouraging parents to read at home the storybooks that will be read in the classroom—in either the child's primary language or in English.

Laura Justice recommends that special needs children be given some control over the activity. By exercising control over aspects of the reading experience—including what is read and the pace at which the interaction takes place—the child's motivation and engagement in the activity will be supported. She also recommends several strategies to support children's linguistic competence, including (a) repeating what the child says verbatim, (b) naming interesting features of illustrations and conceptual features, (c) waiting expectantly for the child to comment or participate, (d) pointing out interesting words or concepts, and (e) praising the child's contributions.

■ *How might teachers offer their children's families with easy access to books and guidance in how to use them?*

Ensuring that all families have access to high-quality books is important to children's language and literacy development. Teachers can ensure early literacy development at home and foster the home–school connection through a classroom lending library. A classroom lending library allows children to check out a new book each day, thus ensuring that all parents have an opportunity to read to their child frequently. Yet another way to encourage family participation and successfully engage and guide parents' literacy interactions with their children is through book bags, bags of three or four books and activities inspired by a specific theme.

LINKING KNOWLEDGE TO PRACTICE

1. Visit an early childhood classroom, and observe a storybook-reading or shared-reading activity. What type of book was being read? How did the teacher introduce the book? Did the teacher read with expression and at a moderate rate? What kinds of questions did the teacher and the children ask during the reading? After reading, was there a thoughtful discussion of the book? Did the children have an opportunity to respond to the story through art activities, drama, or writing?

2. Go with a friend or two to a library or bookstore. Plan to treat yourselves to a whole day of reading children's literature. Take your computers or four- to six-inch note cards with you. Record the bibliographic information and a brief description of the books you read. Be sure to read books for all age groups, infancy through kindergarten, and all kinds. What a wonderful day you will have! End the day browsing the various websites suggested in this chapter.

3. Tape yourself during a read-aloud with a small group of children. Analyze your read-aloud for the strategies suggested in this chapter. What goals would you set for yourself? Do a shared reading of a big book with a group of children. Audio- or videotape yourself reading. (Be sure to gain permission from the children's parents before you do the videotaping. Some parents do not want their children's face to be visible in a videotape. If so, position the camera so it is focused on you and not the children.) Analyze this big-book shared reading using the recommendations in Special Feature 6.2 as the lens through which you view your sharing of this big book.

Go to the Topics Comprehension, English Language Learners, and At Risk and Struggling Readers in the MyEducationLab (www.myeducationlab.com) for your course, where you can:

- Find learning outcomes for Comprehension, English Language Learners, and At Risk and Struggling Readers along with the national standards that connect to these outcomes.
- Complete Assignments and Activities that can help you more deeply understand the chapter content.
- Examine challenging situations and cases presented in the IRIS Center Resources.

Go to the Topic A+RISE in the MyEducationLab (www.myeducationlab.com) for your course. A+RISE® Standards2Strategy™ is an innovative and interactive online resource that offers new teachers in grades K-12 just in time, research-based instructional strategies that:

- Meet the linguistic needs of ELLs as they learn content
- Differentiate instruction for all grades and abilities
- Offer reading and writing techniques, cooperative learning, use of linguistic and nonlinguistic representations, scaffolding, teacher modeling, higher order thinking, and alternative classroom ELL assessment
- Provide support to help teachers be effective through the integration of listening, speaking, reading, and writing along with the content curriculum
- Improve student achievement
- Are aligned to Common Core Elementary Language Arts standards (for the literacy strategies) and to English language proficiency standards in WIDA, Texas, California, and Florida.

Teaching Early Reading Skills

Martha Vasquez, teacher in a "reverse mainstream" preschool classroom in a school district in southwestern Arizona, is in the middle of a thematic unit on water and sea creatures. Today she has decided to center her instruction on syllable segmenting, a phonological awareness skill that is part of her state's Early Learning Standards. She begins by holding up cards with children's first names written on them. She asks the children first to recognize whose name is on the card and then clap and count the number of syllables in the name. The children have become quite good at this, quickly shouting out the names (e.g., "Christopher" is pronounced "kris-tə-fer") and number of syllables ("three"). The children enjoy the activity and are very engaged. Next up is the poster *part of the lesson. Mrs. Vasquez first asks children how many syllables are in the word* poster, *and the children shout out "two!" Then she reads the rhyme poster, which is about a submarine. While the main purpose of the poster is to teach rhyme recognition, Mrs. Vasquez focuses on vocabulary and syllable segmenting. She reads the poster with the children, encouraging them to make motions that go with rhyme (e.g., putting their fingers together to make pretend glasses for the word* periscope). *Then she asks individual children to count the syllables in several words from the story (e.g., sub-mar-ine = 3). Finally, she moves onto the vocabulary phase of the lesson. As before, she asks the children how many syllables are in the word* vocabulary. *She says the word in syllable segments and holds up a finger for each syllable. The children clap each syllable. Four children quickly shout out "five!" Being able to count the syllables in a five-syllable word is quite an accomplishment for 4-year-olds! Next, Mrs. Vasquez holds up picture/word cards that contain words related to the unit theme. She asks the children to say the word and then asks them a question about it. For example, after the children identify the picture of a whale, she asks, "Where would you find a whale?" Several children respond, "In the ocean!" She also has them make motions for the words when appropriate (as with* wave). *When words contain more than one syllable (e.g.,* rainbow), *Mrs. Vasquez asks the children to clap and count syllables. The academic level of these activities is quite high for preschool, especially because two-thirds of the children in this reverse mainstreamed classroom have identified special needs. But all students seem able to successfully participate (two assistant teachers are there to help), and they appear to enjoy showing off their rapidly growing literacy skills.*

Mrs. Vasquez's instruction exemplifies the scientifically based reading research (SBRR) approach to early literacy instruction. She is directly teaching her students skills that will prepare them to learn to read in kindergarten and the primary grades. When she has children recognize their classmates' written names, she is teaching them print awareness. When she has them count the number of syllables in words, she is teaching a phonological awareness skill. When she has children identify, use, and discuss the words on the picture/word cards, she is directly teaching them new vocabulary. Since many of her children are English language learners, this latter skill is particularly important.

It is important to note that this type of direct, focused instruction is only part of the literacy instruction that the children in Mrs. Vasquez's classroom receive. She also reads them several books every day. In addition, the children have an hour-long center time in which they choose what to do. On the day described above, Mrs. Vasquez read the book *The Rainbow Fish* by Marcus Pfister (North-South Books, 1992) class, and children had the following choices: (a) engage in dramatic play in an ocean-theme center, complete with a cardboard boat; (b) play with miniature replicas of sea creatures; (c) play a game where they would "catch" letters with a fishing pole with a string and magnet on the end; (d) make a cut-and-paste picture of the Rainbow Fish with multicolored scales; and (e) read books in the library with the teacher.

Mrs. Vasquez's literacy program is an example of what we refer to as a blended curriculum. It combines emergent literacy strategies (described in Chapters 4 and 6) with science-based instructional strategies. Mrs. Vasquez directly teaches skills contained in typical standards, including the newly published Common Core State Standards, which we highlight in boxed features throughout this chapter. We believe that such a combination is the most effective way to help young children learn to read and write.

In the section that follows, we discuss strategies for teaching the following SBRR skills: phonological and phonemic awareness, alphabet knowledge, phonics, and print awareness.

BEFORE READING THIS CHAPTER, THINK ABOUT . . .

- How you learned the names of the letters of the alphabet. Did you learn by singing the alphabet song?
- How you learned the sounds letters make. Do you remember phonics workbooks or learning phonics rules (e.g., when two vowels go walking, the first one does the talking)?

FOCUS QUESTIONS

- What is the difference between phonological awareness, phonemic awareness, and phonics? In what sequence do young children typically acquire these skills? What does this sequence suggest about classroom instructional strategies?
- How might early childhood teachers introduce young children to the letters of the alphabet?
- How can early childhood teachers reassure the public that they are teaching phonics?

BOX 7.1	**Alphabetic principle:** The idea that letters, or groups of letters, represent phonemes
	Onset: The beginning part of a word
Definition of Terms	**Phoneme:** One of the individual sounds that make up spoken words
	Phonemic awareness: The awareness that spoken words are composed of individual sounds or phonemes
	Phonics: The relationship between sounds and letters in written language
	Phonological awareness: Awareness of the sound structure of oral language
	Print awareness: Children's ability to recognize print and their knowledge of concepts of print
	Rime: The ending part of a word

Phonological and Phonemic Awareness Instruction

A "massive body of work has established that phonological awareness is a critical precursor, correlate, and predictor of reading achievement" (Dickinson, McCabe, Anastaspoulos, Peisner-Feinberg, & Poe, 2003, p. 467), and discriminating units of language (i.e., words, segments, phonemes) is linked to successful reading (National Early Literacy Panel, 2008; National Reading Panel, 2000). Clearly, phonological and phonemic awareness are two important, closely related skills that have an important role in early literacy development. *Phonological awareness* is a broader term, referring to awareness of the sound structure of speech. Phonemic

BOX 7.2

Typical Phonological Awareness Standards

Identifies words in sentences and syllables in words by snapping, clapping, or other rhythmic movement.

Counts words in sentences and syllables in words.

Recognizes words that rhyme in familiar games, songs, and stories.

Produces words that rhyme.

Recognizes when words begin with the same sound.

Produces words that begin with the same sound.

Blends and segments consonants and rimes of spoken words (e.g., /b/-/oat/).

Blends, segments and substitutes phonemes in spoken words (e.g., /h-a-t /= *hat; boat =* /b/-/o/-/t/; change the /b/ to /g/ to make *goat*).

awareness is an advanced subset of phonological awareness that involves awareness that spoken words are composed of individual sounds or phonemes (McGee, 2007). Both are important for all young children to possess if they are to become successful readers. These phonological processing skills lay the foundation for learning phonics, the relationships between letters and the sounds that they represent. Because of their importance to children's success as readers, typical preschool and kindergarten standards have included each of the phonological skills identified in the following discussion as linguistic awareness skills that children should possess by the end of kindergarten. See Box 7.2 for typical phonological awareness standards.

Marilyn Adams (1990) suggests that if children are to succeed at reading, especially if the reading program they meet in the primary grades relies heavily on phonics, phonemic awareness is the most crucial component of an early literacy program. Early childhood teachers must look for ways to help their young children attend to the sounds in the language. This is a new challenge for early childhood teachers. In the past, children have been denied phonological and phonemic awareness instruction because teachers did not realize the importance of this skill. Children were first taught to recognize letters and then taught the sounds associated with the letters (i.e., phonics). Now we know that, before phonics instruction can be fully useful to young children, they need phonemic awareness. They must be aware of the individual sounds in words before they can begin to match these sounds up with letters. By not teaching phonological and phonemic awareness, teachers were making it difficult for many children to learn phonics!

Growth in phonological awareness begins in infancy, so even the teacher of the youngest child is a phonological awareness instructor. Initially, babies hear language "as one big piece of 'BLAH BLAH BLAH.'" However, as discussed in Chapter 2, babies quickly learn to hear the unique phonemes that make up their native language. These early speech lessons occur naturally as most adults use "parentese" to communicate with infants (parentese is an exaggerated, slowed, and highly articulated form of speech that allows infants to see and hear their native language; see Chapter 2). Phonological awareness begins when young children are able to hear the boundaries of words (for example, *Seethekitty* becomes *See the kitty*). As sounds become words that are frequently used in context to label specific objects, the acquisition of word meaning begins.

Research has revealed a developmental continuum in children's acquisition of phonological processing skills (see Figure 7.1). In general the movement is from larger units to smaller units.

FIGURE 7.1

Phonological Awareness Developmental Continuum

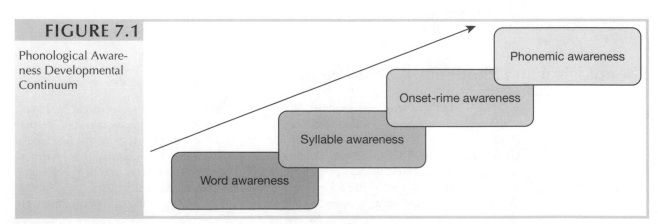

Marilyn Adams (1990) and others (Phillips, Clancy-Menchetti, & Lonigan, 2008) suggest that before young children can become aware of phonemes—the individual sounds that make up spoken words—they first must become aware of larger units of oral language. Thus, children must first realize that spoken language is composed of words, syllables, and sounds. Beth Phillips, Jeanine Clancy-Menchetti, and Christopher Lonigan (2008, p. 5) explain:

> . . . the continuum of skill development moves from the capacity to manipulate words, such as words in phrases and words within compounds (*rain* + *bow* = *rainbow*), to the syllable level (*sister* − */sis* = */ter/*), to onset-rime (*/b/* + *ird* = *bird*), and finally to phonemes (*/m/*+*/o/*+*/p/* = *mop*).

According to these researchers, children's ability to "detect words that rhyme (e.g., *hat* rhymes with *flat* and *cat* but not with *ham*)" (p. 5) is an example of children's understanding of onset-rime awareness, as is children's ability to detect words that begin with the same sound (e.g., *bike* and *bird* both begin with the */b/* sound). As mentioned earlier, the skills identified before phonemes are referred to as phonological awareness. Once these skills are mastered, children can begin to focus on the individual sounds of language and develop phonemic awareness. When children have fully mastered phonemic awareness, they are able to take individual sounds and blend them into whole words, break words down into individual sounds, and even manipulate the sounds in words (e.g., replace the middle sound of a word with another sound, so that *cat* become *cut* and *fan* becomes *fun*).

Phillips, Clancy-Menchetti, and Lonigan add two additional points:

(1) Children's development of phonological awareness "is not a stage model in which a child has to master one level before moving to the next. Rather, children show beginning levels of skills on more complex levels while still working toward mastery of less complex levels" (p. 5). This is important information for teachers to know as they plan phonological awareness activities for their children. A steady diet of activities to develop one skill (e.g., word awareness activities) would not be consistent with the research. Activities to support children's acquisition of various phonological awareness skills are appropriate.

(2) "Children's phonological awareness skill development is across different types of tasks with varied difficulty" (p. 5). Activities that teach phonological and phonemic awareness can ask children to identify ("Do these two words rhyme?"), blend or synthesize ("*/B/* + */at/* makes what word?") or break apart or analyze ("Take the first sound away from *cat* and what word did you make—*at*").

Research is clear that phonological awareness and phonemic awareness are metalinguistic abilities (Adams, 1990). As such, children must not only be able to recite and play with sound units but also must understand that sound units map onto parts of language. While children's initial entry into phonological awareness might be through recitations and playing with sound units, such activities appear to be insufficient. Explicit instruction is required (Pullen & Justice, 2006). In addition, teachers are cautioned against focusing too much attention on rhyming. While rhyme is a good starting point for building awareness of the sounds of language, rhyming has not been found to be a strong predictor of children's reading skills (National Early Literacy Panel, 2008).

In the sections that follow, we describe a number of strategies that teachers can use to increase children's phonological and phonemic awareness. We have ordered these to match the general development continuum of phonological processing.

Phonological Awareness

Phonological awareness activities focus children's attention on the sounds of words. Segmenting activities help children learn to break oral sentences up into individual words and take individual words and break them up into syllables. In rhyming activities, children learn to recognize when words have the same middle and ending sound. In alliteration activities, the focus shifts to the beginning sounds of words. Onset and rime activities involve segmenting initial sounds from ending syllables in selected groups of words. These activities make children aware of the sounds of language and lay the foundation for phonemic awareness.

WORD AND SYLLABLE SEGMENTING. Activities that help children learn how to segment sentences into words and words into syllables help set the stage for full phonemic segmentation—the ability to divide words up into individual sounds:

■ *Word segmenting:* The goal is to develop children's awareness that oral language is made up of strings of individual words. Children initially have difficulty with word boundaries. For example, young children often think that *before* is actually two words (because of syllable segmentation) and that *once upon a time* is one word (because the words are often blended together with little pause in between). Teachers can help children divide speech up into separate words by reciting familiar nursery rhymes (e.g., "Jack and Jill") and inviting the children to join in. The teacher then explains that rhymes are made up of individual words. He or she recites the rhyme again, clapping as each word is spoken. Children then join in, clapping the words along with the teacher. This is continued until the children can clap the words accurately. Finally, the teacher reconstructs the rhyme by inviting each child to say one word of the rhyme in sequence (The Wright Group, 1998). Activities in which children track print, such as the shared reading of big books described in Chapter 6, are also effective ways to help children discover the concept of a word.

■ *Syllable segmenting:* Activities that develop the ability to analyze words into separate syllables take segmenting to the next stage. Syllables are a unit of spoken language larger than a phoneme but smaller than a word. Once children can divide words up into syllables (*begin* can be divided into *be-gin*), full phonemic awareness is just a step away (*begin* can be segmented into *b-e-g-i-n*). The vignette at the beginning of this chapter describes how Martha Vasquez teaches this important skill. She begins by having children clap and count the syllables in their classmates' last names. She then has children clap and count syllables in a rhyme poster and in vocabulary words on picture/word cards. What we like best about Mrs. Vasquez's approach is that she keeps returning to this skill throughout the day, giving children many brief but focused opportunities to practice and perfect it.

ONSET AND RIME SUBSTITUTION. Onset and rimes are often used as an instructional bridge between phonological and phonemic awareness. Onset and rimes are "families" of words that end with the same vowel and consonant cluster (e.g., *-at: bat, cat, fat, hat, mat, rat, sat*). The beginning consonant is referred to as the onset, and the medial vowel and ending consonant are called the rime. Onset and rime substitution activities, in which the child substitutes different onsets with a set rime (*c-ake, b-ake, sh-ake, m-ake*) are easier than phonemic awareness activities because the word is only broken into a beginning and ending part (*f-ake*) rather than into individual phonemes (*f-a-k*). Onsets and rimes also build a foundation for learning the sounds represented by vowels. In the primary grades, onsets and rimes are often used as a way to teach long and short vowel sounds because rimes have consistent letter–sound relationships. The vowel *a* can represent many different sounds, but when it is paired with *ke*, forming the *ake* rime, it almost always represent the long *a* sound. In primary-grade phonics

---

TRADE SECRETS 7.1

An Onset and Rime Activity

New Castle County, Delaware, Head Start teacher Debby Helman uses an onset and rime activity as a transition from circle time to getting-ready-for-lunch time. Ms. Helman begins by telling the children that to leave the circle today they are going to play a game with rhymes. She begins, "Listen to this word: *hop*. Now if I take the /h/ away from *hop* and I put a /p/ on /op/, what new word did I make? /p/-/op/." The children are quiet. Just as she is about to speak, Jemelda shouts, "Pop!" Ms. Helman compliments her and invites her to go wash her hands for lunch. She asks, "Who can put a different letter sound on /op/ and make a different rhyming word? [pause] When you see a red light you___." A child shouts, "Stop!" Ms. Helman says, "Right! /St/ on /op/ makes /st/-/op/." She invites the child who provided the word *stop* to go wash his hands. She says, "We wash up spills with a___*op*." Kathryn says, "Mop!" Ms. Helman says, "Kathryn took the /p/ off /op/, put on an /m/, and made *mop*. Kathryn goes to wash her hands." These examples have helped the children understand how to play this game. Soon the children produce *shop, cop, top, bop, nop,* and more /-op/ words. (Notice that *nop* is a nonsense word. It is acceptable to play this game with nonsense words.)

instruction, rimes are often referred to as phonograms or word families. Trade Secrets 7.1 presents an example of a preschool onset and rime lesson.

Rhyme activities, one kind of onset-rime awareness, focus children's attention on the middle and ending sounds of words (e.g., *fun, sun, run*) (Pullen & Justice, 2006). There are two levels of rhyme awareness: rhyme identification, in which children can indicate which words rhyme, and rhyme production, in which children can, when given examples of rhyming words (*fat, cat, mat*), come up with other words that fit the rhyme pattern (*rat, sat, Laundromat*). Identification is the easier of the two. Research by Fernandez-Fein and Baker (1997) showed that children's knowledge of nursery rhymes and the frequency that they engage in word play were both strong predictors of children's phonological awareness. It is not surprising, therefore, that many research-based strategies for promoting phonological awareness in preschool and kindergarten use playful activities such as singing songs, reciting nursery rhymes, reading books that play with the sounds of language, and gamelike activities (e.g., Adams, Foorman, Lundberg, & Beeler, 1998).

Rhyme identification instruction often begins by inviting children to recite or sing well-known nursery rhymes such as "Jack and Jill," "Humpty Dumpty," or "Hickory Dickory Dock." After children become familiar with the rhyme, the teachers can go back and highlight the rhyming words, pointing out that these special words end with the same sound. Then teachers can help children identify the rhyming words. Once children are able to identify these words, teachers can repeat a rhyme, pausing before the words that rhyme, giving children time to predict the upcoming word ("Humpty Dumpty sat on a wall. Humpty Dumpty had a big___.") (Ericson & Juliebö, 1998). This is the first step toward rhyme production. Ultimately, teachers can present the rhyming words from a story and ask children to supply more words that fit the rhyme pattern ("In this story, *wall* and *fall* rhyme—they end with the same sound. Can you think of other words that rhyme with *wall* and *fall?*").

Games are a fun, enjoyable way for children to consolidate their knowledge of rhyme. Brenda Casillas, a Head Start teacher in San Luis, Arizona, plays a "rhyming basket" game with her children. She begins by showing the children a basket full of pairs of objects that rhyme (e.g., rock and sock). Next, she takes out one object from each rhyming pair (e.g., the rock) and places it in front of her. She also asks the children to identify these objects. Almost all of the children in her class are English language learners, so this step helps build vocabulary as well as set the stage for the game. Finally, Mrs. Casillas passes the basket to the children and asks them to find an object that rhymes with whatever object she points to in front of her. For example, if she points to the rock, then the child is supposed to find the sock and say its name. By the middle of the school year, the 4-year-olds in Mrs. Casillas's class have become quite skilled at this rhyme identification task. This helps the children meet an Arizona Early Learning Standard (*Strand 2 Prereading Processes—Concept 3 Sounds and Rhythms of Spoken Language: a. Recognizes words that rhyme in familiar games, songs, and stories*).

Trade Secrets 7.2 illustrates how kindergarten teacher Grant Clark uses the popular song, *Down by the Bay*, to help children learn to go a step beyond rhyme identification and produce their own rhymes.

TRADE SECRETS 7.2

A Rhyme Production Activity

In a video published by Allyn and Bacon (2000), kindergarten teacher Grant Clark demonstrates how a song/book, *Down by the Bay* by Raffi (Crown, 1987), can be used to help children learn to produce rhyming words that fit a pattern. "Down by the Bay (Polka Dot Tail)" is a predictable song that has the refrain "Did you ever see a goose kissing a moose, Down by the bay?" "Did you ever see a whale with a polka-dot tail, Down by the bay?" Two words always rhyme: *fly-tie, bear-hair*. When Mr. Clark reads the book to the class, he pauses slightly before reading the second word. This enables the children to use their knowledge of rhyme and the clues given by the book illustrations to come up with the second part of the rhyme. After he has finished reading the book, he continues to sing the song with the children, letting the children come up with their own pairs of rhyming words, some which are quite amusing. For example, one girl came up with "Did you ever see a book kissing a hook, Down by the bay?"

"Polka Dot Tail," words and music by Michael Melchiondo and Aaron Freeman © 1997 Warner-Tamerlane Publishing Corp. (BMI), Browndog Music (BMI) and Ver Music (BMI). All rights on behalf of Browndog Music (BMI) and Ver Music (BMI) and administered by Warner-Tamerlane Publishing Corp. (BMI). All rights reserved. Used by permission.

A few words of caution: Beware of providing children *only* with rhyming activities. The research literature clearly shows that children's ability to rhyme is a consistently weak predictor of their later reading comprehension (NELP, 2008).

Alliteration, another kind of onset-rime awareness, occurs when two or more words begin with the same sound (e.g., *Bibbity bobbity bumble bee*). As with rhyme, there are two levels of alliteration awareness: (a) identification—recognizing that several words start with the same sound and (b) production—after hearing several words that begin with the same sound (*sand, sailboat, seal, sun*), children can produce other words that start with the same sound (*sing, snake*). As with rhyme, instruction begins by reading or singing songs and stories that contain examples of alliteration (e.g., "My baby brother Bobby bounced his favorite ball.") As with rhyme, the teacher should first point out and explain the examples of alliteration ("*Baby, brother, Bobby,* and *ball* all start with the same sound, /b/."). Then children can be asked to identify the words that "start alike." Once children can recognize alliteration, they can be helped to come up with other words that start with the same sound.

San Luis Preschool teacher Lisa Lemos systematically introduces her children to a letter and its sound every two weeks using a published program, *Sound, Rhyme and Letter Time* (Wright Group/McGraw-Hill, 2002). For example, she introduced the sound of the letter *S* by showing children a chart that contains pictures of objects that start with this sound (*sun, seal, sailboat, sandwich, sand, sunglasses, seashell*). She began by having the children identify the objects on the poster. As was the case in Brenda Casillas's classroom, most of Mrs. Lemos's children are English language learners, so this helped to build vocabulary as well as phonological awareness. Next, she pointed out the names of all the objects that begin with the same sound: /s/. She then had the children take turns identifying and saying the names of the objects. She then asked if the children know any other words that start with this sound. At the beginning of the school year this was a challenge for the children. On the day that author Jim Christie observed in Mrs. Lemos's classroom, one child was able to come up with a Spanish word, *sol*, that starts with the /s/ sound. Mrs. Lemos praised the child for coming up with such an excellent example, commenting that both *sol* and its English counterpart *sun* start with the /s/ sound. Later that day, she sent a note home with the children, telling their families that the class is studying the letter *S* and requesting objects from home that begin with the /s/ sound. The next day, about half of the children brought objects to share. The children took turns sharing their objects with the class. For example, Alexis showed a small replica of a star and said its name. Mrs. Lemos said, "Yes, *star* begins with the /s/ sound." Then Mrs. Lemos wrote the word *star* on the white board and drew a small picture of a star. Next, Izac shared his stuffed snake (which was a big hit with his classmates), and Mrs. Lemos added *snake* and a drawing of a snake to the white board. After adding the names and drawings of all the objects that the children have brought to share, Mrs. Lemos puts a big sun in the middle of the *S* web. This web remained up for the remainder of the two weeks that the /s/ sound was studied. Through these activities, Mrs. Lemos was helping her children master the Arizona Early Learning Standard *Strand 2 Prereading Processes— Concept 3 Sounds and Rhythms of Spoken Language: d. Recognizes when different words begin or end with the same sound.*

Phonemic Awareness

The phonological awareness exercises described in the preceding section build a base in which children become aware that the words in speech are composed of sequences of individual sounds or phonemes. This conscious awareness of phonemes sets the stage for children to discover the alphabetic principle that there is a relationship between letters and sounds. Learning these letter–sound relationships, in turn, facilitates "sounding out" written words that are in children's oral vocabulary but are not familiar in print (Stanovich, 1986).

On entering school, children's level of phonemic awareness is one of the strongest predictors of success in learning to read (Adams, 1990). In fact, phonemic awareness has been shown to account for 50 percent of the variance in children's reading proficiency at the end of first grade (Adams et al., 1998).

Unfortunately, phonemic awareness is difficult for many young children to acquire. Marilyn Adams and her colleagues (1998, p. 19) report that

Phonemic awareness eludes roughly 25 percent of middle-class first graders and substantially more of those who come from less literacy-rich backgrounds. Furthermore, these children evidence serious difficulty in learning to read and write.

One reason that phonemic awareness is difficult to learn is that there are few clues in speech to signal the separate phonemes that make up words (Ehri, 1997). Instead, phonemes overlap with each other and fuse together into syllabic units. Adams and her colleagues (1998) give the example of *bark*. They point out that this word is not pronounced /b/, /a/, /r/, /k/. Instead, the pronunciation of the medial vowel *a* is influenced by the consonants that precede and follow it. Because phonemes are not discrete units of sound, they are very abstract and are difficult for children to recognize and manipulate. This is why most children need direct instruction on phonemic awareness. The challenge is to make this instruction appropriate for young children. We believe that strategies presented below meet this important criterion.

PHONEME ISOLATION. Phoneme isolation activities focus children's attention on the individual phonemes, the smallest units of sound, that make up words. This is the beginning of true phonemic awareness:

- *Sound matching:* children decide which of several words begins with a specific sound (Yopp & Yopp, 2000). For example, the teacher can show children pictures of familiar objects (*cat, bird, monkey*) and ask which begins with the /b/ sound.

- *Sound isolation:* children are given words and asked to tell what sound occurs at the beginning, middle, or ending (Yopp, 1992). For example, the teacher can ask, "What's the sound that starts these words: *time, turtle, top?*" Or she can ask children to "Say the first little bit of *snap*" (Snow et al., 1998).

PHONEME BLENDING. In blending activities, children combine individual sounds to form words. The game "What am I thinking of?" is a good way to introduce blending to preschoolers (Yopp, 1992). The teacher tells the class that she is thinking of an animal. Then she says the name of the animal in separate phonemes: "/k/-/a/-/t/." Children are then asked to blend the sounds together and come up with the name of the animal.

PHONEME SEGMENTING. Segmenting is the flip side of blending. Here, teachers ask children to break words up into individual sounds (McGee, 2007). Lucy Calkins (1994) calls the ability to segment words "rubber-banding," stretching words out to hear the individual phonemes. For example, the teacher can provide each child with counters and Elkonin boxes, a diagram of three blank squares representing the beginning, middle, and ending sounds in a word (e.g., ☐☐☐). Children are asked to place counters in the boxes to represent each sound in a word. For the word *cat,* a marker would be placed in the left-hand square for /k/, another in the center square for /a/, and a third in the right-hand square for /t/. The concrete props are designed make this abstract task more concrete for children.

PHONEME MANIPULATION. Phoneme manipulation is the most advanced form of phonemic awareness. These activities require children to add or substitute phonemes in words:

- *Phoneme addition:* say a word, and then say it again with a phoneme added at the beginning (*an > fan*) or end (*an > ant*).
- *Phoneme deletion:* say a word, and then say it again without the initial (*farm > arm*) or ending (*farm > far*) sound.
- *Phoneme substitution:* substitute initial sounds in lyrics of familiar songs (*Fe-Fi-Fiddly-i-o > De-Di-Diddly-i-o*) (Yopp, 1992).

In a video published by Allyn and Bacon (2000), kindergarten teacher Grant Clark demonstrates how the book *The Hungry Thing* by Jan Slepian and Ann Seidler (Scholastic, 1971) can be used to teach phoneme manipulation. In the book, a large creature comes into town with a sign saying "Feed me." When asked what it would like to eat, the creature mispronounces the name of a series of foods. For example, if it wants pancakes, it says "shmancakes." The adults try to come up with complicated interpretations (e.g., schmancakes are a strange kind of chicken), but a little boy figures out that one just needs to substitute a different beginning sound to make sense of what the creature is saying (*schmancakes > fancakes > pancakes*). Once the children in his class catch on to the pattern, Mr. Clark pauses and sees if the children can figure out what food the creatures wants (*tickles > pickles*). The children soon are shouting out the correct names of the food as soon as the creature mispronounces the words. After reading the story, Mr. Clark follows up by playing a game. He reaches into a bag, which he says is his lunch bag, and describes a food item, mispronouncing the initial sound like the creature in the story. For example, when he grabs the replica of a clump of grapes, he says, "Oh, these must be napes!" Then he asks the children what they think *napes* are. They quickly catch on and say "grapes!" He then pulls out a simple cardboard replica of a cluster of grapes. Next is *phitza,* and so on.

How can you tell phonological awareness instruction from phonics instruction? Kindergarten teacher Patty Buchanan provided us with the following easy-to-remember response: Phonological awareness instruction can be provided in the dark. Why? Phonological awareness instruction is helping children *hear* the sounds in the language; phonics instruction is helping children associate sounds with letters. Therefore, for phonics instruction the lights must be on so that the children can see the print. Phonics instruction is a form of alphabet instruction. We discuss alphabet instruction next.

Alphabet Instruction

Alphabet identification in kindergarten is a strong predictor of later reading achievement (National Early Literacy Panel, 2008). In addition, research indicates that the phonemic awareness instruction is more effective when it is taught along with alphabet knowledge (Ehri et al., 2001). As discussed above, phonemes are not discrete units in speech (Adams et al., 1998). Instead, phonemes are influenced by adjacent sounds in words. Alphabet letters provide a concrete representation for the "elusive" phonemes that make up words. See Box 7.3 for typical alphabet knowledge standards.

What do children seem to be learning when they begin to name and write alphabet letters? By the time young children say the alphabet letter names, they have begun to make discoveries about the alphabet. Children who have had experiences with print come to understand that the squiggles on the paper are special; they can be named. Toddler Jed, for example, called all letters in his alphabet books or in environmental print signs either *B* or *D* (Lass, 1982). At this very young age, he had already learned that letters were a special form of graphics with names. Three-year-old Frank associated letters with things that were meaningful to him. He argued with his mother to buy him the *fire truck* (not just the car) because "It's like me!" He pointed to the *F*. (Incidentally, his argument was successful.) Giti pointed to the *z* on her blocks and said, "Look, like in the zoo!" (Baghban, 1984, p. 30). These three young children have learned to associate letters with things important to them.

Shayne Piasta and Richard Wagner (2010) suggest that alphabet knowledge can be divided into five subskills: "letter name knowledge, letter sound knowledge, letter name fluency, letter sound fluency, and letter writing" (Piasta & Wagner, 2010, p. 10). To this list, we add letter identification. Alphabet identification involves being able to point out a letter that someone else names. For example, a teacher might ask a child to point to the letter *c* on an alphabet frieze (a chart that lists all of the letters in alphabetical order). Alphabet naming requires naming a letter that someone else points to. For example, the teacher could point to

BOX 7.3 **Typical Alphabet Knowledge Standards**	Understands that letters of the alphabet are special visual graphics that have a name Identifies all upper- and lowercase letters Names all upper- and lowercase letters Names the letters in his or her name Makes sounds associated with some letters

the letter *c* on the alphabet chart and ask, "What's the name of this letter?" Of these two skills, naming is the more difficult. Letter name fluency involves assessing how quickly children can name letters. While some studies assess the speed with which children are able to name letters as an outcome measure, we do *not* recommend implementing activities in preschool or kindergarten classrooms with this as a goal. Alphabet instruction should be embedded in developmentally appropriate activities, not in "drill and kill children's interest" activities. Like Piasta and Wagner, we include phonics—the study of letter–sound relationships—as an alphabet knowledge outcome. Once children have developed phonemic awareness and have begun learn to identify the letters of the alphabet, they can begin to learn the sounds that are associated with those letters. So we have categorized phonics as the most advanced aspect of alphabet learning. Many pre-K and kindergarten teachers make phonics the capstone of their teaching of each letter. What often happens in large group phonics instruction with 4-year-olds is that children with good phonemic awareness learn letter–sound relationships as a result of this teaching, whereas children who are slower in developing phonological processing skills will receive extra exposure to letters and their names. This is not necessarily bad, as long as the teacher understands what each child is expected to get out of the instruction. Of course, a preferable alternative is to use small group instructions tailored to needs of individual children.

Should early childhood teachers expect all children to identify and name all letters of the alphabet by the time the children are 5? Certainly not! However, state early childhood academic standards always include alphabet knowledge as a key instructional outcome. For example, the Arizona Early Learning Standards and the 1999 reauthorization of Head Start (*Good Start, Grow Smart,* 2002, p. 8) both specify that, by the end of preschool, children should be able to *name* at least 10 letters of the alphabet. The more recent Common Core State Standards (2010) suggest that by the end of preschool, children should be able to recognize and name *all* upper- and lowercase letters of the alphabet. This is a tall task indeed! So building alphabet knowledge does need to be a key component of early literacy programs.

While it is generally accepted that alphabet knowledge should be an instructional objective, there is some controversy over which specific letters to teach and the order in which to teach them. Some argue that different letters should be taught to each child. For example, Lea McGee and Don Richgels (2008) believe that it is preferable to teach letters that match children's current interests and activities. To deliver this type of individualized alphabet instruction, teachers need to observe closely to learn about the types of contexts in which children notice letters (e.g., environmental print, computer keyboards, books, friends' T-shirts). These contexts provide wonderful opportunities for informal talk and instruction about the alphabet.

Examples of "informal" alphabet learning activities include

- *Environmental print:* Bring environmental print items to class (empty cereal boxes, cookie bags, and the like) and encourage children to read the print's message and discuss prominent letters (e.g., the letter *C* on a box of corn flakes).

- *Reading and writing children's names:* As discussed in Chapter 4, printed versions of children's names can be used for a variety of functional purposes, including attendance charts, helper charts, sign-up lists, and so on. Names of classmates have inherent high interest. Take advantage of every opportunity to read these names and to call attention to letters in the names ("Look, Jenny's and Jerry's names both start with the same letter. What letter is it?").

- *Traditional manipulatives:* Many traditional early childhood manipulatives can be used to support children's alphabet letter name learning. These manipulatives include alphabet puzzles, magnetic upper- and lowercase letters, felt letters, letter stencils, and chalk and chalkboards.

- *Writing:* Whenever children engage in writing, on their own or with a teacher (e.g., shared writing), their attention can be drawn to the letters of the alphabet. Remember that even if children are using scribbles or another personalized form of script, they are attempting to represent the letters of alphabet and thus are learning about letters.

- *Alphabet books:* Many types of alphabet books are available. For young children who are just learning the alphabet, books with simple letter–object associations (e.g., illustrations that show a letter and objects that begin with the sound associated with the letter) are most appropriate (Raines & Isbell, 1994). Alphabet books offer an enjoyable way to introduce children to letters and the sounds they represent. Research has shown that repeated reading of ABC books can promote young children's letter recognition (Greenewald & Kulig, 1995). It is also beneficial for children to make their own personal alphabet books (Strickland & Schickedanz, 2009). These child-made ABC books typically have a letter at the top of each page. Children then draw pictures and/or cut and paste illustrations of objects that begin with the sound of each letter. They can also write any words they know that contain the target letter. An adult can label the pictures.

■ *Making letters:* Young children enjoy finger painting letters; painting letters on the easel or on the sidewalk on a hot day with a brush dipped in water; rolling and folding clay or Play-Doh to make letters; and making and eating alphabet soup, puzzles, or pretzels. All of these activities provide meaningful, playful contexts within which young children can learn alphabet names.

Other researchers recommend that the alphabet be taught in a systematic order to all children, using more direct forms of instruction. Two basic assumptions underlie this position. First, it is assumed that it is difficult for teachers to individualize alphabet instruction for all the children in their classroom. If this individualization is not done effectively, some children will "fall through the cracks" and not learn much about the alphabet. Second, it is assumed that there is a logical sequence for alphabet instruction. Some letters should be taught before others. For example, Treiman and Kessler (2003) discovered that young children learn letters in about the same order. For example, *O* is one of the easiest letters for children between the ages of 3 and 7 to recognize. Letters such as *D, G, K, L, V,* and *Y* are more difficult for children and typically are among the last children recognize. Hence, McGee (2007) recommends that letters be taught in sets of three, starting with sets of uppercase letters that are the most different from each other (C, O, and T). Teaching several letters at one time helps children learn to discriminate between the shapes of letters.

We strongly recommend a blended approach, providing children with the individualized, informal forms of alphabet learning already described plus systematic instruction on selected letters. The order of the letters can be based on ease of learning or on other curriculum factors. For example, teachers may wish to focus on letters that fit with the stories and experiences highlighted in the curriculum. If the class is going to take a field trip to the fire station, for example, it might be an ideal time for them to learn the letter *F*. This letter will be encountered

Direct, systematic instruction on selected letters promotes alphabet knowledge

on the field trip, in shared reading of books about fires and firefighters, in play activities connected with the theme, and in shared writing.

The following are some of the strategies that we recommend for direct instruction on the alphabet.

Songs

The alphabet song is the way children are most often introduced to letters at home (Adams, 1990). While there are some advantages to learning the names of letters in this fashion (e.g., the names give children a peg on which to attach perceptual information about letters), the song can also lead to misconceptions (e.g., that *lmnop* is one letter). In addition, Schickedanz (1998) argues that learning to recite the alphabet from memory is a trivial accomplishment that contributes little to children's learning to read. Yet the influential report by the National Research Council (Burns, Griffin, & Snow, 1998) suggests singing the alphabet song as one of many activities early childhood teachers should use to support children's literacy learning.

Other songs can also be used to help children learn the alphabet. For example, Marla Chamberlain, who teaches at the San Luis Preschool in Arizona, uses a song with the lyrics

> *Can you find the letter ____?*
> *The letter ____?*
> *The letter ____?*
> *Can you find the letter ____,*
> *Somewhere in this room?*

She writes the lyrics on five large pieces of tagboard with slots to hold different letters. The class currently is studying the letter M, so she has written this letter on four cards that can be placed in these slots. The song now becomes:

> *Can you find the letter M?*
> *The letter M?*
> *The letter M?*
> *Can you find the letter M,*
> *Somewhere in this room?*

Mrs. Chamberlain sings the song with the children and then waits for them to answer the question posed by the song. Most of the children hold up their hands. One child says "monkey," pointing to a picture of a monkey on a poster that has an upper- and lowercase M on it. Another child points to the class calendar and says "Monday." Because of the slots, this song chart can be used for practice in identifying all of the letters that the class studies.

Letter Charts

Letter charts contain a letter (usually its upper- and lowercase forms) and pictures of objects that start with the letter. Teachers can purchase or make these, using pictures from magazines, environmental print, and the like. As already described in the section on teaching alliteration, San Luis Preschool teacher Lisa Lemos systematically introduces her children to a letter and its sound every two weeks, using a published program, *Sound, Rhyme and Letter Time* (Wright Group, 2002). This program provides a letter poster showing pictures of objects that begin with a "target" letter. For example, the letter *S* poster has pictures of a sun, seal, sailboat, sandwich, sand, sunglasses, and a seashell. During the first week, Mrs. Lemos focuses on the sound of the letter, helping children realize that all of the objects on the chart start with the same sound, /s/. She also helps children come up with other words that start with the /s/ sound. During the second week, Mrs. Lemos teaches children about the letter *S*. She begins by reviewing the words represented on the poster, reminding the children that all these words begin with the /s/ sound. Next she writes a label for each picture on a Post-it Note, with the first letter in a different color, and places the labels on the pictures. She points out that all of the words start with the same letter, *S.* Next Mrs. Lemos removes the labels from the poster and has the children put the labels back on the chart next to the corresponding object. When they do this, Mrs. Lemos asks them to say letter name, letter sound, and whole word. This is repeated over several days so that all of the children get several turns. By using this two-week routine with each letter, Mrs. Lemos is helping her children develop phonemic awareness, letter recognition, and phonics.

Alphabet Word Walls

A word wall is a collection of words displayed on a classroom wall that is used for instructional purposes. In an alphabet word wall, large upper- and lowercase letters are arranged on the wall in alphabetical order, and words that begin with each letter are posted below. Each day, one or two special words are selected for placement on the word wall. These words can come from the stories, rhymes, songs, and poems that the class is reading. They can also include children's names, familiar environmental print, and words from thematic units, and they are placed under the letters that they start with. At the pre-K level, teachers often include a picture to go along with each printed word. Picture supports tend to get phased out in kindergarten. The teacher can use the words on the word wall to reinforce letter identification and letter naming. Lisa Lemos uses her word wall during transitions from large group to small group instruction. She asks each child to point to a letter that she says (letter identification), or she will say the name of a letter, hand the pointer to a child, and ask the child to point to the letter (letter naming). Each child gets a turn before going to the next activity, and Mrs. Lemos helps those who have difficulty. Usually children can quickly point to or name the letters because the pictures that go with the words and the familiar environmental print give helpful clues. Trade Secrets 7.3 describes how a kindergarten teacher makes use of an alphabet word wall to teach letters and their sounds.

Games

Games are frequently used in SBRR instruction to provide children with the practice needed to consolidate and retain the skills that are being taught through direct instruction. When practice activities are put into a game format, skill practice can become fun and enjoyable for children. They will persist at games much longer than activities such as worksheets and workbook exercises. On the day that author Jim Christie was observing Martha Vasquez's syllable segmenting instruction described at the beginning of this chapter, Ms. Vasquez had also planned an alphabet game for her preschoolers to play during center time. The game involved fishing for letters that were on little replicas of fish. The children would catch the fish with magnets on strings suspended from small poles. One of Mrs. Vasquez's assistant teachers, Christian Garibay, stationed himself in the dramatic play area so that he could scaffold the children's play with the letters. When children caught a letter, he would ask them to name it. What was remarkable is that a group of five boys spent more than 30 minutes engaging in this letter-naming practice.

At the San Luis Preschool, teacher Lisa Lemos has her children play a game that combines alphabet practice with the traditional "A tisket, a tasket, a red and yellow basket" song. A small group of children sits on the floor, and Mrs. Lemos gives one of them a letter carrier hat and a small basket that contains large pieces of poster paper, each with a letter written on it. While the children sing the "tisket, tasket" song, the "mail carrier" walks around the group and gives one child a letter from the bag. The child who receives the letter then must say the name of the letter. Then this child becomes the mail carrier. Again, the game format and make-believe role-playing ensure high levels of child engagement.

Researcher Judy Schickedanz (1998) recommends two alphabet games that are particularly useful in reinforcing young children's growing alphabet knowledge:

■ *Alphabet-matching puzzles,* in which the children match loose letter tiles with letters printed on a background board;

■ *Alphabet clue game,* in which the teacher draws part of a letter and then asks children to guess which letter he or she is thinking of. After children make their guesses, the teacher adds another piece to the letter and has the children guess again.

TRADE SECRETS 7.3

An Alphabet Word Wall

At the beginning of the kindergarten year, Mrs. Burl begins each school day by asking her class to share any print items they brought from home. These items are usually packages or wrappers from products the children's families use at home. She asks each child who brought an item to read the name of the item to the rest of the class. After the children have read their environmental print, Mrs. Burl selects one of the products, Aim toothpaste, and asks the children where they think the Aim toothpaste container should go on their ABC word wall. The children think for just a moment when Anissa suggests cutting the wrapper into two parts—one part for *Aim* to go under the letter *Aa* on the word wall and the second for *toothpaste* to go under the letter *Tt*. Mrs. Burl asks the class for a thumbs-up (for yes) or thumbs-down (for no) vote. The children give her a unanimous thumbs-up. Mrs. Burl quickly cuts the package, circles the appropriate words, and asks the

child who brought the wrapper to pin each word under the correct letter on the word wall.

The word wall concept allows teachers to stimulate children's awareness of words and knowledge of letters and sounds (Morrow, Tracey, Gee-Woo, & Pressley, 1999; Wagstaff, 1998). Teachers may use a range of word wall activities to reinforce and support young children's growing phonemic abilities and reading skills. Mrs. Burl begins the kindergarten year with an ABC word wall that focuses on the initial letter sounds. Later, when the children's awareness of the sound–symbol relationship grows, she will add blends and consonant digraphs to the ABC word wall (see Figure 7.2).

Mrs. Burl found the word wall concept to be useful for teaching a variety of minilessons and stimulating the children's interest in words and reading. She also found that parents are interested in the word walls because they provide an ongoing visual record of the many lessons Mrs. Burl uses to teach alphabet knowledge and phonemic awareness to her students.

FIGURE 7.2   A Kindergarten ABC Word Wall

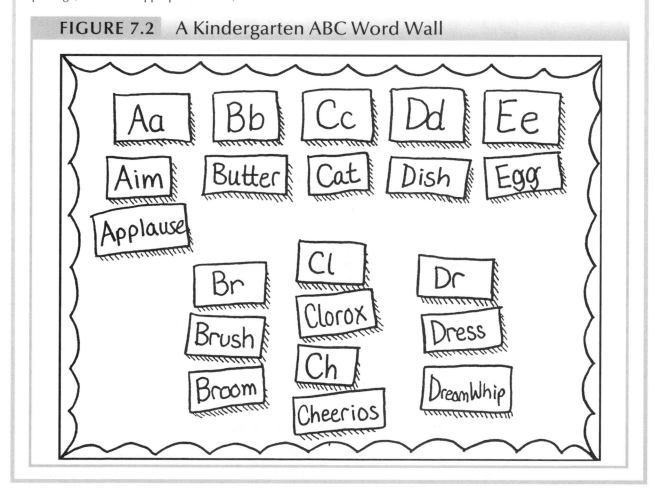

What kinds of alphabet instruction has research found to be most effective? Piasta and Wagner's (2010) extensive review of the current research suggests that school-based instruction had a greater effect on children's alphabet knowledge than home-based instruction, and small group instruction, rather than individual tutoring, had the greater effect on children's alphabet knowledge. Unfortunately, their review did not reveal conclusively exactly how teachers should promote children's alphabet knowledge development. Therefore, teachers are encouraged to use a range of activities, like those described above.

Phonics Instruction

Phonics involves using the alphabetic principle (letters have a relationship with the sounds of oral language) to decode printed words. Young children differ greatly in their need for instruction in this important decoding skill. Stahl (1992, p. 620) explains: "Some will learn to decode on their own, without any instruction. Others will need some degree of instruction, ranging from pointing out of common spelling patterns to intense and systematic instruction." Thus, as in all other aspects of literacy instruction, it is important for phonics teaching to match the needs of individual students.

The children who learn phonics more or less on their own simply need to be provided with the types of meaningful reading and writing activities described in Chapters 4, 6, and 8—functional literacy activities, literacy-enriched play, shared reading, and shared writing. As these children engage in these purposeful literacy activities, they gradually discover the relationship between letters and sounds.

Those who need a moderate amount of assistance profit from what Morrow and Tracey (1997) term "contextual instruction." This type of instruction occurs in conjunction with the same types of activities described in the preceding paragraph—shared reading and writing, literacy-enriched play, and functional literacy activities. The only difference is that while children are engaging in these activities, the teacher draws children's attention to letter–sound relationships that are present.

Morrow and Tracey (1997, p. 647) give an example of how one teacher, Mrs. M., drew her students' attention to the letter *M* and its sound during an activity that involved both shared writing and functional writing:

Because her class had finished putting on a show for their grandparents, Mrs. M. thought it would be a good idea if they wrote a thank-you note to the music teacher who assisted them with the performance. The note was composed by the students with the teacher's help. She wrote the note on the board and sounded out each word to help the students with spelling. After they finished writing, Mrs. M. read the entire note and had the students read the note aloud:

Mrs. M.: How should we start this letter?

Student: Dear Mr. Miller.

Mrs. M.: Very good. [as she writes] "Dear Mr. Miller" has three words. *Dear* is the first word, *Mr.* is the second word, and *Miller* is the third word. I just realized that my name and Mr. Miller's name both begin with the same letter, *M.* Let's say these words together, "Mr. Miller, Mrs. Martinez."

This type of spontaneous teaching can occur in connection with all the literacy learning activities described in Chapters 4 and 6. Of course, such teaching requires a teacher who is on the lookout for teachable moments involving letter–sound relationships. Because most, if not all, preschool and kindergarten classes contain some children who need moderate assistance, we recommend that teachers make an effort to take advantage of these types of teaching opportunities when they arise.

Another way to help children acquire knowledge about phonics is through writing (IRA/NAEYC, 1998; Stahl, 1992). Once children have reached the invented spelling stage in their writing development, they begin to use their knowledge of letter names and letter–sound relationships to spell words. During this stage, children spell words the way that they sound rather than how they are conventionally spelled. For example, a child may spell the word *leave* with the letters *lev* because this is how the word sounds. When children use invented spelling, their attention is naturally focused on letter–sound relationships.

Research indicates that temporary use of invented spelling can promote children's reading development (IRA/NAEYC, 1998). For example, a study by Clarke (1988) found that young children who were encouraged to write with invented spelling scored higher on decoding and reading comprehension tests than children who were encouraged to use conventional spelling.

Finally, teachers can provide preplanned phonics activities to children who have developed an awareness of the sounds that make up spoken words and who can recognize some of the letters of the alphabet. This can be done by adapting the phonemic awareness, letter recognition, and word recognition activities discussed earlier in this chapter so that they focus on letter–sound relationships. We recommend selection of letter–sound relationships that fit in with ongoing class activities or that fit the needs of specific children, rather than using an arbitrary sequence (consonants first, short vowels second, long vowels third, and so on).

Several of the phonemic awareness activities described earlier in this chapter can easily be modified to teach phonics by having children identify which letters represents the various sounds and then writing words so that children can see the letter–sound relationships:

■ *Letter–sound matching:* Show pictures of familiar objects (cat, bird, and monkey), and ask children which begins with the /m/ sound. Then ask which letter *monkey* starts with. Write the word on the chalkboard. Ask the children for other words that start with the /m/ sound, and write these words on the board.

■ *Letter–sound isolation:* Pronounce words, and ask children what sounds are heard at the beginning, middle, or end. For example, ask the children, "What sound is in the middle of *man, cat,* and *Sam?*" Once the sound is identified, ask the children what letter represents the sound. The words can then be written on the chalkboard, along with other short-*a* words.

In a similar fashion, letter recognition activities can be modified to teach phonics by shifting the focus from letters to their sounds:

■ *Environmental print:* Discuss letter–sound relationships that occur in environmental print. For example, if children have brought in cereal boxes from home, the teacher could ask questions such as "What letters make the /ch/ sound in Cheerios?" Children could then be asked to identify other words that start with the /ch/ sound, and these words could be written on the chalkboard.

■ *Reading and writing children's names:* When referring to children's names in attendance charts, helper charts, and other places, call children's attention to letter–sound correspondences in their names. For example, the teacher might say, "Jenny's and Jerry's names start with the same sound. What letter do both their names start with?"

■ *Games:* Create games that enable children to reinforce their growing knowledge of letter–sound relationships in an enjoyable manner. A popular type of phonics game requires children to match letters with pictures that begin with letter sounds. For example, the letter *b* might be matched with a picture of a bird. If you use this type of phonics matching game, be sure to tell the children the word that each picture represents to avoid confusion with other words that the picture could represent. In the example of the *b/bird* item, a child might justifiably believe that the picture of bird represented the word *robin* or *sparrow* rather than *bird.*

Word walls, previously discussed in the section on alphabet knowledge, can also be invaluable aids in helping children learn phonics. The words displayed on a word wall are familiar to children and often have strong personal significance and meaning. These high-meaning words can serve as pegs on which children can attach letter–sound relationships. Teachers should routinely take advantage of these words by linking them with phonics activities and lessons. For example, if children already can identify and name the letter *r,* a teacher may decide to help them learn the *r* letter–sound correspondence by asking them to find words that start with /r/ sound on the word wall (as opposed to finding words that begin with the letter *r*).

Many children will need more direct instruction on letter–sound relationships, but not during the preschool years. Preschool and kindergarten children who need extensive help learning phonics really need more experience with phonemic awareness, letter recognition, and informal types of phonic instruction described in this chapter. These activities will build a foundation that will help these children benefit from more systematic approaches to learning phonics later.

BOX 7.4

Typical Print Awareness Standards

Identifies the front and back covers of books

Knows what the author and illustrator do for books

Follows words from left to right and top to bottom

Understands that words are separated by spaces in print

Understands how speech maps onto print

Print Awareness Instruction

According to the National Research Council (1999, p. 27), "a child's sensitivity to print is a major first step toward reading." Print awareness is a broad term that refers to children's ability to recognize print, ranging from contextualized environmental print (e.g., the word *Cheerios* on a cereal box) to decontextualized written words (e.g., the print in a children's book). Print awareness also encompasses concepts about print, including book concepts (author, illustrator, title, front, back) and conventions of print (directionality, capitalization, punctuation). Research has shown that young children's knowledge of concepts of print is moderately correlated with reading ability in the primary grades (National Early Literacy Panel, 2008), and thus "concepts of print" is an instructional objective of SBRR instruction. See Box 7.4 for typical print awareness standards.

In other chapters, we describe a number of strategies that can be used to promote print awareness, such as functional print (Chapter 4), literacy-enriched play (Chapter 4), shared reading (Chapter 6), and shared writing (Chapter 8). Trade Secrets 7.4 describes another way that shared reading can contribute to children's print awareness. In this strategy, teachers use "print-salient" books and make reference to print during story reading.

In the sections that follow, we describe how print awareness can be taught through direct instruction and the key word method.

Teaching Concepts about Print

Although concepts about print instruction are strongly associated with the emergent literacy approach, print concepts also receive attention in SBRR programs. For example, Early Reading

---

TRADE SECRETS 7.4

Selecting Print-Salient Books

Sonia Cabell and her colleagues (2008) suggest that teachers need to include an explicit focus during storybook reading on print. Laura Justice and Helen Ezell (2009) suggest two approaches for teachers use: Select print-salient books for reading, and incorporate print references in reading interactions.

Print-salient books are books where print is a key component of the design of the book; these are books that make print worth talking about. Some examples include: *Chicka Chicka Boom Boom* by Bill Martin Jr. and John Archambault (1989), *Click, Clack, Moo: Cows That Type* by Doreen Cronin (2000), and *The Crunching Munching Caterpillar* by Sheridan Cain (2000). While reading any book, teachers can do such things as track the print, point to the print within the illustration, and ask questions, like "What do you think I'm reading, the pictures or the word?" or "This word

says 'Danger!'" or "This is the letter *S,* just like in your name," or "What is this letter?" Print-salient books offer special opportunities to invite children to attend to the print in the book. For example, in *Click, Clack, Moo: Cows That Type*, the cows write Farmer Brown a letter demanding electric blankets. One whole page is the letter from the cows to Farmer Brown. Another page contains a letter from the cows telling him that the hens want electric blankets also; they, too, are cold! On other pages, print is embedded into the illustration. For example, on one page, a hen holds a sign "Closed. No milk. No eggs." The hens are on strike. On other pages the word *moo* is enlarged and in bold print. The book provides many opportunities for the teacher to draw the children's attention to its print.

Including print referencing strategies into adult-child or children storybook reading interactions is important to do because when teachers do not reference print during their storybook reading children do not attend to the print in the storybook (Justice, Bowles, & Skibbe, 2006).

First projects are required to teach "print awareness" by providing print-rich classroom environments and teaching book concepts during shared reading. So even though Early Reading First has its roots in the SBRR approach, it also makes use of effective emergent literacy strategies.

Some teachers in Early Reading First projects who are firm believers in the SBRR philosophy also use more direct forms of instruction to teach concepts about print. Head Start teacher Connie Felix uses this approach to help her children in San Luis, Arizona, learn the distinctions among pictures, words, and alphabet letters. Mrs. Felix has prepared a large chart with three columns labeled Picture, Word, and Letter. An example of each is pasted next to the label (e.g., there is photograph next to the label *Picture* and a written word next to the label *Word*). She has put a number of cards into a bag. Each card contains an example of a picture, word, or letter. She begins by explaining each of these concepts. The children are very interested, and several quickly recognize the examples that Mrs. Felix has provided ("That's an *A*," and "It's *cat*"). Children take turns drawing a card out of the basket. When each has drawn a card, he or she tells the class what is on the card, says to which category it belongs, and tapes it to the correct column on the chart. If a child struggles, classmates help out. For example, Angela picks a card with a classmate's name on it. She recognizes the name and says "Elian." Mrs. Felix prompts her with the question, "Which type is it? A picture, word, or letter?" When Angela does not respond, several classmates chime in, "It's a word." Angela then places the card in the correct column and feels proud that she has done this correctly.

Key Words

The key word strategy, developed by Sylvia Ashton-Warner (1963), is another excellent way to build young children's ability to recognize words. It is a very simple and elegant strategy: Children choose words that are personally meaningful and that they would like to learn to read. Real-life experiences, favorite children's books, writing workshop, and language experience stories are primary sources for these key words. Children learn to recognize these words quickly because of their high meaning and personal significance.

The key word strategy is often associated with emergent literacy because of its focus on personal meaning, learning by doing, and social interaction. However, the key word strategy also meets the specifications for an SBRR strategy because it involves direct instruction. It features teacher modeling, guided practice, and independent practice. We have included key words in this section because we believe that it is one of the most effective way to directly teach pre-K and kindergarten children to recognize whole words.

Here is how the key word strategy works: The teacher asks each child in the class to pick a favorite word that he or she would like to learn to read. This word is written on a large card while the child watches. (This is sometimes done in circle time so that the whole class learns about each child's key word.) The children then write their key words plus any other words that they remember. Finally, they engage in various games and practice activities with their key words. For example, all children may be asked to put one of their key words on the floor, upside down. The cards are then scrambled, and the children try to find their key words.

Veatch and her colleagues recommend that children collect key words and keep them in a box or on a ring file known as a "word bank." Another possibility is to have children keep their key words in a word book. In this variation, the teacher writes a word on a card for the child, then the child copies the word into his or her word book. Periodically, the teacher can have children review their words in their word banks or word books. Besides providing opportunities for children to practice recognizing key words, word banks and word books serve other valuable functions. They provide children with a concrete record of their reading vocabulary growth. It is very motivating for children to see their collections of words grow larger and larger. In addition, the words can be used to help children learn about letters and the sounds they are associated with. For example, if children are learning the sound associated with *b,* the teacher can have children find all the words in their collections that begin with that letter.

Trade Secrets 7.5 describes a variation of the word bank strategy in which children write their key words in a word book. Notice how the teacher, Bernadette Watson, prompts Amanda to use letter–sound relationships when she writes Amanda's key word, *elephant,* on the card.

TRADE SECRETS

7.5

My Word Book

Bernadette Watson

As the children entered the classroom, Ms. Watson greeted them, gave them a three- by five-inch card, and asked them, "What is your word for today?" Children answered. Amanda said, "Elephant." Ms. Watson positioned her hand to write elephant on the card. Before she wrote the word, she asked Amanda how she decided on this word as her word for the day. Amanda had seen a program on television about elephants the night before and had decided, right then and there, that elephant would be her word today.

"So," asked Ms. Watson, "what letter do you think *elephant* begins with?"

"I don't know," responded Amanda.

"It's an *E*," said Ms. Watson. "What letter is next?" She stretched the sound, "L-l-l-l-l."

Amanda responded, "*L!*"

"You're right," exclaimed Ms. Watson, "and then it's another *e*, and a *p-h-a-n*. And what do you think the last letter is? T-t-t-t-t."

Amanda said, "*T!*"

"Absolutely," said Ms. Watson.

Amanda took her card with *elephant* written on it with her and set off to locate her word book. Having found it, she sat at a table to copy her word into her book. First she drew a picture of an elephant. Above it, she copied the word *elephant*. At the beginning of the year, that is all she would have done. Now, she also wrote a sentence under the picture: "isnt.v" ("I saw on TV").

When she was done, Amanda took her book to the library center. Here she might read her words to herself or to a friend. The pictures she had drawn greatly help her remember her word for the day.

Strategies for Teaching English Language Learners: Vocabulary and Phonological Awareness

Young English language learners (ELLs) face a large task; they are charged with the task of acquiring a second language while simultaneously developing their first. A recent extensive review of the research on ELL children sponsored by the Institute of Education Sciences and the U.S. Department of Education reported that, despite a paucity of rigorous experimental research, sufficient evidence exists to provide five proven and practical strategies to improve early literacy skills with ELL children (Gersten, Baker, Shanahan, Linan-Thompson, Collins, & Scarcella, 2007, p. 2). These five strategies have been analyzed and reviewed by the *What Works Clearinghouse* (http://ies.ed.gov/ncee/wwc/):

1. Conduct formative assessments with English learners using English language measures of phonological processing, letter knowledge, and word and text reading.
2. Provide focused, intense small group interventions for English learners determined to be at risk for reading problems.
3. Provide high-quality vocabulary instruction throughout the day.
4. Provide curricula and supplementary curricula to accompany core reading and mathematics series . . . . Accompany with relevant training and professional development for the teachers.

5. Ensure that teachers of English learners devote approximately 90 minutes a week to instructional activities in which pairs of students at different ability levels or different English proficiency levels work together on academic tasks.

Note that these recommendations are closely related to the SBRR strategies discussed in this chapter. Instruction and assessment for ELL children should focus on the same "core" early literacy skills that are at the foundation of the science-based approach: phonological awareness, alphabet knowledge, print awareness, and vocabulary. Beyond the ideas recommended in this chapter (several researchers comment on the value of using the activities described in this book with *all* children), are there any evidence-based suggestions specifically for helping young ELL children develop these key language and reading skills?

Vocabulary. Theresa Roberts (2008) discovered that sending books home in the child's primary language for a caregiver to read while the teacher read the same book in English in the classroom helped low-income preschoolers whose primary language was Hmong or Spanish to learn a substantial number of words in English.

Eurydice Bauer and Patrick Manyak (2008) suggest that, to make language comprehensible to children learning a new language, teachers need to accompany oral explanations and read-alouds with visuals, realia, gestures, and dramatization to illustrate key concepts and vocabulary. Such a strategy, of course, is appropriate for use with all children.

(continued)

Researchers point out the importance of connecting learning with the learners' personal experiences (Bear, Invernizzi, Templeton, & Johnston, 2007). A strategy recommended is the use of cognates. When the English word is similar to the first language word (e.g., *colores* and *colors*), the teacher should highlight the similarities.

Phonological Awareness. David Dickinson and his colleagues (Dickinson, McCabe, Clark-Chiarelli, & Wolf, 2004) recommend teaching ELL children whose primary language is Spanish phonological awareness in Spanish; there is a strong transfer of performance on phoneme deletion and rhyme recognition from Spanish to English. What kinds of activities? Hallie Kay Yopp and Lilia Stapleton (2008) suggest engaging in sound play in the Spanish language (for example, pointing out the rhymes in songs and poems or substituting sounds in each repetition of a verse of a song), teaching tongue twisters, selecting Spanish books that "exploit the sounds of the language" (p. 379), including books like *Vamos a Cazar un Oso* (Rosen, 1993), *Albertina anda Arriba: El Abecedario* (Tabor, 1992), and *Los Nanas de Abuelita: Canciones de Cuna, Trabelenguas y Adivinanzas de Suramerica* (Jaramillo, 1994). Whether or not someone in the preschool speaks the child's home language, the parents should be encouraged to engage in these activities to support their children's reading development. And, of course, while reading parents can teach their children new words and concepts about print—all of the key language and literacy skills.

Family Focus: Creating a Book Nook and Author's Corner

Allison Mullady

Parents can help support children's emerging reading and writing skills at home by creating a book nook and/or author's corner. In the corner of a family room or child's bedroom, parents can gather all types of literacy materials. For instance, all the children's books and magazines can be collected and placed on a small bookshelf or placed in baskets for children to peruse.

Parents can include a rocking chair or large pillows to encourage reading.

Parents can also create an author's corner by collecting paper of all types and writing implements such as crayons, markers, and pencils. Some parents have even included safety scissors and tape to encourage more creative books. Parents then can include a writing place, using a small table and chairs. Children can write their own books that can be "published" and placed in the book nook.

Parents who create such special literacy places in their homes report significant increases of literacy activities and more opportunities to encourage young readers and writers.

Strategies for Teaching Children with Special Needs

Karen Burstein and Tanis Bryan

ON YOUR MARK

Teachers in preschools and kindergartens are increasingly likely to have students with special needs in their classrooms. Typically, the majority of these children have speech and/or language impairments, developmental delays, and learning disabilities. A smaller number of these children have mental and or emotional disturbances, sensory disabilities (hearing or visual impairments), and physical and health impairments. The latter reflects increases in the number of children surviving serious chronic conditions (e.g., spina bifida, cystic fibrosis) and attending school as well as increases in the number of children with less life-threatening but nonetheless serious health (e.g., asthma) and socio-cognitive (e.g., autism) problems.

Public policy and law, including the 1997 Individuals with Disabilities Education Act (IDEA), along with humane and ethical considerations, dictate that children with disabilities receive optimal educational programs, given our knowledge bases and resources. Further, IDEA stipulates that children with special needs be provided their education in classes with their age-same peers to the greatest extent possible.

One of the primary goals of early education is to prepare all young children for general education classrooms. Making this a reality for children with

(continued on next page)

(continued)

special needs requires that teachers make accommodations and adaptations that take into account the individual student's special needs. Teachers' willingness to include students with disabilities and their skillfulness in making adaptations are critical determinants of effective instruction. This special feature outlines strategies and suggestions for teachers who have young students with special needs in their classrooms. Our purpose is to provide suggestions for making adaptations so that teachers feel comfortable, confident, and successful including these students in their classrooms.

GET SET

Cognitive, physical, sensory, developmental, physical, emotional—there are so many variations in development! It is not reasonable to expect general education teachers or special education teachers to be experts on every childhood malady. The primary lesson to remember is that children are far more alike than they are different from one another. Whatever their differences, children desire and need the company of other children. They are more likely to develop adaptive behaviors in the presence of peers. Children with special needs can succeed academically and socially in mainstreamed settings (Stainback & Stainback, 1992; Thousand & Villa, 1990).

Setting the stage for an inclusive classroom takes somewhat more planning. Effective planning includes input and support from the school administration, other teachers, parents of children with special needs, and possibly the school nurse. Early and frequent collaboration with your special education colleagues is particularly helpful. There are significant differences between general and special education teachers' perspectives on curriculum and methods of instruction. Sometimes they differ in expectations for children.

Collaboration works when teachers constructively build on these different points of view. For collaboration to work, teachers have to respect different points of view, have good listening skills, and be willing to try something new. Here are some strategies for collaboration:

- Attend the student's multidisciplinary team meeting.
- Keep a copy of the individual family service plan (IFSP) or individualized education plan (IEP), and consult it periodically to ensure that short- and long-term goals are being achieved.
- Arrange to have some shared planning time each week with others who work with students with special needs.
- Brainstorm modifications/adaptations to regular instructional activities.
- Identify who will collect work samples of specific tasks.

- Assess the student's language, reading, and writing strengths, and give brief probes each week to check on progress and maintenance.
- Share copies of student work with your collaborators, and add these artifacts to the student's portfolio.
- Collaborate with families. Parents are children's first and best teachers. Additionally, they possess personal knowledge of their children that far surpasses any assessment data we may collect.

GO

As previously mentioned, the majority of children with special needs have difficulties in language, reading, and written expression. Research indicates that these problems stem from deficits in short-term memory, lack of self-awareness and self-monitoring strategies, lack of mediational strategies, and inability to transfer and generalize learned material to new or novel situations. Hence, many students with special needs may have difficulty in classroom settings that use a high degree of implicit teaching of literacy. These students typically can benefit from explicit instruction. Here are some general teaching strategies that teachers can use to support students with special needs:

- Establish a daily routine on which the student with special needs can depend.
- Allocate more time for tasks to be completed by students with special needs.
- Structure transitions between activities, and provide supervision and guidance for quick changes in activities.
- Adapt the physical arrangement of the room to provide a quiet space free of visual and auditory distractions.
- Plan time for one-on-one instruction at some point in the day.
- Use task analysis to break learning tasks into components.
- Recognize the different learning styles of all students, and prepare materials in different ways—for example, as manipulatives, audio recordings, visual displays, and the like.
- Try cross-ability or reciprocal peer tutoring for practice of learned material.
- Consistently implement behavior change programs.
- Encourage all students to respect and include students with special needs in their academic and play activities.
- Establish a routine means of communication with parents.
- Locate strategies that help parents select materials that are developmentally and educationally appropriate for their students

Summary

This chapter describes a variety of developmentally appropriate strategies that teachers can use to directly teach children the skills needed to learn to read. Each skill has been found to be important to children's success as readers. What have you learned?

■ *What are the differences among phonological awareness, phonemic awareness, and phonics? In what sequence do young children typically acquire these skills? What does this sequence suggest about classroom instructional strategies?*

Phonological awareness (realization that spoken language is composed of words, syllables, and sounds) is broader than phonemic awareness (realization that words are composed of phonemes). Both are important for all young children to possess if they are to become successful readers. Whereas phonological and phonemic awareness just involve sound, phonics involves learning the relationship between letters and the sounds they represent. The instructional sequence now recommended by research is to begin by helping children build the basic concepts of phonological awareness, then to move toward helping children develop awareness that words are composed of phonemes, and finally to help children develop awareness of letter–sound associations. Therefore, the instructional sequence is from broad concepts to smaller and smaller units of sound.

■ *How might early childhood teachers introduce young children to the letters of the alphabet?*

We recommend that early childhood teachers use a combination approach to alphabet instruction. They should used "personalized" instruction to teach their young learners the names of the letters that match specific children's current interests and activities. For example, children can be taught to recognize letters in their names, friends' names, familiar environmental print, and print used in play settings. To deliver this type of individualized alphabet instruction, teachers need to observe closely to learn about the types of contexts in which children notice letters. Teachers should also teach the alphabet to the whole class in a systematic way, using songs, letter charts, ABC word walls, and games. This combination of personalized instruction and direct, systematic instruction will ensure that all children have an opportunity to learn to identify and name the letters of the alphabet.

■ *How can early childhood teachers reassure the public that they are teaching phonics?*

Some children seem to learn phonics on their own; teachers need to provide them with numerous meaningful reading and writing activities that will allow them to discover how our language works. Other children need some phonics instruction; teachers need to offer them the same kind of meaningful reading and writing activities and also need to draw children's attention to letter–sound relationships present in these activities—not once, but often. Teachers need to be alert to teachable moments for drawing children's attention to letter–sound relationships in many reading and writing activities. Remember, phonics instruction is appropriate only when children exhibit phonological and phonemic awareness.

LINKING KNOWLEDGE TO PRACTICE

1. Create descriptions of several developmentally appropriate phonological awareness activities, from the most basic concepts to the more advanced, that might be used with young children. Make copies of your activities for others in your class.
2. Create descriptions of several developmentally appropriate phonemic awareness activities for use with young children. Make copies of your activities for others in your class.
3. Create a description of several developmentally appropriate alphabet recognition activities for use with young children. Make copies of your activities for others in your class.

Go to the Topics Phonemic Awareness and Phonics, English Language Learners, and At Risk and Struggling Readers in the MyEducationLab (www.myeducationlab.com) for your course, where you can:

- Find learning outcomes for Phonemic Awareness and Phonics, English Language Learners, and At Risk and Struggling Readers along with the national standards that connect to these outcomes.
- Complete Assignments and Activities that can help you more deeply understand the chapter content.
- Examine challenging situations and cases presented in the IRIS Center Resources.

Go to the Topic A+RISE in the MyEducationLab (www.myeducationlab.com) for your course. A+RISE® Standards2Strategy™ is an innovative and interactive online resource that offers new teachers in grades K-12 just in time, research-based instructional strategies that:

- Meet the linguistic needs of ELLs as they learn content
- Differentiate instruction for all grades and abilities
- Offer reading and writing techniques, cooperative learning, use of linguistic and nonlinguistic representations, scaffolding, teacher modeling, higher order thinking, and alternative classroom ELL assessment
- Provide support to help teachers be effective through the integration of listening, speaking, reading, and writing along with the content curriculum
- Improve student achievement
- Are aligned to Common Core Elementary Language Arts standards (for the literacy strategies) and to English language proficiency standards in WIDA, Texas, California, and Florida.

Teaching Early Writing

When Carol was 3 and 4, she lived in California, and her beloved Grammy lived in Minnesota. Whenever her mother wrote to her mother, Carol wrote to her grandmother. When she had completed her letter, her mother always asked, "And what did you tell Grammy?" Carol pointed to the scribbles on the page, every scribble, and eagerly told her mother exactly what the letter said. Her mother listened intently, always ending with, "And you wrote all that?" Later, her clever mother inserted a slip of paper into the envelope telling Grammy the gist of Carol's message. Grammy's response to Carol's letter always arrived within a week or two. Carol and her mother snuggled together on the overstuffed green sofa to read Grammy's letter, over and over. When her daddy came home from work, Carol met him with "It's a Grammy letter day!" Then, she'd "read" Grammy's letter to her daddy.

Proponents of emergent literacy contend that children learn written language just like oral language. That is, children learn to read and write simply by having opportunities to see print in use and by engaging in activities where literacy is embedded in the task, just like Carol did in the vignette above. These people believe that children learn without ever knowing they are learning. This view supports the implicit teaching of literacy. Other educators believe that children need instruction to help them focus on the abstract features of our written language, like on letter names and sounds. This perspective supports the explicit teaching of literacy and is consistent with the newer view of literacy learning, the scientifically based reading research (SBRR) view. We believe both views hold merit. Children do need opportunities to see writing in use and to experience the purposes of literacy. Children also need to be directly taught about the functions and features of print. The key is that the activities and experiences that early childhood teachers offer young children must be appropriate for the children's age and stage.

In Chapters 4 through 7 we present the core components of a blended early childhood language and literacy program:

- Multiple language opportunities for children in various classroom contexts (e.g., circle time, learning centers, dramatic play, and language-centered activities) (Chapter 4);
- Interacting with teachers and peers (Chapter 5);
- Sharing of ideas in daily storybook readings by the teacher (Chapter 6);
- Opportunities for children to attempt to read books on their own in the library center (Chapter 4);
- Opportunities to respond to books that are read (Chapter 3 and 6);
- Functional reading and writing activities (Chapter 4);
- Literacy activities linked to play (Chapter 4); and
- Activities designed to explicitly teach early reading skills (e.g., phonological awareness, alphabet letter and sound knowledge) (Chapter 7).

Though some children seem to learn to write simply by engaging in meaningful writing activities, all children profit from some explicit instruction.

This chapter focuses on one other key component of a high-quality early literacy program: writing instruction. In this chapter we describe children's development as writers and provide several effective means for teaching children about writing: shared and interactive writing, writing workshop, and publication. We began the discussion of the teaching of writing to young children in Chapter 4 with the introduction of the writing center as an important center in the preschool and kindergarten classroom and the inclusion of paper and writing tools in all centers in the classroom. The instructional strategies described in this chapter illustrate how early childhood teachers provide their young learners with supports to help them get their ideas down on paper.

Teaching writing to young children has caught the attention of national and state officials, as evidenced in national and state standards. In Box 8.1, we provide examples of the kind of language used in national and state writing standards for young children.

BEFORE READING THIS CHAPTER, THINK ABOUT . . .

■ How you learned to write. Not handwrite, but write. Do you remember writing messages to special people, maybe messages that were lines and lines of scribble? Do you remember writing on walls, much to someone's dismay?

BOX 8.1 **Examples of National and State Writing Standards**	Use a combination of drawing and writing to compose narrative, informative, and persuasive texts.
	Share stories by dictating to an adult.
	With guidance and support from peers and adults, make changes (revisions) to written texts.
	Use technology to produce and publish writing.
	Use inventive spelling to present ideas.
	Produce scribbles and letterlike forms to represent words, convey ideas, or tell stories.
	Use writing to communicate for a variety of purposes and audiences.

FOCUS QUESTIONS

■ What are the key features of children's development as writers?
■ How does shared writing increase a child's understanding of print and facilitate reading development?

■ What is the difference between shared writing and interactive writing?

■ How does a teacher teach during a writing workshop?

■ Why is it important to publish children's writing?

■ How might teachers connect home with early care and kindergarten programs to support young children's development as writers?

BOX 8.2 **Definition of Terms**	**Focus lesson:** Whole-class lessons on writing that typically occur at the beginning of writing workshop **Interactive writing:** An extension of shared writing in which children share the pen with the teacher to write a text **Shared writing:** The teacher works with whole groups, small groups, or individual children to write down the children's oral language stories. These highly contextualized stories are easy for children to read **Writing workshop:** Scheduled time for writing, with the explicit teaching of something about writing in a focus lesson, writing time, and a group share time

Children's Development as Writers

How do children become writers? Over several decades, various researchers have watched young writers at work and play and reported their discoveries. Below we summarize their key findings:

■ *Children first learn about the purposes for writing through real-life experiences.* Reread this chapter's opening vignette. Carol learned about letter writing by watching her mother write to Carol's grandmother. In everyday family activity, Carol's mother wrote for other purposes: grocery lists, reminder notes, telephone messages, invitations, and more. Carol watched, learned about the purposes of writing, and occasionally wrote her own lists, notes, messages, and invitations.

■ *Context plays an important role in determining how young children write.* Karen and Marika are playing in the restaurant play setting in the dramatic play center. Marika is the waitress, with writing pad in hand. Karen, reading the menu, points and says that she wants a hamburger. Marika writes a line of linear scribble. Dashing to the chef, she shouts, "That customer wants a hangaburger, and she wants it right now." She tears the writing from the pad and tosses it aside. Her oral language carried the message, not the marks on the paper. Later in the choice time, Marika works at writing a message to her mother. Karen has invited her for a "play date." The teacher had prepared a "dictionary" of all the children in the class. Each page has a picture of a classmate with his or her name beneath it. Marika uses this resource to copy Karen's name. She asks her teacher, "How do you spell *house?*" The teacher helps her stretch the word to hear the sounds. Marika writes HS. Satisfied that her mother will know what this means, she carefully folds the paper and puts it in her backpack. Clearly, this writing is meant to communicate a message. Note how the context affects Marika's writing.

■ *Children understand the purposes for writing before they can produce conventional forms of writing.* The form of the writing refers to letter formation, spelling, and so forth. Carol wrote in an early form (linear scribble) to tell her grandmother what she had been doing in California. Marika wrote in an early form in the play context (linear scribble) and a more advanced form (invented or phonics-based spelling) in the writing center to tell her mother about a play date with Karen. Carol and Marika demonstrated that they are learning about the functions of written language, even though they cannot yet produce the form conventionally.

■ *Adults play an important role in children's development as writers.* Children's early experimentations with print are mindful of their babblings in oral language. Listening closely, a mother is certain she hears her baby say "Mama." Looking closely, a teacher will be sure she sees a correctly formed letter in a child's letterlike writing. When the adult, mother or teacher, responds enthusiastically to the child's writing, the child responds enthusiastically—and begins to try again. A print-and language rich-context and adults' positive response both work to shape the children's writing so that it resembles the writing of the society in which they live.

■ *Children learn about writing through explicit and implicit instruction.* The opening vignette shows how Carol learned about sending written messages by observing her mother (implicit instruction). Marika learned how to write her message to her mother by sitting beside her teacher who helped her match sounds with the correct symbols in the writing center (explicit instruction). Both kinds of instruction are needed: the explicit instruction of teaching a writing skill and the implicit instruction of observing others who know more engage in a writing event.

■ *"Children need many opportunities to write.* Quality early-childhood writing programs provide many opportunities for children to write independently. Inserting writing tools (paper and writing implements) into all classroom centers, not just the writing center, provides children with many opportunities to use what they know about the forms of written language to create a message.

These research-based features guide our recommendations on the design of a high-quality writing program in early childhood classrooms.

Even the youngest of children like to write—not only on paper, but also on walls and floors. Early childhood teachers, then, must take advantage of this natural urge by providing a variety of writing materials to their young writers, modeling writing through shared and interactive writing experiences, learning to ask the right question at the right time and providing the right instruction at the right time to nudge their young writers' development. Early childhood teachers need to provide children with many opportunities to experiment with creating their text for many different purposes. Before we explore the what and the how of writing instruction in an early childhood classroom, we begin by describing the early forms of children's writing.

Early Forms of Children's Writing

Traditionally, strict criteria have been used to define the onset of writing. Children were not considered to be writing until they had mastered correct letter formation and could spell words conventionally. Children's early tries at writing (scribbles or random groups of letters) were dismissed as insignificant and inconsequential.

As interest in emergent literacy increased during the 1970s, some researchers began focusing attention on these initial attempts at reading and writing (Clay, 1975; Read, 1971). It soon became clear that these early forms appeared to be purposeful and rule governed. Children appeared to construct, test, and perfect hypotheses about written language. Research began to reveal general developmental sequences, with the emergent forms of reading and writing gradually becoming more conventional with age and experience (Ferreiro & Teberosky, 1982; Sulzby et al., 1989).

EMERGENT WRITING. Building on the earlier work of Marie Clay (1975) and of Emilia Ferreiro and Ana Teberosky (1982), Elizabeth Sulzby asked preschool children to write stories and to read what they had written (Sulzby, 1985b, 1990). Based on this research, Sulzby (1990) identified seven broad categories of early writing: drawing as writing, scribble writing, letter-like units, nonphonetic letter strings, copying from environmental print, invented spelling, and conventional writing (see Figure 8.1).

These categories do not form a strict developmental hierarchy. While there is a general movement from less mature forms toward conventional forms, children move back and forth across these forms when composing texts, and they often combine several different types in the same composition. Quinn's writing in Figure 8.1 shows this type of form mixing. Perhaps the

FIGURE 8.1

Sulzby's
Categories
of Emergent
Writing

Drawing as writing—Pictures represent writing.

Message: My soup with a fork, spoon, and knife. It is ready to eat. (Zoe Fragkias)

Scribble writing—Continuous lines represent writing

Letter-like units—A series of separate marks that have some letter-like characteristics

The child began writing using letter-like units. In the last two lines, he switched to scribble writing.

Message: First, I ate at a restaurant. Then, I went to a place to take pictures. (Quinn Peters)

Nonphonetic letter strings—Strings of letters that show no evidence of letter-sound relationships

Message: I like books. (Zithlaly Velazquez)

(continued on next page)

FIGURE 8.1

(continued)

Copying from environmental print—Copying print found in the environment

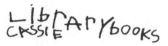

Message: Library books (Cassie Dong)

Invented spelling—Spelling using letter-sound relationships (This can range from using one letter per word to using a letter for several sounds in each word [as in the example]).

Message: I went to my Dad's work. (Quinn Peters)

Conventional spelling—Correct spelling for most of the words

Message: I put on nail polish. (Katja Pils)

first two lines of letter-like units refer to the first picture and the two lines of scribble writing refer to the second picture? Children also appear to adjust their form of writing to the task at hand. Kindergartners tend to use invented or conventional spellings when writing single words. When writing longer pieces of text, they often shift to less mature forms, such as nonphonetic letter strings or scribbles, which require less time and effort (Sulzby & Teale, 1991).

Sulzby cautions teachers against having unrealistic expectations of children's emergent writing capabilities. Case studies of early readers (Baghban, 1984; Bissex, 1980) might lead teachers to expect that invented spelling is a common occurrence among 4- and 5-year-olds. However, longitudinal research revealed that children's writing development is typically much slower, with invented spelling not arriving until late kindergarten for some and not until the end of first grade for others (Sulzby & Teale, 1991). Both groups of children (the early and the late spellers) are normal.

The typical preschooler, then, will not have sufficient skill in writing to capture everything he or she wants to say. So how do preschoolers communicate their meaning? They talk and they draw, with their writing, to share their ideas. In combination, through oral language, writing, and drawing, they say what they mean to say.

In the following sections, we describe a range of activities teachers of young children can use to support children's development as writers. Remember that these activities are in addition to the playful opportunities teachers provide children through infusing writing paper and tools throughout the classroom's centers and by having a writing center for children's use during center time (see Chapter 4).

Shared Writing

The language experience approach, which became popular in the 1970s (Allen, 1976; Veatch et al., 1979), has children read texts composed of their own oral language. Children first dictate a story about a personal experience, and the teacher writes it down. The teacher reads the story back to the children and then gives them the opportunity to read it themselves. Sometimes the children illustrate their dictated sentences. In recent years, this strategy has become known as shared writing.

The shared writing strategy is an excellent means for teachers to demonstrate the relationship between speaking, writing, and reading. It can help children realize that (1) what is said can be written down in print, and (2) print can be read back as oral language.

Like functional print and play-based literacy, the shared writing strategy presents children with a broad array of learning opportunities. At the most basic level, shared writing helps children learn that the purpose of written language is the same as that of oral language: to communicate meaning. For other children, the strategy enables teachers to demonstrate explicitly the structure and conventions of written language. The children watch as the teacher spells words conventionally, leaves spaces between words, uses left-to-right and top-to-bottom sequences, starts sentences and names with capital letters, ends sentences with periods or other terminal punctuation marks, and so on. This is an ideal means to show children how the mechanical aspects of writing work.

Shared writing has the additional advantage of making conventional writing and reading easier for children. By acting as scribe, the teacher removes mechanical barriers to written composition. The children's compositions are limited only by their experiential backgrounds and oral language. Reading is also made easier because the stories are composed of the children's own oral language and are based on their personal experiences. This close personal connection with the story makes it easy for children to predict the identity of unknown words in the text.

A number of variations of shared writing have been developed. In the sections that follow, four that are particularly appropriate for use with young children are described: the shared chart, interactive writing, individual experience stories, and the classroom newspaper.

The Shared Writing Chart

This strategy begins with the class having some type of shared experience: The class takes a field trip to a farm, to a zoo, across the street to the supermarket, to see a play; the class guinea

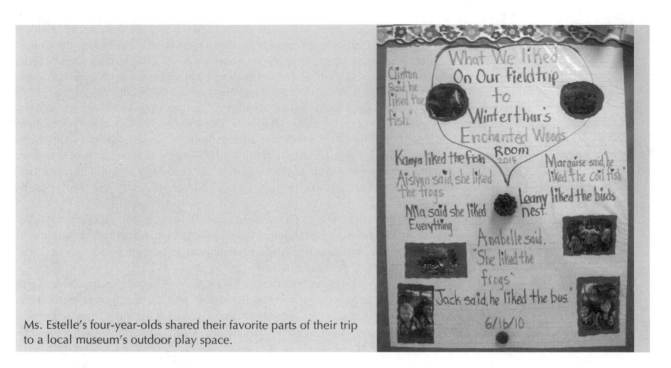

Ms. Estelle's four-year-olds shared their favorite parts of their trip to a local museum's outdoor play space.

pig has babies; the class completes a special cooking activity or other project. Whatever the event, the experience should be shared by many members of the group so that several children can contribute to the story.

The following is a description of how a teacher might engage children in a group shared story-writing experience:

Step 1 The teacher begins by gathering the children on the rug in the whole-group area to record their thoughts about the experiences—to preserve what they recall in print. Teachers often begin with a request to "tell me what you remember about . . . ?"

Step 2 As children share their memories, the teacher records exactly what the children say on a large piece of chart paper, using a felt-tip marker. The teacher does not rephrase or correct what a child says. The teacher records the children's language, just as they use it. The sentence structure, or syntax, is the child's. The spellings, however, are correct.

When doing shared chart stories, the teacher takes sentences from only a small number of students. Taking sentences from all the children would make the sitting time too long for the young learners. If a child's contribution is vague or unclear, the teacher might have to ask the child to clarify the point or may have to do some *minor* editing to make the sentence comprehensible to the rest of the class. The teacher must exercise caution when a child's contribution is in a divergent dialect (e.g., "He be funny."). Changing this utterance to so-called standard English may be interpreted as a rejection of the child's language. This, in turn, might cause the child to cease to participate in future experience stories. In such cases it is usually better to accept the child's language and not change it.

As the teacher writes the chart story, he or she can draw children's attention to a variety of key literacy skills. Below are examples of skills we have woven into our writing of shared writing charts with young children:

▪ "I'm going to start by writing our first word right here" (print concept, demonstrate that writing begins at the top left side of the chart).
▪ "I'm going to write from here to here." (print concept, demonstrate the left-to-right progression of letters and words).

Shared writing is an excellent way to teach the alphabet and concepts about print.

- "So, the sentence we want to write is *We went to the post office*. First I will write the word *We*. Now I will write the word *went*. Watch what I do before I write *went*. [print concept, move marker over to leave a space.] What do you see? What did I do?" (print concept, demonstrate spaces between words).
- Pause before writing a word, say the word slowly, and say *Ppppost*. What sound do you hear at the beginning of that word?" After children isolate the /p/ phoneme, ask, "What letter should I write for that sound?" (alphabet knowledge, demonstrate representing a sound with a letter).
- "Look! I wrote a whole sentence. How many words are in that sentence? Let's count them. Ah, 6 words!" (print concept, sentences are made up of words)

Step 3 When the whole story is created, the teacher rereads it from beginning to end, carefully pointing to each word and emphasizing the left-to-right and return-sweep progression. Then the class reads the story as a group (a practice called choral reading). Often a child points to the words with a pointer as the class reads.

Step 4 The teacher hangs the story in the writing center, low enough so interested children can copy the story. Because the teacher wrote the story on chart paper (teachers' preferred medium for group stories), the story can be stored on the chart stand and reviewed periodically by the class. Sometimes the teacher rewrites each child's sentence on a piece of paper and asks the originator to illustrate his or her sentence. The pages are then collected into a book, complete with a title page listing a title and the authors' names, and placed in the library corner. These books are very popular with the children. Other times, the teacher makes individual copies of the story—via photocopying or word processing—for each child.

Of course, shared writing can also be done with preschoolers. Trade Secrets 8.1 illustrates how Lisa Lemos did a group shared writing activity with her English language learners in her preschool class.

After a shared chart is reread several times, teachers can invite children to use the pointer to point to the words as they are read. Then, the teacher can invite children to circle the capital *W*, or draw a line under the longest sentence, or put a box around a letter that is in their name, or circle in red all the /r/ letters (say the letter sound) in the chart, and so forth. These types of activities are an excellent way to teach early reading skills in a meaningful context.

Interactive Writing

An extension of the shared chart strategy is known as interactive writing. A significant difference is that the teacher shares the pen with the children, inviting them to write some of

TRADE SECRETS 8.1

San Luis preschool teacher Mrs. Lisa Lemos links shared reading with shared writing activities. Today she has just finished reading the big book *There Was an Old Lady Who Swallowed a Fly*, by Simms Taback (Scholastic, 2000). It is one of the children's favorite books. Mrs. Lemos has decided to use the children's enthusiasm for the story as a stimulus for a group experience story, with a twist—it will be a group letter. Lemos starts the lesson by saying, "Maybe today we can write a letter to the Old Lady Who Swallowed the Fly. Who would like to help me write the letter?" Almost all of the children raise their hand and shout out, "Me! Me!" Lemos has already written the beginning of the letter at the top of a large piece of chart paper. She reads this to the children: "Dear Old Lady . . . " Then she says, "Okay, what do we want to say next?" She picks Dileanna, who says, "Don't eat a fly, and don't eat lots of candy." Mrs. Lemos writes down Dileanna's words, repeating them as they are written. Once she has written the words, Mrs. Lemos rereads Dileanna's sentence. Then she asks, "Why shouldn't she eat lots of candy?" and a child responds, "Because it's not good for us!" Mrs. Lemos then says, "What else can we say?" Keetsia volunteers, "Don't eat all of the animals," and Mrs. Lemos writes this down and reads it back to the class. As Mrs. Lemos writes *eat*, Nubia shouts out, "No, Mrs. Lemos, *eat* starts with a *t!*" Mrs. Lemos sounds out the word (/ē-t/) and says, "Yes, *eat* does

have a *t*, but it comes at the end of the word. *Eat* starts with the /ē/ sound. What letter makes that sound?" Several children respond *E*. The children continue contributing things that the Old Lady shouldn't eat: a cow and a spider. Then Mrs. Lemos asks, "Should we put anything else?" and several children mention healthy food. So Mrs. Lemos concludes the story with, "She should eat healthy foods." Nubia again helps with the spelling, pointing out that *healthy* starts with an *h*. Mrs. Lemos then rereads the story:

> *Dear Old Lady,*
> *Don't eat a fly, and don't eat lots of candy.*
> *Don't eat all of the animals.*
> *Don't eat a cow.*
> *Don't eat a spider.*
> *You should eat healthy foods.*

Then Mrs. Lemos writes, "From your friends," and reads it to the class. Dileanna says, "And our names so she knows." Mrs. Lemos responds, "That's a good idea. Each of you can come up and write your name so she knows who wrote this letter. Roberto, would you like to come first?" All of the children then take turns writing their names at the end of the letter. Finally, Mrs. Lemos says, "We're going to read our letter one more time," and reads it again with class. The children have figured out what the print says by this point and are able to read along fluently with Mrs. Lemos.

the letters and words on the chart paper. In Trade Secrets 8.2, Noreen Moore describes how a teacher uses a form of interactive writing, scaffolded writing, with her kindergartners. Ms. Sue used six steps to create the sentence:

1. The teacher and the children agreed upon a short sentence.
2. The children counted the number of words in the sentence on their fingers, putting up one finger for each word spoken.
3. The teacher counted the number of words in the sentence, putting up one finger for each word spoken.
4. The teacher drew a line for each word, repeating each word in the sentence as she drew each line.
5. The teacher invited a child to the chart paper to write a word on the first line. While the child wrote the word on the chart paper, each child wrote the word in his or her hand. (Had the child needed help, Ms. Sue would have stretched the word so the child could hear each of the sounds.)
6. The teacher and children repeated step 5 until the whole sentence was written.

Ms. Sue uses an interactive writing instructional strategy developed by Elena Bodrova and Deborah Leong (2007). Bodrova and Leong called it scaffolded writing. When teachers begin, they draw the lines for the words in the message, provide strong support to the children in the stretching of the words to hear the sounds in each word, and write the words on the lines. When the children become reasonably proficient, they invite the children to draw the lines and write a word on each line. The teacher provides as much support as the children need, just as Ms. Sue did in the description in Trade Secrets 8.2.

TRADE SECRETS 8.2

Scaffolded Interactive Writing

Noreen Moore

Ms. Sue's kindergarten class is clustered attentively around her on the colorful alphabet carpet as she finishes her read aloud of Robert Munsch's *Moira's Birthday*. Ms. Sue asks the children if they can make a text-to-self connection. Immediately hands bolt up the in the air, waving frantically; the children are anxious to share their connections between the text and their own birthdays. Lila describes her cake with pink flowers, Bryce talks about his cake shaped like Mickey Mouse, and Cameron recounts her birthday party at Build-a-Bear.

Ms. Sue takes this opportunity to engage in an interactive writing activity in which children write about their text-to-self connections. Because it is Bryce's birthday today, the children decide to write Bryce's text-to-self connection. Bryce shares his text-to-self connection with the class again. He proudly announces, "My cake was Mickey Mouse."

Ms. Sue asks the children to count the words in Bryce's sentence. All of the children count aloud using their fingers, "one . . . two . . . three . . . four . . . five," as Ms. Sue repeats the sentences and counts on her fingers, "My . . . cake . . . was . . . Mickey . . . Mouse." Next, Ms. Sue draws five lines,

representing each of the words in the sentence, on a piece of chart paper. As she draws the five lines, she repeats Bryce's sentence, "My . . . cake . . . was . . . Mickey . . . Mouse." With the lines clearly displayed, she invites individual children to go to the chart paper and write a word in Bryce's sentence. Jonathan approaches the chart paper first and writes "My" with a capital "M" because it is the first word in the sentence. As a child writes a word on the chart paper, the children sitting on the carpet write the word themselves using a pointer finger in one hand as the pen and the palm of their other hand as the paper. After each word, Ms. Sue praises the child who wrote the word on the chart paper and asks the children sitting on the carpet to show her the "writing" they did on the palm of their hands. The class continues in this way until Bryce's sentence is written.

Next, children write their own text-to-self connections independently at their tables. Many children have mastered drawing lines to represent the words in their writing. They use clothespin space men to help them leave spaces between words. Other children request Ms. Sue's help in drawing the lines to match the words in their sentence after they dictate it to her. Ms. Sue continues to circulate the room checking in on children and talking to them about their writing. Soon, all children have written a successful sentence and they are enjoying illustrating what they have written.

Individual Experience Stories

In an individual experience story, each student meets individually with the teacher and dictates her or his own story. As the child dictates, the teacher writes the sentence or story. Because the story is not intended for use with a group audience, editing can be kept to a minimum, and the child's language can be left largely intact. Once the dictation is completed, the teacher reads the story back to the child. This rereading provides a model of fluent oral reading and gives the child an opportunity to revise the story ("Is there anything you would like to change in your story?"). Finally, the child reads the story.

A variety of media can be used to record individual experience stories, each with its own advantages. Lined writing paper makes it easier for teachers to model neat handwriting and proper letter formation. Story paper and unlined drawing paper provide opportunities for children to draw illustrations to go with their stories. Teachers can also use the classroom computer to make individual experience stories. Children enjoy watching the text appear on the monitor as the teacher keys in their story. Word processing programs make it easy for the teacher to make any changes the children want in their stories. Stories can then be printed to produce a professional-looking text.

Individual experience stories can be used to make child-generated books. One approach is to write children's stories directly into blank books. Blank books are made of sheets of paper stapled between heavy construction paper or bound in hard covers. For example, during the last week of the program, Estelle Turner provided her Head Start children with photographs of each of them engaged in classroom activities over the year. The children selected and pasted photographs of interest to them onto pages in their book, one book for each child. Then, Estelle, her teacher assistant, and a volunteer recorded the children's comments on the appropriate page. This became a special history of their preschool year for them to share with their families. An alternative approach is to staple completed experience stories between pieces of heavy construction paper. For example, books can be made up of one student's stories ("Joey's Book") or of a compilation of different children's stories ("Our Favorite Stories" or "Our Trip to the Fire Station"). Child-authored texts can be placed in the classroom library for others to read. These books tend to be very popular because children like to read what their friends have written.

Individual experience stories have several important advantages over group stories. The direct personal involvement produces high interest and motivation to read the story. There is a perfect match between the child's experiences and the text, making the story very easy to read. Children also feel a sense of ownership of their stories and begin to think of themselves as authors.

The one drawback to this strategy is that the one-to-one dictation requires a considerable amount of teacher time. Many teachers make use of parent volunteers or older students (buddy writers) to overcome this obstacle. Another strategy is to have a tape recorder available for children to dictate their stories. Teachers can then transcribe the children's compositions when time allows. Of course, children miss out on valuable teacher modeling when tape recordings are used.

Classroom Newspaper

The classroom-newspaper strategy (Veatch, 1986) begins with oral sharing in which individual children discuss recent events that have happened to them. For example, Bobby might say, "We went to the lake, and I saw a big fish swimming in the water. I tried to catch it, but I fell in and got all wet." After five or six children have shared their personal experiences, the teacher picks several of the most interesting to put in the classroom newspaper. The teacher then writes these experiences on a piece of chart paper with the date on the top. The teacher rephrases the children's contributions, polishing them up a bit and converting them to the third person. For example, Bobby's contribution might be edited into the following: "Bobby and his family went to the lake. He tried to catch a large fish and fell into the water. He got all wet!" Note that Bobby's thoughts are preserved, but the text is transformed into third-person, newspaper-style writing.

Children then take turns reading the day's news. The charts can be saved and reviewed at the end of the week. Classroom news does not require a shared experience, making it easier to use this technique on a regular basis than to use the group-experience story. This technique also can give quite an ego boost to the children whose experiences are reported. For this reason, an effort should be made to ensure that all children get a turn at having their stories included in the news.

The classroom newspaper is an excellent way to help shift children from first-person narrative style used in individual and group styles to the third-person narrative styles used in many magazines and adult-authored children's books. We describe a variation of this strategy—daily time capsules news—in Trade Secrets 8.3.

TRADE SECRETS 8.3

Just before class is dismissed each day, Cyndy Schmidt asks her kindergartners what they have learned. As children tell their "significant learnings," she lists them on the chalkboard. Next, Cyndy asks the children to pick the one that they are most likely to remember next year. The item picked by the most children becomes the Time Capsule for that day. The Capsule item can be written, along with the day's date, on a large piece of construction paper and illustrated by student volunteers. These Capsules are permanently displayed on the classroom wall. By the end of the year, several rings of Capsules encircle the entire classrooms! Other teachers prefer to put Capsules into a book that is displayed in the library center. Daily Time Capsules can be reviewed occasionally with children to reinforce learning and to give them additional reading practice. Cyndy has found that these Capsules also make a very favorable impression on parents and others who visit the classroom.

The Writing Workshop

The writing workshop was first described by Donald Graves (1983) in his book *Writing: Teachers and Children at Work.* All members of the writing workshop meet to intensively study the art and craft of writing. The workshop typically has the following components:

- *Focus lesson:* A five-minute lesson to teach children about the writing process ("I want to make a change in my writing. I'm going to *revise.* Here's how I'll do it"); a procedural aspect of the writing program ("We help our friends while they write. We say things like, 'Tell me more about your dog. What color is he?'"); a quality of good writing ("I can tell more about my dog by adding his color, black. So I'll write 'I hv a blk dg.'"); a mechanical feature of writing ("Always make *I* a capital, a big letter."); or about why people write ("We need to make a list.").

- *Writing:* A 10- to 15-minute period during which children write and talk with peers and the teacher.

- *Group share:* A 10-minute period during which one or two children read their writing pieces to the group and receive positive feedback and content-related questions.

While the writing workshop was originally designed for the elementary grades, it can be easily adapted for use with younger children. Here is an example of how one kindergarten teacher has used the workshop approach to help her students develop as writers.

Focus Lessons

Focus lessons are short lessons that explicitly teach the children about an aspect of writing. Kindergarten teacher Bernadette Watson uses focus lessons to teach her students how to match letter sounds with the correct letter symbols. In one lesson, she helped the children sound out the spellings of the words in the sentence "I went to New York." She stretched the words out (e.g., w-e-n-t) and focused the children's attention on the sound of each letter ("What letter makes the /w/ sound?) or letter cluster ("How about /ent/?). Because she knows that her children would not fully understand the relationship between sounds and symbols as a result of one lesson, Ms. Watson weaves the content of this lesson into many lessons and reinforces this understanding when she talks with her young writers about their writing.

Writing Time

The focus lesson is followed by a time for the children to write. While the children write, the teacher meets with the young writers about their writing. The opportunity to talk while writing is a critical component of writing workshop. The talk is about the content and the mechanics (usually the letter–sound relationships) of the piece. Through conferences, teachers can give one-on-one instruction, providing the child with just the right help needed at that minute.

Group Share Time

The workshop is culminated by group share time. During the group share session, two or three children sit, one at a time, in the author's chair and share their pieces with the other writers in the class. Typically, the other children are gathered at the sharing writer's feet, listening attentively while the writer reads the piece, preparing to make comments or ask questions. The following describes one group share in Ms. Bernadette Watson's kindergarten classroom:

> ***Demetri:*** "I like your story."
>
> ***Ms. Watson:*** "Remember, Demetri, when we talked about how we tell the writer what we really liked about his or her story? Can you tell Aaron what you liked about his story?"

> *Demetri:* "I really liked the part where you thought you would get a dog, because I want
> a dog, too."
>
> *Aaron:* "Thanks."

The classroom rule is that the writer calls on three children for a question or a comment. The first response is a comment. The other two must be questions. Ms. Watson uses this time to help her children begin to understand the difference between a comment (statement or sentence) and a question. Learning the difference takes lots of practice.

Aaron calls on another child, Luisa, for a question.

> *Luisa:* "Did you draw your picture and write, or write and draw your picture?"
>
> *Aaron:* "I drew the pictures and then wrote." [Aaron calls on Bill.]
>
> *Bill:* "I know how to spell *to*. Do you?"

Aaron is unsure how to respond to Bill's question. He writes a string of letters with no match to letter sounds. According to Elizabeth Sulzby's categories of emergent writing, Aaron's writing is representative of the nonphonetic letter strings.

Ms. Watson understands his confusion and comes to his rescue. She asks, "Bill, can you write *to* on the chart paper for us? [Bill eagerly displays what he knows.] Listen to Aaron's sentence. *I want to get a dog.* Count the number of words in Aaron's sentence." Ms. Watson says the sentence and raises a finger for each word: *I want to get a dog.* [Children respond correctly.] What Bill is saying is that Aaron's third word, *I want to,* is written *t-o.* Should we add that to our word wall? Then you can look at the word wall when you need to write the word *to* in your sentences. [She takes a three- by five-inch card, writes *to* on the card, and ceremoniously adds it to the classroom word wall.] Thanks so much, Aaron and Bill. We learned about Aaron's hope for a birthday present and how to write the word *to* today. Who else would like to share?"

Through group shares, young children learn that writing is meant to be shared with others. Writers write to communicate their thoughts and ideas with their readers. Young children also learn about the how of sharing with others (reading in a loud voice so others can hear, holding their writing so others can see) and about the difference between a question and a comment. Teachers use children's texts and questions and comments as a context to teach about writing.

Some teachers bring a chair unlike any other in the room into the classroom (e.g., a stool, a rocker, a stuffed chair) to serve as the author's chair. When the children or the teacher read to the group, the reader sits in this special chair.

Bernadette Watson's writing workshop is not unlike that described by Eileen Feldgus and Isabell Cardonick in their book, *Kid Writing: A Systematic Approach to Phonics, Journals, and Writing Workshop* (1999). In such writing workshops, teachers explicitly teach such skills as phonemic segmentation, letter-sound associations, onset-rime knowledge—all in the context of children's meaningful written messages.

In Trade Secrets 8.4, we describe how one kindergarten teacher uses Kid Writing in her kindergarten classroom.

Ms. Emerson's children write, share, and publish. Ms. Emerson celebrates what they can do, verbalizing that they are doing ("Oh, you made a capital *B* there, didn't you?), and seems always to be telling the children what good writers they are. She claims that nothing she does is "original"; she borrowed all her ideas from Feldgus and Cardonick. She encourages every teacher of young children to use *Kid Writing*. Kindergarten children can write, and the children in her classroom prove the accuracy of her belief.

How do teachers get writing workshop started? Kathryn Brown (2010) began writing workshop in her kindergarten classroom by inviting the children to explore books. She asked them to consider what they noticed about the books. Her children noticed that books had a title, authors and illustrators, pages, words, photographs, and so forth. With that, Brown gave the children blank books and encouraged them to write and be sure to include all of the elements they had noticed in the books they had just examined. Later she introduced short lessons and conferenced with her young writers as they wrote their books. When books were finished, the children shared their books from the Author's Chair. In this way, Brown filled her kindergarten classroom with writers, young authors.

TRADE SECRETS

8.4

Kid Writing

The children in Ginny Emerson's kindergarten classroom are writers. Several years ago Ms. Emerson "converted" to Eileen Feldgus and Isabell Cardonick's (1999) *Kid Writing* program. As Feldgus and Cardonick suggest, Ms. Emerson introduces her children to written language through journal writing in a writing workshop format.

This classroom is rich with functional print. Ms. Emerson pays particular attention to posting words that the children might need in their writing. For example, the light switches are labeled *Up* and *Down*. The attendance chart is labeled *Boys* and *Girls*, with space for the children to sign in each day. The inside of the classroom door is labeled *Inside*; the outside is labeled *Outside*. Ms. Emerson often reminds the children to use the classroom print as a resource, asking, for example, "Where can you find the word *outside* in our classroom?" There is a word wall. The categories are letters of the alphabet. The words listed are high-frequency words, arranged alphabetically. Words are added to the "Words We Use a Lot" word wall as Ms. Emerson introduces them during minilessons (what some people call focus lessons).

Ms. Emerson watches her young writers to learn what minilessons they need. When she noticed that the children often needed the /ing/ sound in their writing, she followed the Kid Writing authors' suggestion and made a crown with /ing/ written on it. Each day during the writing workshop, a child is assigned to be the "King of /ing/." The child proudly wears the /ing/ crown. When the young writers want to write "shopping" or "going," they use the King of /ing/ to help them remember how to write /ing/. The "Star of are" wears a hat with a star and the word *are* written on it. There is also a "Wiz of is" moving about the classroom.

All this activity, of course, comes after Ms. Emerson gets her *Kid Writing* program going, shortly after the first day of school. To kick off the program, she follows the description of the first day of writing found in *Kid Writing* (p. 33). She demonstrates for the children different ways of writing, from wavy lines to zigzag writing to magic lines to letterlike forms that resemble alphabet letters to alphabet letters. The children "write" in the air. With every stroke they make, Ms. Emerson reinforces what they know with encouragement such as, "You are such great wavy-line writers!" She follows this lesson with a lesson on using a sound (the first, most prominent sound) to write a word. Many subsequent lessons help children stretch out words, listening to the sounds, much like Bernadette Watson's focus lesson. Other lessons, for example, teach children how to use a dash as a placeholder for a word they cannot spell or about using rime to help them spell.

Teachers want to provide young children with opportunities to write for many different purposes and to use different forms (or modes) of writing. Maggie Murphy modeled writing a letter (a form or mode) to stay in contact with people (a purpose) in the writing center. Nancy Edwards demonstrated writing a list (a form or mode) to help her remember (a purpose) in a writing workshop group lesson. In this section, we describe two kinds of writing that are particularly beneficial for beginning writers: dialogue writing and pen pals.

Dialogue Writing

By the time children are 4 or 5 years old, most have become quite proficient at oral dialogue. Teachers can capitalize on this strength by engaging children in written conversations (Watson, 1983). In written conversations, the teacher and child use shared writing paper or dialogue journals to take turns writing to each other and reading each other's comments. This strategy makes children's writing more spontaneous and natural by helping them see the link between written and oral language. In addition, the teacher serves as an authentic audience of children's writing, providing motivation for engaging in the writing process.

The teacher initiates these written conversations by writing brief messages to each student, who in turn reads what the teacher has written and writes a response back to the teacher. The teacher then reads these responses and writes additional comments, and this continues in a chainlike fashion.

Teachers usually begin by making declarative statements about personal experiences rather than by asking children questions. Questions have a tendency to result in brief, stilted replies from children (similar to their oral responses to verbal interrogation by a teacher). For example,

Teacher: Did you do anything nice over the weekend?

Child: No.

On the other hand, when teachers write personal statements to the children, they respond more spontaneously. Nigel Hall and Rose Duffy (1987, p. 527) give the following example:

> *Teacher:* I am upset today.
> *Child:* What is the matr with you?
> *Teacher:* My dog is sick. I took her to the vet, and he gave her some medicine.
> *Child:* I hop she get betr sun did the medsn wok?

Obviously, it is helpful if children can use legible forms of invented spelling to write their messages. However, this strategy can be used even with children who are at the scribble or well-learned unit (random streams of letters) stage of early literacy. With these children, a brief teacher–child conference is needed so that children can read their personal script messages to the teacher.

Pen Pals

Once children get used to engaging in written conversations with their teachers, they will naturally want to engage in written exchanges with their peers. Miriam Martinez and Bill Teale (1987) describe how a "postal system/pen pal" program was successfully implemented in several Texas early childhood classrooms. Children in the morning half-day classes wrote weekly letters to pen pals in the afternoon classes; children in full-day programs were assigned pen pals in other full-day program classrooms. Children were purposely paired with partners who used different writing strategies. For example, a scribble writer was matched with an invented speller. Letters were exchanged once a week and placed in mailboxes located in the writing center. A teacher or aide was at the center to assist in cases where children received letters they could not read. Teachers reported that student response was overwhelmingly positive. Here, real audiences and real purposes for writing are provided.

Publishing Children's Writing

To publish with young children is to take their written texts and do something special with them. To publish is to make the writing public, to present it for others to read. There are many different ways to publish young children's writing. For example:

- Ask each child to bring a clear, plastic eight- by eleven-inch frame to school. (Of course, frames must be purchased for those children whose parents cannot provide them.) Have the children publish their work by mounting their selected pieces, one at a time, in their frames. Hang the frames on the back wall of the classroom on a Wall of Fame.
- String a clothesline across the classroom. Using clothespins, clip the children's writings to the clothesline.
- Punch a hole in the upper left corner of several pages. All pages may be construction paper pages. If not, include a piece of colored construction paper or poster board on the top and bottom of the pile of pages for the book's cover. Thread string, yarn, or a metal ring through the hole to hold the book together.
- Ask each child to bring a light-colored T-shirt to school. (Again, teachers will need to provide T-shirts for children whose parents cannot provide them.) Invite the children to use laundry marking pens and markers to write and illustrate their stories on their T-shirts.
- Purchase a low-cost photo album with large, stick-on plastic sleeves. (These can be found at discount stores and occasionally at flea markets or rummage and garage sales.) Place one page of each child's writing in one of the plastic sleeves. The same photo album can be used over and over as one piece of writing can be substituted for another piece of writing. Occasionally, all children might write on the same topic, and a class book might be created on this topic (e.g., a field trip to the apple orchard). Preserve these special books for the children's reading and rereading.
- While engaging in a special experience, take photographs of the children. Glue the pictures to pieces of colored construction paper. Ask each child to select a photo. Ask the

child to write about the chosen picture on a piece of white paper. Cut the white paper into an interesting shape, and mount it on the construction paper below the photo. Laminate each page, and put the pages together with spiral binding. (Teachers might wish to type and mount the conventionally spelled version of the child's writing on the paper along with the child's personal script. Be sure to include both versions of the writing. If a child's script is not included, the child writer often does not recognize the writing and cannot read the print.)

■ Cover a large bulletin board with bright paper or fabric. In large cut-out letters, label the bulletin board something like "Young Authors" or "Room 101 Authors." Divide the bulletin board evenly into rectangular-shaped sections, one section for each child in the class, using yarn or felt-tipped marker. Label each section with a child's name. Encourage the children to mount one of their pieces of writing in their special section each week. A staple or pushpin might be used to mount the writing.

These are but a few of the many ways that children's writing might be published. We repeat: Publishing with young children means making their writing public—available for others to read. It is important to note that it is developmentally inappropriate to require young children to revise or recopy their writing, though sometimes they are willing to add to their text. Most young children do not have the attention span or interest to make revisions or to recopy the text.

If the child's writing is a personal script—that is, if it is a form of emergent writing that needs the child's reading for meaning to be constructed—the teacher might elect to include a conventionally spelled version of the message with the child's personal script version. As noted above, it is important to include the child's personal script version on the page with the conventionally spelled version to avoid taking ownership from the child.

Handwriting

So far, we have focused on providing young children with opportunities to write. What about handwriting? Drilling young children on how to form the letters of the alphabet correctly is a developmentally inappropriate practice, though certainly teachers can provide a child with explicit instruction when it is requested (Schickedanz & Casbergue, 2009). (p. 37)

Forming letters correctly requires a good bit of manual dexterity, something most young children are developing. Teachers should provide young children with numerous opportunities to engage in activities that help develop their dexterity, like puzzles, sewing cards, table games, cutting, and drawing. Models of appropriately formed letters should be available for the children's reference. This means that teachers should correctly form the upper- and lower-case letters when writing for and with the children, and an alphabet chart of upper- and lower-case letters should be available at eye level for the children's use in the writing center. When children have achieved some control, the teacher might work one-on-one with them.

Because the letters in a child's name are the most important alphabet letters to children, teachers will want to provide many real reasons for children to write their names. For example, signing in each morning is a real reason to write one's name. Early in the year, an effective strategy is to write each child's name on the top of a single sheet of paper. (With 3-year-olds, attach a picture of the child to the sheet for a few months to help with name recognition.) Spread the papers out on a table or two. The children's first task is to find the paper with their name (name recognition) and then to write their name under the model. (Three-year-olds may be able to manage writing just the first letter of their name early in the year, and their script may barely be recognizable as a letter.) Later in the year, the teacher might put blank pieces of paper on the table with a date stamp. The children write their name and stamp the paper with the date. A single sheet of paper then can be used for a whole week. Throughout the year, the teacher can provide one-on-one instruction in letter formation as the children write. Sample pages can be kept to provide a record of the children's handwriting growth over several months.

Children's writing of their name and attention to their classmates' names can spread across the day. Children can sign up for popular centers on chart paper posted outside the center. A child who is ready to move to another center is responsible for alerting the next child on the list of the availability of a space in the center. Similarly, children can sign up to be next for using the tricycles during outdoor play. Activities such as these provide meaningful reasons for learning to write the letters of the alphabet and opportunities for teachers to support children's writing of letters important to each of them.

Family Focus: Connecting Home with Early Care and Kindergarten Programs

Families write for real purposes and audiences regularly. Parents write notes or send e-mail or text messages to young children's older siblings, spouses, friends, relatives and others, reminding them that they'll be home later than usual or of an upcoming date, sharing stories of the day's special events, and so forth. They make lists of items to be collected at the food store. Timothy Rasinski and Nancy Padak (2009) suggest that teachers help parents discover how to use everyday events like these as opportunities for their young children to learn about the power of the pen (or keyboard). Rasinski and Padek prepared a list of ideas for teachers to share with parents of the kinds of writing purposes to which parents might expose their young children. With young children, teachers should encourage parents to describe the type of writing ("I'm making a list") and the purpose ("to help me remember what to get at the grocery store") for the writing. We present our version of their suggestions in Table 8.1.

Young children pay attention to these incidental, "teachable" moments. A rule in the Peters' house was "do not touch Mommy's computer." Thirty-month-old Lauren had watched her mother check and write e-mails since birth. One day, her mother discovered her banging on the keyboard.

Mom: "Lauren, what are you doing?!"
Lauren: "Checkin' my e-mail."

Back in the classroom, they make lists in the housekeeping center of what to purchase in the grocery store or of things they need to do. They write notes in the writing center asking friends to come to their house for play dates. Through incidental teaching at home and explicit teaching in the classroom, young children learn about writing for real purposes and audiences.

Families also are an important audience for children's completed texts. Teachers will send home copies of the shared writing charts, the individual language experience stories, the classroom newspaper, and independently written texts. Teachers should encourage parents to respond enthusiastically to these texts, read them over and over with the child, and place them in a visible place for others to comment about. Teachers might also involve parents in writing for their children. During an open house, Lisa Lang (Evers, Lang, & Smith, 2009), for example, asked parents to write for their children. The children beamed with pride as the pieces their parents had written to them were shared. (Wise teachers will write a note themselves for those children whose parents were unable to attend the open house.)

All children need writing materials at home, and unfortunately many parents face great financial hardships and cannot provide the writing materials each child needs. One way to increase children's access to writing supplies is for teachers to prepare writing briefcases that can be checked out as part of a classroom lending library. The briefcase can be an inexpensive plastic carrying case or a canvas portfolio. Inside the briefcase, the teacher may

TABLE 8.1 Types of Family Writing	Types of Family Writing	Examples of Authentic Purposes
	List writing	Make a list of errands to run, groceries to purchase, favorite books to collect from the library or DVDs from the video store
	Notes, e-mail, or text messages	Write a note on the calendar to remind themselves of birthdays that month, an e-mail to invite the child's grandparents to Grandparents' Day at preschool, send a text message to a sibling to remind him to be home by curfew time
	Journal/diaries	Write a summary of significant events of the day in the new sibling's baby book
	Letters	Write a letter to someone who doesn't live in the home telling about the day's events, write the address on the envelope, and mail it together from the post office

provide writing paper, colored construction paper, markers, pens and pencils, glue, tape—anything that might stimulate a child to write a story, make a greeting card, design a book cover, or create whatever he or she can imagine. Depending on the size of the class, teachers may have seven or eight writing briefcases—enough so that four or five children may check out the materials each day, and two or three extras so that the teacher has time to replenish the briefcase supplies frequently and conveniently. The briefcases are numbered, and each has a library pocket and identification card. The checkout procedures follow the same routine as for library books. The writing briefcase may also contain explicit suggestions that encourage parents to use writing to communicate with their children.

Summary

This chapter and Chapter 7 deal with explicit literacy instruction. This chapter described a variety of developmentally appropriate strategies that teachers can use to directly teach children how to write. What have you learned?

■ *What are the key features of children's development as writers?*

In the early writing development literature, we identified several key features of children's development as writers: (a) Children first learn about the purposes for writing through real life experiences. (b) Context plays an important role in determining how young children write. (c) Children understand the purposes for writing before they can produce conventional forms of writing. (d) Adults play an important role in children's development as writers. (e) Children learn about writing through explicit and implicit instruction. (f) Children need many opportunities to write.

■ *What is emergent writing?*

On their way toward writing conventionally, young children construct, test, and perfect hypotheses about written language. Research has shown general developmental sequences, with children's early forms of writing gradually becoming more conventional with age and experience. These early writing forms are known as emergent. Children using all forms of writing are legitimate writers.

■ *How does shared writing increase a child's understanding of print and facilitate reading development?*

The shared writing strategy involves having the teacher write down stories that children dictate. These child-composed stories are a dynamic means to demonstrate the connections among talking, reading, and writing. As the teacher writes down the children's speech, the children immediately see the one-to-one correspondence between spoken and written words. The teacher also has opportunities to teach alphabet recognition and concepts of print. Because the children are the authors of these highly contextualized stories, they can easily read the stories. Shared writing strategies include chart stories, interactive writing, individual experience stories, and the classroom newspaper.

■ *What is the difference between shared writing and interactive writing?*

In shared writing, the children make up the story and the teacher writes it down. The teacher does all the writing. In interactive writing, the teacher "shares the pen," and both the teacher and children get to write. Interactive writing gives children an opportunity to write with teacher assistance.

■ *How does a teacher teach during a writing workshop?*

Each writing workshop begins with a focus lesson. The goal of these lessons is to teach children about some aspect of writing (e.g., how to make revisions, how to add describing words, or how to spell words). The focus lesson is followed by writing time. During writing time, the teacher talks with individual children about their writing. Here, the teacher might help a child stretch words to hear sounds, add details to the child's drawing, or talk with the child about the topic of the piece. Through conferences, the teacher provides one-on-one instruction. After the writing time, two or three children share their work with their peers and the teacher. Now the teacher and the other children can ask questions about the writing.

■ *Why is it important to publish children's writing?*

Publishing helps young children understand that they write so others can read their thoughts. Making young children's writing efforts public is important. The publishing process need not be complicated.

■ *How might teachers connect home with early care and kindergarten programs to support young children's development as writers?*

Families provide opportunities for children to be involved in writing for real purposes and audiences. At home, young children can see parents write lists, send notes or e-mail messages, record descriptions of special events, and write and send letters. Teachers can send texts written in the classroom home so children can share their writing with their families. Parents might write pieces for their children. Such activities build children's knowledge of the purposes of writing, the audiences for writing, and the children's enthusiasm for engaging in the writing process. Finally, one way that teachers might ensure that all children have access to paper and writing tools at home is to create writing briefcases.

LINKING KNOWLEDGE TO PRACTICE

1. Visit a kindergarten classroom during writing instruction time. How does what the teacher is doing compare with what you read in this chapter? Is the teacher implementing a writing workshop? What evidence is there that the children write regularly?
2. Collect samples of preschoolers' writing. Use Sulzby's emergent forms of writing to categorize the collected writing samples.
3. Use the shared writing procedures to write a shared writing chart with a group of children.

Go to the Topics Writing Development, English Language Learners, and At Risk and Struggling Readers in the MyEducationLab (www.myeducationlab.com) for your course, where you can:

- Find learning outcomes for Writing Development, English Language Learners, and At Risk and Struggling Readers along with the national standards that connect to these outcomes.
- Complete Assignments and Activities that can help you more deeply understand the chapter content.
- Examine challenging situations and cases presented in the IRIS Center Resources.

Go to the Topic A+RISE in the MyEducationLab (www.myeducationlab.com) for your course. A+RISE® Standards2Strategy™ is an innovative and interactive online resource that offers new teachers in grades K-12 just in time, research-based instructional strategies that:

- Meet the linguistic needs of ELLs as they learn content
- Differentiate instruction for all grades and abilities
- Offer reading and writing techniques, cooperative learning, use of linguistic and nonlinguistic representations, scaffolding, teacher modeling, higher order thinking, and alternative classroom ELL assessment
- Provide support to help teachers be effective through the integration of listening, speaking, reading, and writing along with the content curriculum
- Improve student achievement
- Are aligned to Common Core Elementary Language Arts standards (for the literacy strategies) and to English language proficiency standards in WIDA, Texas, California, and Florida.

Assessing Young Children's Language and Early Literacy: Finding Out What They Know and Can Do

Mrs. Saenz is observing 4-year-old Martine and Monique playing together in the post office center. The children are pretending to be post office workers and are busy sorting letters into a mail sorter (a plastic office sorter that is divided into 24 slots, each labeled with an alphabet letter sticker). As she watches the children put the letters in the slots, Mrs. Saenz notices that Martine is accomplishing this task by recognizing the first letter of each name, then matching it to the appropriately labeled slot. She also notices that Monique, who is learning English, is simply putting the letters into the slots without paying any attention to the names on the envelopes. After a few moments, Martine stops Monique.

Martine:	*No, Monique. Look at the name. See the big letter? That letter tells you to put it in this mailbox.*
Monique:	*What it say?*
Martine:	*It says B. I think it is for Bobby. See? [He puts the letter in the B mailbox.]*
Monique:	*Gimme. [She reaches for another letter.] What it say?*
Martine:	*It says R.*
Monique:	*[Thinking for a moment, she starts to sing the alphabet song. She puts her hand on each letter as she sings it.]*
Martine:	*That helps find 'em fast, uh?*

Mrs. Saenz carefully observes this interaction and makes brief anecdotal notes describing what Monique and Martine know and can do. This information will also help her to adjust instruction to better meet both children's learning needs.

In several of the preceding chapters we have presented strategies for implicit and explicit instruction in early literacy. While these instructional activities form the core of an effective language arts program, they cannot stand alone. Two other elements are needed to ensure that the instructional strategies meet the needs of every child in the class, assessment and adaptations of instruction for all children.

We begin this chapter by discussing the goals literacy professionals have identified as those that teachers should help their young learners meet. Then we consider the two general assessment approaches that teachers might use to gather information, ongoing or classroom assessment and on-demand or standardized assessment. We continue to believe in the power of ongoing classroom assessment and encourage teachers to use the various ongoing assessment strategies. However, since the publication of the earlier editions of this book, standardized assessments have become increasingly prevalent across the country, even in early childhood education. Therefore, we agree with Kathy Short, Jean Schroeder, Gloria Kauffman, and Sandy Kaser (2002, p. 1999): "Educators can no longer afford to ignore these tests since the results are often used to make life-altering decisions about students and curriculum and to evaluate teachers and programs."

BEFORE READING THIS CHAPTER, THINK ABOUT . . .

- How your teachers assessed your literacy progress. Did you take spelling tests? Did you read stories and answer comprehension questions? Did you ever evaluate your own progress?
- Your own experiences with standardized tests. Were you required to take a test like the Scholastic Aptitude Test or the Graduate Record Examination and score above a minimum level to gain admission to your undergraduate or graduate program?
- How information about your literacy progress was shared with your parents. Did your parents read your report card? Did your parents attend conferences? Were you involved in sharing information about your progress with your peers or parents?

FOCUS QUESTIONS

- What is important for teachers to know about children's literacy development?
- What are the two general approaches teachers might use to assess their children's literacy learning?
- What types of ongoing assessment tools are used to collect information about children's progress?
- What types of standardized tests are used to assess young children's language and literacy progress?
- How do teachers use the assessment data the collect? How do teachers share assessment information with parents?

BOX 9.1

Definition of Terms

Criterion-referenced test: A test used to compare a student's progress toward mastery of specified content, typically content the student had been taught. The performance criterion is referenced to some criterion level such as a cutoff score (e.g., a score of 60 is required for mastery).

Norm-referenced test: A test that is designed to compare one group of students with another group

On-demand assessment: A type of assessment that occurs during a special time set aside for testing. In most cases, teaching and learning come to a complete stop while the teacher conducts the assessment.

Ongoing assessment: A form of assessment that relies on the regular collection of children's work to illustrate children's knowledge and learning. The children's products are created as they engage in daily classroom activities. Thus, children are learning while they are being assessed.

Reliability: Consistency of the data; if the same test is administered to the same child on consecutive days, the child's score should be the similar

Standardized test: The teacher reads verbatim the scripted procedures to the students. The conditions and directions are the same whenever the test is administered. Standardized tests are one form of on-demand testing.

Validity: Extent to which an assessment really measures what it claims to measure

Determining What Children Know and Can Do

Instruction and assessment are intertwined in excellent literacy instruction. In the opening vignette, Ms. Saenz observed two children with differing levels of alphabet recognition. Ms. Saenz's careful observations are supported by developmental guidelines created by early childhood experts. She knows that though Martine and Monique differ in their ability to recognize alphabet letters, both are making remarkable progress. She also knows that as an English language learner, Monique has made tremendous strides. Further, Ms. Saenz's observations provide her with a better understanding of the different strategies (alphabet song and one-to-one letter matching) Monique is using to learn the name of each of these symbols. The lessons Ms. Saenz will teach tomorrow are guided by the observations she made of what and how her children learned today.

Ms. Sanez is sensitive to the challenges of accurately assessing Monique's language and literacy learning. She knows that the results from the assessment process can be used to make many vital decisions. She wants the conclusions she reaches about her English language learners' (ELLs') development to be valid.

In 2004, the National Association for the Education of Young Children and the National Association of Early Childhood Specialists in State Departments of Education prepared a joint position statement on curriculum, assessment, and program evaluation. These two major early childhood associations agreed that "reliable assessment [should be] a central part of all early childhood programs"; the purpose of assessment, these educators believe, should be to assess children's "strengths, progress, and needs" (NAEYC/NAECS-SDE, 2004, pp. 51, 52). What teachers learn from assessing their children today should determine what they teach tomorrow—the Assess-Plan-Teach-Assess model.

The primary purpose of early childhood assessment, then, is to improve instruction. According to Lorrie Shepard, Sharon Kagan, and Emily Wurtz (1998) the ongoing assessment of children's learning also serves the purpose of guiding teachers in their reflection on their teaching. Assessment helps teachers answer questions about the effectiveness of their curriculum and instruction.

However, increasingly administrators need to collect evidence to document the effectiveness of the instructional program and to assess the program's children's progress toward a set of learning goals. This is assessment, often called testing, for accountability purposes.

What Is Important for Teachers to Know about Children's Literacy Development?

Sheila Valencia (1990) and Grant Wiggins (1993) agree on a primary principle of assessment: Teachers must begin assessment by determining what they value. Teachers must answer these questions: What is important for us to know about our children's development as readers, writers, speakers, and listeners? What do these young learners need to know and be able to do when they exit the preschool years and enter kindergarten and when they exit kindergarten and enter the primary grades?

Today early childhood educators have a new resource to help them answer these questions. Early childhood educators (sometimes with parents, administrators, and higher-education faculty) in nearly every state in the United States have worked together to create language and early literacy standards (or *building blocks*, or *learning foundations*); various terms are used interchangeably. Pre-K standards have also been developed for other subject areas such as mathematics, social and emotional development, science, and social studies.

In addition, some national groups have defined standards or outcomes. For example, Head Start has developed an outcomes framework, defining six framework domains: listening and understanding; speaking and communicating; phonological awareness; print awareness and concepts about book knowledge; early writing; and alphabet knowledge. Two national groups, the National Governors Association and the Council of Chief School Officers, joined together and in spring 2010 released standards in English language arts and mathematics, starting at kindergarten. Readers can have access to the full set of common core state standards at *www.corestandards.org*. The writers of these national standards intended to clearly define what American students needed to learn in order to be prepared for success in college and careers.

In spring 2010, the two organizations began discussions with early childhood experts about creating zero to 5 standards (Gewertz, 2010).

While once there was considerable disagreement in the early childhood field regarding the appropriateness of child outcome standards, today the majority of educators recognize that standards are important because they express shared expectations for children. That is, the educators in each state or national group have agreed on what they value. Further, once stated, all educators have a common language for assessing children's progress toward those goals or outcomes. Not only do standards guide teachers' assessment of children's progress, but they also guide what teachers teach. They tell teachers what the public, parents, school district, or funding agency expect teachers to teach and children to learn (Bowman as referenced in Gewertz, 2010). What was at the heart of the disagreement? The fear was that standards would drive more academically oriented, teacher-directed instruction. Those features of high quality early childhood education (e.g., active learning, opportunities for creativity and imagination, time for socialization) would be replaced with a content-oriented, skill-based curriculum (e.g., paper-and-pencil and drill-on-skills activities). Further, the fear was that high-quality assessment that described a child's progress overtime would be replaced with a single test. Assessment for accountability would become the norm, rather than assessment to gather information on how to adjust the curriculum to meet each child's needs and to measure the curriculum's effectiveness.

We begin this section by exploring the most appropriate ways teachers might gather information about their children's literacy development. We describe the tools for the ongoing gathering of information about children's language and literacy learning, how to store information, and issues involved in interpreting and sharing the information gathered. Readers should know that it is generally believed to be more difficult to determine what young children know and can do than what older children know and can do. Both the nature of early learning and young children's developing language skills provide teachers and caregivers with assessment challenges.

Two Kinds of Assessment

Once teachers have decided what is important for them to know about their children's literacy development, they must then decide how to gather this information. Teachers use two kinds of assessment to measure their children's progress toward the achievement of the state standards, ongoing and on demand. Ongoing assessment occurs in the context of everyday instruction. It includes teachers carefully observing children at work and play during classroom activities, and studying collections of children's work. On-demand assessment, on the other hand, requires that teachers stop teaching to take a formal measure of language or literacy. On-demand assessment requires the teacher to use standardized procedures to gather samples of what their children know.

We begin by considering ongoing assessment because this is the kind of assessment used most frequently by teachers of young children. Engaging in this kind of assessment demands that the teacher be a very careful observer of young children.

Ongoing Assessment

Ongoing assessment relies on regularly collecting artifacts to illustrate children's knowledge and learning. "It is the process of gathering information in the context of everyday class activities to obtain a representative picture of children's abilities and progress" (Dodge, Heroman, Charles, & Maiorca, 2004, p. 21). The artifacts (the children's products) are produced by the children while they engage in their daily classroom activities, such as those described in every chapter in this book. The products of these activities, then, serve the dual purposes of instruction and assessment. Because teachers are gathering *samples* of children's work to illustrate what the children know and can do, ongoing assessment sometimes is called *work sampling*. Ongoing assessment differs from on-demand assessment in several ways:

▇ Children work on their products for varying amounts of time, and the procedures or directions often vary across the classroom or across classes in the building.

- What each child and the teacher select as evidence of literacy learning may be different, not only across the children in the school or center but also across the children in a teacher's class.
- The classroom teacher analyzes each child's performance on the tasks and makes judgments about each child's learning.
- The classroom teacher's judgments are used immediately to define the child's next learning goal. The assessment, then, has an immediate effect on instruction for each child.
- The assessment of the work produced over time in many different contexts permits the teacher and the child to gather more than a quick snapshot of what the child knows and is able to do at a given moment.

Ongoing assessment, then, permits both the teacher and the student to examine the child's knowledge and learning. Young learner Phyllis shares what this means as she uses her journal to describe her growth as a reader and writer:

> I comed to this school a little bit nervous, you know. Nothin'. [She shakes her head for added emphasis.] I couldn't read or write nothin'. Look at this. [She turns to the first few pages of her writing journal.] Not a word! Not a word! [She taps the page and adds an aside.] And the drawin's not too good. Now, look at this. [She turns to the end of the journal.] One, two, three, four. Four pages! And I can read 'em. Listen. [She reads.] Words! [Nodding her head.] Yup! Now I can read and write a lotta words!

Ongoing Assessment Tools

Phyllis's journal is one of several tools her teacher uses to gather information about Phyllis's literacy learning. Like Phyllis, her teacher can compare the writing at the beginning and at the end of the journal to learn about Phyllis's literacy development over time. Each tool used permits teachers to gather information about their children's literacy learning while the children perform the kinds of developmentally appropriate activities described in this book. Below we describe several of these tools.

- *Anecdotal notes:* These are teacher notes describing a child's behavior. In addition to the child's name, the date, and the classroom area, the specific event or product should be described exactly as it was seen and heard. The following is an example of an anecdotal note:

Martia 9/25
M. in the library center "reading" a page in a big book. As she reads, she points to the words. She runs out of words before she is done reading (each syllable = pointed to word). She tries again, and again, and again, and again. She leaves, shaking her head.

Teachers use many different kinds of paper (e.g., notepads, paper in a loose-leaf binder, index cards, Post-it Notes) to make anecdotal records of children's behavior. One technique some teachers have found helpful is to use a sheet of sticky computer labels. They put a child's name on each label. Through the week, they write short notes describing the children's behavior, much like the note above. At the end of the week, they remove the label and attach the note to each child's folder. The next week, they begin again with a blank computer label sheet. A benefit of the computer label sheets is that at a glance teachers can see which children have been observed and which have been overlooked.

Teachers use anecdotal notes to describe such behaviors as the processes children use while they write, the functions of writing children use while they play, and characteristics of children's talk during large-group time. Note that anecdotal notes describe exactly what occurred and what was said verbatim, with no judgment or interpretation applied.

- *Vignettes or teacher reflections:* Vignettes are recordings of recollections of significant events made after the fact, when the teacher is free of distractions. Because vignettes are like anecdotal notes, except that they are prepared some time after a behavior has occurred and are based on a teacher's memory of the event, vignettes are used for purposes such

Teacher observations of children's work provide important information about children's language and literacy progress.

as those identified for anecdotal notes. These after-the-fact descriptions or vignettes can be more detailed than anecdotal notes and are particularly useful when recording literacy behavior that is significant or unique for a specific child.

For example, kindergarten teacher Karen Valentine observed a child attempting to control his peers' behavior by writing a sign and posting it in an appropriate place. She did not have time to record a description of the child's behavior immediately. As soon as the children left for the day, she recorded her recollection of the event:

> For days Jamali had been complaining about the "mess" left by the children getting drinks at the classroom water fountain after outdoor play. "Look at that mess! Water all over the floor!" At his insistence, the class discussed solutions to the problem. While the problem wasn't solved, I thought there was less water on the floor. Evidently, Jamali did not. Today he used the "power of the pen" to attempt to solve the problem. He wrote a sign:
>
> BEWR!! WTR SHUS UP
> ONLE TRN A LITL
> (Beware! Water shoots up. Only turn a little.)
>
> He posted his sign over the water fountain. This was the first time I had observed him using writing in an attempt to control other children's behavior.

Vignettes, then, are recollections of *significant* events. Because teachers can write vignettes when they are free of distractions, they can be more descriptive about the child's concern that drove the literacy-oriented behavior, and they can connect this event to what is known about the child's previous literacy-oriented behaviors.

■ *Checklists:* Checklists are observational aids that specify which behaviors to look for and provide a convenient system for keeping records. They can make observations more systematic and easier to conduct. The number of checklists available to describe children's literacy development seems almost endless! In Figure 9.1, we provide an example of a checklist we have used to assess young children's book-related understandings. When children engage in storybook reading and shared readings (see Chapter 6), teachers can closely and systematically observe children's book-related behaviors and gather important information about children's literacy knowledge and learning. Readers will notice that we have identified the items on our checklist with an asterisk that are like kindergarten standards on the Common Core State Standards. When checklist items are linked to standards, teachers can regularly monitor children's acquisition of key language and literacy behaviors.

FIGURE 9.1

Checklist for Assessing Young Children's Book-Related Under-standings

_____ can
      (child's name)

	Date	Comments
Concepts about Books		
Handle a book without attempting to eat or chew it	_____	_____
Identify the front cover, back cover, and title page of a book*	_____	_____
Turn the pages correctly, holding the book upright	_____	_____
Recognize that the author writes the words and the illustrator draws the pictures*	_____	_____
Conventions of Print		
Follow words from left to right, top to bottom*	_____	_____
Point to where a reader begins reading on a page	_____	_____
Point to the print when asked, "What do people look at when they read?"	_____	_____
Find a requested letter*	_____	_____
Name a requested letter*	_____	_____
Count the number of words in a sentence	_____	_____
Ask questions or make comments about letters	_____	_____
Ask questions or make comments about words*	_____	_____
Read words or phrases	_____	_____
Comprehension of Stories		
Answer and ask literal questions about story		
Ask and answer questions about the details and events of a story*	_____	_____
Answer and ask inferential questions about story		
Ask "what do you think" questions	_____	_____
Asks questions about story or informative text	_____	_____
Use pictures to help to recall details*	_____	_____
Retell, including		
Setting*	_____	_____
Main character(s)*	_____	_____
Theme (what the main character wanted or needed)*	_____	_____
Ending	_____	_____
Sequence of events*	_____	_____
From beginning to middle	_____	_____
From middle to end	_____	_____
Connect information in stories to events in his or her life	_____	_____
Compare and contrast characters' actions in familiar stories*	_____	_____
Locate information in an informative book*	_____	_____
Tell the main ideas presented in an informative book*	_____	_____
Attitude toward Books		
Participate in book-sharing routine with caregiver	_____	_____
Listen attentively to a variety of genre	_____	_____
Voluntarily look at books	_____	_____
Show excitement about books and reading	_____	_____
Ask adults to read to him or her	_____	_____
Use books as a resource for answers to questions	_____	_____

FIGURE 9.2	Name _____		
Early Forms of Writing Developmental Checklist	Forms of Writing	Date(s) Observed	In What Context (eg., dramatic play, writing center, science center)?
	■ uses drawing (might be circular scribbles)	_____	_____
	■ uses drawing and writing	_____	_____
	■ uses linear scribble	_____	_____
	■ uses letterlike shapes	_____	_____
	■ uses random letters	_____	_____
	■ uses invented spellings	_____	_____
	■ uses conventional spellings	_____	_____

The most common writing checklist used in early childhood programs is a version of the early forms of writing scale readers read about in Figure 8.1. Several school districts and child care centers across the United States have transformed this continuum into a checklist for teachers use to track their children's progress toward conventional spelling. Figure 9.2 is an example of such an Early Forms of Writing Developmental Checklist.

Checklists are useful because they provide information that teachers can see at a glance, showing what children can do. Teachers have learned that (1) children sometimes engage in a behavior today that does not reappear for several weeks, and (2) many different variables (e.g., a storybook being read, other children in the group) can affect the literacy behaviors children show. Hence, teachers are careful to record the date of each observation and to use the checklist many times over the year in an attempt to create an accurate picture of their children's literacy development. Knowing when each child demonstrates each literacy accomplishment helps teachers and parents understand that individual child's pattern of development. Reading each child's checklist informs the teacher of the child's strengths and the instructional program that child needs. Collectively reading all children's checklists informs the teacher of the instructional needs of all the children in the class.

■ *Video and audio recordings:* One means of accurately assessing children's knowledge about and use of oral language is to record them talking. Below are guidelines we have used to gather video recordings:

■ Select an activity setting that encourages language interaction. (Dramatic play areas are a good place to start.)

■ Place the camera on a tripod and adjust the zoom lens so that it covers the main area where children will be interacting. Turn the camera on, and check it occasionally to make sure that the camera angle is capturing the significant action.

■ Do a trial recording to make sure that the equipment is working correctly and that the children's language is being clearly recorded. This trial will also help desensitize the children to the equipment.

■ View the recordings as soon as possible so that your memory can help fill in the gaps in unintelligible parts of the recordings.

This is the only way to truly capture the full richness of children's language—but then what? What should a teacher do after the sample has been gathered? The literature suggests that teachers make a verbatim transcription of what is said, along with detailed descriptions of the context in which the language occurred. The transcript can then be analyzed to determine the mean length of sentences used, which forms of language the child used, the pragmatic rules followed, and so forth (see Genishi & Dyson, 1984, for additional suggestions). Unfortunately, such endeavors are very time consuming and not practical for most teachers.

Fortunately, a number of more practical options are available for assessing children's oral language abilities. Each begins with the recording of the children's talk within a classroom context. To illustrate these options, we use an incident observed by two of the authors in a university preschool. Julia is a 4-year-old Korean girl who has been in the United States for about eight months. She participates in classroom activities, especially dramatic play, but rarely speaks either in Korean (she is the only child from Korea in the class) or in English. Chari, Julia's teacher, is playing with several other children at the time of the incident. Chari takes on the role of a customer and asks to use the toy phone in a post office theme center. She picks up the phone and makes a pretend phone call to Buddy, whose behavior is becoming very raucous. Chari says, "Ring, ring, ring . . . Buddy, there's a package waiting here for you in the post office." This is successful in re-directing Buddy away from the rough-and-tumble play that he had been engaging in. Julia is playing by herself in the housekeeping center, pretending to be a parent taking care of a baby (a doll). Julia overhears Chari's pretend phone call to Buddy, but she continues with her solitary play. A few minutes later, Julia picks up a toy phone in the housekeeping cen-ter, and says: "Ring, ring . . . Miss Chari, will you come over to my house?" This is Julia's first complete sentence used in the classroom!

As you review Figure 9.3, what skills has Julia demonstrated?

As Chari observes the videotape after the children have departed, she has several options for recalling Julia's language breakthrough. She might use a checklist. Figure 9.3 is a checklist that might be used in a multilingual classroom. This checklist focuses on Michael Halliday's (1975) functional uses of language (see Table 2.1). Such checklists are easy to use and re-quire little time. This checklist can be easily modified to fit other situations (for example, for a monolingual classroom, the language columns could be eliminated) or to focus on other aspects of language. Such instruments provide a broad view of the language that children use in the classroom. However, much of the richness of the children's actual language is lost.

FIGURE 9.3

Oral Language Checklist

| Child's Name | Language | | | Partner(s) | | | Location | | | | | | | | Function | | | | | | |
	English	Spanish	Other	Child	Several Children	Adult	Library	Writing	Listening	Housekeeping	Theme (play)	Blocks	Math/Sci	Art	Instrumental	Regulatory	Interaction	Personal	Heuristic	Imaginative	Informative
Julia	✓									✓										✓	

Chari might use a less-structured observation-recording form, such as the one illustrated in Figure 9.4. Forms like this allow teachers to record more detailed information about children's language behaviors. Typically such forms have columns for children's names, samples of their speech, and other variables that might be of interest to the teacher. Chari is interested in knowing the context within which her children's language samples are collected and the language forms illustrated. Hence, she added two columns to the observation-recording form she uses in her classroom. Notice that she does not put lines on her observation-recording form. This is intentional. No lines means that Chari can record as much information about each incident as necessary for her to recall each language event. Compare the information on this form to that recorded on the checklist. Notice how the observation-recording form captured much more of the essence of Julia's language accomplishment than did the checklist.

Chari might use an anecdotal record. Anecdotal records (Figure 9.5) are even less structured than an observation-recording form. Here, the teacher writes a brief description of the language incident on a piece of paper, index card, or sticky note. Later, Chari can file these anecdotal notes in individual folders for each of her children. This unstructured format allows Chari to make the most detailed description of Julia's language.

Teachers can use audio and video recordings for other purposes as well. For example, recording circle time or small group time when the children are retelling a narrative story would provide the teacher with valuable information about the children's developing abilities to comprehend stories. Which narrative structures do the children include in their retellings—the initiating event, the main character, the problem, the solution? How much teacher scaffolding is needed to support the children's retelling?

Focusing the video camera's lens on the dramatic play or the writing center also can provide the teacher with information about the children's knowledge of the functions of writing. For example, in the camp site play setting in the dramatic play center in a kindergarten classroom, the video recording showed children writing tickets for camp site speeders and making signs like "DO NOT FEED THE BEARS!" and also revealed the number of a camper's tent location on a slip of paper and drawing a map to the location. The sign making demonstrated that the children knew that a purpose of writing is to control other people's behavior, and the map demonstrated that they knew that a purpose of writing is to inform. Because the teacher was busy interacting with children in other centers, she might have missed this opportunity to understand her children's developing knowledge of the functions of written communication.

FIGURE 9.4

Oral Language Observation Recording Form

Child's Name	Context	What Was Said	Language Forms
Julia	Playing role of mother in house keeping center.	Ring, ring... Miss Chari... Will you come to my house?	Complete sentence!

FIGURE 9.5

Anecdotal
Note

Julia   4/6/95

Julia observed me making a
prentend phone call to Buddy
from the post office center.
Several minutes later she picked
up the toy phone in the
housekeeping center and
said "Ring, ring .. Miss Chari,
will you come to my house?"
It was her first complete
English sentence!

▪ *Products or work samples:* Some products, such as samples of children's writing, can be gathered together in a folder. If the children's original works cannot be saved (e.g., a letter that is sent to its recipient), a photocopy can be made of the product. Other products, such as three-dimensional structures the children have created with labels written by them, might not be conveniently saved. In these cases, a photograph—still or video—can be made. Because memories are short, the teacher should record a brief description of the product or the activity that resulted in the product.

Addressing Storage Problems

Mrs. Saenz has developed an assessment notebook that helps organize information about children's literacy learning. Her notebook consists of several sections. One section contains a checklist she has developed to document children's emergent writing. Another section contains a checklist she created to document emergent reading behaviors, including information about concepts of print and alphabet recognition. Mrs. Saenz's notebook also has a section for writing vignettes. To prompt her memory of an event, Mrs. Saenz uses a digital camera that allows her to take pictures of the children engaging in specific literacy behaviors. Later in the day, she downloads the disk, prints the photo, and writes her interpretation of the event on the bottom margin of the photo. In addition, the camera automatically dates the picture, making it easier for Mrs. Saenz to document this information quickly. Using these various tools will result in the accumulation of many items that will need to be stored someplace.

For teachers to maintain this kind of assessment system, they must be very well organized! Some teachers maintain a folder on each child. Many teachers find that folders with pockets and center clasps for three-hole-punched paper serve as better storage containers than file folders. Checklists, prints of photographs, examples of the child's writing, and other similar papers can be three-hole-punched, thus permitting easy insertion into each child's folder. When anecdotal notes and vignettes are written on computer mailing labels, the labels can be attached to the inside covers of each child's folder. When these notes are written on index cards, the cards can be stored in one of the folder's pockets. Also, a plastic resealing sandwich bag might be stapled inside each child's folder to hold an audiotape or DVD. The self-sealing feature of the bag means that the tape or DVD can be securely held inside the folder. The class's folders might be housed in a plastic container or in hanging files in a file cabinet.

One teacher we know prepared an end-of-year lasting treasure for her children's parents. Minjie Paark's teacher pulled examples of Minjie's literacy behaviors as reflected using the ongoing assessment tools described above and digital photos of Minjie's work, scanned select items, and created an end-of-year digital presentation on a CD for Minjie's parents. Both Minjie and her parents were thrilled to see how her language and literacy skills had progressed during the year.

On-Demand Assessment

Teachers use, or are required to use, another kind of assessment to understand their children's literacy learning. This kind of assessment is often referred to as on-demand assessment (Johnston & Costello, 2005). Think of on-demand assessments like an annual physical checkup. Periodically, we all need to stop what we are doing to take a formal measure of the state of our health. On-demand assessments occur at specific times, like once a year or every three months. For example, on Tuesday all kindergarten children in the school district may be asked to take a pencil-and-paper test. They might be asked to listen to several short stories composed of two or three sentences. Then the children would be asked to put an *X* on the picture that best matches each story. They may be asked to circle the letters said aloud by the teacher. They might be asked to listen to sounds said aloud by the teacher (e.g., *b*) and to circle the letter that makes that sound.

Most readers likely would label these kinds of on-demand assessments as *tests*. On-demand assessments are administered, scored, and interpreted in the same way for all test takers. Each child taking the test hears the same passages and answers the same questions. When all variables are held constant, the assessment would be known as a "standardized" test. These tests should produce reliable and valid data. *Reliability* refers to the consistency of the data; if the same test is administered to the same child on consecutive days, the child's score should be the similar. And if two different teachers administer an assessment to the same child, again the scores should be similar if the assessment is reliable. *Validity* refers to the extent to which an assessment really measures what it claims to measure.

There are two types of standardized tests:

(1) *Criterion-referenced tests* are developed with a specific set of objectives that reflect district, state, federal, or national learning standards. The goal of criterion-referenced tests is for all children to demonstrate mastery of the information and skills they have been taught. In Special Feature 9.1, Tanis Bryan and Cevriye Erfgul describe a criterion-reference assessment procedure known as Curriculum Based Assessment (CBM).

(2) *Norm-referenced tests* are designed to measure the accomplishments of one child relative to the whole class, or to compare one classroom of pre-K children to another classroom within the same school or center, or to compare all the children in all classrooms in a district or project, or to compare all children across the country. Norm-referenced standardized tests can be used to determine whether a school's curriculum reflects national

Curriculum-Based Measurement

Tanis Bryan and Cevriye Erfgul

An important part of teaching early literacy skills is continuous monitoring of children's learning. Although teachers "take in" thousands of bits of information about their students' learning every day, preschool teachers need reliable and valid measures to help them evaluate young children's development of the early literacy skills being taught in their classrooms. Over the past 30 years, curriculum-based measurement (CBM) has been developed to help teachers monitor children's progress. The intent is for teachers to collect technically sound but simple data in a meaningful fashion to document children's growth and determine the necessity for modifying instructional programs.

Critical early literacy skills assessed with preschool CBMs are phonological awareness, alphabet letter naming, and oral vocabulary. CBM test stimuli are drawn from the curriculum. Teachers administer CBMs weekly across the school year and use the data for instructional planning. Teachers find CBM a feasible addition to their schedules because it is fast (two minutes per child weekly), inexpensive, and easy to administer. Because CBM is directly connected to daily instruction, the information is useful to teachers. Teachers use CBM to continuously measure their children's gains, determine if their children are learning at the expected rate, and evaluate their instructional strategies. Ideally, a team of teachers collaborate in each step of doing CBM.

Here is a step-by-step description of how teachers use CBM:

Step 1: Select children. Teachers can select two to four children who are monitored weekly or rotate two to four children each week so that all children in the classroom are monitored monthly. It's important that each cohort includes a child with learning delays or problems, such as a child who has developmental delays or disabilities, and/or a child at risk for disabilities. Include a child with typical achievement and/or a child with high achievement to help figure out if a particular child is having a problem or if all the children are making errors, and the instruction is missing its mark (e.g., the material is too difficult for everyone).

Step 2: Develop CBMs. Teachers take a close look at the curriculum and weekly lesson plans and decide which vocabulary, sounds, and letters will be emphasized each week. Each CBM should assess receptive vocabulary ("Show me"), expressive vocabulary ("Tell me"), letter identification, and alliteration (identification of initial sounds). The CBM should include six to eight words, two to four alphabet letters, and two sounds for alliteration from each week's lesson plan. It is important to use the same number of words, sounds,

and letters each week because this allows teachers to evaluate the children's development across time.

A score sheet is prepared for each child (see Figure 9.6). The score sheet lists the sources for the items, such as the book/page or poster that shows the words in the item, as well as space for comments and descriptions of the types of errors (e.g., okay with initial sounds but unable to pronounce the rest of the word, mispronunciation of the whole word, certain types of mispronunciations of words or letters) or any other event that influenced the child's responses (e.g., off-task behavior, sick, weather too hot).

Step 3: Administer CBMs. CBMs are administered at the same time each week, following the same procedures and wait time for each child. For "receptive vocabulary," the child is shown a poster or page that has several pictures from the lesson and asked to "Show me _____." For "expressive vocabulary" and "letter Identification," the child is shown a poster or book page and asked to name the object or letter pointed to. On "alliteration," the child is shown a card with the target word illustrated at the top of the card and three other illustrations in a row at the bottom of the card. One of the illustrations should have the same initial sound as the target word. Two sample items should be provided. The teacher displays each card and sounds out the words. The child is asked to point to one of the three pictures at the bottom with the same initial sound as the target picture.

Step 4: Analysis. At the end of each week or monthly, each child's scores on each test are summed and a graph is prepared (see Figure 9.7). The horizontal axis indicates the week of the unit, and the vertical axis presents the number of correct responses on each CBM subtest. Graphs give teachers an overview of each child's mastery of the curriculum. Teachers compare the performance of children with special needs, at risk, typical achieving, and high achieving.

Step 5: Using the results. First, teachers establish expectations for children. Should every child get every item on every CBM? Should every child get three of the four items? Teachers reviewing the data should ask: (a) Are one or two children not meeting expectations? (b) Are all children not meeting expectations? or (c) Are all the children exceeding expectations? We recommend that teachers use the performance of the typical or average-achieving children to establish an expectation line. Then teachers can evaluate whether the child with disabilities or at risk for disabilities is learning at about the same rate as typical children or needs additional instruction.

Teachers are encouraged to include parents in the process by sending parents (or discussing) an explanation of CBM, the words and letters being focused on in each exploration or week, and the child's graph. The teacher should explain the graph, noting positive changes in the child's progress. Parents also should be provided activities to do at home that support classroom learning.

SPECIAL FEATURE **9.1** (continued)

FIGURE 9.6 CBM Score Sheet

ACE3 CBM SCORE SHEET – UNIT [VROOM VROOM] /WEEK [One]

Child's Name _____ School _____

Date of Test _____ Examiner _____

Purpose: Track how well the child is learning the vocabulary words and letters you are teaching using DOORS.

Directions: Read the script in the box below. Enter the scores in the box below. Enter the scores on the left side column.

Letter Identification
Letter Card (card with all letters):

D d _____ L l _____ M m _____ J j _____

correct _____

ShowMe
Our Big Book of Driving: Pages 2-3.

Van _____

Bicycle _____

Motorcycle _____

Fire Truck _____

correct _____

Tell Me
Picture Word Cards: Pull the word cards for the following items:

Taxi _____   Bus _____

Tire _____   Stop sign _____

correct _____

Comments:

LETTER IDENTIFICATION:
Present the letter card to the child, and
"Say, "We are going to look at this card with all these letters. Tell me the name of letter I point to."

SCORE:
1 Point = correct answer or self-correction within approximately 3 seconds.
0 Point = incorrect answer.
NA (No Answer) = Asked twice and no answer at the end of three seconds.

SHOW ME (Identification):
Open the lap book version of "Our Big Book of Driving" to pages 2-3. Place the book in front of the child and
Say, "We are going to look at these pictures. Point to the picture that I tell you."
"Show me the _____."

SCORE:
1 Point = correct answer or self-correction within approximately 3 seconds.
0 Point = incorrect answer.
NA (No Answer) = Asked twice and no answer at the end of three seconds.

TELL ME (Production):
Place the word cards in front of the child and
"Say, "We are going to look at these pictures. Tell me the name of the picture I point to."
"Point to each picture and say, "Tell the name of this."

SCORE:
1 Point = correct answer or self-correction within approximately 3 seconds.
0 Point = incorrect answer.
NA (No Answer) = Asked twice and no answer at the end of three seconds.

**ACE3 CBM SCORE SHEET (ALLITERATION)
"VROOM VROOM" / WEEK 1**

Alliteration (Picture cards)

Toy _____   Toilet _____

Toaster _____   Toes _____

correct _____

Comments: _____

ALLITERATION (Identification of initial sounds):
Use alliteration picture cards.
1. Sample item 1
"Say, **"Here is a picture of bread. It starts with the 'b' sound."** Repeat the word and say **"Now look at these pictures. Which one starts with "b,"** Name each bottom picture. If child does not get correct answer, say the top picture's name and correct answer emphasizing initial sounds.
2. Sample item 2
Repeat the instructions of sample item 1 using the pictures' names in this sample.
3. Test items 1 and 2
"Say, **"Here is a picture of a (picture name). Now which one of these pictures starts with the same sound."** Name the top picture and then point to each picture in the bottom and say out loud.

SCORE:
1 Point for each correct answer or self-correction within approximately 3 seconds.
0 Point = incorrect answer.
NA (No Answer) = Asked twice and no answer at the end of three seconds.
Sample responses are not scored.

(continued on next page)

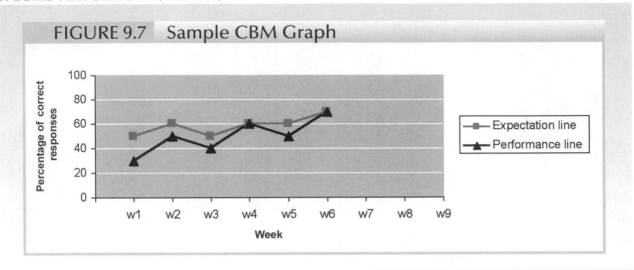

FIGURE 9.7   Sample CBM Graph

expectations of what children should know at a specific age or grade level and to compare children to one another. In Table 9.1, we provide a description of several of the norm-referenced standardized assessments in language and reading currently in use in early childhood programs across the United States.

TABLE 9.1   Standardardized Language and Early Reading Measures Used with Young Children

Title/Publisher	Purpose	Description	When to Use It
Dynamic Indicators of Basic Early Literacy Skills (DIBELS)–Letter-Naming Fluency	To assess fluency with which children identify letter names. To identify children at risk of reading difficulty early before a low reading trajectory is established.	Individually administered, timed phonemic awareness task. Randomly ordered lower- and uppercase letters are presented to children for 1 minute; children are instructed to name as many letters as they can.	Beginning kindergarten through fall of first grade or until children are proficient at accurately producing 40–60 letter names per minute
Phonemic Segmentation Fluency Publisher: CBM Network, School Psychology Program, College of Education, University of Oregon http://dibels.uoregon.edu/	To assess children's ability to segment orally presented words into phonemes. To identify children who may be at risk of reading difficulty.	Individually administered, timed phonological awareness task. Words are orally presented to children for 1 minute; children are instructed to segment each word into individual phonemes (i.e., sounds).	Winter of kindergarten through first grade or until children are proficient at accurately producing 35–45 phonemes per minute
IDEA Proficiency Test (IPT) Publisher: Ballard & Tigh	To determine the English language skills of students who have a non–English language background	Children are assessed on oral language abilities, writing, and reading and asked to write their own stories and respond to a story.	Administered to children K–12
Individual Growth and Developmental Indicators (IGDI) *www.getgotgo.net*	To identify children's phonological awareness strengths and weaknesses	Three components to the test: picture naming, rhyming, and alliteration. Takes approximately 5 minutes to administer.	Used for ages 3–5

Phonological Aware-ness Literacy Screening, Pre-K (PALS Pre-K) http://pals.virginia.edu/ PALS-Instruments/ PALS-PreK.asp	To provide information on children's strengths and weak-nesses	Measures name-writing ability, upper- and lowercase alphabet rec-ognition, letter sound and begin-ning sound production, print and word awareness, rhyme awareness, and nursery rhyme awareness	Used in fall of pre-K and can be used as a measurement of prog-ress in the spring
Peabody Picture Vocabu-lary Test-III (PPVT-III) Publisher: American Guidance Service	To measure receptive vocabu-lary acquisition and serve as a screening test of verbal ability	Student points to the picture that best represents the stimulus word.	Beginning at age 2.5 years to 90+ years
The Phonological Aware-ness Test (PAT) Publisher: LinguiSystems	To assess students' phonologi-cal awareness skills	Five different measures of pho-nemic awareness (segmentation of phonemes, phoneme isolation, phoneme deletion, phoneme substitution, and phoneme blending) and a measure of sensitivity to rhyme	Beginning the second semester of kindergarten through second grade
Test of Preschool Early Literacy (TOPEL) Publisher: Pro-Ed	To identify children at risk of having problems or developing problems in literacy	Individually administered. Pro-vides information about print knowledge, single-word oral vo-cabulary and definitional vocabu-lary, and phonological awareness	Used for ages 3 to 6
Test of Language Devel-opment (TOLD) Publisher: Pearson	To identify children's strengths and weaknesses and major lan-guage disorders	Individually administered. Pro-vides information about recep-tive and expressive vocabulary, grammar, word articulation, word discrimination, and syntax	Primary Version, as-sesses children between 4 and 8.11 years
Assessment of Literacy and Language (ALL) Publisher: Pearson	To detect early signs of lan-guage difficulties	Individually administered. As-sesses verbal and written language in the following areas: listening, comprehension, language compre-hension, semantics, syntax, phono-logical awareness, alphabetic prin-ciples, and concepts about print.	Used for preschool, kindergarten, and first grade children

Special Feature 9.2 by Karen Burstein, an evaluation expert, provides useful information about both types of standardized assessments. In addition, Dr. Burstein describes the range of assess-ments used in the Arizona Centers of Excellence, an Early Reading First Project.

Using Assessment Data to Plan Early Literacy Instruction

Karen Burstein identified four reasons for assessing children. In our view, the last reason, to inform teachers of children's instructional needs, is the most important reason:

We strongly agree that no single test score should be used alone to judge a child's progress in language, reading, and writing development. However, *if* most of the children in a classroom do not perform as expected on a standardized test, then teachers must be prepared to reconsider their methods of teaching language, reading, and writing. Teachers need to ask themselves, What could I have done better or differently? Did I not spend enough time explicitly teaching phonological

SPECIAL FEATURE 9.2

Standardized Assessment of Young Children

Karen Burstein

During the past 20 years, assessment of young children has assumed increased prominence. Today early childhood teachers are frequently expected to administer and interpret multiple standardized tests as well as to conduct informal evaluations of children across the year. The notion of testing young children evokes passionate debate among teachers and scholars. To some it provides reliable measures for examining programs and attainment of standards; to others it conjures up negative images of subjecting children to trying experiences of questionable value. That said, there continues to be a push to test children to track their progress in preschool. What are early childhood educators to do?

Because early childhood educators are being asked to systematically observe, record, and conduct standardized assessments in their classrooms, a basic understanding of the types of tests and their limitations is important, as is familiarity with the language of assessment. The Early Childhood Education Assessment section of the Council of Chief State Schools Officers coordinated the aggregation of a web-based glossary of common language around assessment and standards (*www.ccsso.org/projects/scass/projects/ early_childhood_education_assessment_consortium/ publications_and_products/2838.cfm*).

REASONS FOR TESTING

As assessments of young children are increasing, teachers and scholars ask why. The driving force behind assessment lies in the results: What information does the assessment yield? Who can use it? What is the benefit to the child? There are four primary reasons for assessment (Shepard, Kagan, & Wurtz, 1998):

1. *To compare districts/schools with one another:* Districts/schools are compared across communities, and the question posed is whether they are achieving state standards or benchmarks. For this purpose, early childhood programs are likely to be using Dynamic Indicators of Basic Early Literacy Skills (DIBELS), its preschool counterpart *Get It Got It Go* (Individual Growth and Development Indicators), and AIMS Web. These are standardized, individually teacher-administered measures of early reading skills that are responsive to the implementation of teaching methods consistent with scientifically based reading research. These tests provide districts and schools with benchmark information and teachers with child-specific skills attainment. The instruments are administered approximately three times annually and yield results on children's acquisition of skills in sound (phonemic awareness), alphabet, letter, vocabulary, and oral reading fluency.

2. *To determine which children need additional support services:* Since the implementation of IDEA (formerly P.L. 94-142) in 1975, the most common reason for administering standardized assessments to young children is to assist in determining children's eligibility for special services. These tests include standardized measures of IQ, such as the Wechsler Preschool and Primary Scale of Intelligence (WPPSI) or the Stanford-Binet Intelligence Scales for Early Childhood (Early SB5), and measures of different areas of child development such as the Vineland Social-Emotional Early Childhood Scales and Peabody Picture Vocabulary Test-III. All of these tests are individually administered, and some require special training or advanced credentials to administer and interpret. Children's raw scores are usually converted into standard scores that fall along a continuum that allows for comparisons of individuals to a "normal" distribution of same-age children. They typically do not indicate academic strengths or weaknesses and generally do not help teachers develop instructional plans. The advantage of standardized assessments is that they expedite the process of determining eligibility for special services. However, important educational decisions should be based on multiple sources of information including observations, work samples, and family interviews.

3. *To monitor children's progress and assess the overall effectiveness of programs:* One of the most prevalent and high-profile models of program evaluation is the Head Start National Reporting System (NRS). Early in 2003, the Bush administration announced its intention to require all 4- and 5-year-olds in the federal Head Start program to be assessed at the beginning and end of each program year. The NRS assessments were standardized and measure a limited set of skills that include expressive and receptive English vocabulary, uppercase letter naming, and early math skills such as number identity and simple addition and subtraction. Teachers administered the NRS, but it was scored by an external organization that sends reports of overall program outcomes to Head Start and local administrations. It is important to understand that the primary focus of the NRS was the overall progress that groups of children make in each Head Start program. The NRS was not designed to assess the school readiness of individual children (Head Start In Focus, April 2003).

Programs can also be evaluated at the local level. For example, all Early Reading First projects are required to have an evaluation plan to measure their effectiveness in boosting pre-K children's school readiness. The Arizona Centers of Excellence in Early Education developed an evaluation model that included semiannual administration of a battery of standardized assessments, semimonthly systematic classroom observations, and weekly curriculum-based measurements. Many adequate "skills-specific" measures exist, so assessments were selected based on reliability and validity reported by test publishers and the test "fit" with the population of children being assessed (i.e., the populations were represented in the norm-

ing samples). A team of local substitute teachers were trained to be the examiners. The ACE3 assessment battery provided the following information about each child: an English Language Fluency level, a baseline of initial sounds and rhymes, areas of competence in print awareness, a measure of receptive vocabulary,

FIGURE 9.8   ACE Preschool Continuum of Progress

ACE Preschool Continuum of Progress: Niño at a glance!

Child Name _____   Program Year _____

Teacher: _____   Center/Site: _____

The purpose of this form is to assist parents and teachers to make appropriate educational goals for children enrolled in the ACE program and to track progress across the school year. It concludes with a summary and end-of-the-year report to families.

Curriculum Based Assessment Results (initial, midyear, end of year)

Letter Identification   1) _____ 2) _____ 3) _____

Initial Sounds (alliteration) 1) _____ 2) _____ 3) _____

Rhyming   1) _____ 2) _____ 3) _____

Get Ready to Read   1) _____ 2) _____ 3) _____

CBM Quarterly   1- Letter name) _____ Show Me) _____ Tell Me) _____ Alliteration) _____

2- Letter name) _____ Show Me) _____ Tell Me) _____ Alliteration) _____

3- Letter name) _____ Show Me) _____ Tell Me) _____ Alliteration) _____

4- Letter name) _____ Show Me) _____ Tell Me) _____ Alliteration) _____

Developmental assessment (name) _____ Brief summary _____

_____

_____

Summary of teacher observations and anecdotal records _____

_____

_____

_____

Parent Goals (What the parent wants the child to work on during the program year): _____

_____

_____

IEG Individual Education Goals: _____

   1) _____

   2) _____

Goals from IEP to be supported in the classroom: _____

_____

Monthly Explorations/Theme:

September _____

Circle each of the letter names that the child has learned. Letter names learned: F   M

Instructional Modifications: 0) no modification necessary   1) modify classroom   2) more instruction

          3) more practice   4) more structured play   5) more parent involvement   6) other _____

Social development activities:

Activities sent home:

[Note: Page 2 contains reports on the remaining monthly explorations and themes, and page 3 contains reports of the parent conferences that are conducted in the fall and spring.]

(continued on next page)

and the number and names of the letters recognized. Upon completion of the battery, teachers received the ACE Preschool Continuum of Progress (see Figure 9.8), an easy-to-understand summary of each child's assessment results and a set of graphs of overall class results. Parents were provided with similar information and, at the end of the year, an exit summary of their child's skills in each area.

4. *To provide information to teachers about each child's instructional needs:* From the teacher's perspective, the most important reason for assessment is to obtain accurate information about the instructional needs of their students. The assess-plan-teach-assess model of instruction directs teachers to:

- Know the content of the Early Childhood Education Standards in their community;
- Align their classroom curriculum to these standards;
- Assess each child's skill attainment on these standards;
- Plan instruction that is responsive to children's assessed needs and skills;

- Deliver instruction that explicitly targets needs; and
- Reassess to ensure that children are learning the content that was delivered.

Within this model, assessment is a critical step in good instruction. As the call for assessment has increased, there is now a plethora of measures covering a myriad of skills. Even curriculum developers have begun to develop standardized measures aligned with their materials. However, the vast majority of standardized assessments are limited in their scope and number of items. Couple this limitation with the dramatic developmental variations in young children, and one can begin to understand the consequences of trying to use standardized assessments to fully inform teachers of the needs of their students. Teachers need specific information from multiple models of assessment to develop effective plans and activities for their classes. Each teacher's skill repertoire should include not only standardized assessment but knowledge about child development and strong skills in observation techniques, work sampling, parent interviewing and collaboration, curriculum alignment, and curriculum-based measurement (see Special Feature 9.1).

---

awareness? Did I not support my children's language development by explicitly teaching vocabulary and expanding or elaborating on their talk? Others certainly will raise these questions. Teachers must be able to respond by defending their teaching practices and by learning what legitimately needs revising to support children's language, reading, and writing development. Teacher need to study the data to understand what their children could do well and what was challenging for their children. These data can guide teachers' examination of their teaching practices.

What do I teach tomorrow? Early childhood teachers do not teach a program; they teach children. Information must be gathered, using on-demand and ongoing assessment procedures, to help teachers know what their young children know and can do—and cannot do. This information, then, determines what the teacher teachers tomorrow.

Strategies for Teaching English Language Learners: Assessing Young English Language Learners' Language and Literacy

Sohyun Han

Research suggests that assessment problems often stem from a lack of training, awareness, and sensitivity (Santos, 2004). To do a good job of assessing young children whose home language is not English, skill, sensitivity, and knowledge of the children's culture and language are required. The best-practice recommendations for appropriate assessment of young children whose home language is not English are as follows:

1. *Consider each English language learner's unique language background.* ELL children's competency

in two languages varies by contexts (Langdon & Wiig, 2009; Valdés & Figueroa, 1994). They choose different words or speak a combination of words from the two languages based on the topic and situation. Gather as much evidence as possible of ELL children's language and literacy competency in their home language and in English.

2. *Carefully choose linguistically and developmentally appropriate and culturally sensitive assessment instruments.* Study the items on the instrument before using it with the children to determine if any items are inappropriate for use with the particular group of ELL children to be assessed.

3. *Select tools that are appropriate for the purpose of the assessment.* Different measures can be used for a variety of purposes; for example: (a) determining a child's eligibility for services, (b) meeting accountability requirements, (c) planning classroom instruction, or (d) monitoring a child's progress. For example, because standardized

(continued)

norm-referenced tests can be administered only a few times a year, they are inappropriate for monitoring progress in classrooms. On the other hand, curriculum-based measurements (CBMs) cannot be used for screening purposes because they do not provide norm references.

4. *Be sure to assess all aspects of a child's language and literacy proficiency: receptive and expressive language, phonological awareness, letter knowledge, and print concept.* Teachers should not overemphasize one dimension of children's language and literacy skills. It is possible, for example, that while an ELL's oral language skills are less proficient than his or her English-speaking peers, the child can name all of the English alphabet letters, both upper- and lowercase. All aspects of language and literacy are important for later reading development. To plan appropriately for each child, teachers need information on all the aspects of each child's language and literacy skill development.

5. *Multiple factors beyond language proficiency may interact with ELLs' performance* (Spinelli, 2008). ELLs, for example, may have fewer experiences than their English-speaking peers in taking tests. This may make them more anxious or distracted than their English-speaking peers (Meisels, 2001). Examiners are advised to be friendly and to build rapport with ELL children to gain their trust (Spinelli, 2008). ELLs from low-income families may have nutrition issues (Ortiz, 2003). The assessment of their language and literacy performance might be negatively affected when they are hungry. Consider these factors, and do your best to meet each child's unique needs.

6. *When possible, modify the testing conditions for ELLs.* When testers who speak the child's home language are available, which various groups and researchers suggest is optimal (AERA, APA, & NCME, 1999; Noland, 2009), it might be permissible to translate the test's directions into each child's home language. When a test is administered only in English, the testers might consider

administering the missed items later in children's home language. Though not calculated in the children's score, this information could prove helpful for teachers as they design plans to meet each child's needs. The teacher might be able to use the language and literacy knowledge that the ELL children possess in their home language to assist them in mastering these skills in English.

7. *When acceptable, reword the test's directions and ensure that ELLs understand what is being asked of them before proceeding with the administration of the test.* Perhaps the items and directions can be presented through graphics and pictorial representations. Be sure to allow sufficient response time for the children to process the question (Spinelli, 2008).

8. *Determine whether further testing is needed; consider follow-up classroom observations and conversations with family members.* The goal is to confirm the interpretations of the child's behavior during the assessment process.

9. *Interpret the results of standardized tests with caution.* A prominent problem with using standardized or norm-referenced tests with ELL children is that few tests have norms for ELL children. Therefore, the use of these tests for ELLs can be a stretch (Noland, 2009). Although the use of such tests often is unavoidable for screening purposes to determine the eligibility for governmental services, careful interpretation is required.

10. *Adopt an in-depth approach beyond standardized tests to support individualized intervention planning for ELL children* (Langdon & Wiig, 2009; Roseberry-McKibbin & O'Hanlon, 2005). Interview family members to obtain language history information. Include alternative assessments such as language samples, anecdotal notes, criterion-referenced tests, observations, journals, and portfolios for dynamic and authentic assessment procedures. Aim to obtain a picture of what ELL children *know* and *can* do, not just what they do not know and cannot do.

Family Focus: Sharing Assessment Results with Parents

There is one more important reason for assessing children's language and literacy progress: to share information with parents about their children's language and literacy growth. In the following section, we describe how teachers might use parent conferences to build parent–teacher partnerships and to share the details of children's language and literacy progress.

Children are complex, social individuals who must function appropriately in two very different cultures, school and home. Parents need to understand how a child uses his or her social skills to become a productive member of the school community. Likewise, experienced teachers appreciate the child's home life and recognize its significant influence on a child's behavior and ability to learn. Partnerships reach their full potential when parents and teachers share information about the child from their unique perspectives, value the child's individual needs and strengths, and work together for the benefit of the child.

(continued on next page)

(continued)

The best opportunity teachers have for engaging parents in this type of discussion is during parent–teacher conferences. Conferences should feature a two-way exchange of information. There are generally two types of parent–teacher conferences: preestablished conferences that review the child's classroom progress and spontaneous conferences that deal with a range of specific concerns that occur throughout the year.

PROGRESS REVIEW CONFERENCES. The progress review conference is an opportunity for parents and teachers to share information about children's social interactions, emotional maturity, and cognitive development. One way to help a parent and teacher prepare to share information during the conference is a preconference questionnaire. The teacher sends the questionnaire home to the parent to complete and return prior to the conference. In Figure 9.9, we present the notes made by Manuel's mother as she prepared for her conference with Ms. Jones, her son's kindergarten teacher. The information Mrs. Rodriguez provides also tells Ms. Jones what concerns she has; therefore, Ms. Jones

has a better idea about how to focus the conference. Remember, it may be necessary to have this letter and questionnaire translated into the language spoken in the home.

During a progress review conference, the teacher shares information about the child's academic progress. In addition to academic progress, most parents want to know about their children's social interactions and classroom behavior. The observational data that the teacher has recorded helps provide a more complete picture of the child in the classroom context.

When working with parents, teachers are encouraged to use a structured format during the progress review conference. The structure keeps the conference focused and increases the chance of both teachers' and parents' concerns being adequately discussed.

The success of the parent–teacher relationship depends on the teacher's ability to highlight the child's academic and social strengths and progress. When areas of concern are discussed, it is important to provide examples of the child's work or review the

---

FIGURE 9.9

Preconference Questionnaire

Dear Parent,

To help us make the most of our time, I am sending this questionnaire to help facilitate our progress review conference. Please read and complete the questions. If you have any other concerns, simply write them down on the questionnaire, and we will discuss any of your inquiries during our time together. I look forward to getting to know both you and your child better.

1. How is your child's overall health?
   Good, but Manuel gets colds alot.
2. Are there specific health concerns that the teacher should know about? (include allergies)
   Colds and sometimes ear infections.
3. How many hours of sleep does your child typically get?
   About 9
4. Does your child take any medication on a regular basis? If so, what type?
   He takes penicillin when he has ear infections.
5. What are the names and ages of other children who live in your home?
   Maria, 9; Rosalina, 7; Carlos, 3.
6. How would you describe your child's attitude toward school?
   He likes school.
7. What school activity does your child enjoy most?
   P.E. and art
8. What school activity does your child enjoy least?
   Math
9. What are your child's favorite TV shows?
   Power Rangers, Ninja Turtles
   How many hours of TV will your child generally watch each night?
   Three
10. What is the title of your child's favorite storybook?
    Where the Wild Things Are.
11. How often do you read to your child?
    His sisters read to him most nights.
12. What other activities does your child enjoy?
    Playing soccer.
Other concerns:
    I can't read his writing. His sisters' was good in Kindergarten.

observational data to illustrate the point. Often, the issues the parents reveal are directly related to the concerns the teacher has. Whenever possible, connect these concerns, as this reinforces the feeling that the teacher and the parents have the same goals for helping the child learn. It is essential to solicit the parents' views and suggestions for helping the child and also to provide concrete examples about how they might help the child learn.

To make sure both teacher and parents reach a common understanding, briefly review the main ideas and suggestions that were discussed during the conference. Allow parents to orally discuss their views of the main ideas of the conference. Check the parents' perceptions. Finally, briefly record the parents' oral summary on the conference form.

Figure 9.10 is a progress review conference form from Manuel's conference.

CHILD–PARENT–TEACHER CONFERENCES. A somewhat new innovation in progress review conferences is the inclusion of the child. The child participates equally—sharing work, discussing areas in which he or she has noticed improvement, and establishing academic and/or social goals. This type of conference requires that the children are active participants in selecting what work will be featured during the conference. Child–parent–teacher conferences are a natural outgrowth of frequent child–teacher conferences.

Because a three-way conference may be a new experience for parents, it is important for the teacher

FIGURE 9.10

Progress Review Conference Form

Student's name: Manuel Romero   Parent's name: Mary Romero

Conference date: Nov. 1   Time: 4:30 p.m.

Positive Statement: Manuel is so eager to learn

Review Conference steps:
Our conference today will consist of three parts. First, I will ask you to review your child's progress, sharing with me both academic/social strengths and areas of concern. Next, I'll review Manuel's work with you and discuss his academic/social strengths and areas in which we will want to help him grow. Finally, we will discuss the main points we discussed today and review the strategies we decided would help Manuel continue to make progress.

1. **Ask for Parent Input:** What have you observed about Manuel this year that makes you feel good about his learning? (Take notes as parent is sharing)
Manuel likes school, drawing, friends, stoves.

What are your main concerns?
His writing looks like scribbles. He's not reading yet but he likes stories read to him.

2. **Teacher Input:** I would like to share some observations about Manuel's work and review both areas of strengths and skills that need to be refined. Manuel interest in reading is wonderful. He is eager to write in class journal. Though his printing is still developing, he is beginning to use "invented" spelling. Look at this example in his portfolio.

MT M p N PR RG2

Mighty Morphin Power Rangers

Notice how he is separating the words. Ask him to read his work for you if you are having difficulty decoding or deciphering it. His printing skills will improve naturally with time and encouragement. He is really progressing well. Sometimes young girls develop finger muscles sooner. We need to support his efforts. Manuel enjoys sharing his writing in class with his friends and his art work is full of detail. Manuel has many friends and gets along easily with others.

3. **Closure:** Let's review those things we talked about that will facilitate continued success. (Teacher needs to write down this information as the parent talks)

a. Manuel's printing is "Okay" for him.

b. Manuel is writing. I am surprised to see that he really is writing. I just need to have him read for me. Then it's easier for me to figure out what his

c. letters say.

(continued on next page)

(continued)

to establish guidelines for parents and children. A letter sent home explaining the format of the conference and discussing each person's role is essential. Parents are encouraged to ask open-ended questions, such as:

"What did you learn the most about?"

"What did you work the hardest to learn?"

"What do you want to learn more about?"

Questions such as these encourage children to analyze their own learning and also help them to set new goals. Parents should not criticize the child's work or focus on any negative aspect of any material that is presented during the conference. Negative comments, particularly from parents, will only inhibit learning and dampen excitement about school.

Perhaps you are thinking that young children could not possibly discuss their learning during child–parent–teacher conferences. Some years ago, Bernadette Watson's kindergartners did just that. With their teacher's assistance, they looked at the work samples the teacher had collected over the year, noticed what they could do now that they couldn't do in September, and planned what they would tell their parent or parents about what they had learned—and what they liked to do best of all in kindergarten.

When parents and teachers share information, the child benefits.

Exactostock/SuperStock

Summary

The earlier chapters in the book presented the instructional strategies that create the framework for an effective early childhood language arts curriculum. However, these strategies by themselves are not sufficient to construct a program that ensures optimal language and literacy learning for all children. This chapter presents the other key ingredient: assessment.

◼ *What is important for teachers to know about children's literacy development?*

Teachers must begin assessment by asking themselves what is important for them to know about their young learners' development as readers, writers, speakers, and listeners. A useful resource to help them answer this question is their state and national standards.

■ *What are the two general approaches teachers might use to assess their children's literacy learning?*

Teachers use two kinds of assessment to measure their children's progress toward the achievement of the state standards, ongoing and on demand.

■ *What types of ongoing assessment tools are used to collect information about children's progress?*

Changes in what we know about literacy learning have necessitated major changes in our ways of measuring young children's literacy accomplishments and progress. In addition to on-demand assessments that provide samples of student literacy behavior, teachers rely on ongoing assessment procedures that are connected with the daily literacy activities that take place in the classroom. This ongoing assessment makes heavy use of systematic observation and the collection of samples of children's work. Every component of the day (large group, small group, center time) and every area within the classroom (dramatic play, writing, blocks) are ideal for this type of assessment, and anecdotal notes, vignettes, video and audio recordings, and checklists provide effective ways to record data.

■ *What types of standardized tests are used to assess young children's language and literacy progress?*

There are two types of on-demand, standardized tests used to assessment children's literacy progress, criterion referenced and norm referenced. Criterion-referenced tests assess children's progress toward achieving specific objectives or standards. Norm-referenced tests compare children's progress with that of other children.

■ *How do teachers use the information they collect? How do teachers share assessment information with parents?*

Teachers often store the collected information in notebooks or folders. These types of authentic assessments provide just the type of information that teachers need to know to provide effective literacy learning experiences for every child.

Teachers also use the information they collect to share with parents. Parents need to know how their children are progressing, and most parents need to have concrete examples with explicit information provided by the teacher to see how their child's early literacy efforts will develop into conventional reading and writing. Teachers use the gathered information during parent–teacher conferences to illustrate what the children can do.

LINKING KNOWLEDGE TO PRACTICE

1. One way teachers determine what they want and need to know about children's literacy development is by reviewing national, state, and local standards. Contact your state and a local school district to obtain a copy of the local standards for language arts at the pre-K and kindergarten levels. Search to learn if the Council for Chief School Officers and the National Governors Association have prepared pre-K standards. Given what you have learned about children's early literacy development in this textbook, do these standards appear to be reasonable goals for language arts instruction at these levels?

2. Interview a pre-K or kindergarten teacher about the information-gathering tools that he or she typically uses to collect information about children's literacy development. How does the teacher organize this information to share with parents?

Go to the Topics Assessment, English Language Learners, and At Risk and Struggling Readers in the MyEducationLab (www.myeducationlab.com) for your course, where you can:

- Find learning outcomes for Assessment, English Language Learners, and At Risk and Struggling Readers along with the national standards that connect to these outcomes.
- Complete Assignments and Activities that can help you more deeply understand the chapter content.
- Examine challenging situations and cases presented in the IRIS Center Resources.

Go to the Topic A+RISE in the MyEducationLab (*www.myeducationlab.com*) for your course. A+RISE® Standards2Strategy™ is an innovative and interactive online resource that offers new teachers in grades K-12 just in time, research-based instructional strategies that:

- Meet the linguistic needs of ELLs as they learn content
- Differentiate instruction for all grades and abilities
- Offer reading and writing techniques, cooperative learning, use of linguistic and nonlinguistic representations, scaffolding, teacher modeling, higher order thinking, and alternative classroom ELL assessment
- Provide support to help teachers be effective through the integration of listening, speaking, reading, and writing along with the content curriculum
- Improve student achievement
- Are aligned to Common Core Elementary Language Arts standards (for the literacy strategies) and to English language proficiency standards in WIDA, Texas, California, and Florida.

At-HOME ACTIVITIES!

Music in the house and the car

Why Important!
Singing and playing musical toys stimulates auditory, cognitive and motor connections in the brain. Language and self-esteem also are developed.

ACTIVITY

1

Freeze Dance

MATERIALS NEEDED: Portable CD player and examples of music (CDs)

1. Play music, and have your child make movements while the music is playing and freeze when it stops.

2. You can have your child dance and make his or her own moves, or help the child with ideas (e.g., dance with your arms, dance in a circle, dance with your head, and the like).

3. You can also talk about why the child chooses to move in a different way. Talk about how music makes you feel, show the face that expresses the feeling the song gives you. Is the music slow/fast, high/low?

Relates to AZ Readiness Standards: LS-R2, LS-R5, 1WP-R1, 1AM-R2, 1AM-R3, 2AM-R2, 2AM-R3, 3AM-R2, LS-R3, VP-R3
Relates to AZ ECD Standards: SED 1.2; PD 1.1, 1.3; LL 1.3; A 1.1, 1.2, 1.3

ACTIVITY

2

Discovering Rhymes

Music in the house and the car

MATERIALS NEEDED: Portable CD player or car stereo and examples of music (CDs, tapes, and/or radio music)

1. Play music for your child.
2. Listen for and talk about rhyming words you hear in the song lyrics.
3. What is the pattern of the rhyming words? Are the rhyming words at the beginning, middle, or end of the line of the song?

Relates to AZ Readiness Standard: LS-R2, LS-R3, R-R4, 1AM-R1, 1AM-R2
Relates to AZ ECD Standards: LL 1.3, 2.6; A 1.1, 1.2

Why Important!
Singing and playing musical toys stimulates auditory, cognitive and motor connections in the brain. Language and self-esteem also are developed.

Music in the house and the car

Why Important!
Singing and playing musical toys stimulates auditory, cognitive, and motor connections in the brain. Language and self-esteem also are developed.

ACTIVITY

3

Singing Together!

MATERIALS NEEDED: Your child, you, and your singing voice

While performing regular daily routines, take the time to sing to and with your child. Singing together is a fun way to enjoy each other's company.

1. While driving in the car, sing "The Wheels on the Bus."
2. While cooking together in the kitchen, sing "Patty Cake, Patty Cake Baker's Man."
3. While watching the rainfall from a window, sing "The Itsy Bitsy Spider."
4. While looking at the stars together, sing "Twinkle, Twinkle, Little Star."

Enjoy singing other favorite family songs or rhymes together! When possible include your child's name in the song.

Relates to AZ Readiness Standard: 1AM-R1
Relates to AZ ECD Standards: SED 2.1; LL 2.6; A 1.1, 1.2

ACTIVITY

4

Kitchen Drummers!

MATERIALS NEEDED: Safe kitchen utensils, such as a large plastic bowl or pot, pair of wooden spoons

1. Have your child sit in a safe location in the kitchen.
2. Hand her a large plastic bowl turned upside down and a pair of wooden spoons.
3. Allow her to create all kinds of drumming "music" and rhythms with her instruments.

Join your child to make music!

Relates to AZ Readiness Standard: 1AM-R2
Relates to AZ ECD Standards: SED 2,1, 3.2; PD 1.3; A 1.1, 1.2

Why Important!
Singing and playing musical toys stimulates auditory, cognitive and motor connections in the brain. Language and self-esteem also are developed.

Outside
and in the
Environment

Why Important!
Arts and crafts activities encourage creativity, decision-making, oral language, and self-esteem skills.

ACTIVITY

Sidewalk Chalk and Talk!

5

MATERIALS NEEDED: Jumbo-sized chalk for sidewalk drawing

1. Show your child how to mark on the sidewalk, and even draw along with her on the concrete.
2. Show her how to make lines, shapes, and even the letters of her name. While you draw, talk about the drawings.
3. You could draw a simple hopping square and play a game together.
4. Also allow your child to freely try out the chalk.

Your child should not be left alone with the chalk or other objects that could cause a potential choking risk.

Enjoy talking, drawing, and hopping with your child.

Relates to AZ Readiness Standard: 1AV-R1, 1AV-R2
Relates to AZ ECD Standards: SED 2.1, 3.2 PD 1.3; LL 3.1, 3.2; A 1.1

ACTIVITY

6   Sensational Squirt Bottles!

MATERIALS NEEDED: Plastic squirt bottles, water, food coloring, paper

1. Add 1 ½ cups of water to each plastic squirt bottle.
2. Add 8 drops of liquid food coloring into each bottle.
3. Make as many different colors as you can with your child.
4. Take a piece of paper outdoors. Put it down on the sidewalk or in the grass. You may want to use some small rocks to hold down the paper to prevent it from blowing away.
5. Encourage your child to squirt the colored water on the paper, creating unique and colorful designs, letters, shapes, or his own name.

Congratulate and support his artistic talents.

Relates to AZ Readiness Standard: 1AV-R1, 2AV-R3, 1SC-R5
Relates to AZ ECD Standards: SED 2.1, 3.2; PD 1.3; LL 3.1, 3.2; A 1.1

Why Important!
Arts and crafts activities encourage creativity, decision-making, oral language, and self-esteem skills.

Outside and in the Environment

Why Important!
Finding letters in everyday situations helps children understand the functions of print. They begin to see how symbols are useful and important.

ACTIVITY

7

Grocery Store Hunt!

MATERIALS NEEDED: Your child and you on a trip to the grocery store

Did you know that you can go on a hunt with your child while you are grocery shopping? As you both are going down the aisles in store, you may want to play this game.

1. When you come to a familiar aisle, such as the cereal aisle, play the "I Spy Game" with your "helper."

2. Say, "I spy a box that is orange, has a bee on the front, and it starts with the letter C" (fill in any descriptors that match the item you are trying to have her locate).

3. Allow her to look for the clues you are giving her to help her guess what it is you are looking for. You can also give her hints such as: "You're getting closer" or "You're almost there, just two more steps to the left."

Have fun together as you hunt for items.

Relates to AZ Readiness Standard: VP-R1, LS-R2, R-R5, 2M-R1
Relates to AZ ECD Standards: SED 2.1; LL 2.3, 2.4, 2.5; M 5.1, 2.2

Outside and in the Environment

Why Important!
Finding letters in everyday situations helps children understand the functions of print. They begin to see how symbols are useful and important.

ACTIVITY

8   Observation Walk!

MATERIALS NEEDED: Your child and you

1. Take a walk with your child. As you walk, ask your child to look at the different ways people are moving.

2. Ask your child to tell you how the people are moving, for example, walking, running, biking, driving, and the like. During your walk, suggest finding and naming things that grow, such as trees, flowers, weeds, cats, people, dogs, and so on. Ask, "Do rocks, streets, or cars grow?"

3. Talk about the day. Is it sunny, cloudy, rainy, hot, cold? Compare today to yesterday, and predict what tomorrow might be like and why.

Relates to AZ Readiness Standards: LS-R3, LS-R5, 1SC-R2, 1SC-R6, 4SC-R1 2M-R2, LS-R2, LS-R3, 1SC-R2, 1SC-R2, 1SC-R3, 6SC-R1
Relates to AZ ECD Standards: SED 2.1, 4.4; LL 1.2, 1.3; M 3.2, 5.1

Outside and in the Environment

Why Important!
Games that practice learning colors, numbers, letters, and shapes help build concept development and confidence. Games also continue to build bonding relationship between parent and child. This also builds problem-solving and spatial skills.

ACTIVITY

9

I Spy . . . while Driving!

When your child is safely buckled into the backseat of your car, the game can begin.

1. While you are driving with her, you will both be looking for objects that are of a particular color or looking for a predetermined number. For instance if you wanted to practice colors with her you might say, "Who can be the first person to find something red?" Then both of you will be looking for an object that matches that description. When you or your child finds that color, say, "I spy . . ."

2. As soon as one of you finds something that is red, that will count as one red object, and you keep looking for another red object.

3. The goal is to count and find as many red objects as you can on that car trip.

4. When you desire, you can change colors or start looking for letters. You can also look for numbers or shapes that can be found on signs and license plates.

Have fun looking for and counting letters, colors, shapes, and numbers together.

Relates to AZ Readiness Standards: 2M-R2, 3M-R2, 4M-R2, LS-R2, LS-R3
Relates to AZ ECD Standards: SED 2.1, 4.4; LL 1.3, 2.4; M 2.1, SC 1.1

ACTIVITY

10

Zoo Fun!

Are you ready for a day of fun at the zoo?

1. Look for familiar animals and classify them into groups. You can classify them by type of animal, color, number of legs, or whether they have wings.

2. Have your child follow along with the map. Ask him to find animals of his choice.

3. Ask your child to describe which animals he liked best and why.

4. Spend some time at the petting zoo.

Discuss how the animals feel and smell. Ask your children how this makes them feel. Do they enjoy petting the animals?
Have fun together at the zoo.

Relates to AZ Readiness Standards: 2M-R2, 3M-R2, 4M-R2, LS-R2, LS-R3
Relates to AZ ECD Standards: SED 2.1, 4.4; LL 1.3, 2.4; M 2.1, SC 1.1

Why Important!
Games that practice learning colors, numbers, letters, and shapes help build concept development and confidence. Games also continue to build bonding relationship between parent and child. This also builds problem-solving and spatial skills.

Outside
and in the
Environment

Why Important!
These types of
activities encourage
reading and writing.
They also increase
opportunities for
meaningful language
experiences and
early mathematical
thinking. This also
encourages imagina-
tion and creativity!

ACTIVITY

Environmental Print Game!

11

MATERIALS NEEDED: Labels from familiar products in your environment, scissors, a writing tool (crayon, nontoxic marker or pencil); notebook binder is optional

1. Find some labels from products in your everyday environment, such as a Coca Cola label or the label from M&M's candy. Use labels from products that you have or use in your home that your child should be able to recognize.

2. Cut them out and place them in a notebook or picture book by stapling them or gluing them in.

3. Show these pictures to your child, and ask him if he recognizes any of these products.

4. Repeat this activity. Your child will display early signs of reading, once he begins to recognize these products.

Also, enjoy this game together!

Relates to AZ Readiness Standard: VP-R1, LS-R2, R-R5, 2M-R1
Relates to AZ ECD Standards: SED 2.1; LL 2.3, 2.4, 2.5; M 5.1, 2.2

Outside and in the Environment

ACTIVITY

12

Trip to the Library!

1. Take your child to the library.
2. Have her *pick out* books that *she* is interested in and excited about reading with you. Avoid picking out books for her!
3. Choose a corner in the library to sit and read the books with your child for periods of 15 minutes. Some children have a hard time sitting still for longer periods of time.
4. Ask your child open-ended questions about the book. For example, ask her what did she like about the story, who was her favorite character, and what did she see in the pictures.
5. Be sure to interact with your child when you read the book. Stop and talk about the pages of the book as you read, and include your child while you read! This is especially helpful with children who have a hard time sitting still.

Attain a library card at your local library if you wish to check out books and take them home with you to read. This is an inexpensive way to read new books to your child!

Relates to AZ Readiness Standards: W-R1, R-R5, R-R1, R-R2, LS-R3, LS-R4, LS-R5, R-R5
Relates to AZ ECD Standards: SED 2.1; LL 1.2, 1.3, 2.1, 2.3, 2.6, 2.7

Why Important!
These types of activities encourage reading and writing. They also increase opportunities for meaningful language experiences and early mathematical thinking. This also encourages imagination and creativity!

Outside and in the Environment

Why Important!
These types of activities build motor development and problem-solving skills. Engaging with your child also increases opportunities for meaningful language experiences and early mathematical thinking.

Making Play Dough!

1. As your child's fine motor skills develop, it is important to provide him with the opportunity to practice mixing materials together to make and play with play dough.
2. First make your play dough by following the recipe below.
3. Be sure that the play dough is not sticky. If it feels sticky, add more flour as needed.
4. Ask your child what you need to make play dough. Have your child put the ingredients into a bowl and mix it together with his hands.
5. Be sure to interact with your child while you make the play dough. Ask such questions as: How many ingredients were needed to make the play dough? What kind of objects can you make?
6. Have your child make different objects with his play dough. Have your child mold and roll play dough into balls, using the palms of the hands facing each other and with fingers curled slightly towards the palm.

Play Dough Recipe

4 cups flour	1 cup salt
2 tablespoons alum powder (a spice)	2 tablespoons oil
2 cup warm water	

Mix ingredients together. Add extra flour if needed. You can add food coloring or tempera paint if you wish to have color—Store in a plastic bag or airtight container when finished.

Relates to AZ Readiness standards: 5M-R1, 1SC-R5
Relates to AZ ECD Standards: SED 2.1, 3.2; PD 1.3; M 3.1; A 1.1

ACTIVITY

14   Come Pot a Plant with Me!

MATERIALS NEEDED: Pot, small flower or plant, potting soil, rocks, and water

1. As your child's fine motor skills develop, it is important to provide her with the opportunity to practice using small muscles in her body. Planting a flower in a pot is a great opportunity to increase fine motor skills.
2. Get a small pot with a hole at the bottom to allow water to drain.
3. Have your child place three or four small rocks in the bottom to allow the water to drain through the hole.
4. Then have her put a small amount of soil in the bottom of the pot.
5. Next, have your child place the flower into the pot.
6. Fill in the remainder of the pot with soil. Fill to the top and pat down firmly. Water the plant.

Also, enjoy this activity together by potting your own plant!

Relates to AZ Readiness standards: 5M-R1, 1SC-R5
Relates to AZ ECD Standards: SED 2.1, 3.2; PD 1.3; M 3.1; A 1.1

Why Important!
These types of activities build motor development and problem-solving skills. Engaging with your child also increases opportunities for meaningful language experiences and early mathematical thinking.

REFERENCES

Adams, M. (1990). *Beginning to read: Thinking and learning about print.* Cambridge, MA: MIT Press.

Adams, M., Foorman, B., Lundberg, I., & Beeler, T. (1998). The elusive phoneme: Why phonemic awareness is so important and how to help children develop it. *American Educator, 21* (1&2), 18–29.

Allen, R. (1976). *Language experiences in communication.* Boston: Houghton Mifflin.

Albers, C. A., Kenyon, D. M., & Boals, T. J., (2009). Measures for determining English language proficiency and the resulting implications for instructional provision and intervention. *Assessment for Effective Intervention, 34*(2), 74–85.

Altwerger, B., Diehl-Faxon, J., & Dockstader-Anderson, K. (1985). Read-aloud events as meaning construction. *Language Arts, 62,* 476–484.

American Educational Research Association, American Psychological Association, & National Council on Measurement in Education. (1999). *Standards for educational and psychological testing.* Washington, DC: Authors.

Anderson, D., Huston, A., Linebarger, K., & Wright, J. (2002). Early childhood viewing and adolescent behavior. *Monograph for the Society for Research in Child Development, 66* (serial number 264).

Anderson, G., & Markle, A. (1985). Cheerios, McDonald's and Snickers: Bringing EP into the classroom. *Reading Education in Texas, 1,* 30–35.

Ashton-Warner, S. (1963). *Teacher.* New York: Simon & Schuster.

Askov, E. N., Grinder, E. L., & Kassab, C. (2005). Impact of family literacy on children. *Family Literacy Forum, 4*(1), 38–39.

August, D. & Hakuta, K. (Eds.) (1997). *Improving schooling for language-minority children: A research agenda.* National Research Council and Institute of Medicine. Washington, DC: National Academy Press.

Baghban, M. (1984). *Our daughter learns to read and write.* Newark, DE: International Reading Association.

Baker, L., Serpell, R., & Sonnenschein, S. (1995). Opportunities for literacy learning in homes of urban preschoolers. In L. Morrow (Ed.), *Family literacy: Connections in schools and communities* (pp. 236–252). Newark, DE: International Reading Association.

Barbour, A. (1998–1999). Home literacy bags: Promote family involvement. *Childhood Education, 75*(2), 71–75.

Barclay, K. H. (2010). Using song picture books to support early literacy development. *Childhood Education, 86,* 138–145.

Barrentine, S. (1996). Engaging with reading through interactive read-alouds. *The Reading Teacher, 50,* 36–43.

Bateson, G. (1979). *Mind and nature.* London: Wildwood House.

Bauer, E., & Manyak, P. (2008). Creating language-rich instruction for English language learners. *The Reading Teacher, 62,* 176–178.

Bear, D., Invernizzi, M., Templeton, S., & Johnston, F. (2008). *Words their way: Word study for phonics, vocabulary, and spelling instruction* (4th ed.). Upper Saddle River, NJ: Merrill.

Beck, I. L. McKeown, M. G. (2007). Increasing young low-income children's oral vocabulary repertoires through rich and focused instruction. *The Elementary School Journal, 107*(3), 251–271.

Beck, I., McKeown, M. G., & Kucan, L. (2002). *Bringing new words to life: Robust vocabulary instruction.* New York: Guilford.

Becker, H., & Epstein, J. (1982). Parent involvement: A study of teacher practices. *Elementary School Journal, 83,* 85–102.

Bhavnagri, N., & Gonzalez-Mena, J. (1997). The cultural context of infant caregiving. *Childhood Education, 74,* 2–8.

Bialystok, E. (Ed.) (1991). *Language processing in bilingual children.* Cambridge, UK: Cambridge University Press.

Biemiller, A. (2001) Teaching vocabulary: Early, direct, and sequential. *American Educator* (25), 24–29.

Biemiller, A., & Boote, C. (2006). An effective method for building meaning vocabulary in primary grades. *Journal of Education Psychology, 98*(1). 44–62.

Biemiller, A., and Slonim, N. (2001). Estimating root word vocabulary growth in normative and advantaged populations: Evidence for a common sequence of vocabulary acquisition. *Journal of Educational Psychology, 93,* 498–520.

Bissex, G. (1980). *GNYS AT WRK: A child learns to read and write.* Cambridge, MA: Harvard University Press.

Black, J. (2003). Environment and development of the nervous system. In M. Gallagher & R. Nelson (Eds.), *Handbook of psychology Vol. 3: Biological psychology* (pp. 655–668). Hoboken, NJ: Wiley.

Black, J., Puckett, M., & Bell, M. (1992). *The young child: Development from prebirth through age eight.* New York: Merrill.

Bodrova, E., & Leong, C. (2007). *Tools of the mind: The Vygotskian approach to early childhood education* (2nd Ed.). Upper Saddle River, NJ: Prentice Hall.

Booth-Church, E. (1998). From greeting to goodbye. *Scholastic Early Childhood Today, 13*(1), 51–53.

Boroski, L. (1998). The what, how, and why of interactive writing. In S. Collom (Ed.), *Sharing the pen: Interactive writing with young children.* Fresno, CA: San Joaquin Valley Writing Project.

Bowman, B. (2006). Standards: At the heart of educational equity. *Young Children, 61,* 42–48.

Brabham, E., & Lynch-Brown, C. (2002). Effects of teachers' reading-aloud styles on vocabulary acquisition and comprehension of students in the early elementary grades. *Journal of Education Psychology, 94,* 3, 465–472.

Bredekamp, S. (1989). *Developmentally appropriate practice.* Washington, D.C.: National Association for the Education of Young Children of Young Children.

Brock, D., & Dodd, E. (1994). A family lending library: Promoting early literacy development. *Young Children, 49*(3), 16–21.

Bromley, K. (1988). *Language arts: Exploring connections.* Boston: Allyn & Bacon.

Brooks, R., & Meltzoff, (2005). The development of gaze following and its relation to language. *Developmental Science* 8(6). 535–543.

Brown, J. (1994). Parent workshops: Closing the gap between parents and teachers. *Focus on Early Childhood Newsletter, 7*(1).

Brown, K. M. (2010). Young authors: Writing workshop in kindergarten. *Young Children, 65,* 24–29.

Bruer, J., & Greenough, W. (2001). The subtle science of how experience affects the brain. In D. B. Bailey Jr., J. T. Bruer, F. J. Symons, & J. W. Lichtman (Eds.), *Critical thinking about critical periods* (pp. 209–232). Baltimore: Paul H. Brookes.

Bruner, J. (1983). Play, thought, and language. *Peabody Journal of Education, 60*(3), 60–69.

Burns, M. S,, Griffin, P., & Snow, C. (Eds.). (1999). *Starting out right: A guide to promoting children's reading success.* Washington, DC: National Academy Press.

Bus, A., van Izendoorn, M., & Pellegrini, A. (1995). Joint book reading makes for success in learning to read: A meta-analysis on intergenerational transmission of literacy. *Review of Educational Research, 65,* 1–21.

Butler, A., & Turbill, J. (1984). *Towards a reading-writing classroom.* Portsmouth, NH: Heinemann.

Cabell, S., Justice, L., Vukelich, C., Buell, M., & Han, M. (2008). Strategic and intentional shared storybook reading. In L. Justice & C. Vukelich (Eds.), *Achieving excellence in preschool literacy instruction* (pp. 198–220). New York: Guilford Press.

Calkins, L. (1994). *The art of teaching writing.* Portsmouth, NH: Heinemann.

Camaioni, L., Perucchini, P., Bellagamba, F., & Colonnesi, C. (2004). The role of declarative pointing in developing a theory of mind. *Infancy, 5,* 291–308.

Canizares, S. (1997). Sharing stories. *Scholastic Early Childhood Today, 12,* 46–48.

Cannella, G. (2002). *Kidworld: Childhood studies, global perspectives, and education.* New York: Peter Lang Publishers.

Carey, S. (1979). The child as word learner. In M. Halle, J. Bresnan, & G. Miller (Eds.), *Linguistic theory and psychological reality* (pp. 264–293). Cambridge, MA: MIT Press.

Casbergue, R., McGee, L., & Bedford, A. (2008). Characteristics of classroom environments associated with accelerated literacy development. In L. Justice & C. Vukelich (Eds.), *Achieving excellence in preschool literacy instruction* (pp. 167–181). New York: Guilford.

Cazden, C. (1976). Play with language and meta-linguistic awareness: One dimension of language experience. In J. Bruner, A. Jolly, & K. Sylva (Eds.), *Play: Its role in development and evolution* (pp. 609–618). New York: Basic Books.

Cazden, C. (1988). *Classroom discourse.* Portsmouth, NH: Heinemann.

Census Bureau of U.S. Citizenship and Immigration Services (formerly the Immigration and Naturalization Service). (2001). Immigrants, fiscal year 2001. Washington, DC: Census Bureau.

Cole, J. (1989). Anna Banana: 101 Jump Rope Rhymes. NY: HarperCollins.

Common Core State Standards Initiative. *Common Core State Standards: English language arts and literacy in history/social studies & science.* (2010). Retrieved July 13, 2010, from:.www.corestandards.org.

Chomsky, N. (1965). *Aspects of the theory of syntax.* Cambridge, MA: MIT Press.

Chris, T., & Wang, C. (2010). Bridging the vocabulary gap: What the research tells us about vocabulary instruction in early childhood. *Young Children.* 84–91.

Christian, K., Morrison, F., & Bryant, F. (1998). Predicting kindergarten academic skills: Interaction among child-care, maternal education, and family literacy environments. *Early Childhood Research Quarterly, 13,* 501–521.

Christie, J. (2008). The SBRR approach to early literacy instruction. In L. M. Justice & C. Vukelich (Eds.), *Achieving excellence in preschool literacy instruction* (pp. 25–40). New York: Guilford.

Christie, J., Johnsen, E. P., & Peckover, R. (1988). The effects of play period duration on children's play patterns. *Journal of Research in Childhood Education, 3,* 123–131.

Christie, J., & Stone, S. (1999). Collaborative literacy activity in print-enriched play centers: Exploring the "zone" in same-age and multi-age groupings. *Journal of Literacy Research, 31,* 109–131.

Christie, J., & Wardle, F. (1992). How much time is needed for play? *Young Children,* 47 (93), 28–32.

Chukovsky, K. (1976). The sense of nonsense verse. In J. Bruner, A. Jolly, & K. Sylva (Eds.), *Play: Its role in development and evolution* (pp. 596–602). New York: Basic Books.

Clark, E. (1983). Meanings and concepts. In J. Flavell & E. Markman (Eds.), *Handbook of child psychology: Vol. 3. Cognitive development* (4th ed. pp. 787–840.). New York: Wiley.

Clarke, A., & Kurtz-Costes, B. (1997). Television viewing, educational quality of the home environment, and school readiness. *Journal of Educational Research, 90,* 279–285.

Clarke, L. (1988). Invented spelling versus traditional spelling in first graders' writing: Effects on learning to spell and read. *Research in the Teaching of English, 22,* 281–309.

Clay, M. (1975). *What did I write?* Auckland, NZ: Heinemann.

Clay, M. (1985). *The early detection of reading difficulties* (3rd ed.). Portsmouth, NH: Heinemann.

Clay, M. (1989). Telling stories. *Reading Today, 6*(5), 24.

Clay, M. (1991). *Becoming literate.* Portsmouth, NH: Heinemann Books.

Clements, D., & Sarama, J. (2003). Young children and technology: What *does* the research say? *Young Children, 58,* 34–41.

Cochran-Smith, M. (1984). *The making of a reader.* Norwood, NJ: Ablex.

Cochran-Smith, M., Kahn, J., & Paris, C. (1986, March). *Play with it; I'll help you with it; Figure it out; Here's what it can do for you.* Paper presented at the Literacy Research Center Speaker Series, Graduate School of Education, University of Pennsylvania. Philadelphia.

Collier, V. (1987). The effect of age on acquisition of a second language for school. *New Focus,* 1 (2).

Collin, B. (1992). *Read to me: Raising kids who love to read.* New York: Scholastic.

Collins, M. (1997). Sounds like fun. In B. Farber (Ed.), *The parents' and teachers' guide to helping young children learn* (pp. 213–218). Cutchoque, NY: Preschool Publications.

Collins, M. (2005). ESL preschoolers' English vocabulary acquisition from storybook reading. *Reading Research Quarterly, 40,* 406–408.

Comer, J. P., & Haynes, N. (1991). Parent involvement in schools: An ecological approach. *The Elementary School Journal, 91*(3), 271–277.

Coody, B. (1997). *Using literature with young children.* Chicago: Brown & Benchmark Publishing.

Copeland, J., & Gleason, J. (1993). *Causes of speech disorders and language delays.* Tucson: University of Arizona Speech and Language Clinic.

Corballis, M. C. (1991). *The lopsided ape: Evolution of the generative mind.* New York: Oxford University Press.

Council of Chief State School Officers and National Governors Association. (2002). *Common core standards-English language arts.* Retrieved from www.corestandards.org.

Cowley, F. (1997, Spring/Summer). The language explosion. *Newsweek: Your Child,* 16–18, 21–22.

Cromer, A. (1997). *Connected knowledge: Science, philosophy, and education.* New York: Oxford University Press.

Crystal, D. (1995). *Cambridge encyclopedia of the English language.* New York: Cambridge University Press.

Cummins, J. (1994). Primary language instruction and the education of language minority students. In California State Department of Education (Ed.), *Schooling and language minority students: A theoretical framework* (2nd ed., pp. 3–46). Los Angeles: Evaluation, Dissemination, and Assessment Center, California State University, Los Angeles.

Cunningham, A., & Stanovich, K. (1998). What reading does for the mind. *American Educator, 21*(1&2), 8–15.

Curtiss, S. (1977). *Genie: A psycholinguistic study of a modern-day "wild child."* New York: Academic Press.

Danst, C., Lowe, L., & Bartholomew, P. (1990). Contingent social responsiveness, family ecology, and infant communicative competence. *National Student Speech-Language-Hearing Association Journal, 17*(1), 39–49.

Degarmo, D. S., Forgatch, M., & Martinez, C. (1999). Parenting of divorced mothers as a link between social status and boys' academic outcomes: Unpacking the effects of socioeconomic status. *Child Development, 70,* 1231–1245.

Delpit, L. (1997). Ebonics and cultural responsive instruction. *Rethinking School Journal, 12*(1), 6–7.

DeLoache, J., (1984). *What's this? Maternal questions in joint picture book reading with toddlers.* Paper presented at the Annual Meeting of the American Educational Research Association, New Orleans, LA.

Demo, D. (2000). *Dialects in education* (ERIC/CLL Resources Guide online). Washington, DC: ERIC: Clearinghouse on Language and Linguistics.

Dewey, J. (1938). *Experiences and education.* New York: Collier Books.

Dickinson, D. K. (2010, April). *Too precious to get it wrong: Trends, challenges and directions in early literacy intervention.* Paper presented at the Literacy Development for Young Children Research Forum. Chicago: International Reading Association.

Dickinson, D. K., Darrow, C. L., & Tinubu, T. A. (2008). Patterns of teacher–child conversations in Head Start classrooms: Implications for an empirically grounded approach to professional development. *Early Education and Development, 19*(3), 396–429.

Dickinson, D. K., McCabe, A., Anastaspoulos, L., Peisner-Feinberg, E. S., & Poe, M. D. (2003). The comprehensive language approach to early literacy: The interrelationships among vocabulary, phonological sensitivity, and print knowledge among preschool-aged children. *Journal of Educational Psychology, 95*(3), 465–481.

Dickinson, D., McCabe, A., Clark-Chiarelli, N., & Wolf, A. (2004). Cross-language transfer of phonological awareness in low-income Spanish and English bilingual preschool children. *Applied Psycholinguistics, 25,* 323–347.

Dickinson, D., & Smith, M. W. (1994). Long-term effects of preschool teachers' book readings on low-income children's vocabulary and story comprehension. *Reading Research Quarterly, 29,* 104–122.

Dickinson, D., & Tabors, P. (Eds.) (2001). *Beginning literacy and language: Young children learning at home and in school.* Baltimore: Brookes.

Dodd, B., & Bradford, A. (2000). A comparison of three therapy methods for children with different types of developmental phonological disorder. *International Journal of Language and Communication Disorders. 35,* 189–209.

Dodge & Coker, (2010). The Creative Curriculum for Early Childhood Education Silver Spring, MD

Dodge, D., Heroman, C., Charles, J., & Maiorca, J. (2004). Beyond outcomes, how ongoing assessment supports children's learning and leads to meaningful curriculum. *Young Children, 59(1),* 20–28.

Duke, N. (2000). For the rich it's richer: Print experiences and environments offered to children in very low- and very high-SES first grade classrooms. *American Educational Research Journal, 37,* 441–478.

Dunn, L., & Dunn, L. (1997). *Peabody Picture Vocabulary Test III.* Circle Pines, MN: American Guidance Service.

Durkin, D. (1966). *Children who read early.* New York: Teachers College Press.

Early Childhood Research Institute on Measuring Growth and Development. (2000). Individual Growth and Development Indicator (IGDI). The *Young Exceptional Children Monograph* Series #4. Longmont, Co: Sopris West Publisher.

Edelman, G. (1995, June). Cited in Swerdlow, J. Quiet miracles of the brain. *National Geographic, 187*(6), 2–41.

Ehri, L. (1997). Phonemic awareness and learning to read. *Literacy Development in Young Children, 4*(2) 2–3.

Ehri, L., Nunes, S., Willows, D., Schuster, B., Yaghoub-Zadeh, Z., & Shanahan, T. (2001). Phonemic awareness instruction helps children learn to read: Evidence from the National Reading Panel's meta-analysis. *Reading Research Quarterly, 36,* 250–287.

Ehri, L., & Roberts, T. (2006). The roots of learning to read: Acquisition of letters and phonemic awareness. In S. Neuman & D. Dickinson (Eds.), *Handbook of early literacy research* (2nd ed., pp. 113–131). New York: Guilford.

Enz, B. (1992). *Love, laps, and learning to read.* Paper presented at International Reading Association Southwest Regional Conference, Tucson, AZ.

Enz, B. (2003). The ABC's of Family Literacy. In A. DeBruin-Pareki and B. Krol-Sinclair (Eds.), *Family literacy: From theory to practice.* (pp. 50–67). Newark, DE. International Reading Association.

Enz, B., & Christie, J. (1997). Teacher play interaction styles: Effects on play behavior and relationships with teacher training and experience. *International Journal of Early Childhood Education, 2,* 55–69.

Enz, B., & Foley, D. (2009). Sharing a Language and Literacy Legacy—A Middle-Class Family's Experience. In Guofang Li (Ed)., *Multicultural families, home literacies, and mainstream schooling* (pp. 153–174). Charlotte, NC: New Age Information.

Enz, B., Kortman, S., & Honaker, C. (2002). *Trade secrets: For primary/elementary teachers.* (2nd ed., pp. 36–44). Dubuque, IA: Kendall-Hunt Publishers,

Enz, B., & Morrow, L. M. (2009). *Assessing preschool literacy development.* Newark, DE: International Reading Association.

Enz, B., Rhodes, M. & LaCount, M. (2008). Easing the transition: Family support programs and early school success. In M. Cornish (Ed.). *Promising practices for partnering with families the early year* (pp. 59–78). Charlotte, NC: Information Age Publishing.

Enz, B., & Searfoss, L. (1995). Let the circle be unbroken: Teens as literacy teachers and learners. In L. M. Morrow (Ed.), *Family literacy: Multiple perspectives* (pp. 115–128). Reston, VA: International Reading Association.

Epstein, J. (1986). Parents' reactions to teacher practices of parent involvement. *Elementary School Journal, 86,* 277–294.

Epstein, J. (1996). School/family/community partnerships: Caring for the children we share. *Phi Delta Kappa, 76,* 701–712.

Ericson, L., & Juliebö, M. (1998). *The phonological awareness handbook for kindergarten and primary teachers.* Newark, DE: International Reading Association.

Evers, A. J., Lang, L. F., & Smith, S. V. (2009). An ABC literacy journey: Anchoring in texts, bridging language and creating stories. *The Reading Teacher, 62,* 461–470.

Ezell, H. K., & Justice, L. M. (2005). *Shared storybook reading: Building young children's language & emergent literacy skills.* Baltimore: Brookes Publishing Co.

Faltis, C. (2001). *Joinfostering: Teaching and learning in multilingual classrooms* (3rd ed.). New York: Prentice Hall.

Fein, G., Ardila-Rey, A., & Groth, L. (2000). The narrative connection: Story and literacy. In K. Roskos & J. Christie (Eds.), *Play and literacy in early childhood: Research from multiple perspectives* (pp. 27–43). Mahwah, NJ: Erlbaum.

Feitelson, D., & Goldstein, Z. (1986). Patterns of book ownership and reading to young children in Israeli school-oriented and nonschool-oriented families. *The Reading Teacher, 39,* 924–930.

Feldgus, E., & Cardonick, I. (1999). *Kid Writing: A systematic approach to phonics, journals, and writing workshop.* Bothell, WA: The Wright Group/McGraw-Hill.

Fennell, C. T., Byers-Heinlein, K. & Werker, J. F. (2007). Using speech sounds to guide word learning: The case of bilingual infants. *Child Development, 78*(5), 1510–1525.

Fernandez-Fein, S., & Baker, L. (1997). Rhyme and alliteration sensitivity and relevant experiences among preschoolers from diverse backgrounds. *Journal of Literacy Research, 29,* 433–459.

Ferreiro, E., & Teberosky, A. (1982). *Literacy before schooling.* Exeter, NH: Heinemann.

Fessler, R. (1998). Room for talk: Peer support for getting into English in an ESL kindergarten. *Early Childhood Research Quarterly, 13,* 379–410.

Field, T., Woodson, R., Greenberg, R., & Cohen, D. (1982). Discrimination and imitation of facial expressions by neonates. *Science, 218,* 179–181.

Fisher, B. (1995). Things take off: Note taking in the first grade. In P. Cordeiro (Ed.), *Endless possibilities: Generating curriculum in social studies and literacy* (pp. 21–32). Portsmouth, NH: Heinemann.

Flom, R., Deák, G. O., Phill, C., & Pick, A. D. (2003). Nine-month-olds' shared visual attention as a function of gesture and object location. *Infant Behavior and Development, 27,* 181–194.

Foley, D. (2010). *Instructional strategies and their role in the achievement of first grade students' literacy skills as measured by benchmark assessments.* Unpublished doctoral dissertation, Arizona State University.

Forrest, K. (2002). Are oral-motor exercises useful in the treatment of phonological/articulatory disorders? *Seminars in Speech and Language, 23,* 15–25.

Fractor, J., Woodruff, M., Martinez, M., & Teale, W. (1993). Let's not miss opportunities to promote voluntary reading: Classroom libraries in the elementary school. *The Reading Teacher, 46*, 476–484.

Francis, D., Rivera, M., Lesaux, N., Kieffer, M., & Rivera, H. (2006). *Practical guidelines for the education of English language learners: Research based recommendations for instruction and academic interventions.* Portsmouth, NH: RMC Research Corporation, Center on Instruction. Available at: www.centeroninstruction.org/files/ELL1-Interventions.pdf.

Freeman, Y., & Freeman, D. (1994). Whole language learning and teaching for second language learners. In C. Weaver (Ed.), *Reading process and practice: From sociopsycholinguistics to whole language.* (pp. 558–629). Portsmouth, NH: Heinemann.

Galda, L., Cullinan, B., & Strickland, D. (1993). *Language, literacy, and the child.* Fort Worth, TX: Harcourt Brace Jovanovich.

Gallas, K. (1992). When the children take the chair: A study of sharing in a primary classroom. *Language Arts, 69*, 172–182.

Garvey, C. (1977). *Play.* Cambridge, MA: Harvard University Press.

Gelfer, J. (1991). Teacher–parent partnerships: Enhancing communications. *Childhood Education, 67*, 164–167.

Geller, L. (1982). Linguistic consciousness-raising: Child's play. *Language Arts, 59*, 120–125.

Genishi, C. (1987). Acquiring oral language and communicative competence. In C. Seefeldt (Ed.), *The early childhood curriculum: A review of current research.* (pp. 75–106). New York: Teachers College Press.

Genishi, C., & Dyson, A. (1984). *Language assessment in the early years.* Norwood, NJ: Ablex.

Gersten, R., Baker, S. K., Shanahan, T., Linan-Thompson, S., Collins, P., & Scarcella, R. (2007). *Effective literacy and English language instruction for English learners in the elementary grades: A practice guide* (NCEE 2007-4011). Washington, DC: National Center for Education Evaluation and Regional Assistance, Institute of Education Sciences, U.S. Department of Education. Retrieved from http://ies.ed.gov/ncee/wwc/publications/practiceguides.

Gewertz, C. (April 7, 2010). Potential for both value and harm seen in K–3 common standards. *Education Week, 29*, 1, 20.

Glazer, J., & Giorgis, C. (2008). *Literature for young children: Supporting emergent literacy, ages 0-8.* New York: Prentice Hall.

Gleason, J. B. (1967, June). *Do children imitate?* Paper presented at International Conference on Oral Education of the Deaf, Lexington School for the Deaf, New York City.

Goldenberg, C. (2008, Summer). Teaching English-language learners: What the research does—and does not—say. *American Educator*, 8–24.

Golinkoff, R. (1983). The preverbal negotiation of failed messages: Insights into the transition period. In R. Golinkoff (Ed.), *The transition from prelinguistic to linguistic communication.* Hillsdale, NJ: Erlbaum.

Golinkoff, R. M., & Hirsh-Pasek, K. (1999). *How babies talk: The magic and mystery of language in the first three years of life.* New York: Dutton Publishers.

González, V., Oviedo, M. D., & O'Brien de Ramirez, K. (2001). Developmental, SES, and linguistic factors affecting bilingual and monolingual children's cognitive performance. *Bilingual Research Journal* 25 (1 & 2). http://www.tandf.co.uk/journals/ubrj

Gonzalez-Mena, J. (1997). *Multicultural issues in childcare* (2nd ed.). Mountain View, CA: Mayfield Publishing Company.

Good start, grow smart: The Bush administration's early childhood initiative. (2002). Washington, DC: The White House.

Gopnik, A., Meltzoff, A., & Kuhl, P. (2001). *The scientist in the crib.* New York: Harper-Collins.

Graves, D. (1983). *Writing: Teachers and children at work.* Portsmouth, NH: Heinemann.

Greenewald, M. J., & Kulig, R. (1995). Effects of repeated readings of alphabet books on kindergartners' letter recognition. In K. Hinchman, D. Leu, & C. Kinzer (Eds.), *Perspectives on literacy research and practice: Forty-fourth yearbook of the National Reading Conference* (pp. 231–234). Chicago: National Reading Conference.

Greenough, W., & Black, J. (1999). Experience, neural plasticity, and psychological development. In N. Fox, L. Leavitt, & J. Warhol (Eds.), *Proceedings of the 1999 Johnson & Johnson pediatric round table: The role of early experience in infant development* (pp. 29–40). Johnson & Johnson Consumer Companies, Inc. New Brunswick, New Jersey. Greenough, W., Black, J., & Wallace, C. (1987). Experience and brain development. *Child Development, 58,* 539–559.

Gregory, A. E., & Cahill, M. A. (2010). Kindergartners can do it, too! Comprehension strategies for early readers. *The Reading Teacher, 63,* 515–520.

Griffin, E., & Morrison, F. (1997). The unique contribution of home literacy environment to differences in early literacy skills. *Early Child Development and Care* (127–128), 233–243.

Grinder, E., Longoria Saenz, E., Askov, E., & Aldemir, J. (2005). What's happening during the parent–child interactive literacy component of family literacy programs? *Family Literacy Forum, 4*(1), 12–18.

Grosjean, F. (1982). *Life with two languages.* Cambridge, MA: Harvard University Press.

Gump, P. (1989). Ecological psychology and issues of play. In M. Bloch & A. Pellegrini (Eds.), *The ecological context of children's play* (pp. 35–36). Norwood, NJ: Ablex.

Hall, N. (1999). Real literacy in a school setting: Five-year-olds take on the world. *The Reading Teacher, 52,* 8–17.

Hall, N., & Duffy, R. (1987). Every child has a story to tell. *Language Arts, 64,* 523–529.

Hall, N., & Robinson, A. (1995). *Exploring writing and play in the early years.* London: David Fulton.

Halliday, M. (1975). *Learning how to mean: Explorations in the development of language.* London: Edward Arnold.

Hansen, C. (1998). *Getting the picture: Talk about story in a kindergarten classroom.* Unpublished doctoral dissertation, Arizona State University.

Hart, B., & Risley, T. (1995). *Meaningful differences in the everyday experience of young American children.* Baltimore, MD: Paul H. Brookes Publishing Company.

Hart, B., & Risley, T. (2003). The early catastrophe. *American Educator, 27*(4), 6–9.

Hazen, K. (October, 2001). *Teaching about dialects.* Educational Resources Information Center, ERIC: Clearinghouse on Language and Linguistics. EDO-FL-01-01. Washington, DC.

Head Start Bulletin # 78, (2005). English Language Learners. Washington, DC: Head Start Bureau

Healy, J. M. (1994). *Your child's growing mind: A practical guide to brain development and learning from birth to adolescence.* New York: Doubleday.

Healy, J. (1997, August–September). Current brain research. *Scholastic Early Childhood Today,* 42–43.

Heath, S. (1982). What no bedtime story means: Narrative skills at home and school. *Language in Society, 11,* 49–76.

Heath, S. (1983). *Ways with words.* Cambridge, UK: Cambridge University Press.

Hemmeter, M., Ostrosky, M., Artman, K., & Kinder, K. (2008). Moving right along: Planning transitions to prevent challenging behaviors. *Young Children, 63*(3), 18–25.

Henderson, A. T., & Berla, N. (1994). *A new generation of evidence: The family is critical to student achievement.* Washington, DC: National Committee for Citizens in Education. (ERIC Document No. ED 375 968).

Hetherington, E., Parke, R., and Otis, V. (2003). *Child psychology: A contemporary viewpoint* (5th ed.). New York: McGraw-Hill.

Hicks, D., & Mahaffeys, S. (1997). *Flannelboard classic tales.* Chicago: American Library Association.

Hirsch, E. D. (2003). Reading comprehension requires knowledge of words and the world. *American Educator, 27*(1), 10–14.

Hirschler, J. (1994). Preschool children's help to second language learners. *Journal of Educational Issues of Language Minority Students, 14*, 227–240.

Hoff, E. (2003). The specificity of environmental influence: Socioeconomic status affects of early vocabulary development via maternal speech. *Child Development, 74*(5). 1368–1378.

Hoffman, J., Roser, N., & Battle, J. (1993). Reading aloud in classrooms: From modal toward a "model." *The Reading Teacher, 46*, 496–503.

Holdaway, D. (1979). *The foundations of literacy.* Sydney: Ashton Scholastic.

Howard, S., Shaughnessy, A., Sanger, D., & Hux, K. (1998). Let's talk! Facilitating language in early elementary classrooms. *Young Children, 53*(3), 34–39.

Huck, C., Kiefer, B., Hepler, S., & Hickman, J. (2004). *Children's literature in the elementary school.* New York: The McGraw-Hill Company.

Huey, E. (1908). *The psychology and pedagogy of reading.* New York: Macmillan.

Huttenlocher, J. (1991). Early vocabulary growth: Relations to language input and gender. *Developmental Psychology, 27*(2), 236–248.

Huttenlocher, P. (1999). Synaptogenesis in human cerebral cortex and the concept of critical periods. In N. Fox, L. Leavitt, & J. Warhol (Eds.), *Proceedings of the 1999 Johnson & Johnson pediatric round table: The role of early experience in infant development* (pp. 15–28). Johnson & Johnson Consumer Companies, Inc. New Brunswick, New Jersey.

Iannucci, C. K. (2007). *Repeated interactive read-alouds in preschool and kindergarten.* Retrieved on April 6, 2010, from:.www.readingrockets.org/article/16287.

International Reading Association/National Association for the Education of Young Children (IRA/NAEYC). (1998). Learning to read and write: Developmentally appropriate practices for young children. *Young Children, 53*(4), 30–46.

International Reading Association/National Council of Teachers of English (IRA/NCTE). (1994). *Standards for the assessment of reading and writing.* Newark, DE, and Urbana, IL: International Reading Association and National Council of Teachers of English.

Invernizzi, M., Meier, J., Swank, L. & Juel, C. (1999). *Phonological Awareness Literacy Screening teacher's manual.* Charlottesville, NC: University Printing Services.

Isenberg, J. P., & Jalongo, M. R. 1993. *Creative expression and play in the early childhood curriculum.* New York: Macmillan.

Jackman, H. (1997). *Early education curriculum: A child's connection to the world.* Albany, NY: Delmar.

Jacobs, B., Schall, M., & Scheibel, A. B. (1993). A quantitative dendritic analysis of Wernicke's area in humans: II. Gender, hemispheric, and environmental factors. *Journal of Comparative Neurology, 327*, 97–111.

Jalongo, M. (1995). Promoting active listening in the classroom. *Childhood Education, 72*(1), 13–18.

Johnson, J., Christie, J., & Wardle, F. (2005). *Play, development, and early education.* New York: Allyn & Bacon.

Johnson, J., Christie, J., & Yawkey, T. (1999). *Play and early childhood development* (2nd ed.). Glenview, IL: Scott, Foresman.

Johnston, E., & Costello, P. (2005). Principles for literacy assessment. *Reading Research Quarterly, 40*(2), 256–267.

Jones, E., & Reynolds, G. (1992). *The play's the thing: Teachers' roles in children's play.* New York: Teachers College Press.

Justice, L. (2002). Word exposure conditions and preschoolers' novel word learning during shared storybook reading. *Reading Psychology, 23*, 87–106.

Justice, L., Bowles, R., & Skibbe, L. (2006). Measuring preschool attainment of print concepts: A study of typical and at-risk 3- to 5-year-old children. *Language, Speech, and Hearing Services in Schools, 37*, 1–12.

Justice, L., & Ezell, H. (2000). Enhancing children's print and word awareness through home-based parent intervention. *American Journal of Speech-Language Pathology, 9*, 257–269.

Justice, L., & Ezell, H. (2002). Use of storybook reading to increase print awareness in at-risk children. *American Journal of Speech-Language Pathology, 11*, 17–29.

Justice, L., Kaderavek, J., Fan, X., Sofka, A., & Hunt, A. (2009). Accelerating preschoolers' early literacy development through classroom-based teacher-child storybook reading and explicit print referencing. *Language, Speech, and Hearing Services in Schools, 40*, 67–85.

Justice, L., & Pence, K. (2005). *Scaffolding with storybooks: A Guide for Enhancing Young Children's Language and Literacy Achievement.* Newark, DE: International Reading Association.

Justice, L., Pullen, P., & Pence, K. (2008). Influence of verbal and nonverbal references to print on preschoolers' visual attention to print during storybook reading. *Developmental Psychology, 44*, 855–866.

Kalb, C. & Namuth, T. (1997, Spring/Summer). When a child's silence isn't golden. *Newsweek: Your Child*, 23.

Kim, K., Relkin, N., Lee, K., & Hirsch, J. (1997). Distinct cortical areas associated with native and second languages. *Nature* 388, 171–174.

Kotulak, R. (1997). *Inside the brain: Revolutionary discoveries of how the mind works.* Kansas City, MO: Andrews McMeel Publishing.

Krashen, S. (1981). Bilingual education and second language acquisition theory. California State Department of Education (Ed.), *Schooling and language minority students: A theoretical framework* (pp. 51–79). Los Angeles: Evaluation, Dissemination, and Assessment Center.

Krashen, S. (1987). Encouraging free reading. In M. Douglass (Ed.), *51st Claremont Reading Conference Yearbook.* Claremont, CA: Center for Developmental Studies.

Kuhl, P. (1993). *Life language.* Seattle: University of Washington.

Kuhl, P. K. (1999). The role of experience in early language development: Linguistic experience alters the perception and production of speech. In N. Fox, L. Leavitt, & J. Warhol (Eds.), *Proceedings of the 1999 Johnson & Johnson Pediatric Round Table, "The role of early experience in infant development"* (pp. 101–125). Johnson & Johnson Consumer Companies, Inc.

Kuhl, P. (2000). The role of experience in early language development: Linguistic experience alters the perception and production of speech. In N. Fox, L. Leavitt, & J. Warhol (Eds.), *Proceedings of the 1999 Johnson & Johnson pediatric round table: The role of early experience in infant development* (pp. 101–125). New Brunswick, New Jersey.

Kuhl, P. (2004). Early language acquisition: Cracking the speech code. *Nature Reviews, 5*, 831–843.

Kuhl, P., Tsao, F., Liu, H. M., Zhang, Y., & de Boer, B. (2001). Language/culture/mind/brain: Progress at the margins between disciplines. In A. Damasio (Ed.), *Unity of knowledge: The convergence of natural and human science* (pp. 136–174). New York: The New York Academy of Sciences.

Kupetz, B., & Green, E. (1997). Sharing books with infants and toddlers: Facing the challenges. *Young Children, 52*(2), 22–27.

Labbo, L. (2005). Books and computer response activities that support literacy development. *Reading Teacher, 59*, 288–292.

Langdon, H. W. & Wiig, E. H. (2009). Multicultural issues in test interpretation. *Seminars in Speech and Language, 30* (4), 261–278.

Lapointe, A. (1986). The state of instruction in reading and writing in U.S. elementary schools. *Phi Delta Kappan, 68*, 135–138.

Lass, B. (1982). Portrait of my son as an early reader. *The Reading Teacher, 36*, 20–28.

Lessow-Hurley, J. (2000). *The foundations of dual language instruction.* New York: Longman.

Levin, D., & Carlsson-Paige, N. (1994). Developmentally appropriate television: Putting children first. *Young Children, 49*, 38–44.

Lewis, R., & Doorlag, D. (1999). *Teaching special students in general education classrooms.* Columbus, OH: Prentice Hall.

Lindfors, J. (1987). *Children's language and learning* (2nd ed.). Englewood Cliffs, NJ: Prentice Hall.

Linver, M. R., Brooks-Gunn, J., & Kohen, D. E. (2002). Family processes and pathways from income to young children's development. *Development Psychology, 38,* 719–734.

Luke, A., & Kale, J. (1997). Learning through difference: Cultural practices in early childhood language socialization. In E. Gregory (Ed.), *One child, many worlds: Early learning in multicultural communities* (pp. 11–29). New York: Teachers College Press.

MacLean, P. (1978). A mind of three minds: Educating the triune brain. In J. Chall & A. Mirsky (Eds.), *Education and the brain: 77th yearbook of the National Society for the Study of Education* (pp. 308–342). Chicago: University of Chicago Press.

Malloch, S., & Trevarthen, C. (2010*). Communicative musicality: Exploring the basis of human companionship.* London: Oxford University Press.

Manning-Kratcoski, A., & Bobkoff-Katz, K. (1998). Conversing with young language learners in the classroom. *Young Children, 53*(3), 30–33.

Marcus, G. (2003). *The birth of the mind: How a tiny number of genes creates the complexities of human thought.* New York: Basic Books.

Martinez, M., & Roser, N. (1985). Read it again: The value of repeated readings during storytime. *The Reading Teacher, 38,* 782–786.

Martinez, M., & Teale, W. (1987). The ins and outs of a kindergarten writing program. *The Reading Teacher, 40,* 444–451.

Martinez, M., & Teale, W. (1988). Reading in a kindergarten classroom library. *The Reading Teacher, 41,* 568–572.

Mayberry, R. I., Lock, E., & Kazmi, H. (2001). Linguistic ability and early language exposure. *Nature, 4.* 17–38.

Mayberry, R. I., & Nicoladis, E. (2000). Gesture reflects language development: Evidence from bilingual children. *Current Directions in Psychological Science, 9,* 192–196.

McCardle, P., & Chhabra, V. (2004). *The voice of evidence in reading research.* Baltimore: Brookes.

McGee, L. (2005). The role of wisdom in evidence-based preschool literacy curricula. In B. Maloch, J. Hoffman, D. J., Schallert, C. D., Fairbanks, & J. Worthy (Eds.), *54th Yearbook of the National Reading Conference* (pp. 1–21). Oak Creek, WI: National Reading Conference.

McGee, L. (2007). *Transforming literacy practices in preschool.* New York: Scholastic.

McGee, L.M., & Richgels, D.J. (1996). *Literacy's beginnings: Supporting young readers and writers* (2nd ed.). Boston, MA: Allyn and Bacon.

McGee, L., & Richgels, D. (2008). *Literacy's beginnings: Supporting young readers and writers* (5th ed.). Boston, MA: Allyn and Bacon.

McKeown, M., & Beck, I. (2006). Encouraging young children's language interactions with stories. In D. Dickenson & S. Neuman (Eds.), *Handbook of Early Literacy Research Vol. 2* (pp. 281–294). New York: Guilford.

McNeal, R. B. Jr. (1999). Parental involvement as social capital: Differential effectiveness on science achievement, truancy, and dropping out. *Social Forces, 78*(1), 117–144.

Mehan, H. (1979). *Learning lessons: Social organization in the classroom.* Cambridge: Harvard University Press.

Meisels, S. (2001). Fusing assessment and intervention: Changing parents' and providers' views of young children. *Zero to Three, 21* (4), 4–10.

Menyuk, P. (1988). *Language development: Knowledge and use.* Glenview, IL: Scott, Foresman.

Miller, S. (1997). Family television viewing: How to gain control. *Childhood Education, 74*(1), 38–40.

Moffett, J., & Wagner, B. (1983). *Student-centered language arts and reading, K–13: A handbook for teachers* (3rd ed.). Boston: Houghton Mifflin.

Moir, A., & Jessel, D. (1991). *Brain sex: The real differences between men and women.* New York: Carol Publishing Group.

Morisset, C. (1995). Language development: Sex differences within social risk. *Developmental Psychology,* 851–865.

Morrow, L. (1982). Relationships between literature programs, library corner designs, and children's use of literature. *Journal of Educational Research, 75*, 339–344.

Morrow, L. (1983). Home and school correlates of early interest in literature. *Journal of Educational Research, 76*, 221–230.

Morrow, L. (1985). Reading and retelling stories: Strategies for emergent readers. *The Reading Teacher, 38*, 870–875.

Morrow, L. (1988). Young children's responses to one-to-one story readings in school settings. *Reading Research Quarterly, 23*, 89–107.

Morrow, L. (2005). *Literacy development in the early years.* New York: Pearson.

Morrow, L. (2009). *Literacy development in the early years: Helping children read and write* (6th ed.). New York: Pearson.

Morrow, L., Freitag, E., & Gambrell, L. (2009). *Using children's literature in preschool to develop comprehension: Understanding and enjoying books.* Newark, DE: International Reading Association.

Morrow, L., & Tracey, D. (1997). Strategies used for phonics instruction in early childhood classrooms. *The Reading Teacher, 50*, 644–651.

Morrow, L., Tracey, D., Gee-Woo, D., & Pressley, M. (1999). Characteristics of exemplary first-grade literacy instruction. *The Reading Instructor, 52*, 462–476.

Morrow, L., & Weinstein, C. (1982). Increasing children's use of literature through program and physical changes. *Elementary School Journal, 83*, 131–137.

Mowery, A. (1993). *Qualifying paper on early childhood parent education programs.* Unpublished manuscript, University of Delaware, Newark, DE.

Namy, L., & Waxman, S. (2000). Naming and exclaiming: Infants' sensitivity to naming contexts. *Journal of Cognition and Development, 1*, 405–428.

National Early Literacy Panel (NELP). (2008). *Developing early literacy: Report of the National Early Literacy Panel: A scientific synthesis of early literacy development and implications for intervention.* Washington, DC: National Center for Family Literacy.

National Association for the Education of Young Children (NAEYC) & NAECS/SDE. (2004). Where we stand: On curriculum, assessment, and program evaluation. *Young Children, 59*, 51–54.

National Reading Panel. (2000). *Teaching children to read: An evidence-based assessment of the scientific research literature on reading and its implications for reading instruction.* Washington, DC: U.S. Government Printing Office.

National Research Council. (1999). *Starting out right: A guide to promoting children's reading success.* Washington, DC: National Academy Press.

Neuman, S. (1988). The displacement effect: Assessing the relationship between television viewing and reading performance. *Reading Research Quarterly, 23*, 414–440.

Neuman, S. (1995). *Linking literacy and play.* Newark, DE: International Reading Association.

Neuman, S. (1999). Books make a difference: A study of access to literacy. *Reading Research Quarterly, 34*(3), 286–311.

Neuman, S., & Celano, D. (2001). Access to print in low-income and middle-income communities: An ecological study of four neighborhoods. *Reading Research Quarterly, 30*, 8–26.

Neuman, S., Copple, C., & Bredekamp, S. (1998). *Learning to read and write: Developmentally appropriate practices.* (A joint position paper of the International Reading Association and the National Association for the Education of Young Children). Retrieved on June 19, 2010, from: www.pbs.org/teacherline/courses/rdla155/pdfs/c2s2_5devapprop.pdf. Retrieved on June 19, 2010.

Neuman, S., & Dwyer, J. (2009). Missing in action: Vocabulary instruction in Pre-K. *The Reading Teacher, 62*(5).

Neuman, S., & Roskos, K. (1993). *Language and literacy learning in the early years: An integrated approach.* Fort Worth, TX: Harcourt Brace Jovanovich.

Neuman, S., & Roskos, K. (1997). Literacy knowledge in practice: Contexts of participation for young writers and readers. *Reading Research Quarterly, 32,* 10–32.

Neuman, S., & Roskos. K. (2005). The state of the state prekindergarten standards. *Early Childhood Research Quarterly 20.* 125–145.

Neuman, S., & Roskos, K. (2007). *Nurturing knowledge: Building a foundation for school success by linking early literacy to math, science, art, and social studies.* New York: Scholastic.

Neuman, S., Roskos, K., Wright, T., & Lenhart, L. (2007). *Nurturing knowledge: Building a foundation for school success by linking early literacy to math, science, art, and social studies.* New York: Scholastic.

Newport, E. L., Bavelier, D., & Neville, H. J. (2001). Critical thinking about critical periods: Perspectives on a critical period for language acquisition. In E. Dupoux (Ed.), *Language, brain and cognitive development* (pp. 481–502). Cambridge, MA: MIT Press.

Noland, R. M. (2009). When no bilingual examiner is available: Exploring the use of ancillary examiners as a viable testing solution. *Journal of Psychoeducational Assessment, 27* (1). 29–45.

Nord, C. W., Lennon, J., Liu, B., & Chandler, K. (2000). *Home literacy activities and signs of children's emerging literacy, 1993 and 1999* [NCES Publication 2000–026]. Washington, DC: National Center for Education Statistics.

Norris, A., & Hoffman, P. (1990). Language intervention with naturalistic environments. *Language, Speech, and Hearing Services in the Schools, 21,* 72–84.

Orellana, M., & Hernández, A. (1999). Taking the walk: Children reading urban environmental print. *The Reading Teacher, 52,* 612–619.

Ortiz, A. A. (2003). English language learners with special needs: Effective instructional strategies. ERIC Number ED469207. Washington DC: ERIC Clearinghouse on Language and Linguistics.

Ostrosky, M., Jung, E., & Hemmeter, M. (2008). *What works briefs: Helping children make transitions between activities.* Retrieved on June 4, 2008, from www.vanderbilt.edu/csefel/briefs.

Otto, B., (2006). *Language development in early childhood* (2nd ed.). Upper Saddle River, NJ: Merrill, Prentice Hall.

Paley, V. (1990). *The boy who would be a helicopter.* Cambridge, MA: Harvard University Press.

Penno, J., Wilkinson, I., & Moore, D. (2002). Vocabulary acquisition from teacher explanation and repeated listening to stories: Do they overcome the Matthew effect? *Journal of Educational Psychology, 94,* 1, 23–33.

Pentimonti, J., Zucker, T., & Justice, L. (in press). What are preschool teachers reading in their classrooms? *Reading Psychology.*

Pentimonti, J., Zucker, T., Justice, L., & Kaderavek, J. (2010). Informational text use in preschool classroom read-alouds. *The Reading Teacher, 63,* 656–665.

Phillips, B., Clancy-Menchetti, J., & Lonigan, C. (2008). Successful phonological awareness instruction with preschool children: Lessons from the classroom. *Topics in Early Childhood Special Education, 28,* 3–17.

Piasta, S., & Wagner, R. (2010). Developing early literacy skills: A meta-analysis of alphabet learning and instruction. *Reading Research Quarterly, 45,* 8–39.

Pinker, S. (1995). *The language instinct.* Hammersmith UK: Perennial (HarperCollins).

Piper, T. (1993). *Language for all our children.* New York: Macmillan.

Power, B. (1998). Author! Author! *Scholastic Early Childhood Today, 12,* 30–37.

Price, LH., van Kleeck, A., & Huberty, C.J. (2009). Talk during book sharing between parents and preschool children: A comparison between storybook and expository book conditions *Reading Research Quarterly, 44,* 171–194

Prior, J., & Gerard, M. (2004). *Environmental print in the classroom: Meaningful connections for learning to read.* Newark, DE: International Reading Association.

Pullen, P., & Justice, L. (2006). Enhancing phonological awareness, print awareness, and oral language skills in preschool children. In G. Moss & T. Swain (Eds.), *Early childhood and elementary literacy* (pp. 39–40). Dubuque, IA: McGraw-Hill/Dushkin.

Raines, S., & Isbell, R. (1994). *Stories: Children's literature in early education.* Albany, NY: Delmar.

Ramachandran, V. S. (2000). Mirror neurons and imitation learning as the driving force behind "the great leap forward" in human evolution. *Social Neuroscience Abstracts.* Vol. 133, No. 2, 310–327

Ramey, C. T., & Ramey, S. L. (1999). Beginning school for children at risk. In *The transition to kindergarten* (pp. 217–251). Baltimore: Paul H. Brookes Publishing Co.

Rasinski, T., & Padak, N. (2009). Write soon! *The Reading Teacher, 62,* 618–620.

Read, C. (1971). Pre-school children's knowledge of English phonology. *Harvard Educational Review, 41,* 1–34.

Reaney, L. M., Denton, K. L., & West, J. (2002, April). *Enriching environments: The relationship of home educational activities, extracurricular activities and community resources to kindergartners' cognitive performance.* Paper presented at the annual conference of the American Educational Research Association, New Orleans.

Rhodes, M., Enz, B., & LaCount, M. (2006). Leaps and bounds: Preparing parents for kindergarten. *Young Children, 61*(1), 50–51.

Rice, M., Huston, A., Truglio, R., and Wright, J. (1990) Words from *Sesame Street:* Learning vocabulary while viewing. *Development Psychology, 26,* 421–428.

Richgels, D. & Wold, L. (1998). Literacy on the road: Backpacking partnerships between school and home. *The Reading Teacher, 52,* 18–29.

Ritchie, S., James-Szanton, J., & Howes, C. (2002). Emergent literacy practices in early childhood classrooms. In C. Howes (Ed.), *Teaching 4- to 8-year-olds: Literacy, math, multiculturalism, and classroom community* (pp. 71–92). Baltimore: Brookes Publishing Co.

Roberts, T. (2008). Home storybook reading in primary or second language with preschool children: Evidence of equal effectiveness for second-language vocabulary acquisition. *Reading Research Quarterly, 43,* 103–130.

Roseberry-McKibbin, C. & O'Hanlon, L. (2005). Nonbiased assessment of English language learners: A tutorial. *Communication Disorders Quarterly, 26*(3), 178–185.

Rosenblatt, L. (1978). *The reader, the text, the poem: The transactional theory of the literary work.* Carbondale: Southern Illinois University Press.

Roser, N., & Martinez, M. (1985). Roles adults play in preschoolers' response to literature. *Language Arts, 62,* 485–490.

Roskos, K., & Christie, J. (Eds.). (2000). *Play and literacy in early childhood: Research from multiple perspectives.* Mahwah, NJ: Lawrence Erlbaum.

Roskos, K., & Christie, J. (Eds.). (2007a). *Play and literacy in early childhood: Research from multiple perspectives* (2nd ed.). Mahwah, NJ: Lawrence Erlbaum.

Roskos, K., & Christie, J. (2007b). Play in the context of the new preschool basics. In K. Roskos & J. Christie (Eds.), *Play and literacy in early childhood: Research from multiple perspectives* (2nd ed., pp. 83–100). Mahwah, NJ: Lawrence Erlbaum.

Roskos, K., Christie, J., Widman, S., & Holding, A. (2010). Three decades in: Priming for meta-analysis in play-literacy research. *Journal of Early Childhood Literacy, 10,* 55–96.

Roskos, K., & Neuman, S. (1993). Descriptive observations of adults' facilitation of literacy in play. *Early Childhood Research Quarterly, 8,* 77–97.

Roskos, K., Tabor, P., & Lenhart, L. (2004). *Oral language and early literacy in preschool.* Reston, VA: International Reading Association.

Sachs, J., Bard, B., & Johnson, M. L. (1981). Language learning with restricted input: Case studies of two hearing children of deaf parents. *Applied Psycholinguistics, 2,* 33–54.

Sakai, K. (2005). Language acquisition and brain development. *Science, 310* (4), 815–819.

Saville-Troike, M. (1988). Private speech: Evidence for second language learning strategies in the "silent period." *Journal of Child Language, 15,* 567–90.

Schickedanz, J. (1986). *Literacy development in the preschool* [sound filmstrip]. Portsmouth, NH: Heinemann.

Schickedanz, J. (1998). What is developmentally appropriate practice in early literacy? Considering the alphabet. In S. Neuman & K. Roskos (Eds.), *Children achieving: Best practices in early literacy* (pp. 20–37). Newark, DE: International Reading Association.

Schickedanz, J. A., & Casbergue, R. M. (2009). *Writing in preschool: Learning to orchestrate meaning and marks.* Newark, DE: IRA.

Schnabel, J. (2009). The black box. *Nature, 459,* 765–768.

Schon, D. (1983). *The reflective practitioner: How professionals think in action.* New York: Basic Books.

Schunk, D. H. (2003). *Learning theories: An educational perspective* (4th ed). Upper Saddle River, NJ: Prentice Hall.

Schwartz, J. (1983). Language play. In B. Busching & J. Schwartz (Eds.), *Integrating the language arts in the elementary school* (pp. 81–89). Newark, DE: International Reading Association.

Segal, M., & Adcock, D. (1986). *Your child at play: Three to five years.* New York: Newmarket Press.

Sénéchal, M., & LeFevre, J. (2002), Parental involvement in the development of children's reading skill: A five-year longitudinal study. *Child Development, 73*(2), 445–460.

Sénéchal, M., Ouellette, G., & Rodney, D. (2006). The misunderstood giant: On the predictive role of early vocabulary to future reading. In D. Dickinson & S. Neuman (Eds.), *Handbook of early literacy research* (Vol. 2, pp. 173–184). New York: Guilford Press.

Shepard, L., Kagan, S., & Wurtz, E. (1998). Goal 1 early childhood assessments resource group recommends. *Young Children, 53,* 52–54.

Shevell, M. (2005). Outcomes at school age of preschool children with developmental language impairment. *Pediatric Neurology, 32*(4): 264–69.

Shore, R. (1997). *Rethinking the brain: New insights into early development.* New York: Families and Work Institute.

Siegler, R. S. (2005). Children's learning. *American Psychologist, 60,* 769–778.

Silverman, R., & Dibara-Crandell, J. (2010). Vocabulary practices in prekindergarten and kindergarten classrooms. *Reading Research Quarterly, 45*(3), 318–340.

Skinner, B. (1957). *Verbal behavior.* East Norwalk, CT: Appleton-Century-Crofts.

Smith, F. (1988). *Understanding reading* (4th ed.). Hillsdale, NJ: Erlbaum.

Smith, M., & Dickinson, D. (1994). Describing oral language opportunities and environments in Head Start and other preschool classrooms. *Early Childhood Research Quarterly, 9,* 345–366.

Smith, M. W., Brady, J. P., & Anastasopoulos, L. (2008). *Early language & literacy classroom observation: Pre-K tool.* Baltimore: Brookes Publishing Co.

Smith, M. W., & Dickinson, D. K. (2002). *Early Language and Literacy Classroom Observation Toolkit.* Baltimore: Brookes Publishing Co.

Snow, C. (2002). Second language learners and understanding the brain. A. Galaburda, S. Kosslyn, & C. Yves (Eds.), *The languages of the brain* (pp. 151–165). Cambridge, MA: Harvard University Press.

Snow, C., Burns, M., & Griffin, P. (1998). *Preventing reading difficulties in young children.* Washington, DC: National Academy Press.

Snow, C., Chandler, J., Lowry, H., Barnes, W., & Goodman, I. (1991). *Unfilled expectations: Home and school influences on literacy.* Cambridge, MA: Harvard University Press.

Snow, C., & Ninio, A. (1986). The contracts of literacy: What children learn from learning to read books. In W. Teale & E. Sulzby (Eds.), *Emergent literacy: Writing and reading.* (pp. 116–137). Norwood, NJ: Ablex.

Spinelli, C. G. (2008). Addressing the issue of cultural and linguistic diversity and assessment: Informal evaluation measures for English language learners. *Reading & Writing Quarterly, 24,* 101–118.

Sprenger, M. (1999). *Learning and memory: The brain in action.* Alexandria, VA: Association for Supervision and Curriculum Development.

Stahl, S. (1992). Saying the "p" word: Nine guidelines for exemplary phonics instruction. *The Reading Teacher, 45,* 618–625.

Stahl, S. (2003). How words are learned incrementally over multiple exposures. *American Educator, 27*(1), 18–19, 44.

Stahl, S., & Nagy, W. E. (2006). *Teaching word meaning.* Mahwah, NJ: Lawrence Erlbaum.

Stainback, S., & Stainback, W. (1992). *Curriculum considerations in inclusive classrooms.* Baltimore: Brookes.

Stanovich, K. (1986). Matthew effects in reading: Some consequences of individual differences in the acquisition of literacy. *Reading Research Quarterly, 21,* 360–407.

Stevens, R. J., Van Meter, P., & Warcholak, N. D. (2010). The effects of explicitly teaching story structure to primary grad children. *Journal of Literacy Research, 42,* 159–198.

Strickland, D., & Schickedanz, J. (2009). *Learning about print in preschool: Working with letters, words, and beginning links with phonemic awareness.* Newark, DE: International Reading Association.

Sulzby, E. (1985a). Children's emergent reading of favorite storybooks: A developmental study. *Reading Research Quarterly, 20,* 458–481.

Sulzby, E. (1985b). Kindergartners as writers and readers. In M. Farr (Ed.), *Advances in writing research, Vol. 1: Children's early writing development* (pp. 127–200). Norwood, NJ: Ablex.

Sulzby, E. (1990). Assessment of emergent writing and children's language while writing. In L. Morrow & J. Smith (Eds.), *Assessment for instruction in early literacy* (pp. 83–109). Englewood Cliffs, NJ: Prentice Hall.

Sulzby, E., & Barnhart, J. (1990). The developing kindergartner: All of our children emerge as writers and readers. In J. McKee (Ed.), *The developing kindergarten: Programs, children, and teachers* (pp. 169–189). Ann Arbor: Michigan Association for the Education of Young Children.

Sulzby, E., Barnhart, J., & Hieshima, J. (1989). Forms of writing and rereading from writing: A preliminary report. In J. Mason (Ed.), *Reading and writing connections* (pp. 31–63). Boston: Allyn and Bacon.

Sulzby, E., & Teale, W. (1991). Emergent literacy. In R. Barr, M. Kamil, P. Mosenthal, & P. D. Pearson (Eds.), *Handbook of reading research* (Vol. 2, pp. 727–757).). New York: Longman.

Swanborn, M., & de Glopper, K. (1999). Incidental word learning while reading: A meta-analysis. *Review of Educational Research, 69,* 261–285.

Sylwester, R. (1995). *A celebration of neurons: An educator's guide to the human brain.* Alexandria, VA: Association for Supervision and Curriculum Development.

Tabors, P. (1997). *One child, two languages.* Baltimore, MD: Paul Brookes.

Tabors, P. (1998). What early childhood educators need to know: Developing effective programs for linguistically and culturally diverse children and families. *Young Children, 53*(6), 20–26.

Tabors, P., & Snow, C. (1994). English as a second language in preschool programs. In F. Genesee (Ed.), *Educating second language children: The whole child, the whole curriculum, the whole community* (pp. 103–126). New York: Cambridge University Press.

Tabors, P., Snow, C., & Dickinson, D. (2001). Homes and schools together: Supporting language and literacy development. In D. Dickinson & P. Tabors (Eds.). *Beginning literacy with language: Young children learning at home and school* (pp. 313–334). Baltimore: Paul H. Brookes.

Taylor, D., & Dorsey-Gaines, C. (1988). *Growing up literate: Learning from inner-city families.* Portsmouth, NH: Heinemann.

Taylor, D., & Strickland, D. (1986). Family storybook reading. Exeter, NH: Heinemann.

Teale, W. (1986). Home background and young children's literacy development. In W. Teale & E. Sulzby (Eds.), *Emergent literacy: Writing and reading* (pp. 173–205). Norwood, NJ: Ablex.

Teale, W. (1987). Emergent literacy: Reading and writing development in early childhood. In J. Readence and R. Baldwin (Eds.), *Research in literacy: Merging perspectives.* (pp. 45–74). Thirty-sixth Yearbook of the National Reading Conference. Rochester, NY: National Reading Conference.

Teale, W. (2003). Reading aloud to young children as a classroom instructional activity: Insights from research and practice. In A. van Kleeck, S. Stahl, & E. Bauer (Eds.), *On reading books to children* (pp. 114–139). Mahwah, NJ: Erlbaum.

Teale, W., & Martinez, M. (1996). Reading aloud to young children: Teachers' reading styles and kindergartners' text comprehension. In C. Pontecorvo, M. Orsolini, B. Burge, & L. Resnick (Eds.), *Children's early text construction* (pp. 321–344). Mahwah, NJ: Erlbaum.

Thomas, W., & Collier, V. (1997). Two languages are better than one. *Educational Leadership, 55* (4), 23–26.

Thompson, R. (2001). Sensitive periods in attachment? In D. Bailey Jr., J. T. Bruer, F. Symons, & J. Lichtman (Eds.), *Critical thinking about critical periods* (pp. 83–106). Baltimore: Paul H. Brookes.

Thompson, R., & Nelson, C. (2001). Developmental science and the media: Early brain development. *American Psychologist, 56*, 5–15.

Thousand, J., & Villa, R. (1990). Sharing expertise and responsibilities through teacher teams. In W. Stainback & S. Stainback (Eds.), *Support networks for inclusive schooling: Interdependent integrated education* (pp. 151–166). Baltimore: Brookes.

Tincoff, R., & Jusczyk, P.W. (1999). Mama! Dada! Origins of word meaning. *Psychological Science* 10(2), 172–175.

Towell, J. (1998). Fun with vocabulary. *Reading Teacher, 51*, 356.

Trelease, J. (2006). *The read-aloud handbook.* New York: Macmillan.

Treiman, R., & Kessler, B. (2003). The role of letter names in the acquisition of literacy. In R. Kail (Ed.), *Advances in Child Development and Behavior, 31*, 105–135.

Tychsen, L. (2001). Critical periods for development of visual acuity, depth perception, and eye tracking. In D. Bailey Jr., J. Bruer, F. Symons, & J. Lichtman (Eds.), *Critical thinking about critical periods* (pp. 67–80). Baltimore: Paul H. Brookes.

Valdés, G., & Figueroa, R. A. (1994). *Bilingualism and testing: A special case of bias.* Norwood.

Valencia, S. (1990). A portfolio approach to classroom reading assessment: The whys, whats, and hows. *The Reading Teacher, 43*, 338–340.

van Manen, M. (1995). On the epistemology of reflective practice: Teachers and teaching. *Theory and Practice, 1*, 33–50.

Veatch, J. (1986). *Whole language in the kindergarten.* Tempe, AZ: Jan V Productions.

Veatch, J., Sawicki, F., Elliot, G., Flake, E., & Blakey, J. (1979). *Key words to reading: The language experience approach begins.* Columbus, OH: Merrill.

Vernon-Feagans, L. V. (1996). *Children's talk in communities and classrooms.* Cambridge, MA: Blackwell Publishers.

Vouloumanos, A., & Werker, J. F. (2007). Listening to language at birth: Evidence for a bias for speech in neonates. *Developmental Science, 10*, 159–164.

Vukelich, C. (1993). Play: A context for exploring the functions, features, and meaning of writing with peers. *Language Arts, 70*, 386–392.

Vukelich, C. (1994). Effects of play interventions on young children's reading of environmental print. *Early Childhood Research Quarterly, 9*, 153–170.

Vukelich, C., & Christie, J. (2009). *Building a foundation for preschool literacy: Effective instruction for children's reading and writing development* (2nd ed.). Newark, DE: International Reading Association.

Vygotsky, L. (1962). *Thought and language.* Cambridge, MA: MIT Press.

Vygotsky, L. (1978). *Mind in society: The development of psychological processes.* Cambridge, MA: Harvard University Press.

Wagstaff, J. (1998). Building practical knowledge of letter–sound correspondences: A beginner's word wall and beyond. *The Reading Teacher, 51*, 298–304.

Walker, D., Greenwood, C., Hart, B., & Carta, J. (1994). Prediction of school outcomes based on early language production and socio-economic factors. *Child Development, 65*, 606–621.

Wanerman, T. (2010). Using story drama with young preschoolers. *Young Children, 65*, 20–28

Wasik, B., & Bond, M. (2001). Beyond the pages of a book: Interactive book reading and language development in preschool classrooms. *Journal of Educational Psychology, 93*(2), 243–250.

Watson, R. (2001). Literacy and oral language: Implications for early literacy acquisition. In S.B. Neuman & D.K. Dickinson. *Handbook on early literacy research,* Vol. 1, (pp. 43–53). New York: Guildford Press.

Werker, J., & Byers-Heinlein, K. (2008). The youngest bilinguals: First steps in perception and comprehension of language. *Trends in Cognitive Sciences, 12*(4), 144–151.

Werker, J., & Tees, R. (2005). Speech perception as a window for understanding plasticity and commitment in language systems of the brain. *Developmental Psychobiology, 46*(3), 233–251.

Werker, J., & Yeung, H. (2005). Infant speech perception bootstraps word learning. *Trends in Cognitive Science. 9*(11), 519–527.

Weir, R. (1962). *Language in the crib.* The Hague, Netherlands: Mouton.

Weizman, Z., & Snow C. (2001). Lexical input as related to children's vocabulary acquisition: Effects of sophisticated exposure and support for meaning. *Developmental Psychology, 37*(2), 265–279.

Wells, G. (1986). *The meaning makers: Children learning language and using language to learn.* Portsmouth, NH: Heinemann.

White, B. (1985). *The first three years of life.* Englewood Cliffs, NJ: Prentice-Hall.

Whitehurst, G,, Arnold, D., Epstein, J., Angell, A., Smith, M., & Fiscehl, J. (1994). A picture of book reading intervention in day care and home for children from low-income families. *Developmental Psychology, 30*(5), 679–689.

Whitehurst, G., Falco, F., Lonigan, C., Fischel, J., DeBaryshe, B., Valdez-Menchaca, M., & Caulfield, M. (1988). Accelerating language development through picture book reading. *Developmental Psychology, 24*, 552–559.

Whitehurst, G. J., & Lonigan, C. J. (1998). Child development and emergent literacy. *Child Development, 69*, 848–872.

Wien, C., & Kirby-Smith, S. (1998). Untiming the curriculum: A case study of removing clocks from the program. *Young Children, 53*(5), 8–13.

Wiggins, G. (1993). *Assessing student performance.* San Francisco: Jossey-Bass.

Wilder, D., Chen, L., Atwell, J., Pritchard, J., & Weinstein, P. (2006). Brief functional analysis and treatment of tantrums associated with transitions in preschool children. *Journal of Applied Behavior Analysis, 39*, 103–107. Retrieved on June 27, 2008 from www.pubmedcentral .nih.gov.

Winters, D., Saylor, C., & Phillips, C. (2003). Full-day kindergarten: A story of successful adoption and initial implementation. *Young Children, 58*, 54–57.

Wong-Fillmore, L. (1991a). Second-language learning in children: A model of language learning in social context. In E. Bialystok (Ed.), *Language processing in bilingual children* (pp. 49–69). New York: Cambridge University Press.

Wong-Fillmore, L. (1991b). When learning a second language means losing the first. *Early Childhood Research Quarterly*, 6, 232–346.

Wong-Fillmore, L., & Snow, C. (April, 2000). *What teachers need to know about language.* Educational Resources Information Center, ERIC Clearinghouse on Language and Linguistics. ED-99-CO-0008. Washington DC.

Woodward, A., & Guajardo, J. (2002). Infants' understanding of the point gesture as an object-directed action. *Cognitive Development.* 17, 1061–1084.

Woodard, C. (1984). Guidelines for facilitating sociodramatic play. *Childhood Education, 60*, 172–177.

Wright Group/McGraw-Hill. (2002). *Doors to Discovery.* Bothell, WA: The Wright Group.

The Wright Group. (1998). *Phonemic awareness handbook.* Bothell, WA: The Wright Group.

The Wright Group/McGraw-Hill. (2002). *Sound, rhyme and letter time.* Bothell, WA: The Wright Group.

Yaden, D., Enz, B. J. & Perry, N. (2010). Home literacy and school readiness: What factors contribute to success? Technical Report for Phoenix, AZ: First Things First.

Yaden, D., Smolkin, L., & Conlon, A. (1989). Preschoolers' questions about pictures, print conventions, and story text during reading aloud at home. *Reading Research Quarterly, 24*, 188–214.

Yopp, H. (1992). Developing phonemic awareness in young children. *The Reading Teacher, 45*, 696–703.

Yopp, H., & Stapleton, L. (2008). Conciencia fonémica en Español (Phonemic awareness in Spanish). *The Reading Teacher, 61*, 374–382.

Yopp, H., & Yopp, R. (2000). Supporting phonemic awareness development in the classroom. *The Reading Teacher, 54*, 130–143.

Yopp, R. H., & Yopp, H. K. (2006). Informational texts as read-alouds in school and home. *Journal of Literacy Research, 38*, 37–51.

Zimmerman, F., Christakis, D., & Meltzoff, A. (2007). Associations between media viewing and language development in children under age 2 years. *Journal of Pediatrics, 151*(40): 364–368.

CHILDREN'S LITERATURE

A You're Adorable. Alexander, M. (1994). New York: Scholastic

Albertina Anda Arriba: El Abecedario (Albertina Goes Up: An Alphabet Book) Tabor, N. (1992). Watertown, MA: Charlesbridge Publishing

Alexander and the Terrible, Horrible, No Good, Very Bad Day. Viorst, J. (1987). New York: Aladdin Library

Baby Animals Black and White. Tildes, P. (1998). Watertown, MA: Charlesbridge Publishing

Baby Faces. Miller, M. (1998). New York: Little Simon

Best Word Book Ever. Scarry, R. (1980). New York: Western Publishing Company

Black on White. Hoban, T. (1993). New York: Greenwillow Books

Blue's Treasure Hunt Notebook. Santomero, A. (1999). New York: Simon Spotlight

Blueberries for Sal, McCloskey, R. (1963). New York: Puffin Books

Bread and Jam for Francis. Hoban, R. (1964). New York: Scholastic

Brown Bear, Brown Bear. Carle, E. (1992). New York: Henry Holt & Company

Buster's Bedtime. Campbell, R. (2000). London: Campbell Books

Caps for Sale. Slobodkina, E. (1947). New York: HarperCollins

The Carrot Seed. Krauss, R. (1945). New York: HarperCollins

The Cheerios Animal Play Book. Wade, L. (1999). New York: Simon and Schuster Merchandise

The Cheerios Play Book. Wade, L. (1998). New York: Little Simon

Chicka Chicka Boom Boom. Martin, B., & Archambault, J. (1989). New York: Simon & Schuster Children's Publishing

Chicken Soup with Rice. Sendak, M. (1962). New York: HarperCollins

Chicks and Salsa. Reynolds, A. (2005). New York: Bloomsbury Publishing

Click, Clack, Moo: Cows That Type. Cronin, D. (2000). New York: Scholastic

Counting Crocodiles. Hillanbrand, W. (1997). Orlando, FL: Harcourt Brace

Crayon World. Santomero, A. (1999). New York: Simon Spotlight

Crunching Munching Caterpillar. Cain, S. (2000). Wilton, CT: Tiger Tales

The Disappearing Alphabet. Wilbur, R. (1997). Orlando, FL: Harcourt Children's Books

Down By the Bay. Raffi, & Westcott, N. B. (1990). New York: Crown Publishers

Each Peach Pear Plum. Ahlberg, A. & Ahlberg, J. (1978). London: Penguin Books Ltd

Faces. Miglis, J. (2002). New York: Simon Spotlight

Feelings. Miglis, J. (2002). New York: Simon Spotlight

Figure Out Blue's Clues. Perello, J. (1999) New York: Simon Spotlight

Find the Kitten. Cox, P. (2001). Newton, MA: EDC Publications

Find the Puppy. Cox, P. (2001). London: Usborne Publishing Ltd.

Firefighters A to Z. Demarest, C. L. (2000). New York: Margaret K. McElderry Books.

Fit-A-Shape: Clothes. (2001). Philadelphia, PA: Running Press

Fit-A-Shape: Food. (2001). Philadelphia, PA: Running Press

Fit-A-Shape: Shapes. (2000). Philadelphia, PA: Running Press

Five Little Ducks. Raffi (1999). New York: Crown Publishers

Five Little Monkeys Jumping on the Bed. Christelow, E. (1998). New York: Houghton Mifflin

Five Little Monkeys Sitting in a Tree. Christelow, E. (1993). St. Louis, MO: Clarion

Froggy Gets Dressed. London, J. (1997). New York: Viking Children's Press

Get in Shape to Write. Bongiorno, P. (1998). New York: Pen Notes

The Gingerbread Boy. Galdone, P. (1975). New York: Houghton Mifflin

The Gingerbread Man. Arno, E. (1970). New York: Scholastic

Glad Monster, Sad Monster: A Book about Feelings. Emberley, E., & Miranda, A. (1997). New York: Scholastic

The Going to Bed Book. Boynton, S. (1995). New York: Little Simon

Goodnight Moon. Wise, M. (1947). New York: HarperCollins

Happy Colors. Weeks, S. (2001). New York: Reader's Digest Children's Books

Harold and the Purple Crayon. Johnson, C. (1981). New York: HarperCollins

Harold's Fairy Tale: Further Adventures With the Purple Crayon. Johnson, C. (1994). New York: Harper Trophy

Harold's Trip to the Sky. Johnson, C. (1981). New York: HarperCollins

Herman the Helper. Kraus, R. (1974). New York: Windmill

Hershey's Counting Board Book. Barbieri-McGrath, B. (1998). Wellesley, MA: Corporate Board Book

I Love Colors. Miller, M. (1999). New York: Little Simon

In the Small, Small Pond. Fleming, D. (1998). New York: Henry Holt and Company

In the Tall, Tall Grass. Fleming, D. (1993). New York: Henry Holt and Company

Inch by Inch. Leonni, L. (1962). New York: Astor Honor Publishing

The Itsy Bitsy Spider. Trapani, I. (1993). Watertown, MA: Charlesbridge Publishing

Jesse Bear, What Will You Wear? Degen, B. (1996). New York: Simon & Schuster Children's Publishing

Kellogg's Froot Loops! Counting Fun Book. McGrath, B. B. (2000). New York: Harper Festival

Kipper's Sticky Paws. Inkpen, M. (2001). London: Hodder Children's Books

Las Nanas de Abuelita (Grandmother's Nursery Rhymes): *Canciones De Cuna, Trabalenguas Y Adivinanzas De Suramerica (Lullabies, Tongue Twisters, and Riddles from South America.)* Jaramillo, N. P. (1994). New York: Henry Holt and Company

Let's Learn to Write Letters: A Wipe-It-Off Practice Book. Troll Books (1994). Memphis, TN: Troll Association

Let's Learn to Write Numbers: A Wipe-It-Off Practice Book. Troll Books (1994). Memphis, TN: Troll Association

Little Blue and Little Yellow. Lionni, L. (1995). New York: Mulberry Books

Little Cloud. Carle, E. (1996). New York: Scholastic

M & M's Counting Book. McGrath Barbieri, B. (1994). Watertown, MA: Charlesbridge Publishing

Match Shapes with Me. Hood, S. (1999). New York: Reader's Digest Children's Books

Messages in the Mailbox: How to Write a Letter. Leedy, L. (1994). New York: Holiday House

Miss Bindergarten Gets Ready for Kindergarten. Slate, J. (1996). New York: Scholastic.

Miss Spider's Tea Party. Kirk, D. (1994). New York: Scholastic Editions

Moira's Birthday, Munsch, R. (1987). New York: Firefly Books

Moo, Baa, La La La. Boynton, S. (1982). New York: Little Simon

Night, Night Baby. Birkinshaw, M. (2002). London: Ladybird Books

No, David! Shannon, D. (1998). New York: Scholastic Trade

No Dragons for Tea: Fire Safety for Kids (and Dragons). Pendziwol, J. (1999). Toronto ON: Kids Can Press

Oh, A-Hunting We Will Go. Langstaff, J. (1974). New York: Macmillan

Old Hat, New Hat. Berenstain, S. & Berenstain, J. (1976). New York: Random House

The Oreo Cookie Counting Book. Albee, S. (2000). New York: Little Simon

Out and About at the Fire Stations. Dubois, M. L. (2003). Mankato, MN: Picture Window Books

Pancakes for Breakfast. dePaola, T. (1978). New York: Harcourt, Brace, Jovanovich

Pepperidge Farm Goldfish Fun Book. McGrath, B.B. (2000). New York: Harper Festival

Pepperidge Farm Goldfish Counting Fun Book. McGrath, B.B. (2000). New York: Harper Festival

A Picture for Harold's Room. Johnson, C. (1960). New York: HarperCollins.

Quack, Quack, Who's That? Noel, D. & Galloway, R. (2002). London: Little Tiger Press

The Rainbow Fish by Marcus Pfister (1992). New York: North-South Books

Rain Makes Applesauce. Scheer, J. (1964). New York: Holiday House

Red, Blue, Yellow Shoe. Hoban, T. (1986). New York: Greenwillow Books

Silly Sally. Wood, A. (1992). Orlando: FL: Harcourt Brace

Spot Looks at Colors. Hill, E. (1986). New York: Putnam Publishing Group

Strega Nona. dePaola, T. (1975). New York: Simon and Schuster Children's Publishing

Tabby Tiger Taxi Driver. Cowley, J. (2001) Bothall, MA: The Wright Group-McGraw-Hill

That's Not My Puppy. Watt, F. & Wells, R. (1999). London: Usborne Publishing Ltd.

That's Not My Teddy. Watt, F. & Wells, R. (1999). London: Usborne Publishing Ltd.

The Three Bears. Galdone, P. (1979). New York: Houghton Mifflin

The Three Billy Goats Gruff. Galdone, P. (1973). New York: Houghton Mifflin

Pokéman Book of Colors. Muldrow, D. (2000). New York: Golden Books Company

Pokéman Counting Book. Muldrow, D. (1999). New York: Golden Books Company

Popcorn Book. dePaola, T. (1978). New York: Holiday House

Princess and the Goblin. MacDonald, G. (1872). London: Puffin Books

Selfish Crocodile. Charles, F. & Terry, M. (2000). New York: Scholastic

Sun-Maid Raisins Playbook. Weir, A. (1999). New York: Little Simon

There Was An Old Lady Who Swallowed A Fly. Taback, S. (1997).New York: Penguin Books

This Old Man. Jones, C. (1990). New York: Houghton Mifflin

Touch and Feel: Baby Animals. Kindersley, D. (1999). New York: Dorling Kindersley Publishing

Touch and Feel: Bedtime. Kindersley, D. (2001). New York: Dorling Kindersley Publishing

Touch and Feel: Clothes. Kindersley, D. (1998). New York: Dorling Kindersley Publishing

Touch and Feel: Home. Kindersley, D. (1998). New York: Dorling Kindersley Publishing

Touch and Feel: Kitten. Kindersley, D. (1999). New York: Dorling Kindersley Publishing

Touch and Feel: Pets. Kindersley, D. (2001). New York: Dorling Kindersley Publishing

Touch and Feel: Puppy. Kindersley, D. (1999). New York: Dorling Kindersley Publishing

Touch and Feel: Shapes. Kindersley, D. (2000). New York: Dorling Kindersley Publishing

Touch and Talk: Make Me Say Moo! Greig, E. (2002). Bristol, PA: Sandvick Innovations

Vamos a Cazar un Oso. (Going on a Bear Hunt) Rosen, M. (1993). London: Walker Book

The Very Busy Spider. Carle, E (1984). New York: Philomel Books

The Very Hungry Caterpillar. Carle, E. (1969). New York: Penguin Young Readers

The Very Hungry Thing. Slepian, J., & Seidler, A. (1971). New York: Scholastic

What Is That? Hoban, T. (1994). New York: Greenwillow Books

What Will I Do If I Can't Tie My Shoe? Regan, D. (1998). New York: Scholastic

The Wheels on the Bus. Stanley, M. (2002). Bristol, PA: Baby's First Book Club

Where Is Baby's Belly Button? Katz, K. (2000). New York: Little Simon

Where Is Baby's Mommy? Katz, K. (2001). New York: Little Simon

Where the Wild Things Are. Sendak, M. (1988). New York: Harper Trophy

Where's My Fuzzy Blanket? Carter, N. (2001). New York: Scholastic Paperbacks

White on Black. Hoban, T. (1993). New York: Greenwillow Books

Who Are They? Hoban, T. (1994). New York: Greenwillow Books

Who Stole the Cookies from the Cookie Jar? Manning, J. (2001). New York: Harper Festival

Winnie the Pooh: Feelings. Smith, R. (2000). New York: Random House Disney

WOW! Babies. Gentieu, P. (2000). New York: Crown Publisher

AUTHOR INDEX

SUBJECT INDEX